"Vos estis sal terrae...

Vos estis lux mundi"

(Mt 5, 13-14)

Joannes Paulus II

The Gospel according to Matthew

Évangile selon Matthieu

el Evangelio según Mateo

il Vangelo secondo Matteo

This booklet has been published by the Canadian Bible Society. The Canadian Bible Society exists to promote and encourage, without doctrinal note or comment, the translation, publication, distribution and use of the Scriptures throughout Canada and Bermuda, and to cooperate with the United Bible Societies in its worldwide work. The vision of the Canadian Bible Society is to reach every man, woman and child with the life-giving Word of God and to encourage its use.

Ce livret est publié par la Société biblique canadienne. La Société biblique canadienne existe afin de promouvoir et d'encourager une diffusion et une utilisation accrues des Écritures saintes, sans notes doctrinales ni commentaires doctrinaux, partout au Canada, et de coopérer avec l'Alliance biblique universelle dans son travail mondial. La vision de la Société biblique canadienne est d'atteindre toute personne avec la Parole de Dieu, source de Vie, et encourager son usage.

CANADIAN **BIBLE** SOCIETY   SOCIÉTÉ **BIBLIQUE** CANADIENNE

10 Carnforth Road, Toronto, ON M4A 2S4 Canada
Tel: 416-757-4171   Fax: 416-757-3376
www.biblesociety.ca   www.societebiblique.ca

This edition / Cette édition
© 2002 Canadian Bible Society / Société Biblique Canadienne

Cover / Couverture:
St. Matthew and the Angel
Guido Reni (Oil on Canvas)
Vatican Museums

Product No. 3XX301001
CBS/SBC - 2002-300M

ISBN 0-88834-113-X

Printed in Canada

The Gospel According to
MATTHEW

God our Father,
Jesus your Son calls us to be salt of the earth and light of the
world. May the light of your justice shine in our lives; so
that our actions and words can bring the taste of the Gospel
to the world, and that our lives can reflect Jesus, Light of the
World. We ask this of you, through Jesus Christ our Lord,
who lives and rules with You, in unity with the Holy Spirit,
for ever and ever. Amen.

The Gospel according to Matthew
English text from the Good News Translation
© American Bible Society, 1992

Introduction

Jesus called disciples to follow him. He lived with them, teaching the crowd and performing miracles, helping them understand his mission and the opposition that he would encounter. God responded to the shame of the cross by resurrecting Jesus, and glorifying him as Christ and Lord.

The mystery of death becoming life had to be proclaimed to the entire world as a "gospel", that is, as "good news". The disciples of Jesus had witnessed his miracles, his acts of mercy, his passion and the Easter experience. It was important to make these words and events meaningful to the various communities who listened to their teaching; and the Evangelists (writers of the Gospels) drew on the oral and written traditions of these communities. Thus were born the four Gospels that the Church recognizes as true witnesses to the life of Jesus Christ, and to faith in him: the Gospels according to Matthew, Mark, Luke and John.

The Gospel according to Matthew

A Church Distinct from the Synagogue

Matthew probably drafted his Gospel in Antioch, between the years 80 and 90 AD. Christian Jews had founded this church now characterized by an open and forward-looking mentality in the late 30s.

This Community was not only separate from the synagogue, but it was also involved in a heated debate with the Jewish leaders. The series of seven statements in chapter 23, verses 13-36 – How terrible for you, teachers of the Law and Pharisees! You hypocrites! – clearly shows how deeply divided these groups were.

A Church in Search of Identity

Two competing concerns pulled the early Christians in opposite directions. How could they remain faithful to the Jewish heritage of the Old Testament, while accepting that the salvation proclaimed by the Resurrected Christ was meant for all people?

Before Matthew's Gospel was written, the church at Antioch was already experiencing tensions between its open-minded founders and the conservative "brothers" from Jerusalem. Should the Church, rooted in Judaism, guardian of the Old Testament, open itself to the vast non-Jewish world? On what basis? The Gospel of Matthew represents an attempt at reconciliation between the conflicting traditions inherited by the early Christians. Matthew affirms that the good news of salvation is meant for all, and that it is not necessary for people to be circumcised or observe the Jewish dietary rules.

Matthew attempts to preserve the old heritage and at the same time present the new message of the Gospel. He tries to find the middle ground, where the Jewish tradition intersects with the global future. He also raises the profile of Peter, the leader of the Church (16.18-19). For him, Peter represents a moderate position – more conservative than that of Saint Paul in his letters to the Galatians and the Romans, but more open to non-Jews, than that of Saint James in his letter. It is not surprising, then, that the Gospel of Matthew, which establishes the framework for Christian unity, by bringing together the major doctrinal positions of the time, became very popular in a short period of time.

CONCLUSION

Today, globalization is a hot issue for Christians. All barriers between nations, cultures and even religions are falling. It is clear that this *sign of the times*, of which WYD (World Youth Day) is a powerful example, forces us to be more open to others. But how can we preserve our Christian identity, while respecting the identity and values of others?

The early Christians debated a similar distressing problem – the balance between the particular sense of identity that the Jewish people enjoyed and the all-embracing appeal of the Gospel. Their search for a solution, alluded to by Matthew, can inspire us today.

The Gospel according to
MATTHEW

The Ancestors of Jesus Christ

1 ¹This is the list of the ancestors of Jesus Christ, a descendant of David, who was a descendant of Abraham.

2-6a From Abraham to King David, the following ancestors are listed: Abraham, Isaac, Jacob, Judah and his brothers; then Perez and Zerah (their mother was Tamar), Hezron, Ram, Amminadab, Nahshon, Salmon, Boaz (his mother was Rahab), Obed (his mother was Ruth), Jesse, and King David.

6b-11 From David to the time when the people of Israel were taken into exile in Babylon, the following ancestors are listed: David, Solomon (his mother was the woman who had been Uriah's wife), Rehoboam, Abijah, Asa, Jehoshaphat, Jehoram, Uzziah, Jotham, Ahaz, Hezekiah, Manasseh, Amon, Josiah, and Jehoiachin and his brothers.

12-16 From the time after the exile in Babylon to the birth of Jesus, the following ancestors are listed: Jehoiachin, Shealtiel, Zerubbabel, Abiud, Eliakim, Azor, Zadok, Achim, Eliud, Eleazar, Matthan, Jacob, and Joseph, who married Mary, the mother of Jesus, who was called the Messiah.

17 So then, there were fourteen generations from Abraham to David, and fourteen from David to the exile in Babylon, and fourteen from then to the birth of the Messiah.

The Birth of Jesus Christ

18 This was how the birth of Jesus Christ took place. His mother Mary was engaged to Joseph, but before they were married, she found out that she was going to have a baby by the Holy Spirit. 19 Joseph was a man who always did what was right, but he did not want to disgrace Mary publicly; so he made plans to break the engagement privately. 20 While he was thinking about this, an angel of the Lord appeared to him in a dream and said, "Joseph, descendant of David, do not be afraid to take Mary to be your wife. For it is by the Holy Spirit that she has conceived. 21 She will have a son, and you will name him Jesus — because he will save his people from their sins."

22 Now all this happened in order to make come true what the Lord had said through the prophet, 23 "A virgin will become pregnant and have a son, and he will be called Immanuel" (which means, "God is with us").

24 So when Joseph woke up, he married Mary, as the angel of the Lord had told him to. 25 But he had no sexual relations with her before she gave birth to her son. And Joseph named him Jesus.

Visitors from the East

2 [1]Jesus was born in the town of Bethlehem in Judea, during the time when Herod was king. Soon afterward, some men who studied the stars came from the East to Jerusalem [2]and asked, "Where is the baby born to be the king of the Jews? We saw his star when it came up in the east, and we have come to worship him."

[3]When King Herod heard about this, he was very upset, and so was everyone else in Jerusalem. [4]He called together all the chief priests and the teachers of the Law and asked them, "Where will the Messiah be born?"

[5]"In the town of Bethlehem in Judea," they answered. "For this is what the prophet wrote:

[6] 'Bethlehem in the land of Judah,
you are by no means the least
of the leading cities of Judah;
for from you will come a leader
who will guide
my people Israel.'"

[7]So Herod called the visitors from the East to a secret meeting and found out from them the exact time the star had appeared. [8]Then he sent them to Bethlehem with these instructions: "Go and make a careful search for the child; and when you find him, let me know, so that I too may go and worship him."

[9-10]And so they left, and on their way they saw the same star they had seen in the East. When they saw it, how happy they were, what joy was theirs! It went ahead of them until it stopped over the place where the child was. [11]They went into the house, and when they saw the child with his mother Mary, they knelt down and worshiped him. They brought out their gifts of gold, frankincense, and myrrh, and presented them to him.

[12]Then they returned to their country by another road, since God had warned them in a dream not to go back to Herod.

The Escape to Egypt

[13]After they had left, an angel of the Lord appeared in a dream to Joseph and said, "Herod will be looking for the child in order to kill him. So get up, take the child and his mother and escape to Egypt, and stay there until I tell you to leave."

[14]Joseph got up, took the child and his mother, and left during the night for Egypt, [15]where he stayed until Herod died. This was done to make come true what the Lord had said through the prophet, "I called my Son out of Egypt."

The Killing of the Children

[16]When Herod realized that the visitors from the East had tricked him, he was furious. He gave orders to kill all the boys in Bethlehem and its neighborhood who were two years old and younger—this was done in accordance with what he had learned from the visitors about the time when the star had appeared.

[17]In this way what the prophet Jeremiah had said came true:
[18] "A sound is heard in Ramah,
the sound of bitter weeping.

Rachel is crying for her children;
    she refuses to be comforted,
      for they are dead."

The Return from Egypt

19 After Herod died, an angel of the
Lord appeared in a dream to Joseph in
Egypt 20 and said, "Get up, take the
child and his mother, and go back to
the land of Israel, because those who
tried to kill the child are dead." 21 So
Joseph got up, took the child and his
mother, and went back to Israel.

22 But when Joseph heard that
Archelaus had succeeded his father
Herod as king of Judea, he was afraid
to go there. He was given more instructions in a dream, so he went to
the province of Galilee 23 and made his
home in a town named Nazareth. And
so what the prophets had said came
true: "He will be called a Nazarene.'"

The Preaching of John the Baptist

3 1 At that time John the Baptist
came to the desert of Judea and
started preaching. 2 "Turn away from
your sins," he said, "because the
Kingdom of heaven is near!" 3 John
was the man the prophet Isaiah was
talking about when he said,

"Someone is shouting
    in the desert,
  'Prepare a road for the Lord;
    make a straight path for him
      to travel!'"

4 John's clothes were made of
camel's hair; he wore a leather belt
around his waist, and his food was
locusts and wild honey. 5 People came
to him from Jerusalem, from the
whole province of Judea, and from all
over the country near the Jordan
River. 6 They confessed their sins, and
he baptized them in the Jordan.

7 When John saw many Pharisees
and Sadducees coming to him to be
baptized, he said to them, "You
snakes— who told you that you could
escape from the punishment God is
about to send? 8 Do those things that
will show that you have turned from
your sins. 9 And don't think you can
escape punishment by saying that
Abraham is your ancestor. I tell you
that God can take these rocks and
make descendants for Abraham! 10 The
ax is ready to cut down the trees at the
roots; every tree that does not bear
good fruit will be cut down and
thrown in the fire. 11 I baptize you
with water to show that you have
repented, but the one who will come
after me will baptize you with the
Holy Spirit and fire. He is much
greater than I am; and I am not good
enough even to carry his sandals. 12 He
has his winnowing shovel with him to
thresh out all the grain. He will gather
his wheat into his barn, but he will
burn the chaff in a fire that never goes
out."

The Baptism of Jesus

13 At that time Jesus arrived from
Galilee and came to John at the Jordan
to be baptized by him. 14 But John tried
to make him change his mind. "I
ought to be baptized by you," John
said, "and yet you have come to me!"

15 But Jesus answered him, "Let it
be so for now. For in this way we shall

do all that God requires." So John agreed.

16 As soon as Jesus was baptized, he came up out of the water. Then heaven was opened to him, and he saw the Spirit of God coming down like a dove and lighting on him. 17 Then a voice said from heaven, "This is my own dear Son, with whom I am pleased."

The Temptation of Jesus

4 1 Then the Spirit led Jesus into the desert to be tempted by the Devil. 2 After spending forty days and nights without food, Jesus was hungry. 3 Then the Devil came to him and said, "If you are God's Son, order these stones to turn into bread."

4 But Jesus answered, "The scripture says, 'Human beings cannot live on bread alone, but need every word that God speaks.'"

5 Then the Devil took Jesus to Jerusalem, the Holy City, set him on the highest point of the Temple, 6 and said to him, "If you are God's Son, throw yourself down, for the scripture says,

'God will give orders to his angels
    about you;
they will hold you up
    with their hands,
so that not even your feet
    will be hurt on the stones.'"

7 Jesus answered, "But the scripture also says, 'Do not put the Lord your God to the test.'"

8 Then the Devil took Jesus to a very high mountain and showed him all the kingdoms of the world in all their greatness. 9 "All this I will give you," the Devil said, "if you kneel down and worship me."

10 Then Jesus answered, "Go away, Satan! The scripture says, 'Worship the Lord your God and serve only him!'"

11 Then the Devil left Jesus; and angels came and helped him.

Jesus Begins His Work in Galilee

12 When Jesus heard that John had been put in prison, he went away to Galilee. 13 He did not stay in Nazareth, but went to live in Capernaum, a town by Lake Galilee, in the territory of Zebulun and Naphtali. 14 This was done to make come true what the prophet Isaiah had said,
15 "Land of Zebulun
    and land of Naphtali,
    on the road to the sea,
    on the other side of the Jordan,
    Galilee, land of the Gentiles!
16 The people who live in darkness
    will see a great light.
    On those who live
    in the dark land of death
    the light will shine."

17 From that time Jesus began to preach his message: "Turn away from your sins, because the Kingdom of heaven is near!"

Jesus Calls Four Fishermen

18 As Jesus walked along the shore of Lake Galilee, he saw two brothers who were fishermen, Simon (called Peter) and his brother Andrew, catching fish in the lake with a net. 19 Jesus said to them, "Come with me, and I will teach you to catch people."

20 At once they left their nets and went with him.

21 He went on and saw two other brothers, James and John, the sons of Zebedee. They were in their boat with their father Zebedee, getting their nets ready. Jesus called them, 22 and at once they left the boat and their father, and went with him.

Jesus Teaches, Preaches, and Heals

23 Jesus went all over Galilee, teaching in the synagogues, preaching the Good News about the Kingdom, and healing people who had all kinds of disease and sickness. 24 The news about him spread through the whole country of Syria, so that people brought to him all those who were sick, suffering from all kinds of diseases and disorders: people with demons, epileptics, and paralytics — and Jesus healed them all. 25 Large crowds followed him from Galilee and the Ten Towns, from Jerusalem, Judea, and the land on the other side of the Jordan.

The Sermon on the Mount

5 1 Jesus saw the crowds and went up a hill, where he sat down. His disciples gathered around him, 2 and he began to teach them:

True Happiness

3 "Happy are those who know
    they are spiritually poor;
the Kingdom of heaven
    belongs to them!

4 "Happy are those who mourn;
God will comfort them!

5 "Happy are those who are humble;
they will receive
    what God has promised!

6 "Happy are those
    whose greatest desire is to do
    what God requires;
God will satisfy them fully!

7 "Happy are those
    who are merciful to others;
God will be merciful to them!

8 "Happy are the pure in heart;
    they will see God!

9 "Happy are those
    who work for peace;
God will call them his children!

10 "Happy are those
    who are persecuted
    because they do what God requires;
    the Kingdom of heaven
    belongs to them!

11 "Happy are you when people insult you and persecute you and tell all kinds of evil lies against you because you are my followers. 12 Be happy and glad, for a great reward is kept for you in heaven. This is how the prophets who lived before you were persecuted.

Salt and Light

13 "You are like salt for the whole human race. But if salt loses its saltiness, there is no way to make it salty again. It has become worthless, so it is thrown out and people trample on it.

14 "You are like light for the whole world. A city built on a hill cannot be hid. 15 No one lights a lamp and puts it under a bowl; instead it is put on the

lampstand, where it gives light for everyone in the house. 16In the same way your light must shine before people, so that they will see the good things you do and praise your Father in heaven.

Teaching about the Law

17"Do not think that I have come to do away with the Law of Moses and the teachings of the prophets. I have not come to do away with them, but to make their teachings come true. 18Remember that as long as heaven and earth last, not the least point nor the smallest detail of the Law will be done away with — not until the end of all things. 19So then, whoever disobeys even the least important of the commandments and teaches others to do the same, will be least in the Kingdom of heaven. On the other hand, whoever obeys the Law and teaches others to do the same, will be great in the Kingdom of heaven. 20I tell you, then, that you will be able to enter the Kingdom of heaven only if you are more faithful than the teachers of the Law and the Pharisees in doing what God requires.

Teaching about Anger

21"You have heard that people were told in the past, 'Do not commit murder; anyone who does will be brought to trial.' 22But now I tell you: if you are angry with your brother you will be brought to trial, if you call your brother 'You good-for-nothing!' you will be brought before the Council, and if you call your brother a worthless fool you will be in danger of going to the fire of hell. 23So if you are about to offer your gift to God at the altar and there you remember that your brother has something against you, 24leave your gift there in front of the altar, go at once and make peace with your brother, and then come back and offer your gift to God.

25"If someone brings a lawsuit against you and takes you to court, settle the dispute while there is time, before you get to court. Once you are there, you will be turned over to the judge, who will hand you over to the police, and you will be put in jail. 26There you will stay, I tell you, until you pay the last penny of your fine.

Teaching about Adultery

27"You have heard that it was said, 'Do not commit adultery.' 28But now I tell you: anyone who looks at a woman and wants to possess her is guilty of committing adultery with her in his heart. 29So if your right eye causes you to sin, take it out and throw it away! It is much better for you to lose a part of your body than to have your whole body thrown into hell. 30If your right hand causes you to sin, cut it off and throw it away! It is much better for you to lose one of your limbs than to have your whole body go off to hell.

Teaching about Divorce

31"It was also said, 'Anyone who divorces his wife must give her a written notice of divorce.' 32But now I tell you: if a man divorces his wife for any cause other than her unfaithfulness, then he is guilty of making her commit adultery if she marries again; and the man who marries her commits adultery also.

Teaching about Vows

33 "You have also heard that people were told in the past, 'Do not break your promise, but do what you have vowed to the Lord to do.' 34 But now I tell you: do not use any vow when you make a promise. Do not swear by heaven, for it is God's throne; 35 nor by earth, for it is the resting place for his feet; nor by Jerusalem, for it is the city of the great King. 36 Do not even swear by your head, because you cannot make a single hair white or black. 37 Just say 'Yes' or 'No' — anything else you say comes from the Evil One.

Teaching about Revenge

38 "You have heard that it was said, 'An eye for an eye, and a tooth for a tooth.' 39 But now I tell you: do not take revenge on someone who wrongs you. If anyone slaps you on the right cheek, let him slap your left cheek too. 40 And if someone takes you to court to sue you for your shirt, let him have your coat as well. 41 And if one of the occupation troops forces you to carry his pack one mile, carry it two miles. 42 When someone asks you for something, give it to him; when someone wants to borrow something, lend it to him.

Love for Enemies

43 "You have heard that it was said, 'Love your friends, hate your enemies.' 44 But now I tell you: love your enemies and pray for those who persecute you, 45 so that you may become the children of your Father in heaven. For he makes his sun to shine on bad and good people alike, and gives rain to those who do good and to those who do evil. 46 Why should God reward you if you love only the people who love you? Even the tax collectors do that! 47 And if you speak only to your friends, have you done anything out of the ordinary? Even the pagans do that! 48 You must be perfect — just as your Father in heaven is perfect.

Teaching about Charity

6 1 "Make certain you do not perform your religious duties in public so that people will see what you do. If you do these things publicly, you will not have any reward from your Father in heaven.

2 "So when you give something to a needy person, do not make a big show of it, as the hypocrites do in the houses of worship and on the streets. They do it so that people will praise them. I assure you, they have already been paid in full. 3 But when you help a needy person, do it in such a way that even your closest friend will not know about it. 4 Then it will be a private matter. And your Father, who sees what you do in private, will reward you.

Teaching about Prayer

5 "When you pray, do not be like the hypocrites! They love to stand up and pray in the houses of worship and on the street corners, so that everyone

will see them. I assure you, they have already been paid in full. 6But when you pray, go to your room, close the door, and pray to your Father, who is unseen. And your Father, who sees what you do in private, will reward you.

7"When you pray, do not use a lot of meaningless words, as the pagans do, who think that their gods will hear them because their prayers are long. 8Do not be like them. Your Father already knows what you need before you ask him. 9This, then, is how you should pray:

'Our Father in heaven:
May your holy name be honored;
10 may your Kingdom come;
may your will be done on earth
as it is in heaven.
11 Give us today the food we need.
12 Forgive us the wrongs we have done,
as we forgive the wrongs
that others have done to us.
13 Do not bring us to hard testing,
but keep us safe from the Evil One.'

14"If you forgive others the wrongs they have done to you, your Father in heaven will also forgive you. 15But if you do not forgive others, then your Father will not forgive the wrongs you have done.

Teaching about Fasting

16"And when you fast, do not put on a sad face as the hypocrites do. They neglect their appearance so that everyone will see that they are fasting. I assure you, they have already been paid in full. 17When you go without food, wash your face and comb your hair, 18so that others cannot know that you are fasting—only your Father, who is unseen, will know. And your Father, who sees what you do in private, will reward you.

Riches in Heaven

19"Do not store up riches for yourselves here on earth, where moths and rust destroy, and robbers break in and steal. 20Instead, store up riches for yourselves in heaven, where moths and rust cannot destroy, and robbers cannot break in and steal. 21For your heart will always be where your riches are.

The Light of the Body

22"The eyes are like a lamp for the body. If your eyes are sound, your whole body will be full of light; 23but if your eyes are no good, your body will be in darkness. So if the light in you is darkness, how terribly dark it will be!

God and Possessions

24"You cannot be a slave of two masters; you will hate one and love the other; you will be loyal to one and despise the other. You cannot serve both God and money.

25"This is why I tell you: do not be worried about the food and drink you need in order to stay alive, or about clothes for your body. After all, isn't life worth more than food? And isn't the body worth more than clothes? 26Look at the birds: they do not plant seeds, gather a harvest and put it in barns; yet your Father in heaven takes care of them! Aren't you worth much more than birds? 27 Can any of you live a bit longer by worrying about it?

28 "And why worry about clothes? Look how the wild flowers grow: they do not work or make clothes for themselves. 29 But I tell you that not even King Solomon with all his wealth had clothes as beautiful as one of these flowers. 30 It is God who clothes the wild grass — grass that is here today and gone tomorrow, burned up in the oven. Won't he be all the more sure to clothe you? What little faith you have!

31 "So do not start worrying: 'Where will my food come from? or my drink? or my clothes?' 32 (These are the things the pagans are always concerned about.) Your Father in heaven knows that you need all these things. 33 Instead, be concerned above everything else with the Kingdom of God and with what he requires of you, and he will provide you with all these other things. 34 So do not worry about tomorrow; it will have enough worries of its own. There is no need to add to the troubles each day brings.

Judging Others

7 1 "Do not judge others, so that God will not judge you, 2 for God will judge you in the same way you judge others, and he will apply to you the same rules you apply to others. 3 Why, then, do you look at the speck in your brother's eye and pay no attention to the log in your own eye? 4 How dare you say to your brother,

'Please, let me take that speck out of your eye,' when you have a log in your own eye? 5 You hypocrite! First take the log out of your own eye, and then you will be able to see clearly to take the speck out of your brother's eye.

6 "Do not give what is holy to dogs — they will only turn and attack you. Do not throw your pearls in front of pigs — they will only trample them underfoot.

Ask, Seek, Knock

7 "Ask, and you will receive; seek, and you will find; knock, and the door will be opened to you. 8 For everyone who asks will receive, and anyone who seeks will find, and the door will be opened to those who knock. 9 Would any of you who are fathers give your son a stone when he asks for bread? 10 Or would you give him a snake when he asks for a fish? 11 As bad as you are, you know how to give good things to your children. How much more, then, will your Father in heaven give good things to those who ask him!

12 "Do for others what you want them to do for you: this is the meaning of the Law of Moses and of the teachings of the prophets.

The Narrow Gate

13 "Go in through the narrow gate, because the gate to hell is wide and the road that leads to it is easy, and there are many who travel it. 14 But the gate to life is narrow and the way that leads to it is hard, and there are few people who find it.

A Tree and Its Fruit

15 "Be on your guard against false prophets; they come to you looking like sheep on the outside, but on the inside they are really like wild wolves. 16 You will know them by what they do. Thorn bushes do not bear grapes, and briers do not bear figs. 17 A healthy tree bears good fruit, but a poor tree bears bad fruit. 18 A healthy tree cannot bear bad fruit, and a poor tree cannot bear good fruit. 19 And any tree that does not bear good fruit is cut down and thrown in the fire. 20 So then, you will know the false prophets by what they do.

I Never Knew You

21 "Not everyone who calls me 'Lord, Lord' will enter the Kingdom of heaven, but only those who do what my Father in heaven wants them to do. 22 When the Judgment Day comes, many will say to me, 'Lord, Lord! In your name we spoke God's message, by your name we drove out many demons and performed many miracles!' 23 Then I will say to them, 'I never knew you. Get away from me, you wicked people!'

The Two House Builders

24 "So then, anyone who hears these words of mine and obeys them is like a wise man who built his house on rock. 25 The rain poured down, the rivers flooded over, and the wind blew hard against that house. But it did not fall, because it was built on rock.

26 "But anyone who hears these words of mine and does not obey them is like a foolish man who built his house on sand. 27 The rain poured down, the rivers flooded over, the wind blew hard against that house, and it fell. And what a terrible fall that was!"

The Authority of Jesus

28 When Jesus finished saying these things, the crowd was amazed at the way he taught. 29 He wasn't like the teachers of the Law; instead, he taught with authority.

Jesus Heals a Man

8 1 When Jesus came down from the hill, large crowds followed him. 2 Then a man suffering from a dreaded skin disease came to him, knelt down before him, and said, "Sir, if you want to, you can make me clean."

3 Jesus reached out and touched him. "I do want to," he answered. "Be clean!" At once the man was healed of his disease. 4 Then Jesus said to him, "Listen! Don't tell anyone, but go straight to the priest and let him examine you; then in order to prove to everyone that you are cured, offer the sacrifice that Moses ordered."

Jesus Heals a Roman Officer's Servant

5 When Jesus entered Capernaum, a Roman officer met him and begged for help: 6 "Sir, my servant is sick in bed at home, unable to move and suffering terribly."

7 "I will go and make him well," Jesus said.

8 "Oh no, sir," answered the officer. "I do not deserve to have you come into my house. Just give the order, and my servant will get well. 9 I, too, am a man under the authority of superior officers, and I have soldiers under me. I order this one, 'Go!' and he goes; and I order that one, 'Come!' and he comes; and I order my slave, 'Do this!' and he does it."

10 When Jesus heard this, he was surprised and said to the people following him, "I tell you, I have never found anyone in Israel with faith like this. 11 I assure you that many will come from the east and the west and sit down with Abraham, Isaac, and Jacob at the feast in the Kingdom of heaven. 12 But those who should be in the Kingdom will be thrown out into the darkness, where they will cry and gnash their teeth." 13 Then Jesus said to the officer, "Go home, and what you believe will be done for you."

And the officer's servant was healed that very moment.

Jesus Heals Many People

14 Jesus went to Peter's home, and there he saw Peter's mother-in-law sick in bed with a fever. 15 He touched her hand; the fever left her, and she got up and began to wait on him.

16 When evening came, people brought to Jesus many who had demons in them. Jesus drove out the evil spirits with a word and healed all who were sick. 17 He did this to make come true what the prophet Isaiah had said, "He himself took our sickness and carried away our diseases."

The Would-Be Followers of Jesus

18 When Jesus noticed the crowd around him, he ordered his disciples to go to the other side of the lake. 19 A teacher of the Law came to him. "Teacher," he said, "I am ready to go with you wherever you go."

20 Jesus answered him, "Foxes have holes, and birds have nests, but the Son of Man has no place to lie down and rest."

21 Another man, who was a disciple, said, "Sir, first let me go back and bury my father."

22 "Follow me," Jesus answered, "and let the dead bury their own dead."

Jesus Calms a Storm

23 Jesus got into a boat, and his disciples went with him. 24 Suddenly a fierce storm hit the lake, and the boat was in danger of sinking. But Jesus was asleep. 25 The disciples went to him and woke him up. "Save us, Lord!" they said. "We are about to die!"

26 "Why are you so frightened?" Jesus answered. "What little faith you have!" Then he got up and ordered the winds and the waves to stop, and there was a great calm.

27 Everyone was amazed. "What kind of man is this?" they said. "Even the winds and the waves obey him!"

Jesus Heals
Two Men with Demons

28 When Jesus came to the territory of Gadara on the other side of the lake, he was met by two men who came

out of the burial caves there. These men had demons in them and were so fierce that no one dared travel on that road. 29 At once they screamed, "What do you want with us, you Son of God? Have you come to punish us before the right time?"

30 Not far away there was a large herd of pigs feeding. 31 So the demons begged Jesus, "If you are going to drive us out, send us into that herd of pigs."

32 "Go," Jesus told them; so they left and went off into the pigs. The whole herd rushed down the side of the cliff into the lake and was drowned.

33 The men who had been taking care of the pigs ran away and went into the town, where they told the whole story and what had happened to the men with the demons. 34 So everyone from the town went out to meet Jesus; and when they saw him, they begged him to leave their territory.

Jesus Heals a Paralyzed Man

9 1 Jesus got into the boat and went back across the lake to his own town, 2 where some people brought to him a paralyzed man, lying on a bed. When Jesus saw how much faith they had, he said to the paralyzed man, "Courage, my son! Your sins are forgiven."

3 Then some teachers of the Law said to themselves, "This man is speaking blasphemy!"

4 Jesus perceived what they were thinking, and so he said, "Why are you thinking such evil things? 5 Is it easier to say, 'Your sins are forgiven,' or to say, 'Get up and walk'? 6 I will prove to you, then, that the Son of Man has authority on earth to forgive sins." So he said to the paralyzed man, "Get up, pick up your bed, and go home!"

7 The man got up and went home. 8 When the people saw it, they were afraid, and praised God for giving such authority to people.

Jesus Calls Matthew

9 Jesus left that place, and as he walked along, he saw a tax collector, named Matthew, sitting in his office. He said to him, "Follow me."

Matthew got up and followed him.

10 While Jesus was having a meal in Matthew's house, many tax collectors and other outcasts came and joined Jesus and his disciples at the table. 11 Some Pharisees saw this and asked his disciples, "Why does your teacher eat with such people?"

12 Jesus heard them and answered, "People who are well do not need a doctor, but only those who are sick. 13 Go and find out what is meant by the scripture that says: 'It is kindness that I want, not animal sacrifices.' I have not come to call respectable people, but outcasts."

The Question about Fasting

14 Then the followers of John the Baptist came to Jesus, asking, "Why is it that we and the Pharisees fast often, but your disciples don't fast at all?"

15 Jesus answered, "Do you expect the guests at a wedding party to be sad as long as the bridegroom is with them?

Of course not! But the day will come when the bridegroom will be taken away from them, and then they will fast.

16 "No one patches up an old coat with a piece of new cloth, for the new patch will shrink and make an even bigger hole in the coat. 17 Nor does anyone pour new wine into used wineskins, for the skins will burst, the wine will pour out, and the skins will be ruined. Instead, new wine is poured into fresh wineskins, and both will keep in good condition."

The Official's Daughter and the Woman Who Touched Jesus' Cloak

18 While Jesus was saying this, a Jewish official came to him, knelt down before him, and said, "My daughter has just died; but come and place your hands on her, and she will live."

19 So Jesus got up and followed him, and his disciples went along with him.

20 A woman who had suffered from severe bleeding for twelve years came up behind Jesus and touched the edge of his cloak. 21 She said to herself, "If only I touch his cloak, I will get well."

22 Jesus turned around and saw her, and said, "Courage, my daughter! Your faith has made you well." At that very moment the woman became well.

23 Then Jesus went into the official's house. When he saw the musicians for the funeral and the people all stirred up, 24 he said, "Get out, everybody! The little girl is not dead — she is only sleeping!" Then they all started making fun of him. 25 But as soon as the people had been put out, Jesus went into the girl's room and took hold of her hand, and she got up. 26 The news about this spread all over that part of the country.

Jesus Heals Two Blind Men

27 Jesus left that place, and as he walked along, two blind men started following him. "Have mercy on us, Son of David!" they shouted.

28 When Jesus had gone indoors, the two blind men came to him, and he asked them, "Do you believe that I can heal you?"

"Yes, sir!" they answered.

29 Then Jesus touched their eyes and said, "Let it happen, then, just as you believe!" — 30 and their sight was restored. Jesus spoke sternly to them, "Don't tell this to anyone!"

31 But they left and spread the news about Jesus all over that part of the country.

Jesus Heals a Man Who Could Not Speak

32 As the men were leaving, some people brought to Jesus a man who could not talk because he had a demon. 33 But as soon as the demon was driven out, the man started talking, and everyone was amazed. "We have never seen anything like this in Israel!" they exclaimed.

34 But the Pharisees said, "It is the chief of the demons who gives Jesus the power to drive out demons."

Jesus Has Pity for the People

35 Jesus went around visiting all the towns and villages. He taught in the

synagogues, preached the Good News about the Kingdom, and healed people with every kind of disease and sickness. 36As he saw the crowds, his heart was filled with pity for them, because they were worried and helpless, like sheep without a shepherd. 37So he said to his disciples, "The harvest is large, but there are few workers to gather it in. 38Pray to the owner of the harvest that he will send out workers to gather in his harvest."

The Twelve Apostles

10 1Jesus called his twelve disciples together and gave them authority to drive out evil spirits and to heal every disease and every sickness. 2These are the names of the twelve apostles: first, Simon (called Peter) and his brother Andrew; James and his brother John, the sons of Zebedee; 3Philip and Bartholomew; Thomas and Matthew, the tax collector; James son of Alphaeus, and Thaddaeus; 4Simon the Patriot, and Judas Iscariot, who betrayed Jesus.

The Mission of the Twelve

5These twelve men were sent out by Jesus with the following instructions: "Do not go to any Gentile territory or any Samaritan towns. 6Instead, you are to go to the lost sheep of the people of Israel. 7Go and preach, 'The Kingdom of heaven is near!' 8Heal the sick, bring the dead back to life, heal those who suffer from dreaded skin diseases, and drive out demons. You have received without paying, so give without being paid.

9Do not carry any gold, silver, or copper money in your pockets; 10do not carry a beggar's bag for the trip or an extra shirt or shoes or a walking stick. Workers should be given what they need.

11"When you come to a town or village, go in and look for someone who is willing to welcome you, and stay with him until you leave that place. 12When you go into a house, say, 'Peace be with you.' 13If the people in that house welcome you, let your greeting of peace remain; but if they do not welcome you, then take back your greeting. 14And if some home or town will not welcome you or listen to you, then leave that place and shake the dust off your feet. 15I assure you that on the Judgment Day God will show more mercy to the people of Sodom and Gomorrah than to the people of that town!

Coming Persecutions

16"Listen! I am sending you out just like sheep to a pack of wolves. You must be as cautious as snakes and as gentle as doves. 17Watch out, for there will be those who will arrest you and take you to court, and they will whip you in the synagogues. 18For my sake you will be brought to trial before rulers and kings, to tell the Good News to them and to the Gentiles. 19When they bring you to trial, do not worry about what you are going to say or how you will say it; when the time comes, you will be given what you will say. 20For the words you will speak will not be yours; they will come from the Spirit of your Father speaking through you.

21 "People will hand over their own brothers to be put to death, and fathers will do the same to their children; children will turn against their parents and have them put to death. 22Everyone will hate you because of me. But whoever holds out to the end will be saved. 23When they persecute you in one town, run away to another one. I assure you that you will not finish your work in all the towns of Israel before the Son of Man comes.

24 "No pupil is greater than his teacher; no slave is greater than his master. 25So a pupil should be satisfied to become like his teacher, and a slave like his master. If the head of the family is called Beelzebul, the members of the family will be called even worse names!

Whom to Fear

26 "So do not be afraid of people. Whatever is now covered up will be uncovered, and every secret will be made known. 27What I am telling you in the dark you must repeat in broad daylight, and what you have heard in private you must announce from the housetops. 28Do not be afraid of those who kill the body but cannot kill the soul; rather be afraid of God, who can destroy both body and soul in hell. 29For only a penny you can buy two sparrows, yet not one sparrow falls to the ground without your Father's consent. 30As for you, even the hairs of your head have all been counted.

31So do not be afraid; you are worth much more than many sparrows!

Confessing and Rejecting Christ

32 "Those who declare publicly that they belong to me, I will do the same for them before my Father in heaven. 33But those who reject me publicly, I will reject before my Father in heaven.

Not Peace, but a Sword

34 "Do not think that I have come to bring peace to the world. No, I did not come to bring peace, but a sword. 35I came to set sons against their fathers, daughters against their mothers, daughters-in-law against their mothers-in-law; 36your worst enemies will be the members of your own family.

37 "Those who love their father or mother more than me are not fit to be my disciples; those who love their son or daughter more than me are not fit to be my disciples. 38Those who do not take up their cross and follow in my steps are not fit to be my disciples. 39Those who try to gain their own life will lose it; but those who lose their life for my sake will gain it.

Rewards

40 "Whoever welcomes you welcomes me; and whoever welcomes me welcomes the one who sent me. 41Whoever welcomes God's messenger because he is God's messenger, will share in his reward. And whoever welcomes a good man because he is good, will share in his reward. 42You can be sure that whoever gives even a drink of cold

water to one of the least of these my followers because he is my follower, will certainly receive a reward."

The Messengers from John the Baptist

11 ¹When Jesus finished giving these instructions to his twelve disciples, he left that place and went off to teach and preach in the towns near there.

²When John the Baptist heard in prison about the things that Christ was doing, he sent some of his disciples to him. ³ "Tell us," they asked Jesus, "are you the one John said was going to come, or should we expect someone else?"

⁴Jesus answered, "Go back and tell John what you are hearing and seeing: ⁵the blind can see, the lame can walk, those who suffer from dreaded skin diseases are made clean, the deaf hear, the dead are brought back to life, and the Good News is preached to the poor. ⁶How happy are those who have no doubts about me!"

⁷While John's disciples were leaving, Jesus spoke about him to the crowds: "When you went out to John in the desert, what did you expect to see? A blade of grass bending in the wind? ⁸What did you go out to see? A man dressed up in fancy clothes? People who dress like that live in palaces! ⁹Tell me, what did you go out to see? A prophet? Yes indeed, but you saw much more than a prophet. ¹⁰For John is the one of whom the scripture says: 'God said, I will send my messenger ahead of you to open the way for you.'

¹¹I assure you that John the Baptist is greater than anyone who has ever lived. But the one who is least in the Kingdom of heaven is greater than John. ¹²From the time John preached his message until this very day the Kingdom of heaven has suffered violent attacks, and violent men try to seize it. ¹³Until the time of John all the prophets and the Law of Moses spoke about the Kingdom; ¹⁴and if you are willing to believe their message, John is Elijah, whose coming was predicted. ¹⁵Listen, then, if you have ears!

¹⁶ "Now, to what can I compare the people of this day? They are like children sitting in the marketplace. One group shouts to the other, ¹⁷ 'We played wedding music for you, but you wouldn't dance! We sang funeral songs, but you wouldn't cry!' ¹⁸When John came, he fasted and drank no wine, and everyone said, 'He has a demon in him!' ¹⁹When the Son of Man came, he ate and drank, and everyone said, 'Look at this man! He is a glutton and wine drinker, a friend of tax collectors and other outcasts!' God's wisdom, however, is shown to be true by its results."

The Unbelieving Towns

²⁰The people in the towns where Jesus had performed most of his miracles did not turn from their sins, so he reproached those towns. ²¹ "How terrible it will be for you, Chorazin! How terrible for you too, Bethsaida! If the miracles which were performed in you had been performed in Tyre and Sidon, the people there would have

long ago put on sackcloth and sprinkled ashes on themselves, to show that they had turned from their sins! 22I assure you that on the Judgment Day God will show more mercy to the people of Tyre and Sidon than to you! 23And as for you, Capernaum! Did you want to lift yourself up to heaven? You will be thrown down to hell! If the miracles which were performed in you had been performed in Sodom, it would still be in existence today! 24You can be sure that on the Judgment Day God will show more mercy to Sodom than to you!"

Come to Me and Rest

25At that time Jesus said, "Father, Lord of heaven and earth! I thank you because you have shown to the unlearned what you have hidden from the wise and learned. 26Yes, Father, this was how you were pleased to have it happen.

27"My Father has given me all things. No one knows the Son except the Father, and no one knows the Father except the Son and those to whom the Son chooses to reveal him.

28"Come to me, all of you who are tired from carrying heavy loads, and I will give you rest. 29Take my yoke and put it on you, and learn from me, because I am gentle and humble in spirit; and you will find rest. 30For the yoke I will give you is easy, and the load I will put on you is light."

The Question about the Sabbath

12 1Not long afterward Jesus was walking through some wheat fields on a Sabbath. His disciples were hungry, so they began to pick heads of wheat and eat the grain. 2When the Pharisees saw this, they said to Jesus, "Look, it is against our Law for your disciples to do this on the Sabbath!"

3Jesus answered, "Have you never read what David did that time when he and his men were hungry? 4He went into the house of God, and he and his men ate the bread offered to God, even though it was against the Law for them to eat it—only the priests were allowed to eat that bread. 5Or have you not read in the Law of Moses that every Sabbath the priests in the Temple actually break the Sabbath law, yet they are not guilty? 6I tell you that there is something here greater than the Temple. 7The scripture says, 'It is kindness that I want, not animal sacrifices.' If you really knew what this means, you would not condemn people who are not guilty; 8for the Son of Man is Lord of the Sabbath."

The Man with a Paralyzed Hand

9Jesus left that place and went to a synagogue, 10where there was a man who had a paralyzed hand. Some people were there who wanted to accuse Jesus of doing wrong, so they asked him, "Is it against our Law to heal on the Sabbath?"

11Jesus answered, "What if one of you has a sheep and it falls into a deep hole on the Sabbath? Will you not take hold of it and lift it out? 12And a human being is worth much more than a sheep! So then, our Law does allow us to help someone on the Sabbath." 13Then he said to the man with the paralyzed hand, "Stretch out your hand."

He stretched it out, and it became well again, just like the other one. 14Then the Pharisees left and made plans to kill Jesus.

God's Chosen Servant

15When Jesus heard about the plot against him, he went away from that place; and large crowds followed him. He healed all the sick 16and gave them orders not to tell others about him. 17He did this so as to make come true what God had said through the prophet Isaiah:
18"Here is my servant,
　whom I have chosen,
　the one I love,
　and with whom I am pleased.
I will send my Spirit upon him,
　and he will announce
　my judgment to the nations.
19He will not argue or shout,
　or make loud speeches
　in the streets.
20He will not break off a bent reed,
　nor put out a flickering lamp.
He will persist
　until he causes justice to triumph,
21and on him
　all peoples will put their hope."

Jesus and Beelzebul

22Then some people brought to Jesus a man who was blind and could not talk because he had a demon. Jesus healed the man, so that he was able to talk and see. 23The crowds were all amazed at what Jesus had done. "Could he be the Son of David?" they asked.

24When the Pharisees heard this, they replied, "He drives out demons only because their ruler Beelzebul gives him power to do so."

25Jesus knew what they were thinking, and so he said to them, "Any country that divides itself into groups which fight each other will not last very long. And any town or family that divides itself into groups which fight each other will fall apart. 26So if one group is fighting another in Satan's kingdom, this means that it is already divided into groups and will soon fall apart! 27You say that I drive out demons because Beelzebul gives me the power to do so. Well, then, who gives your followers the power to drive them out? What your own followers do proves that you are wrong! 28No, it is not Beelzebul, but God's Spirit, who gives me the power to drive out demons, which proves that the Kingdom of God has already come upon you.

29"No one can break into a strong man's house and take away his belongings unless he first ties up the strong man; then he can plunder his house.

30"Anyone who is not for me is really against me; anyone who does not help me gather is really scattering. 31For this reason I tell you: people can be forgiven any sin and any evil thing they say; but whoever says evil things against the Holy Spirit will not be forgiven. 32Anyone who says something against the Son of Man can be forgiven; but whoever says something against the Holy Spirit will not be forgiven — now or ever.

A Tree and Its Fruit

33 "To have good fruit you must have a healthy tree; if you have a poor tree, you will have bad fruit. A tree is known by the kind of fruit it bears. 34 You snakes — how can you say good things when you are evil? For the mouth speaks what the heart is full of. 35 A good person brings good things out of a treasure of good things; a bad person brings bad things out of a treasure of bad things.

36 "You can be sure that on the Judgment Day you will have to give account of every useless word you have ever spoken. 37 Your words will be used to judge you — to declare you either innocent or guilty."

The Demand for a Miracle

38 Then some teachers of the Law and some Pharisees spoke up. "Teacher," they said, "we want to see you perform a miracle."

39 "How evil and godless are the people of this day!" Jesus exclaimed. "You ask me for a miracle? No! The only miracle you will be given is the miracle of the prophet Jonah. 40 In the same way that Jonah spent three days and nights in the big fish, so will the Son of Man spend three days and nights in the depths of the earth. 41 On the Judgment Day the people of Nineveh will stand up and accuse you, because they turned from their sins when they heard Jonah preach; and I tell you that there is something here greater than Jonah! 42 On the Judgment Day the Queen of Sheba will stand up and accuse you, because she traveled all the way from her country to listen to King Solomon's wise teaching; and I assure you that there is something here greater than Solomon!

The Return of the Evil Spirit

43 "When an evil spirit goes out of a person, it travels over dry country looking for a place to rest. If it can't find one, 44 it says to itself, 'I will go back to my house.' So it goes back and finds the house empty, clean, and all fixed up. 45 Then it goes out and brings along seven other spirits even worse than itself, and they come and live there. So when it is all over, that person is in worse shape than at the beginning. This is what will happen to the evil people of this day."

Jesus' Mother and Brothers

46 Jesus was still talking to the people when his mother and brothers arrived. They stood outside, asking to speak with him. 47 So one of the people there said to him, "Look, your mother and brothers are standing outside, and they want to speak with you."

48 Jesus answered, "Who is my mother? Who are my brothers?" 49 Then he pointed to his disciples and said, "Look! Here are my mother and my brothers! 50 Whoever does what my Father in heaven wants is my brother, my sister, and my mother."

The Parable of the Sower

13 [1] That same day Jesus left the house and went to the lakeside, where he sat down to teach. [2] The crowd that gathered around him was so large that he got into a boat and sat in it, while the crowd stood on the shore. [3] He used parables to tell them many things.

"Once there was a man who went out to sow grain. [4] As he scattered the seed in the field, some of it fell along the path, and the birds came and ate it up. [5] Some of it fell on rocky ground, where there was little soil. The seeds soon sprouted, because the soil wasn't deep. [6] But when the sun came up, it burned the young plants; and because the roots had not grown deep enough, the plants soon dried up. [7] Some of the seed fell among thorn bushes, which grew up and choked the plants. [8] But some seeds fell in good soil, and the plants bore grain: some had one hundred grains, others sixty, and others thirty."

[9] And Jesus concluded, "Listen, then, if you have ears!"

The Purpose of the Parables

[10] Then the disciples came to Jesus and asked him, "Why do you use parables when you talk to the people?"

[11] Jesus answered, "The knowledge about the secrets of the Kingdom of heaven has been given to you, but not to them. [12] For the person who has something will be given more, so that he will have more than enough; but the person who has nothing will have taken away from him even the little he has. [13] The reason I use parables in talking to them is that they look, but do not see, and they listen, but do not hear or understand." So the prophecy of Isaiah applies to them:

'This people will listen and listen,
     but not understand;
they will look and look,
     but not see,
[15] because their minds are dull,
     and they have stopped up their ears
     and have closed their eyes.
Otherwise,
     their eyes would see,
     their ears would hear,
     their minds would understand,
and they would turn to me,
     says God,
and I would heal them.'

[16] "As for you, how fortunate you are! Your eyes see and your ears hear. [17] I assure you that many prophets and many of God's people wanted very much to see what you see, but they could not, and to hear what you hear, but they did not.

Jesus Explains the Parable of the Sower

[18] "Listen, then, and learn what the parable of the sower means. [19] Those who hear the message about the Kingdom but do not understand it are like the seeds that fell along the path. The Evil One comes and snatches away what was sown in them. [20] The seeds that fell on rocky ground stand for those who receive the message gladly as soon as they hear it. [21] But it

does not sink deep into them, and they don't last long. So when trouble or persecution comes because of the message, they give up at once. 22 The seeds that fell among thorn bushes stand for those who hear the message; but the worries about this life and the love for riches choke the message, and they don't bear fruit. 23 And the seeds sown in the good soil stand for those who hear the message and understand it: they bear fruit, some as much as one hundred, others sixty, and others thirty."

The Parable of the Weeds

24 Jesus told them another parable: "The Kingdom of heaven is like this. A man sowed good seed in his field. 25 One night, when everyone was asleep, an enemy came and sowed weeds among the wheat and went away. 26 When the plants grew and the heads of grain began to form, then the weeds showed up. 27 The man's servants came to him and said, 'Sir, it was good seed you sowed in your field; where did the weeds come from?' 28 'It was some enemy who did this,' he answered. 'Do you want us to go and pull up the weeds?' they asked him. 29 'No,' he answered, 'because as you gather the weeds you might pull up some of the wheat along with them. 30 Let the wheat and the weeds both grow together until harvest. Then I will tell the harvest workers to pull up the weeds first, tie them in bundles and burn them, and then to gather in the wheat and put it in my barn.'"

The Parable of the Mustard Seed

31 Jesus told them another parable: "The Kingdom of heaven is like this. A man takes a mustard seed and sows it in his field. 32 It is the smallest of all seeds, but when it grows up, it is the biggest of all plants. It becomes a tree, so that birds come and make their nests in its branches."

The Parable of the Yeast

33 Jesus told them still another parable: "The Kingdom of heaven is like this. A woman takes some yeast and mixes it with a bushel of flour until the whole batch of dough rises."

Jesus' Use of Parables

34 Jesus used parables to tell all these things to the crowds; he would not say a thing to them without using a parable. 35 He did this to make come true what the prophet had said,

"I will use parables
    when I speak to them;
I will tell them things
    unknown since the creation
    of the world."

Jesus Explains the Parable of the Weeds

36 When Jesus had left the crowd and gone indoors, his disciples came to him and said, "Tell us what the parable about the weeds in the field means."

37 Jesus answered, "The man who sowed the good seed is the Son of Man; 38 the field is the world; the good seed is the people who belong to the

Kingdom; the weeds are the people who belong to the Evil One; 39and the enemy who sowed the weeds is the Devil. The harvest is the end of the age, and the harvest workers are angels. 40Just as the weeds are gathered up and burned in the fire, so the same thing will happen at the end of the age: 41the Son of Man will send out his angels to gather up out of his Kingdom all those who cause people to sin and all others who do evil things, 42and they will throw them into the fiery furnace, where they will cry and gnash their teeth. 43Then God's people will shine like the sun in their Father's Kingdom. Listen, then, if you have ears!

The Parable of the Hidden Treasure

44"The Kingdom of heaven is like this. A man happens to find a treasure hidden in a field. He covers it up again, and is so happy that he goes and sells everything he has, and then goes back and buys that field.

The Parable of the Pearl

45"Also, the Kingdom of heaven is like this. A man is looking for fine pearls, 46and when he finds one that is unusually fine, he goes and sells everything he has, and buys that pearl.

The Parable of the Net

47"Also, the Kingdom of heaven is like this. Some fishermen throw their net out in the lake and catch all kinds of fish. 48When the net is full, they pull it to shore and sit down to divide the fish: the good ones go into the buckets, the worthless ones are thrown away. 49It will be like this at the end of the age: the angels will go out and gather up the evil people from among the good 50and will throw them into the fiery furnace, where they will cry and gnash their teeth.

New Truths and Old

51"Do you understand these things?" Jesus asked them.

"Yes," they answered.

52So he replied, "This means, then, that every teacher of the Law who becomes a disciple in the Kingdom of heaven is like a homeowner who takes new and old things out of his storage room."

Jesus Is Rejected at Nazareth

53When Jesus finished telling these parables, he left that place 54and went back to his hometown. He taught in the synagogue, and those who heard him were amazed. "Where did he get such wisdom?" they asked. "And what about his miracles? 55Isn't he the carpenter's son? Isn't Mary his mother, and aren't James, Joseph, Simon, and Judas his brothers? 56Aren't all his sisters living here? Where did he get all this?" 57And so they rejected him.

Jesus said to them, "A prophet is respected everywhere except in his hometown and by his own family." 58Because they did not have faith, he did not perform many miracles there.

The Death of John the Baptist

14 1At that time Herod, the ruler of Galilee, heard about Jesus.

2"He is really John the Baptist, who has come back to life," he told his officials. "That is why he has this power to perform miracles."

3For Herod had earlier ordered John's arrest, and he had him tied up and put in prison. He had done this because of Herodias, his brother Philip's wife. 4For some time John the Baptist had told Herod, "It isn't right for you to be married to Herodias!" 5Herod wanted to kill him, but he was afraid of the Jewish people, because they considered John to be a prophet.

6On Herod's birthday the daughter of Herodias danced in front of the whole group. Herod was so pleased 7that he promised her, "I swear that I will give you anything you ask for!"

8At her mother's suggestion she asked him, "Give me here and now the head of John the Baptist on a plate!"

9The king was sad, but because of the promise he had made in front of all his guests he gave orders that her wish be granted. 10So he had John beheaded in prison. 11The head was brought in on a plate and given to the girl, who took it to her mother. 12John's disciples came, carried away his body, and buried it; then they went and told Jesus.

Jesus Feeds Five Thousand

13When Jesus heard the news about John, he left there in a boat and went to a lonely place by himself. The people heard about it, and so they left their towns and followed him by land. 14Jesus got out of the boat, and when he saw the large crowd, his heart was filled with pity for them, and he healed their sick.

15That evening his disciples came to him and said, "It is already very late, and this is a lonely place. Send the people away and let them go to the villages to buy food for themselves."

16"They don't have to leave," answered Jesus. "You yourselves give them something to eat!"

17"All we have here are five loaves and two fish," they replied.

18"Then bring them here to me," Jesus said. 19He ordered the people to sit down on the grass; then he took the five loaves and the two fish, looked up to heaven, and gave thanks to God. He broke the loaves and gave them to the disciples, and the disciples gave them to the people. 20Everyone ate and had enough. Then the disciples took up twelve baskets full of what was left over. 21The number of men who ate was about five thousand, not counting the women and children.

Jesus Walks on the Water

22Then Jesus made the disciples get into the boat and go on ahead to the other side of the lake, while he sent the people away. 23After sending the people away, he went up a hill by himself to pray. When evening came, Jesus was there alone; 24and by this time the boat was far out in the lake, tossed about by the waves, because the wind was blowing against it.

25Between three and six o'clock in the morning Jesus came to the disciples, walking on the water.

26When they saw him walking on the water, they were terrified. "It's a ghost!" they said, and screamed with fear.

27Jesus spoke to them at once. "Courage!" he said. "It is I. Don't be afraid!"

28Then Peter spoke up. "Lord, if it is really you, order me to come out on the water to you."

29"Come!" answered Jesus. So Peter got out of the boat and started walking on the water to Jesus. 30But when he noticed the strong wind, he was afraid and started to sink down in the water. "Save me, Lord!" he cried.

31At once Jesus reached out and grabbed hold of him and said, "What little faith you have! Why did you doubt?"

32They both got into the boat, and the wind died down. 33Then the disciples in the boat worshiped Jesus. "Truly you are the Son of God!" they exclaimed.

Jesus Heals the Sick in Gennesaret

34They crossed the lake and came to land at Gennesaret, 35where the people recognized Jesus. So they sent for the sick people in all the surrounding country and brought them to Jesus. 36They begged him to let the sick at least touch the edge of his cloak; and all who touched it were made well.

The Teaching of the Ancestors

15 1Then some Pharisees and teachers of the Law came from Jerusalem to Jesus and asked him, 2"Why is it that your disciples disobey the teaching handed down by our ancestors? They don't wash their hands in the proper way before they eat!"

3Jesus answered, "And why do you disobey God's command and follow your own teaching? 4For God said, 'Respect your father and your mother,' and 'If you curse your father or your mother, you are to be put to death.' 5But you teach that if people have something they could use to help their father or mother, but say, 'This belongs to God,' 6they do not need to honor their father. In this way you disregard God's command, in order to follow your own teaching. 7You hypocrites! How right Isaiah was when he prophesied about you!

8 'These people, says God,
     honor me with their words,
   but their heart
     is really far away from me.
9 It is no use for them to worship me,
     because they teach human rules
     as though they were my laws!'"

The Things That Make a Person Unclean

10Then Jesus called the crowd to him and said to them, "Listen and understand! 11It is not what goes into your mouth that makes you ritually unclean; rather, what comes out of it makes you unclean."

12Then the disciples came to him and said, "Do you know that the Pharisees had their feelings hurt by what you said?"

13"Every plant which my Father in heaven did not plant will be pulled up," answered Jesus. 14"Don't worry about them! They are blind leaders of the blind; and when one blind man leads another, both fall into a ditch."

15Peter spoke up, "Explain this saying to us."

16Jesus said to them, "You are still no more intelligent than the others. 17Don't you understand? Anything that goes into your mouth goes into your stomach and then on out of your body. 18But the things that come out of the mouth come from the heart, and these are the things that make you ritually unclean. 19For from your heart come the evil ideas which lead you to kill, commit adultery, and do other immoral things; to rob, lie, and slander others. 20These are the things that make you unclean. But to eat without washing your hands as they say you should—this doesn't make you unclean."

A Woman's Faith

21Jesus left that place and went off to the territory near the cities of Tyre and Sidon. 22A Canaanite woman who lived in that region came to him. "Son of David!" she cried out. "Have mercy on me, sir! My daughter has a demon and is in a terrible condition."

23But Jesus did not say a word to her. His disciples came to him and begged him, "Send her away! She is following us and making all this noise!"

24Then Jesus replied, "I have been sent only to the lost sheep of the people of Israel."

25At this the woman came and fell at his feet. "Help me, sir!" she said.

26Jesus answered, "It isn't right to take the children's food and throw it to the dogs."

27"That's true, sir," she answered, "but even the dogs eat the leftovers that fall from their masters' table."

28So Jesus answered her, "You are a woman of great faith! What you want will be done for you." And at that very moment her daughter was healed.

Jesus Heals Many People

29Jesus left there and went along by Lake Galilee. He climbed a hill and sat down. 30Large crowds came to him, bringing with them the lame, the blind, the crippled, the dumb, and many other sick people, whom they placed at Jesus' feet; and he healed them. 31The people were amazed as they saw the dumb speaking, the crippled made whole, the lame walking, and the blind seeing; and they praised the God of Israel.

Jesus Feeds Four Thousand

32Jesus called his disciples to him and said, "I feel sorry for these people, because they have been with me for three days and now have nothing to eat. I don't want to send them away without feeding them, for they might faint on their way home."

33The disciples asked him, "Where will we find enough food in this desert to feed this crowd?"

34"How much bread do you have?" Jesus asked.

"Seven loaves," they answered, "and a few small fish."

35 So Jesus ordered the crowd to sit down on the ground. 36 Then he took the seven loaves and the fish, gave thanks to God, broke them, and gave them to the disciples; and the disciples gave them to the people. 37 They all ate and had enough. Then the disciples took up seven baskets full of pieces left over. 38 The number of men who ate was four thousand, not counting the women and children.

39 Then Jesus sent the people away, got into a boat, and went to the territory of Magadan.

The Demand for a Miracle

16 1 Some Pharisees and Sadducees who came to Jesus wanted to trap him, so they asked him to perform a miracle for them, to show that God approved of him. 2 But Jesus answered, "When the sun is setting, you say, 'We are going to have fine weather, because the sky is red.' 3 And early in the morning you say, 'It is going to rain, because the sky is red and dark.' You can predict the weather by looking at the sky, but you cannot interpret the signs concerning these times! 4 How evil and godless are the people of this day! You ask me for a miracle? No! The only miracle you will be given is the miracle of Jonah."

So he left them and went away.

The Yeast of the Pharisees and Sadducees

5 When the disciples crossed over to the other side of the lake, they forgot to take any bread. 6 Jesus said to them,

"Take care; be on your guard against the yeast of the Pharisees and Sadducees."

7 They started discussing among themselves, "He says this because we didn't bring any bread."

8 Jesus knew what they were saying, so he asked them, "Why are you discussing among yourselves about not having any bread? What little faith you have! 9 Don't you understand yet? Don't you remember when I broke the five loaves for the five thousand men? How many baskets did you fill? 10 And what about the seven loaves for the four thousand men? How many baskets did you fill? 11 How is it that you don't understand that I was not talking to you about bread? Guard yourselves from the yeast of the Pharisees and Sadducees!"

12 Then the disciples understood that he was not warning them to guard themselves from the yeast used in bread but from the teaching of the Pharisees and Sadducees.

Peter's Declaration about Jesus

13 Jesus went to the territory near the town of Caesarea Philippi, where he asked his disciples, "Who do people say the Son of Man is?"

14 "Some say John the Baptist," they answered. "Others say Elijah, while others say Jeremiah or some other prophet."

15 "What about you?" he asked them. "Who do you say I am?"

16 Simon Peter answered, "You are the Messiah, the Son of the living God."

17 "Good for you, Simon son of John!" answered Jesus. "For this truth did not come to you from any human being, but it was given to you directly by my Father in heaven. 18 And so I tell you, Peter: you are a rock, and on this rock foundation I will build my church, and not even death will ever be able to overcome it. 19 I will give you the keys of the Kingdom of heaven; what you prohibit on earth will be prohibited in heaven, and what you permit on earth will be permitted in heaven."

20 Then Jesus ordered his disciples not to tell anyone that he was the Messiah.

Jesus Speaks about His Suffering and Death

21 From that time on Jesus began to say plainly to his disciples, "I must go to Jerusalem and suffer much from the elders, the chief priests, and the teachers of the Law. I will be put to death, but three days later I will be raised to life."

22 Peter took him aside and began to rebuke him. "God forbid it, Lord!" he said. "That must never happen to you!"

23 Jesus turned around and said to Peter, "Get away from me, Satan! You are an obstacle in my way, because these thoughts of yours don't come from God, but from human nature."

24 Then Jesus said to his disciples, "If any of you want to come with me, you must forget yourself, carry your cross, and follow me. 25 For if you want to save your own life, you will lose it; but if you lose your life for my sake, you

will find it. 26 Will you gain anything if you win the whole world but lose your life? Of course not! There is nothing you can give to regain your life. 27 For the Son of Man is about to come in the glory of his Father with his angels, and then he will reward each one according to his deeds. 28 I assure you that there are some here who will not die until they have seen the Son of Man come as King."

The Transfiguration

17 1 Six days later Jesus took with him Peter and the brothers James and John and led them up a high mountain where they were alone. 2 As they looked on, a change came over Jesus: his face was shining like the sun, and his clothes were dazzling white. 3 Then the three disciples saw Moses and Elijah talking with Jesus. 4 So Peter spoke up and said to Jesus, "Lord, how good it is that we are here! If you wish, I will make three tents here, one for you, one for Moses, and one for Elijah."

5 While he was talking, a shining cloud came over them, and a voice from the cloud said, "This is my own dear Son, with whom I am pleased — listen to him!"

6 When the disciples heard the voice, they were so terrified that they threw themselves face downward on the ground. 7 Jesus came to them and touched them. "Get up," he said. "Don't be afraid!" 8 So they looked up and saw no one there but Jesus.

9 As they came down the mountain, Jesus ordered them, "Don't tell

anyone about this vision you have seen until the Son of Man has been raised from death."

10Then the disciples asked Jesus, "Why do the teachers of the Law say that Elijah has to come first?"

11"Elijah is indeed coming first," answered Jesus, "and he will get everything ready. 12But I tell you that Elijah has already come and people did not recognize him, but treated him just as they pleased. In the same way they will also mistreat the Son of Man."

13Then the disciples understood that he was talking to them about John the Baptist.

Jesus Heals a Boy with a Demon

14When they returned to the crowd, a man came to Jesus, knelt before him, 15and said, "Sir, have mercy on my son! He is an epileptic and has such terrible attacks that he often falls in the fire or into water. 16I brought him to your disciples, but they could not heal him."

17Jesus answered, "How unbelieving and wrong you people are! How long must I stay with you? How long do I have to put up with you? Bring the boy here to me!" 18Jesus gave a command to the demon, and it went out of the boy, and at that very moment he was healed.

19Then the disciples came to Jesus in private and asked him, "Why couldn't we drive the demon out?"

20"It was because you do not have enough faith," answered Jesus. "I assure you that if you have faith as big as a mustard seed, you can say to this hill, 'Go from here to there!' and it will go. You could do anything!"

Jesus Speaks Again about His Death

22When the disciples all came together in Galilee, Jesus said to them, "The Son of Man is about to be handed over to those 23who will kill him; but three days later he will be raised to life."

The disciples became very sad.

Payment of the Temple Tax

24When Jesus and his disciples came to Capernaum, the collectors of the Temple tax came to Peter and asked, "Does your teacher pay the Temple tax?"

25"Of course," Peter answered.

When Peter went into the house, Jesus spoke up first, "Simon, what is your opinion? Who pays duties or taxes to the kings of this world? The citizens of the country or the foreigners?"

26"The foreigners," answered Peter.

"Well, then," replied Jesus, "that means that the citizens don't have to pay. 27But we don't want to offend these people. So go to the lake and drop in a line. Pull up the first fish you hook, and in its mouth you will find a coin worth enough for my Temple tax and yours. Take it and pay them our taxes."

Who Is the Greatest?

18 1At that time the disciples came to Jesus, asking, "Who is the greatest in the Kingdom of heaven?"

2So Jesus called a child to come and stand in front of them, 3and said, "I assure you that unless you change and become like children, you will never enter the Kingdom of heaven. [4]The greatest in the Kingdom of heaven is the one who humbles himself and becomes like this child. [5]And whoever welcomes in my name one such child as this, welcomes me.

Temptations to Sin

[6]"If anyone should cause one of these little ones to lose his faith in me, it would be better for that person to have a large millstone tied around his neck and be drowned in the deep sea. [7]How terrible for the world that there are things that make people lose their faith! Such things will always happen — but how terrible for the one who causes them!

[8]"If your hand or your foot makes you lose your faith, cut it off and throw it away! It is better for you to enter life without a hand or a foot than to keep both hands and both feet and be thrown into the eternal fire. [9]And if your eye makes you lose your faith, take it out and throw it away! It is better for you to enter life with only one eye than to keep both eyes and be thrown into the fire of hell.

The Parable of the Lost Sheep

[10]"See that you don't despise any of these little ones. Their angels in heaven, I tell you, are always in the presence of my Father in heaven.

[12]"What do you think a man does who has one hundred sheep and one of them gets lost? He will leave the other ninety-nine grazing on the hillside and go and look for the lost sheep. [13]When he finds it, I tell you, he feels far happier over this one sheep than over the ninety-nine that did not get lost. [14]In just the same way your Father in heaven does not want any of these little ones to be lost.

When Someone Sins

[15]"If your brother sins against you, go to him and show him his fault. But do it privately, just between yourselves. If he listens to you, you have won your brother back. [16]But if he will not listen to you, take one or two other persons with you, so that 'every accusation may be upheld by the testimony of two or more witnesses,' as the scripture says. [17]And if he will not listen to them, then tell the whole thing to the church. Finally, if he will not listen to the church, treat him as though he were a pagan or a tax collector.

Prohibiting and Permitting

[18]"And so I tell all of you: what you prohibit on earth will be prohibited in heaven, and what you permit on earth will be permitted in heaven.

[19]"And I tell you more: whenever two of you on earth agree about anything you pray for, it will be done for you by my Father in heaven. [20]For where two or three come together in my name, I am there with them."

The Parable of the Unforgiving Servant

[21]Then Peter came to Jesus and asked, "Lord, if my brother keeps on sinning against me, how many times

do I have to forgive him? Seven times?"

22 "No, not seven times," answered Jesus, "but seventy times seven, 23 because the Kingdom of heaven is like this. Once there was a king who decided to check on his servants' accounts. 24 He had just begun to do so when one of them was brought in who owed him millions of dollars. 25 The servant did not have enough to pay his debt, so the king ordered him to be sold as a slave, with his wife and his children and all that he had, in order to pay the debt. 26 The servant fell on his knees before the king. 'Be patient with me,' he begged, 'and I will pay you everything!' 27 The king felt sorry for him, so he forgave him the debt and let him go.

28 "Then the man went out and met one of his fellow servants who owed him a few dollars. He grabbed him and started choking him. 'Pay back what you owe me!' he said. 29 His fellow servant fell down and begged him, 'Be patient with me, and I will pay you back!' 30 But he refused; instead, he had him thrown into jail until he should pay the debt. 31 When the other servants saw what had happened, they were very upset and went to the king and told him everything. 32 So he called the servant in. 'You worthless slave!' he said. 'I forgave you the whole amount you owed me, just because you asked me to. 33 You should have had mercy on your fellow servant, just as I had mercy on you.' 34 The king was very angry, and he sent the servant to jail to be punished until he should pay back the whole amount."

35 And Jesus concluded, "That is how my Father in heaven will treat every one of you unless you forgive your brother from your heart."

Jesus Teaches about Divorce

19 1 When Jesus finished saying these things, he left Galilee and went to the territory of Judea on the other side of the Jordan River. 2 Large crowds followed him, and he healed them there.

3 Some Pharisees came to him and tried to trap him by asking, "Does our Law allow a man to divorce his wife for whatever reason he wishes?"

4 Jesus answered, "Haven't you read the scripture that says that in the beginning the Creator made people male and female? 5 And God said, 'For this reason a man will leave his father and mother and unite with his wife, and the two will become one.' 6 So they are no longer two, but one. No human being must separate, then, what God has joined together."

7 The Pharisees asked him, "Why, then, did Moses give the law for a man to hand his wife a divorce notice and send her away?"

8 Jesus answered, "Moses gave you permission to divorce your wives because you are so hard to teach. But it was not like that at the time of creation. 9 I tell you, then, that any man who divorces his wife for any cause other than her unfaithfulness, commits adultery if he marries some other woman."

10 His disciples said to him, "If this is how it is between a man and his wife, it is better not to marry."

11 Jesus answered, "This teaching does not apply to everyone, but only to those to whom God has given it. 12 For there are different reasons why men cannot marry: some, because they were born that way; others, because men made them that way; and others do not marry for the sake of the Kingdom of heaven. Let him who can accept this teaching do so."

Jesus Blesses Little Children

13 Some people brought children to Jesus for him to place his hands on them and to pray for them, but the disciples scolded the people. 14 Jesus said, "Let the children come to me and do not stop them, because the Kingdom of heaven belongs to such as these."

15 He placed his hands on them and then went away.

The Rich Young Man

16 Once a man came to Jesus. "Teacher," he asked, "what good thing must I do to receive eternal life?"

17 "Why do you ask me concerning what is good?" answered Jesus. "There is only One who is good. Keep the commandments if you want to enter life."

18 "What commandments?" he asked.

Jesus answered, "Do not commit murder; do not commit adultery; do not steal; do not accuse anyone falsely; 19 respect your father and your mother; and love your neighbor as you love yourself."

20 "I have obeyed all these commandments," the young man replied. "What else do I need to do?"

21 Jesus said to him, "If you want to be perfect, go and sell all you have and give the money to the poor, and you will have riches in heaven; then come and follow me."

22 When the young man heard this, he went away sad, because he was very rich.

23 Jesus then said to his disciples, "I assure you: it will be very hard for rich people to enter the Kingdom of heaven. 24 I repeat: it is much harder for a rich person to enter the Kingdom of God than for a camel to go through the eye of a needle."

25 When the disciples heard this, they were completely amazed. "Who, then, can be saved?" they asked.

26 Jesus looked straight at them and answered, "This is impossible for human beings, but for God everything is possible."

27 Then Peter spoke up. "Look," he said, "we have left everything and followed you. What will we have?"

28 Jesus said to them, "You can be sure that when the Son of Man sits on his glorious throne in the New Age, then you twelve followers of mine will also sit on thrones, to rule the twelve tribes of Israel. 29 And everyone who has left houses or brothers or sisters or father or mother or children or fields for my sake, will receive a hundred times more and will be given eternal

life. 30But many who now are first will be last, and many who now are last will be first.

The Workers in the Vineyard

20 1"The Kingdom of heaven is like this. Once there was a man who went out early in the morning to hire some men to work in his vineyard. 2He agreed to pay them the regular wage, a silver coin a day, and sent them to work in his vineyard. 3He went out again to the marketplace at nine o'clock and saw some men standing there doing nothing, 4so he told them, 'You also go and work in the vineyard, and I will pay you a fair wage.' 5So they went. Then at twelve o'clock and again at three o'clock he did the same thing. 6It was nearly five o'clock when he went to the marketplace and saw some other men still standing there. 'Why are you wasting the whole day here doing nothing?' he asked them. 7'No one hired us,' they answered. 'Well, then, you go and work in the vineyard,' he told them.

8"When evening came, the owner told his foreman, 'Call the workers and pay them their wages, starting with those who were hired last and ending with those who were hired first.' 9The men who had begun to work at five o'clock were paid a silver coin each. 10So when the men who were the first to be hired came to be paid, they thought they would get more; but they too were given a silver coin each. 11They took their money and started grumbling against the employer. 12'These men who were hired last worked only one hour,' they said, 'while we put up with a whole day's work in the hot sun—yet you paid them the same as you paid us!' 13'Listen, friend,' the owner answered one of them, 'I have not cheated you. After all, you agreed to do a day's work for one silver coin. 14Now take your pay and go home. I want to give this man who was hired last as much as I gave you. 15Don't I have the right to do as I wish with my own money? Or are you jealous because I am generous?'"

16And Jesus concluded, "So those who are last will be first, and those who are first will be last."

Jesus Speaks a Third Time about His Death

17As Jesus was going up to Jerusalem, he took the twelve disciples aside and spoke to them privately, as they walked along. 18"Listen," he told them, "we are going up to Jerusalem, where the Son of Man will be handed over to the chief priests and the teachers of the Law. They will condemn him to death 19and then hand him over to the Gentiles, who will make fun of him, whip him, and crucify him; but three days later he will be raised to life."

A Mother's Request

20Then the wife of Zebedee came to Jesus with her two sons, bowed before him, and asked him for a favor.

21 "What do you want?" Jesus asked her.

She answered, "Promise me that these two sons of mine will sit at your right and your left when you are King."

22 "You don't know what you are asking for," Jesus answered the sons. "Can you drink the cup of suffering that I am about to drink?"

"We can," they answered.

23 "You will indeed drink from my cup," Jesus told them, "but I do not have the right to choose who will sit at my right and my left. These places belong to those for whom my Father has prepared them."

24 When the other ten disciples heard about this, they became angry with the two brothers. 25 So Jesus called them all together and said, "You know that the rulers of the heathen have power over them, and the leaders have complete authority. 26 This, however, is not the way it shall be among you. If one of you wants to be great, you must be the servant of the rest; 27 and if one of you wants to be first, you must be the slave of the others — 28 like the Son of Man, who did not come to be served, but to serve and to give his life to redeem many people."

Jesus Heals Two Blind Men

29 As Jesus and his disciples were leaving Jericho, a large crowd was following. 30 Two blind men who were sitting by the road heard that Jesus was passing by, so they began to shout, "Son of David! Have mercy on us, sir!"

31 The crowd scolded them and told them to be quiet. But they shouted even more loudly, "Son of David! Have mercy on us, sir!"

32 Jesus stopped and called them. "What do you want me to do for you?" he asked them.

33 "Sir," they answered, "we want you to give us our sight!"

34 Jesus had pity on them and touched their eyes; at once they were able to see, and they followed him.

The Triumphant Entry into Jerusalem

21 1 As Jesus and his disciples approached Jerusalem, they came to Bethphage at the Mount of Olives. There Jesus sent two of the disciples on ahead 2 with these instructions: "Go to the village there ahead of you, and at once you will find a donkey tied up with her colt beside her. Untie them and bring them to me. 3 And if anyone says anything, tell him, 'The Master needs them'; and then he will let them go at once."

4 This happened in order to make come true what the prophet had said:
5 "Tell the city of Zion,
Look, your king is coming to you!
He is humble
    and rides on a donkey
    and on a colt,
    the foal of a donkey."

6 So the disciples went and did what Jesus had told them to do: 7 they brought the donkey and the colt, threw their cloaks over them, and Jesus got on. 8 A large crowd of people spread their cloaks on the road while others cut branches from the trees and spread them on the road. 9 The

crowds walking in front of Jesus and those walking behind began to shout, "Praise to David's Son! God bless him who comes in the name of the Lord! Praise be to God!"

10 When Jesus entered Jerusalem, the whole city was thrown into an uproar. "Who is he?" the people asked.

11 "This is the prophet Jesus, from Nazareth in Galilee," the crowds answered.

Jesus Goes to the Temple

12 Jesus went into the Temple and drove out all those who were buying and selling there. He overturned the tables of the moneychangers and the stools of those who sold pigeons, 13 and said to them, "It is written in the Scriptures that God said, 'My Temple will be called a house of prayer.' But you are making it a hideout for thieves!"

14 The blind and the crippled came to him in the Temple, and he healed them. 15 The chief priests and the teachers of the Law became angry when they saw the wonderful things he was doing and the children shouting in the Temple, "Praise to David's Son!" 16 So they asked Jesus, "Do you hear what they are saying?"

"Indeed I do," answered Jesus. "Haven't you ever read this scripture? 'You have trained children and babies to offer perfect praise.'"

17 Jesus left them and went out of the city to Bethany, where he spent the night.

Jesus Curses the Fig Tree

18 On his way back to the city early next morning, Jesus was hungry. 19 He saw a fig tree by the side of the road and went to it, but found nothing on it except leaves. So he said to the tree, "You will never again bear fruit!" At once the fig tree dried up.

20 The disciples saw this and were astounded. "How did the fig tree dry up so quickly?" they asked.

21 Jesus answered, "I assure you that if you believe and do not doubt, you will be able to do what I have done to this fig tree. And not only this, but you will even be able to say to this hill, 'Get up and throw yourself in the sea,' and it will. 22 If you believe, you will receive whatever you ask for in prayer."

The Question about Jesus' Authority

23 Jesus came back to the Temple; and as he taught, the chief priests and the elders came to him and asked, "What right do you have to do these things? Who gave you such right?"

24 Jesus answered them, "I will ask you just one question, and if you give me an answer, I will tell you what right I have to do these things. 25 Where did John's right to baptize come from: was it from God or from human beings?"

They started to argue among themselves, "What shall we say? If we answer, 'From God,' he will say to us, 'Why, then, did you not believe John?' 26 But if we say, 'From human beings,' we are afraid of what the people might do, because they are all convinced that John was a prophet." 27So they answered Jesus, "We don't know."

And he said to them, "Neither will I tell you, then, by what right I do these things.

The Parable of the Two Sons

28"Now, what do you think? There was once a man who had two sons. He went to the older one and said, 'Son, go and work in the vineyard today.' 29'I don't want to,' he answered, but later he changed his mind and went. 30Then the father went to the other son and said the same thing. 'Yes, sir,' he answered, but he did not go. 31Which one of the two did what his father wanted?"

"The older one," they answered.

So Jesus said to them, "I tell you: the tax collectors and the prostitutes are going into the Kingdom of God ahead of you. 32For John the Baptist came to you showing you the right path to take, and you would not believe him; but the tax collectors and the prostitutes believed him. Even when you saw this, you did not later change your minds and believe him.

The Parable of the Tenants in the Vineyard

33"Listen to another parable," Jesus said. "There was once a landowner who planted a vineyard, put a fence around it, dug a hole for the wine press, and built a watchtower. Then he rented the vineyard to tenants and left home on a trip. 34When the time came to gather the grapes, he sent his slaves to the tenants to receive his share of the harvest. 35The tenants grabbed his slaves, beat one, killed another, and stoned another. 36Again the man sent other slaves, more than the first time, and the tenants treated them the same way. 37Last of all he sent his son to them. 'Surely they will respect my son,' he said. 38But when the tenants saw the son, they said to themselves, 'This is the owner's son. Come on, let's kill him, and we will get his property!' 39So they grabbed him, threw him out of the vineyard, and killed him.

40"Now, when the owner of the vineyard comes, what will he do to those tenants?" Jesus asked.

41"He will certainly kill those evil men," they answered, "and rent the vineyard out to other tenants, who will give him his share of the harvest at the right time."

42Jesus said to them, "Haven't you ever read what the Scriptures say?

'The stone which the builders
    rejected as worthless
turned out to be
    the most important of all.
This was done by the Lord;
    what a wonderful sight it is!'

43"And so I tell you," added Jesus, "the Kingdom of God will be taken away from you and given to a people who will produce the proper fruits."

45The chief priests and the Pharisees heard Jesus' parables and knew that he was talking about them, 46so they tried to arrest him. But they were afraid of the crowds, who considered Jesus to be a prophet.

The Parable of the Wedding Feast

22 ¹Jesus again used parables in talking to the people. ²"The Kingdom of heaven is like this. Once there was a king who prepared a wedding feast for his son. ³He sent his servants to tell the invited guests to come to the feast, but they did not want to come. ⁴So he sent other servants with this message for the guests: 'My feast is ready now; my steers and prize calves have been butchered, and everything is ready. Come to the wedding feast!' ⁵But the invited guests paid no attention and went about their business: one went to his farm, another to his store, ⁶while others grabbed the servants, beat them, and killed them. ⁷The king was very angry; so he sent his soldiers, who killed those murderers and burned down their city. ⁸Then he called his servants and said to them, 'My wedding feast is ready, but the people I invited did not deserve it. ⁹Now go to the main streets and invite to the feast as many people as you find.' ¹⁰So the servants went out into the streets and gathered all the people they could find, good and bad alike; and the wedding hall was filled with people.

¹¹"The king went in to look at the guests and saw a man who was not wearing wedding clothes. ¹²'Friend, how did you get in here without wedding clothes?' the king asked him. But the man said nothing. ¹³Then the king told the servants, 'Tie him up hand and foot, and throw him outside in the dark. There he will cry and gnash his teeth.'"

¹⁴And Jesus concluded, "Many are invited, but few are chosen."

The Question about Paying Taxes

¹⁵The Pharisees went off and made a plan to trap Jesus with questions. ¹⁶Then they sent to him some of their disciples and some members of Herod's party. "Teacher," they said, "we know that you tell the truth. You teach the truth about God's will for people, without worrying about what others think, because you pay no attention to anyone's status. ¹⁷Tell us, then, what do you think? Is it against our Law to pay taxes to the Roman Emperor, or not?"

¹⁸Jesus, however, was aware of their evil plan, and so he said, "You hypocrites! Why are you trying to trap me? ¹⁹Show me the coin for paying the tax!"

They brought him the coin, ²⁰and he asked them, "Whose face and name are these?"

²¹"The Emperor's," they answered.

So Jesus said to them, "Well, then, pay to the Emperor what belongs to the Emperor, and pay to God what belongs to God."

²²When they heard this, they were amazed; and they left him and went away.

The Question about Rising from Death

²³That same day some Sadducees came to Jesus and claimed that people will not rise from death. ²⁴"Teacher,"

they said, "Moses said that if a man who has no children dies, his brother must marry the widow so that they can have children who will be considered the dead man's children. 25Now, there were seven brothers who used to live here. The oldest got married and died without having children, so he left his widow to his brother. 26The same thing happened to the second brother, to the third, and finally to all seven. 27Last of all, the woman died. 28Now, on the day when the dead rise to life, whose wife will she be? All of them had married her."

29Jesus answered them, "How wrong you are! It is because you don't know the Scriptures or God's power. 30For when the dead rise to life, they will be like the angels in heaven and will not marry. 31Now, as for the dead rising to life: haven't you ever read what God has told you? He said, 32'I am the God of Abraham, the God of Isaac, and the God of Jacob.' He is the God of the living, not of the dead."

33When the crowds heard this, they were amazed at his teaching.

The Great Commandment

34When the Pharisees heard that Jesus had silenced the Sadducees, they came together, 35and one of them, a teacher of the Law, tried to trap him with a question. 36"Teacher," he asked, "which is the greatest commandment in the Law?"

37Jesus answered, "'Love the Lord your God with all your heart, with all your soul, and with all your mind.'

38This is the greatest and the most important commandment. 39The second most important commandment is like it: 'Love your neighbor as you love yourself.' 40The whole Law of Moses and the teachings of the prophets depend on these two commandments."

The Question about the Messiah

41When some Pharisees gathered together, Jesus asked them, 42"What do you think about the Messiah? Whose descendant is he?"

"He is David's descendant," they answered.

43"Why, then," Jesus asked, "did the Spirit inspire David to call him 'Lord'? David said,

44'The Lord said to my Lord:
    Sit here at my right side
        until I put your enemies
            under your feet.'

45If, then, David called him 'Lord,' how can the Messiah be David's descendant?"

46No one was able to give Jesus any answer, and from that day on no one dared to ask him any more questions.

Jesus Warns against the Teachers of the Law and the Pharisees

23 1Then Jesus spoke to the crowds and to his disciples. 2"The teachers of the Law and the Pharisees are the authorized interpreters of Moses' Law. 3So you must obey and follow everything they tell you to do; do not, however, imitate their actions, because they don't

practice what they preach. 4 They tie onto people's backs loads that are heavy and hard to carry, yet they aren't willing even to lift a finger to help them carry those loads. 5 They do everything so that people will see them. Look at the straps with scripture verses on them which they wear on their foreheads and arms, and notice how large they are! Notice also how long are the tassels on their cloaks! 6 They love the best places at feasts and the reserved seats in the synagogues; 7 they love to be greeted with respect in the marketplaces and to have people call them 'Teacher.' 8 You must not be called 'Teacher,' because you are all equal and have only one Teacher. 9 And you must not call anyone here on earth 'Father,' because you have only the one Father in heaven. 10 Nor should you be called 'Leader,' because your one and only leader is the Messiah. 11 The greatest one among you must be your servant. 12 Whoever makes himself great will be humbled, and whoever humbles himself will be made great.

Jesus Condemns Their Hypocrisy

13 "How terrible for you, teachers of the Law and Pharisees! You hypocrites! You lock the door to the Kingdom of heaven in people's faces, but you yourselves don't go in, nor do you allow in those who are trying to enter!

15 "How terrible for you, teachers of the Law and Pharisees! You hypocrites! You sail the seas and cross whole countries to win one convert; and when you succeed, you make him twice as deserving of going to hell as you yourselves are!

16 "How terrible for you, blind guides! You teach, 'If someone swears by the Temple, he isn't bound by his vow; but if he swears by the gold in the Temple, he is bound.' 17 Blind fools! Which is more important, the gold or the Temple which makes the gold holy? 18 You also teach, 'If someone swears by the altar, he isn't bound by his vow; but if he swears by the gift on the altar, he is bound.' 19 How blind you are! Which is the more important, the gift or the altar which makes the gift holy? 20 So then, when a person swears by the altar, he is swearing by it and by all the gifts on it; 21 and when he swears by the Temple, he is swearing by it and by God, who lives there; 22 and when someone swears by heaven, he is swearing by God's throne and by him who sits on it.

23 "How terrible for you, teachers of the Law and Pharisees! You hypocrites! You give to God one tenth even of the seasoning herbs, such as mint, dill, and cumin, but you neglect to obey the really important teachings of the Law, such as justice and mercy and honesty. These you should practice, without neglecting the others. 24 Blind guides! You strain a fly out of your drink, but swallow a camel!

25 "How terrible for you, teachers of the Law and Pharisees! You hypocrites! You clean the outside of your cup and plate, while the inside is full

of what you have gotten by violence and selfishness. 26Blind Pharisee! Clean what is inside the cup first, and then the outside will be clean too!

27 "How terrible for you, teachers of the Law and Pharisees! You hypocrites! You are like whitewashed tombs, which look fine on the outside but are full of bones and decaying corpses on the inside. 28In the same way, on the outside you appear good to everybody, but inside you are full of hypocrisy and sins.

Jesus Predicts Their Punishment

29 "How terrible for you, teachers of the Law and Pharisees! You hypocrites! You make fine tombs for the prophets and decorate the monuments of those who lived good lives; 30and you claim that if you had lived during the time of your ancestors, you would not have done what they did and killed the prophets. 31So you actually admit that you are the descendants of those who murdered the prophets! 32Go on, then, and finish up what your ancestors started! 33You snakes and children of snakes! How do you expect to escape from being condemned to hell? 34And so I tell you that I will send you prophets and wise men and teachers; you will kill some of them, crucify others, and whip others in the synagogues and chase them from town to town. 35As a result, the punishment for the murder of all innocent people will fall on you, from the murder of innocent Abel to the murder of Zechariah son of Berechiah, whom you murdered between the Temple and the altar. 36I tell you indeed: the punishment for all these murders will fall on the people of this day!

Jesus' Love for Jerusalem

37 "Jerusalem, Jerusalem! You kill the prophets and stone the messengers God has sent you! How many times I wanted to put my arms around all your people, just as a hen gathers her chicks under her wings, but you would not let me! 38And so your Temple will be abandoned and empty. 39From now on, I tell you, you will never see me again until you say, 'God bless him who comes in the name of the Lord.'"

Jesus Speaks of the Destruction of the Temple

24 1Jesus left and was going away from the Temple when his disciples came to him to call his attention to its buildings. 2"Yes," he said, "you may well look at all these. I tell you this: not a single stone here will be left in its place; every one of them will be thrown down."

Troubles and Persecutions

3As Jesus sat on the Mount of Olives, the disciples came to him in private. "Tell us when all this will be," they asked, "and what will happen to show that it is the time for your coming and the end of the age."

4Jesus answered, "Watch out, and do not let anyone fool you. 5Many men, claiming to speak for me, will come and say, 'I am the Messiah!' and they will fool many people. 6 You are going to hear the noise of battles close by and the news of battles far away; but do not be troubled. Such things must happen, but they do not mean that the end has come. 7 Countries will fight each other; kingdoms will attack one another. There will be famines and earthquakes everywhere. 8 All these things are like the first pains of childbirth.

9 "Then you will be arrested and handed over to be punished and be put to death. Everyone will hate you because of me. 10 Many will give up their faith at that time; they will betray one another and hate one another. 11 Then many false prophets will appear and fool many people. 12 Such will be the spread of evil that many people's love will grow cold. 13 But whoever holds out to the end will be saved. 14 And this Good News about the Kingdom will be preached through all the world for a witness to all people; and then the end will come.

The Awful Horror

15 "You will see 'The Awful Horror' of which the prophet Daniel spoke. It will be standing in the holy place." (Note to the reader: understand what this means!) 16 "Then those who are in Judea must run away to the hills. 17 Someone who is on the roof of a house must not take the time to go down and get any belongings from the house. 18 Someone who is in the field must not go back to get a cloak.

19 How terrible it will be in those days for women who are pregnant and for mothers with little babies! 20 Pray to God that you will not have to run away during the winter or on a Sabbath! 21 For the trouble at that time will be far more terrible than any there has ever been, from the beginning of the world to this very day. Nor will there ever be anything like it again. 22 But God has already reduced the number of days; had he not done so, nobody would survive. For the sake of his chosen people, however, God will reduce the days.

23 "Then, if anyone says to you, 'Look, here is the Messiah!' or 'There he is!' — do not believe it. 24 For false Messiahs and false prophets will appear; they will perform great miracles and wonders in order to deceive even God's chosen people, if possible. 25 Listen! I have told you this ahead of time.

26 "Or, if people should tell you, 'Look, he is out in the desert!' — don't go there; or if they say, 'Look, he is hiding here!' — don't believe it. 27 For the Son of Man will come like the lightning which flashes across the whole sky from the east to the west.

28 "Wherever there is a dead body, the vultures will gather.

The Coming of the Son of Man

29 "Soon after the trouble of those days, the sun will grow dark, the moon will no longer shine, the stars will fall from heaven, and the powers in space will be driven from their courses. 30 Then the sign of the Son of

Man will appear in the sky; and all the peoples of earth will weep as they see the Son of Man coming on the clouds of heaven with power and great glory. 31 The great trumpet will sound, and he will send out his angels to the four corners of the earth, and they will gather his chosen people from one end of the world to the other.

The Lesson of the Fig Tree

32 "Let the fig tree teach you a lesson. When its branches become green and tender and it starts putting out leaves, you know that summer is near. 33 In the same way, when you see all these things, you will know that the time is near, ready to begin. 34 Remember that all these things will happen before the people now living have all died. 35 Heaven and earth will pass away, but my words will never pass away.

No One Knows the Day and Hour

36 "No one knows, however, when that day and hour will come — neither the angels in heaven nor the Son; the Father alone knows. 37 The coming of the Son of Man will be like what happened in the time of Noah. 38 In the days before the flood people ate and drank, men and women married, up to the very day Noah went into the boat; 39 yet they did not realize what was happening until the flood came and swept them all away. That is how it will be when the Son of Man comes. 40 At that time two men will be working in a field: one will be taken away, the other will be left behind. 41 Two women will be at a mill grinding meal: one will be taken away, the other will be left behind. 42 Watch out, then, because you do not know what day your Lord will come. 43 If the owner of a house knew the time when the thief would come, you can be sure that he would stay awake and not let the thief break into his house. 44 So then, you also must always be ready, because the Son of Man will come at an hour when you are not expecting him.

The Faithful or the Unfaithful Servant

45 "Who, then, is a faithful and wise servant? It is the one that his master has placed in charge of the other servants to give them their food at the proper time. 46 How happy that servant is if his master finds him doing this when he comes home! 47 Indeed, I tell you, the master will put that servant in charge of all his property. 48 But if he is a bad servant, he will tell himself that his master will not come back for a long time, 49 and he will begin to beat his fellow servants and to eat and drink with drunkards. 50 Then that servant's master will come back one day when the servant does not expect him and at a time he does not know. 51 The master will cut him in pieces and make him share the fate of the hypocrites. There he will cry and gnash his teeth.

The Parable of the Ten Young Women

25 1 "At that time the Kingdom of heaven will be like this.

Once there were ten young women who took their oil lamps and went out to meet the bridegroom. [2] Five of them were foolish, and the other five were wise. [3] The foolish ones took their lamps but did not take any extra oil with them, [4] while the wise ones took containers full of oil for their lamps. [5] The bridegroom was late in coming, so they began to nod and fall asleep.

[6] "It was already midnight when the cry rang out, 'Here is the bridegroom! Come and meet him!' [7] The ten young women woke up and trimmed their lamps. [8] Then the foolish ones said to the wise ones, 'Let us have some of your oil, because our lamps are going out.' [9] 'No, indeed,' the wise ones answered, 'there is not enough for you and for us. Go to the store and buy some for yourselves.' [10] So the foolish ones went off to buy some oil; and while they were gone, the bridegroom arrived. The five who were ready went in with him to the wedding feast, and the door was closed.

[11] "Later the others arrived. 'Sir, sir! Let us in!' they cried out. [12] 'Certainly not! I don't know you,' the bridegroom answered."

[13] And Jesus concluded, "Watch out, then, because you do not know the day or the hour.

The Parable of the Three Servants

[14] "At that time the Kingdom of heaven will be like this. Once there was a man who was about to leave home on a trip; he called his servants and put them in charge of his property.

[15] He gave to each one according to his ability: to one he gave five thousand gold coins, to another he gave two thousand, and to another he gave one thousand. Then he left on his trip. [16] The servant who had received five thousand coins went at once and invested his money and earned another five thousand. [17] In the same way the servant who had received two thousand coins earned another two thousand. [18] But the servant who had received one thousand coins went off, dug a hole in the ground, and hid his master's money.

[19] "After a long time the master of those servants came back and settled accounts with them. [20] The servant who had received five thousand coins came in and handed over the other five thousand. 'You gave me five thousand coins, sir,' he said. 'Look! Here are another five thousand that I have earned.' [21] 'Well done, you good and faithful servant!' said his master. 'You have been faithful in managing small amounts, so I will put you in charge of large amounts. Come on in and share my happiness!' [22] Then the servant who had been given two thousand coins came in and said, 'You gave me two thousand coins, sir. Look! Here are another two thousand that I have earned.' [23] 'Well done, you good and faithful servant!' said his master. 'You have been faithful in managing small amounts, so I will put you in charge of large amounts. Come on in and share my happiness!' [24] Then the servant who had received one thousand coins came in and said, 'Sir,

I know you are a hard man; you reap harvests where you did not plant, and you gather crops where you did not scatter seed. 25 I was afraid, so I went off and hid your money in the ground. Look! Here is what belongs to you.' 26 'You bad and lazy servant!' his master said. 'You knew, did you, that I reap harvests where I did not plant, and gather crops where I did not scatter seed? 27 Well, then, you should have deposited my money in the bank, and I would have received it all back with interest when I returned. 28 Now, take the money away from him and give it to the one who has ten thousand coins. 29 For to every person who has something, even more will be given, and he will have more than enough; but the person who has nothing, even the little that he has will be taken away from him. 30 As for this useless servant — throw him outside in the darkness; there he will cry and gnash his teeth.'

The Final Judgment

31 "When the Son of Man comes as King and all the angels with him, he will sit on his royal throne, 32 and the people of all the nations will be gathered before him. Then he will divide them into two groups, just as a shepherd separates the sheep from the goats. 33 He will put the righteous people at his right and the others at his left. 34 Then the King will say to the people on his right, 'Come, you that are blessed by my Father! Come and possess the kingdom which has been prepared for you ever since the creation of the world. 35 I was hungry and you fed me, thirsty and you gave me a drink; I was a stranger and you received me in your homes, 36 naked and you clothed me; I was sick and you took care of me, in prison and you visited me.' 37 The righteous will then answer him, 'When, Lord, did we ever see you hungry and feed you, or thirsty and give you a drink? 38 When did we ever see you a stranger and welcome you in our homes, or naked and clothe you? 39 When did we ever see you sick or in prison, and visit you?' 40 The King will reply, 'I tell you, whenever you did this for one of the least important of these followers of mine, you did it for me!'

41 "Then he will say to those on his left, 'Away from me, you that are under God's curse! Away to the eternal fire which has been prepared for the Devil and his angels! 42 I was hungry but you would not feed me, thirsty but you would not give me a drink; 43 I was a stranger but you would not welcome me in your homes, naked but you would not clothe me; I was sick and in prison but you would not take care of me.' 44 Then they will answer him, 'When, Lord, did we ever see you hungry or thirsty or a stranger or naked or sick or in prison, and we would not help you?' 45 The King will reply, 'I tell you, whenever you refused to help one of these least important ones, you refused to help me.' 46 These, then, will be sent off to eternal punishment, but the righteous will go to eternal life."

The Plot against Jesus

26 [1] When Jesus had finished teaching all these things, he said to his disciples, [2] "In two days, as you know, it will be the Passover Festival, and the Son of Man will be handed over to be crucified."

[3] Then the chief priests and the elders met together in the palace of Caiaphas, the High Priest, [4] and made plans to arrest Jesus secretly and put him to death. [5] "We must not do it during the festival," they said, "or the people will riot."

Jesus Is Anointed at Bethany

[6] Jesus was in Bethany at the house of Simon, a man who had suffered from a dreaded skin disease. [7] While Jesus was eating, a woman came to him with an alabaster jar filled with an expensive perfume, which she poured on his head. [8] The disciples saw this and became angry. "Why all this waste?" they asked. [9] "This perfume could have been sold for a large amount and the money given to the poor!"

[10] Jesus knew what they were saying, and so he said to them, "Why are you bothering this woman? It is a fine and beautiful thing that she has done for me. [11] You will always have poor people with you, but you will not always have me. [12] What she did was to pour this perfume on my body to get me ready for burial. [13] Now, I assure you that wherever this gospel is preached all over the world, what she has done will be told in memory of her."

Judas Agrees to Betray Jesus

[14] Then one of the twelve disciples—the one named Judas Iscariot—went to the chief priests [15] and asked, "What will you give me if I betray Jesus to you?" They counted out thirty silver coins and gave them to him. [16] From then on Judas was looking for a good chance to hand Jesus over to them.

Jesus Eats the Passover Meal with His Disciples

[17] On the first day of the Festival of Unleavened Bread the disciples came to Jesus and asked him, "Where do you want us to get the Passover meal ready for you?"

[18] "Go to a certain man in the city," he said to them, "and tell him: 'The Teacher says, My hour has come; my disciples and I will celebrate the Passover at your house.'"

[19] The disciples did as Jesus had told them and prepared the Passover meal.

[20] When it was evening, Jesus and the twelve disciples sat down to eat. [21] During the meal Jesus said, "I tell you, one of you will betray me."

[22] The disciples were very upset and began to ask him, one after the other, "Surely, Lord, you don't mean me?"

[23] Jesus answered, "One who dips his bread in the dish with me will betray me. [24] The Son of Man will die as the Scriptures say he will, but how terrible for that man who will betray the Son of Man! It would have been better for that man if he had never been born!"

25 Judas, the traitor, spoke up. "Surely, Teacher, you don't mean me?" he asked.

Jesus answered, "So you say."

The Lord's Supper

26 While they were eating, Jesus took a piece of bread, gave a prayer of thanks, broke it, and gave it to his disciples. "Take and eat it," he said; "this is my body."

27 Then he took a cup, gave thanks to God, and gave it to them. "Drink it, all of you," he said; 28 "this is my blood, which seals God's covenant, my blood poured out for many for the forgiveness of sins. 29 I tell you, I will never again drink this wine until the day I drink the new wine with you in my Father's Kingdom."

30 Then they sang a hymn and went out to the Mount of Olives.

Jesus Predicts Peter's Denial

31 Then Jesus said to them, "This very night all of you will run away and leave me, for the scripture says, 'God will kill the shepherd, and the sheep of the flock will be scattered.' 32 But after I am raised to life, I will go to Galilee ahead of you."

33 Peter spoke up and said to Jesus, "I will never leave you, even though all the rest do!"

34 Jesus said to Peter, "I tell you that before the rooster crows tonight, you will say three times that you do not know me."

35 Peter answered, "I will never say that, even if I have to die with you!"

And all the other disciples said the same thing.

Jesus Prays in Gethsemane

36 Then Jesus went with his disciples to a place called Gethsemane, and he said to them, "Sit here while I go over there and pray." 37 He took with him Peter and the two sons of Zebedee. Grief and anguish came over him, 38 and he said to them, "The sorrow in my heart is so great that it almost crushes me. Stay here and keep watch with me."

39 He went a little farther on, threw himself face downward on the ground, and prayed, "My Father, if it is possible, take this cup of suffering from me! Yet not what I want, but what you want."

40 Then he returned to the three disciples and found them asleep; and he said to Peter, "How is it that you three were not able to keep watch with me for even one hour? 41 Keep watch and pray that you will not fall into temptation. The spirit is willing, but the flesh is weak."

42 Once more Jesus went away and prayed, "My Father, if this cup of suffering cannot be taken away unless I drink it, your will be done." 43 He returned once more and found the disciples asleep; they could not keep their eyes open.

44 Again Jesus left them, went away, and prayed the third time, saying the same words. 45 Then he returned to the disciples and said, "Are you still sleeping and resting? Look! The hour has come for the Son of Man to be handed over to the power of sinners. 46 Get up, let us go. Look, here is the man who is betraying me!"

The Arrest of Jesus

47 Jesus was still speaking when Judas, one of the twelve disciples, arrived. With him was a large crowd armed with swords and clubs and sent by the chief priests and the elders. 48 The traitor had given the crowd a signal: "The man I kiss is the one you want. Arrest him!"

49 Judas went straight to Jesus and said, "Peace be with you, Teacher," and kissed him.

50 Jesus answered, "Be quick about it, friend!"

Then they came up, arrested Jesus, and held him tight. 51 One of those who were with Jesus drew his sword and struck at the High Priest's slave, cutting off his ear. 52 "Put your sword back in its place," Jesus said to him. "All who take the sword will die by the sword. 53 Don't you know that I could call on my Father for help, and at once he would send me more than twelve armies of angels? 54 But in that case, how could the Scriptures come true which say that this is what must happen?"

55 Then Jesus spoke to the crowd, "Did you have to come with swords and clubs to capture me, as though I were an outlaw? Every day I sat down and taught in the Temple, and you did not arrest me. 56 But all this has happened in order to make come true what the prophets wrote in the Scriptures."

Then all the disciples left him and ran away.

Jesus before the Council

57 Those who had arrested Jesus took him to the house of Caiaphas, the High Priest, where the teachers of the Law and the elders had gathered together. 58 Peter followed from a distance, as far as the courtyard of the High Priest's house. He went into the courtyard and sat down with the guards to see how it would all come out. 59 The chief priests and the whole Council tried to find some false evidence against Jesus to put him to death; 60 but they could not find any, even though many people came forward and told lies about him. Finally two men stepped up 61 and said, "This man said, 'I am able to tear down God's Temple and three days later build it back up.'"

62 The High Priest stood up and said to Jesus, "Have you no answer to give to this accusation against you?" 63 But Jesus kept quiet. Again the High Priest spoke to him, "In the name of the living God I now put you under oath: tell us if you are the Messiah, the Son of God."

64 Jesus answered him, "So you say. But I tell all of you: from this time on you will see the Son of Man sitting at the right side of the Almighty and coming on the clouds of heaven!"

65 At this the High Priest tore his clothes and said, "Blasphemy! We don't need any more witnesses! You have just heard his blasphemy! 66 What do you think?"

They answered, "He is guilty and must die."

67 Then they spat in his face and beat him; and those who slapped him 68 said, "Prophesy for us, Messiah! Guess who hit you!"

Peter Denies Jesus

⁶⁹Peter was sitting outside in the courtyard when one of the High Priest's servant women came to him and said, "You, too, were with Jesus of Galilee."

⁷⁰But he denied it in front of them all. "I don't know what you are talking about," he answered, ⁷¹and went on out to the entrance of the courtyard. Another servant woman saw him and said to the men there, "He was with Jesus of Nazareth."

⁷²Again Jesus denied it and answered, "I swear that I don't know that man!"

⁷³After a little while the men standing there came to Peter. "Of course you are one of them," they said. "After all, the way you speak gives you away!"

⁷⁴Then Peter said, "I swear that I am telling the truth! May God punish me if I am not! I do not know that man!"

Just then a rooster crowed, ⁷⁵and Peter remembered what Jesus had told him: "Before the rooster crows, you will say three times that you do not know me." He went out and wept bitterly.

Jesus Is Taken to Pilate

27 ¹Early in the morning all the chief priests and the elders made their plans against Jesus to put him to death. ²They put him in chains, led him off, and handed him over to Pilate, the Roman governor.

The Death of Judas

³When Judas, the traitor, learned that Jesus had been condemned, he repented and took back the thirty silver coins to the chief priests and the elders. ⁴"I have sinned by betraying an innocent man to death!" he said.

"What do we care about that?" they answered. "That is your business!"

⁵Judas threw the coins down in the Temple and left; then he went off and hanged himself.

⁶The chief priests picked up the coins and said, "This is blood money, and it is against our Law to put it in the Temple treasury." ⁷After reaching an agreement about it, they used the money to buy Potter's Field, as a cemetery for foreigners. ⁸That is why that field is called "Field of Blood" to this very day.

⁹Then what the prophet Jeremiah had said came true: "They took the thirty silver coins, the amount the people of Israel had agreed to pay for him, ¹⁰and used the money to buy the potter's field, as the Lord had commanded me."

Pilate Questions Jesus

¹¹Jesus stood before the Roman governor, who questioned him. "Are you the king of the Jews?" he asked.

"So you say," answered Jesus. ¹²But he said nothing in response to the accusations of the chief priests and elders.

¹³So Pilate said to him, "Don't you hear all these things they accuse you of?"

¹⁴But Jesus refused to answer a single word, with the result that the Governor was greatly surprised.

Jesus Is Sentenced to Death

¹⁵At every Passover Festival the Roman governor was in the habit of

setting free any one prisoner the crowd asked for. 16 At that time there was a well-known prisoner named Jesus Barabbas. 17 So when the crowd gathered, Pilate asked them, "Which one do you want me to set free for you? Jesus Barabbas or Jesus called the Messiah?" 18 He knew very well that the Jewish authorities had handed Jesus over to him because they were jealous.

19 While Pilate was sitting in the judgment hall, his wife sent him a message: "Have nothing to do with that innocent man, because in a dream last night I suffered much on account of him."

20 The chief priests and the elders persuaded the crowd to ask Pilate to set Barabbas free and have Jesus put to death. 21 But Pilate asked the crowd, "Which one of these two do you want me to set free for you?"

"Barabbas!" they answered.

22 "What, then, shall I do with Jesus called the Messiah?" Pilate asked them.

"Crucify him!" they all answered.

23 But Pilate asked, "What crime has he committed?"

Then they started shouting at the top of their voices: "Crucify him!"

24 When Pilate saw that it was no use to go on, but that a riot might break out, he took some water, washed his hands in front of the crowd, and said, "I am not responsible for the death of this man! This is your doing!"

25 The whole crowd answered, "Let the responsibility for his death fall on us and on our children!"

26 Then Pilate set Barabbas free for them; and after he had Jesus whipped, he handed him over to be crucified.

The Soldiers Make Fun of Jesus

27 Then Pilate's soldiers took Jesus into the governor's palace, and the whole company gathered around him. 28 They stripped off his clothes and put a scarlet robe on him. 29 Then they made a crown out of thorny branches and placed it on his head, and put a stick in his right hand; then they knelt before him and made fun of him. "Long live the King of the Jews!" they said. 30 They spat on him, and took the stick and hit him over the head. 31 When they had finished making fun of him, they took the robe off and put his own clothes back on him. Then they led him out to crucify him.

Jesus Is Crucified

32 As they were going out, they met a man from Cyrene named Simon, and the soldiers forced him to carry Jesus' cross. 33 They came to a place called Golgotha, which means, "The Place of the Skull." 34 There they offered Jesus wine mixed with a bitter substance; but after tasting it, he would not drink it.

35 They crucified him and then divided his clothes among them by throwing dice. 36 After that they sat there and watched him. 37 Above his head they put the written notice of the accusation against him: "This is Jesus, the King of the Jews." 38 Then they crucified two bandits with Jesus, one on his right and the other on his left.

39 People passing by shook their heads and hurled insults at Jesus: 40 "You were going to tear down the Temple and build it back up in three

days! Save yourself if you are God's Son! Come on down from the cross!"

41 In the same way the chief priests and the teachers of the Law and the elders made fun of him: 42 "He saved others, but he cannot save himself! Isn't he the king of Israel? If he will come down off the cross now, we will believe in him! 43 He trusts in God and claims to be God's Son. Well, then, let us see if God wants to save him now!"

44 Even the bandits who had been crucified with him insulted him in the same way.

The Death of Jesus

45 At noon the whole country was covered with darkness, which lasted for three hours. 46 At about three o'clock Jesus cried out with a loud shout, *"Eli, Eli, lema sabachthani?"* which means, "My God, my God, why did you abandon me?"

47 Some of the people standing there heard him and said, "He is calling for Elijah!" 48 One of them ran up at once, took a sponge, soaked it in cheap wine, put it on the end of a stick, and tried to make him drink it.

49 But the others said, "Wait, let us see if Elijah is coming to save him!"

50 Jesus again gave a loud cry and breathed his last.

51 Then the curtain hanging in the Temple was torn in two from top to bottom. The earth shook, the rocks split apart, 52 the graves broke open, and many of God's people who had died were raised to life. 53 They left the graves, and after Jesus rose from death, they went into the Holy City, where many people saw them.

54 When the army officer and the soldiers with him who were watching Jesus saw the earthquake and everything else that happened, they were terrified and said, "He really was the Son of God!"

55 There were many women there, looking on from a distance, who had followed Jesus from Galilee and helped him. 56 Among them were Mary Magdalene, Mary the mother of James and Joseph, and the wife of Zebedee.

The Burial of Jesus

57 When it was evening, a rich man from Arimathea arrived; his name was Joseph, and he also was a disciple of Jesus. 58 He went into the presence of Pilate and asked for the body of Jesus. Pilate gave orders for the body to be given to Joseph. 59 So Joseph took it, wrapped it in a new linen sheet, 60 and placed it in his own tomb, which he had just recently dug out of solid rock. Then he rolled a large stone across the entrance to the tomb and went away. 61 Mary Magdalene and the other Mary were sitting there, facing the tomb.

The Guard at the Tomb

62 The next day, which was a Sabbath, the chief priests and the Pharisees met with Pilate 63 and said, "Sir, we remember that while that liar was still alive he said, 'I will be raised to life three days later.' 64 Give orders, then, for his tomb to be carefully guarded until the third day, so that his disciples will not be

able to go and steal the body, and then tell the people that he was raised from death. This last lie would be even worse than the first one."

65 "Take a guard," Pilate told them; "go and make the tomb as secure as you can."

66 So they left and made the tomb secure by putting a seal on the stone and leaving the guard on watch.

The Resurrection

28 ¹After the Sabbath, as Sunday morning was dawning, Mary Magdalene and the other Mary went to look at the tomb. ²Suddenly there was a violent earthquake; an angel of the Lord came down from heaven, rolled the stone away, and sat on it. ³His appearance was like lightning, and his clothes were white as snow. ⁴The guards were so afraid that they trembled and became like dead men.

⁵The angel spoke to the women. "You must not be afraid," he said. "I know you are looking for Jesus, who was crucified. ⁶He is not here; he has been raised, just as he said. Come here and see the place where he was lying. ⁷Go quickly now, and tell his disciples, 'He has been raised from death, and now he is going to Galilee ahead of you; there you will see him!' Remember what I have told you."

⁸So they left the tomb in a hurry, afraid and yet filled with joy, and ran to tell his disciples.

⁹Suddenly Jesus met them and said, "Peace be with you." They came up to him, took hold of his feet, and worshiped him. ¹⁰"Do not be afraid," Jesus said to them. "Go and tell my brothers to go to Galilee, and there they will see me."

The Report of the Guard

¹¹While the women went on their way, some of the soldiers guarding the tomb went back to the city and told the chief priests everything that had happened. ¹²The chief priests met with the elders and made their plan; they gave a large sum of money to the soldiers ¹³and said, "You are to say that his disciples came during the night and stole his body while you were asleep. ¹⁴And if the Governor should hear of this, we will convince him that you are innocent, and you will have nothing to worry about."

¹⁵The guards took the money and did what they were told to do. And so that is the report spread around by the Jews to this very day.

Jesus Appears to His Disciples

¹⁶The eleven disciples went to the hill in Galilee where Jesus had told them to go. ¹⁷When they saw him, they worshiped him, even though some of them doubted. ¹⁸Jesus drew near and said to them, "I have been given all authority in heaven and on earth. ¹⁹Go, then, to all peoples everywhere and make them my disciples: baptize them in the name of the Father, the Son, and the Holy Spirit, ²⁰and teach them to obey everything I have commanded you. And I will be with you always, to the end of the age."

Évangile selon
MATTHIEU

Dieu notre Père,
Jésus ton Fils nous appelle à être sel de la terre et lumière
du monde. Que la lumière de ta justice brille dans nos vies ;
alors nos gestes et nos paroles pourront apporter au monde
une saveur d'Évangile, et nos vies seront le reflet de Jésus,
Lumière du monde. Nous te le demandons par Jésus le
Christ notre Seigneur, qui vit et règne avec Toi, dans l'unité
du Saint-Esprit, pour les siècles des siècles. Amen.

L'Évangile selon Matthieu
Texte français de la Bible en français courant
© Société biblique française, 1997

INTRODUCTION

Jésus invita des disciples à le suivre. Il vécut avec eux, les instruisant sur sa mission et sur son affrontement avec les autorités juives. Au scandale de la croix, Dieu répondit en ressuscitant Jésus, qu'Il glorifia comme Christ et Seigneur.

Ce mystère de mort transfigurée en résurrection devait être proclamé à l'univers entier comme «l'Évangile», c'est-à-dire «La Bonne Nouvelle». Les disciples de Jésus, ses témoins oculaires, conservèrent la mémoire des enseignements, des miracles, des gestes de miséricorde, de la passion et de la résurrection de Jésus.

C'est à ces traditions orales et écrites que puisèrent les évangélistes. Dans différentes communautés chrétiennes apparurent quatre évangiles. L'Église reconnaît ces quatre livres comme des témoignages authentiques de la personne et de la vie de Jésus-Christ : Évangile selon Matthieu, selon Marc, selon Luc et selon Jean.

L'ÉVANGILE DE MATTHIEU

UNE ÉGLISE DISTINCTE DE LA SYNAGOGUE

Matthieu rédigea probablement son Évangile à Antioche, entre les années 80 et 90. Des juifs chrétiens fondèrent l'Église de cette ville vers la fin des années 30. L'esprit libéral et avant-gardiste dominait dans cette Église.

Cette Communauté était non seulement séparée de la synagogue, mais elle était engagée dans une polémique acerbe avec les chefs juifs. La série des sept déclarations *Malheur à vous, maîtres de la loi et Pharisiens, hypocrites!* (Mt 23.13-36) supposent une vive opposition entre les deux groupes.

UNE ÉGLISE À LA RECHERCHE DE SON IDENTITÉ

Deux pôles attiraient les premiers chrétiens dans des directions différentes. Comment pouvaient-ils être fidèles à l'héritage juif de l'Ancien Testament, tout en s'ouvrant à l'universalité du salut proclamée par le Christ Ressuscité ?

L'Église d'Antioche avait subi, avant Matthieu, des tensions entre ses fondateurs libéraux et les « frères » conservateurs en provenance de Jérusalem. L'Église, enracinée dans le Judaïsme, gardien de l'Ancien Testament, devait-elle s'ouvrir à l'immense monde païen ? À quelles conditions ?

L'Évangile de Matthieu représente un essai de compromis entre les traditions divergentes héritées des premiers chrétiens. En accord avec Paul, Matthieu conclut à la claire légitimité de la mission universelle, sans l'exigence de la circoncision et sans l'obligation d'observer les prescriptions alimentaires juives.

Matthieu essaie de conserver à la fois l'héritage ancien et la nouveauté de l'Évangile. Il cherche une voie modérée entre la tradition juive et l'avenir universel. Aussi il exalte la figure de Pierre, chef de l'Église (16.18-19). Pierre représente pour lui une position médiane, plus conservatrice que celle de saint Paul, à gauche, dans ses épîtres aux Galates et aux Romains, mais plus ouverte aux païens que celle de saint Jacques, à droite, dans son épître. Quoi d'étonnant que l'Évangile de Matthieu, qui harmonisait les principales tendances pour favoriser l'unité chrétienne, ait connu rapidement une large popularité !

CONCLUSION

Le phénomène crucial de la mondialisation pose actuellement aux chrétiens un problème aigu. Toutes les barrières tombent entre les nations, les cultures et même les religions. Les communications favorisent la compréhension mutuelle et les échanges. Il est évident que ce signe des temps, dont les JMJ (Journées Mondiales de la Jeunesse) sont un exemple éloquent, nous oblige à nous ouvrir aux autres. Mais comment conserver notre identité chrétienne, tout en respectant les autres et leurs valeurs ?

Les premiers chrétiens ont vécu ce problème angoissant, entre le particularisme juif et l'universalisme évangélique. Leur recherche d'une solution, que reflète l'évangéliste Matthieu, est de nature à nous inspirer aujourd'hui.

MATTHIEU

Les ancêtres de Jésus

1 ¹Voici la liste des ancêtres de Jésus-Christ, descendant de David, lui-même descendant d'Abraham.

²Abraham fut père d'Isaac, Isaac de Jacob, Jacob de Juda et de ses frères; ³Juda fut père de Pérès et de Zéra – leur mère était Tamar –, Pérès fut père de Hesron, Hesron de Ram; ⁴Ram fut père d'Amminadab; Amminadab de Nachon; Nachon de Salman; ⁵Salman fut père de Booz – Rahab était sa mère –, Booz fut père d'Obed – Ruth était sa mère –, Obed fut père de Jessé, ⁶et Jessé du roi David.

David fut père de Salomon – sa mère avait été la femme d'Urie –; ⁷Salomon fut père de Roboam, Roboam d'Abia, Abia d'Asaf; ⁸Asaf fut père de Josaphat, Josaphat de Joram, Joram d'Ozias; ⁹Ozias fut père de Yotam, Yotam d'Akaz, Akaz d'Ézékias; ¹⁰Ézékias fut père de Manassé, Manassé d'Amon, Amon de Josias; ¹¹Josias fut père de Yekonia et de ses frères, à l'époque où les Israélites furent déportés à Babylone.

¹²Après que les Israélites eurent été déportés à Babylone, Yekonia fut père de Chéaltiel et Chéaltiel de Zorobabel; ¹³Zorobabel fut père d'Abihoud, Abihoud d'Éliakim; Éliakim d'Azor; ¹⁴Azor fut père de Sadok, Sadok d'Achim; Achim d'Élioud; ¹⁵Élioud fut père d'Éléazar, Éléazar de Matthan, Matthan de Jacob; ¹⁶Jacob fut père de Joseph, l'époux de Marie; c'est d'elle qu'est né Jésus, appelé le Messie.

¹⁷Il y eut donc en tout quatorze générations depuis Abraham jusqu'à David, puis quatorze depuis David jusqu'à l'époque où les Israélites furent déportés à Babylone, et quatorze depuis cette époque jusqu'à la naissance du Messie.

La naissance de Jésus-Christ

¹⁸Voici dans quelles circonstances Jésus-Christ est né. Marie, sa mère, était fiancée à Joseph; mais avant qu'ils aient vécu ensemble, elle se trouva enceinte par l'action du Saint-Esprit. ¹⁹Joseph, son fiancé, était un homme droit et ne voulait pas la dénoncer publiquement; il décida de rompre secrètement ses fiançailles. ²⁰Comme il y pensait, un ange du Seigneur lui apparut dans un rêve et lui dit: «Joseph, descendant de David, ne crains pas d'épouser Marie, car c'est par l'action du Saint-Esprit qu'elle attend un enfant. ²¹Elle mettra au monde un fils, que tu appelleras Jésus, car il sauvera son peuple de ses péchés.»

²²Tout cela arriva afin que se réalise ce que le Seigneur avait dit par le prophète:

23 «La vierge sera enceinte
　　et mettra au monde un fils,
　　qu'on appellera Emmanuel.»

– Ce nom signifie «Dieu est avec nous». –

24 Quand Joseph se réveilla, il agit comme l'ange du Seigneur le lui avait ordonné et prit Marie comme épouse. 25 Mais il n'eut pas de relations avec elle jusqu'à ce qu'elle ait mis au monde son fils, que Joseph appela Jésus.

Des savants viennent voir Jésus

2 1 Jésus naquit à Bethléem, en Judée, à l'époque où Hérode était roi. Après sa naissance, des savants, spécialistes des étoiles, vinrent d'Orient. Ils arrivèrent à Jérusalem 2 et demandèrent: «Où est l'enfant qui vient de naître, le roi des Juifs? Nous avons vu son étoile apparaître en Orient et nous sommes venus l'adorer.» 3 Quand le roi Hérode apprit cette nouvelle, il fut troublé, ainsi que toute la population de Jérusalem. 4 Il convoqua tous les chefs des prêtres et les maîtres de la loi, et leur demanda où le Messie devait naître. 5 Ils lui répondirent: «A Bethléem, en Judée. Car voici ce que le prophète a écrit:
6 "Et toi, Bethléem, au pays de Juda,
　　tu n'es certainement pas
　　la moins importante des localités
　　de Juda ;
　　car c'est de toi que viendra un chef
　　qui conduira mon peuple, Israël." »
7 Alors Hérode convoqua secrètement les savants et s'informa auprès d'eux du moment précis où l'étoile était apparue. 8 Puis il les envoya à Bethléem, en leur disant: «Allez chercher des renseignements précis sur l'enfant ; et quand vous l'aurez trouvé, faites-le-moi savoir, afin que j'aille, moi aussi, l'adorer.»

9 Après avoir reçu ces instructions du roi, ils partirent. Ils virent alors l'étoile qu'ils avaient déjà remarquée en Orient: elle allait devant eux, et quand elle arriva au-dessus de l'endroit où se trouvait l'enfant, elle s'arrêta. 10 Ils furent remplis d'une très grande joie en la voyant là. 11 Ils entrèrent dans la maison et virent l'enfant avec sa mère, Marie. Ils se mirent à genoux pour adorer l'enfant ; puis ils ouvrirent leurs bagages et lui offrirent des cadeaux: de l'or, de l'encens et de la myrrhe. 12 Ensuite, Dieu les avertit dans un rêve de ne pas retourner auprès d'Hérode ; ils prirent alors un autre chemin pour rentrer dans leur pays.

La fuite en Égypte

13 Quand les savants furent partis, un ange du Seigneur apparut à Joseph dans un rêve et lui dit: «Debout, prends avec toi l'enfant et sa mère et fuis en Égypte ; restes-jusqu'à ce que je te dise de revenir. Car Hérode va rechercher l'enfant pour le faire mourir.» 14 Joseph se leva donc, prit avec lui l'enfant et sa mère, en pleine nuit, et se réfugia en Égypte. 15 Il y resta jusqu'à la mort d'Hérode. Cela arriva afin que se réalise ce que le Seigneur avait dit par le prophète : «J'ai appelé mon fils à sortir d'Égypte.»

Le massacre des enfants

16 Quand Hérode se rendit compte que les savants l'avaient trompé, il entra dans une grande colère. Il donna l'ordre

de tuer, à Bethléem et dans les environs, tous les garçons de moins de deux ans ; cette limite d'âge correspondait aux indications que les savants lui avaient données. 17Alors se réalisa ce qu'avait déclaré le prophète Jérémie :

18 «On a entendu une plainte à Rama,
des pleurs
et de grandes lamentations.
C'est Rachel qui pleure ses enfants,
elle ne veut pas être consolée,
car ils sont morts.»

Le retour d'Égypte

19Après la mort d'Hérode, un ange du Seigneur apparut dans un rêve à Joseph, en Égypte. 20Il lui dit : «Debout, prends avec toi l'enfant et sa mère et retourne au pays d'Israël, car ceux qui cherchaient à faire mourir l'enfant sont morts.» 21Joseph se leva donc, prit avec lui l'enfant et sa mère et retourna au pays d'Israël. 22Mais il apprit qu'Archélaos avait succédé à son père Hérode comme roi de Judée ; alors il eut peur de s'y rendre. Il reçut de nouvelles indications dans un rêve, et il partit pour la province de Galilée. 23Il alla s'établir dans une ville appelée Nazareth. Il en fut ainsi pour que se réalise cette parole des prophètes : «Il sera appelé Nazaréen.»

La prédication de Jean-Baptiste

3 1En ce temps-là, Jean-Baptiste parut dans le désert de Judée et se mit à prêcher : 2«Changez de comportement, disait-il, car le Royaume des cieux s'est approché !» 3Jean est celui dont le prophète Ésaïe a parlé lorsqu'il a dit :

«Un homme crie dans le désert :
Préparez le chemin du Seigneur,
faites-lui des sentiers bien droits !»
4Le vêtement de Jean était fait de poils de chameau et il portait une ceinture de cuir autour de la taille ; il mangeait des sauterelles et du miel sauvage. 5Les habitants de Jérusalem, de toute la Judée et de toute la région voisine de la rivière, le Jourdain, allaient à lui. 6Ils confessaient publiquement leurs péchés et Jean les baptisait dans le Jourdain.

7Jean vit que beaucoup de Pharisiens et de Sadducéens venaient à lui pour être baptisés ; il leur dit alors : «Bande de serpents ! Qui vous a enseigné à vouloir échapper au jugement de Dieu, qui est proche ? 8Montrez par des actes que vous avez changé de mentalité 9et ne pensez pas qu'il suffit de dire en vous-mêmes : "Abraham est notre ancêtre." Car je vous déclare que Dieu peut utiliser les pierres que voici pour en faire des descendants d'Abraham ! 10La hache est déjà prête à couper les arbres à la racine : tout arbre qui ne produit pas de bons fruits va être coupé et jeté au feu. 11Moi, je vous baptise avec de l'eau pour montrer que vous changez de comportement ; mais celui qui vient après moi vous baptisera avec le Saint-Esprit et avec du feu. Il est plus puissant que moi : je ne suis pas même digne d'enlever ses chaussures. 12Il tient en sa main la pelle à vanner et séparera le grain de la paille. Il amassera son grain dans le grenier, mais il brûlera la paille dans un feu qui ne s'éteint jamais.»

Le baptême de Jésus

13Alors Jésus vint de la Galilée au Jourdain ; il arriva auprès de Jean pour être baptisé par lui. 14Jean s'y opposait et lui disait : «C'est moi qui devrais être baptisé par toi et c'est toi qui viens à moi !» 15Mais Jésus lui répondit : «Accepte qu'il en soit ainsi pour le moment. Car voilà comment nous devons accomplir tout ce que Dieu demande.» Alors Jean accepta. 16Dès que Jésus fut baptisé, il sortit de l'eau. Au même moment le ciel s'ouvrit pour lui : il vit l'Esprit de Dieu descendre comme une colombe et venir sur lui. 17Et une voix venant du ciel déclara : «Celui-ci est mon Fils bien-aimé ; je mets en lui toute ma joie.»

La tentation de Jésus

4 1Ensuite l'Esprit de Dieu conduisit Jésus dans le désert pour qu'il y soit tenté par le diable. 2Après avoir passé quarante jours et quarante nuits sans manger, Jésus eut faim. 3Le diable, le tentateur, s'approcha et lui dit : «Si tu es le Fils de Dieu, ordonne à ces pierres de se changer en pains.» 4Jésus répondit : «L'Écriture déclare : "L'homme ne vivra pas de pain seulement, mais de toute parole que Dieu prononce."»

5Alors le diable l'emmena jusqu'à Jérusalem, la ville sainte, le plaça au sommet du temple 6et lui dit : «Si tu es le Fils de Dieu, jette-toi en bas ; car l'Écriture déclare :

"Dieu donnera pour toi des ordres à ses anges
et ils te porteront sur leurs mains pour éviter que ton pied
ne heurte une pierre."»

7Jésus lui répondit : «L'Écriture déclare aussi : "Ne mets pas à l'épreuve le Seigneur ton Dieu."»

8Le diable l'emmena encore sur une très haute montagne, lui fit voir tous les royaumes du monde et leur splendeur, 9et lui dit : «Je te donnerai tout cela, si tu te mets à genoux devant moi pour m'adorer.» 10Alors Jésus lui dit : «Va-t'en, Satan ! Car l'Écriture déclare : "Adore le Seigneur ton Dieu et ne rends de culte qu'à lui seul."» 11Cette fois le diable le laissa. Des anges vinrent alors auprès de Jésus et se mirent à le servir.

Jésus commence son oeuvre en Galilée

12Quand Jésus apprit que Jean avait été mis en prison, il s'en alla en Galilée. 13Il ne resta pas à Nazareth, mais alla demeurer à Capernaüm, ville située au bord du lac de Galilée, dans la région de Zabulon et de Neftali. 14Il en fut ainsi afin que se réalisent ces paroles du prophète Ésaïe :

15«Région de Zabulon,
région de Neftali,
en direction de la mer,
de l'autre côté du Jourdain,
Galilée qu'habitent des non-Juifs !
16Le peuple qui vit dans la nuit
verra une grande lumière !
Pour ceux qui vivent
dans le sombre pays de la mort,
la lumière apparaîtra !»

17Dès ce moment, Jésus se mit à prêcher : «Changez de comportement, disait-il, car le Royaume des cieux s'est approché !»

Jésus appelle quatre pêcheurs

18 Jésus marchait le long du lac de Galilée, lorsqu'il vit deux frères qui étaient pêcheurs, Simon, surnommé Pierre, et son frère André ; ils pêchaient en jetant un filet dans le lac. 19 Jésus leur dit : « Venez avec moi et je ferai de vous des pêcheurs d'hommes. » 20 Aussitôt, ils laissèrent leurs filets et le suivirent. 21 Il alla plus loin et vit deux autres frères, Jacques et Jean, les fils de Zébédée. Ils étaient dans leur barque avec Zébédée, leur père, et réparaient leurs filets. Jésus les appela ; 22 aussitôt, ils laissèrent la barque et leur père et ils le suivirent.

Jésus enseigne et guérit

23 Jésus allait dans toute la Galilée ; il enseignait dans les synagogues de la région, proclamait la Bonne Nouvelle du Royaume et guérissait les gens de toutes leurs maladies et de toutes leurs infirmités. 24 L'on entendit parler de lui dans tout le pays de Syrie et on lui amena tous ceux qui souffraient de diverses maladies ou étaient tourmentés par divers maux : ceux qui étaient possédés d'un esprit mauvais, ainsi que les épileptiques et les paralysés. Et Jésus les guérit. 25 De grandes foules le suivirent ; elles venaient de Galilée, de la région des Dix Villes, de Jérusalem, de Judée et du territoire situé de l'autre côté du Jourdain.

Le sermon sur la montagne (chap. 5 à 7)

5 1 Quand Jésus vit ces foules, il monta sur une montagne et s'assit. Ses disciples vinrent auprès de lui 2 et il se mit à leur donner cet enseignement :

Le vrai bonheur

3 « Heureux ceux qui se savent
    pauvres en eux-mêmes,
  car le Royaume des cieux
    est à eux !
4 Heureux ceux qui pleurent,
  car Dieu les consolera !
5 Heureux ceux qui sont doux,
  car ils recevront la terre
    que Dieu a promise !
6 Heureux ceux qui ont faim et soif
    de vivre comme Dieu
    le demande,
  car Dieu exaucera leur désir !
7 Heureux ceux qui ont
    de la compassion pour autrui,
  car Dieu aura de la compassion
    pour eux !
8 Heureux ceux qui ont le coeur pur,
  car ils verront Dieu !
9 Heureux ceux qui créent la paix
    autour d'eux,
  car Dieu les appellera ses fils !
10 Heureux ceux qu'on persécute
    parce qu'ils agissent
    comme Dieu le demande,
  car le Royaume des cieux
    est à eux !

11 Heureux êtes-vous si les hommes vous insultent, vous persécutent et disent faussement toute sorte de mal contre vous parce que vous croyez en moi. 12 Réjouissez-vous, soyez heureux, car une grande récompense vous attend dans les cieux. C'est ainsi, en effet, qu'on a persécuté les prophètes qui ont vécu avant vous. »

Le sel et la lumière

¹³«C'est vous qui êtes le sel du monde. Mais si le sel perd son goût, comment pourrait-on le rendre de nouveau salé ? Il n'est plus bon à rien ; on le jette dehors, et les gens marchent dessus.

¹⁴«C'est vous qui êtes la lumière du monde. Une ville construite sur une montagne ne peut pas être cachée. ¹⁵On n'allume pas une lampe pour la mettre sous un seau. Au contraire, on la place sur son support, d'où elle éclaire tous ceux qui sont dans la maison. ¹⁶C'est ainsi que votre lumière doit briller devant les hommes, afin qu'ils voient le bien que vous faites et qu'ils louent votre Père qui est dans les cieux.»

Enseignement au sujet de la loi

¹⁷«Ne pensez pas que je sois venu supprimer la loi de Moïse et l'enseignement des prophètes. Je ne suis pas venu pour les supprimer mais pour leur donner tout leur sens. ¹⁸Je vous le déclare, c'est la vérité : aussi longtemps que le ciel et la terre dureront, ni la plus petite lettre ni le plus petit détail ne seront supprimés de la loi, et cela jusqu'à la fin de toutes choses. ¹⁹C'est pourquoi, celui qui écarte même le plus petit des commandements et enseigne aux autres à faire de même, sera le plus petit dans le Royaume des cieux. Mais celui qui l'applique et enseigne aux autres à faire de même, sera grand dans le Royaume des cieux. ²⁰Je vous l'affirme : si vous n'êtes pas plus fidèles à la volonté de Dieu que les maîtres de la loi et les Pharisiens, vous

ne pourrez pas entrer dans le Royaume des cieux.»

Enseignement au sujet de la colère

²¹«Vous avez entendu qu'il a été dit à nos ancêtres : "Tu ne commettras pas de meurtre ; tout homme qui en tue un autre mérite de comparaître devant le juge." ²²Eh bien, moi je vous déclare : tout homme qui se met en colère contre son frère mérite de comparaître devant le juge ; celui qui dit à son frère : "Imbécile !" mérite d'être jugé par le Conseil supérieur ; celui qui lui dit : "Idiot !" mérite d'être jeté dans le feu de l'enfer. ²³Si donc tu viens à l'autel présenter ton offrande à Dieu et que là tu te souviennes que ton frère a une raison de t'en vouloir, ²⁴laisse là ton offrande, devant l'autel, et va d'abord faire la paix avec ton frère ; puis reviens et présente ton offrande à Dieu.

²⁵«Si tu es en procès avec quelqu'un, dépêche-toi de te mettre d'accord avec lui pendant que vous êtes encore en chemin. Tu éviteras ainsi que ton adversaire ne te livre au juge, que le juge ne te remette à la police et qu'on ne te jette en prison. ²⁶Je te le déclare, c'est la vérité : tu ne sortiras pas de là tant que tu n'auras pas payé ta dette jusqu'au dernier centime.»

Enseignement au sujet de l'adultère

²⁷«Vous avez entendu qu'il a été dit : "Tu ne commettras pas d'adultère." ²⁸Eh bien, moi je vous déclare : tout homme qui regarde la

femme d'un autre en la désirant a déjà commis l'adultère avec elle en lui-même. 29Si donc c'est à cause de ton œil droit que tu tombes dans le péché, arrache-le et jette-le loin de toi : il vaut mieux pour toi perdre une seule partie de ton corps que d'être jeté tout entier dans l'enfer. 30Si c'est à cause de ta main droite que tu tombes dans le péché, coupe-la et jette-la loin de toi : il vaut mieux pour toi perdre un seul membre de ton corps que d'aller tout entier en enfer. »

Enseignement au sujet du divorce

31« Il a été dit aussi : "Celui qui renvoie sa femme doit lui donner une attestation de divorce." 32Eh bien, moi je vous déclare : tout homme qui renvoie sa femme, alors qu'elle n'a pas été infidèle, lui fait commettre un adultère si elle se remarie ; et celui qui épouse une femme renvoyée par un autre commet aussi un adultère. »

Enseignement au sujet des serments

33« Vous avez aussi entendu qu'il a été dit à nos ancêtres : "Ne romps pas ton serment, mais accomplis ce que tu as promis avec serment devant le Seigneur." 34Eh bien, moi je vous dis de ne faire aucun serment : n'en faites ni par le ciel, car c'est le trône de Dieu ; 35ni par la terre, car elle est un escabeau sous tes pieds ; ni par Jérusalem, car c'est la ville du grand Roi. 36N'en fais pas non plus par ta tête, car tu ne peux pas rendre blanc ou noir un seul de tes cheveux. 37Si c'est oui, dites "oui", si c'est non, dites "non", tout simplement ; ce que l'on dit en plus vient du Mauvais. »

Enseignement au sujet de la vengeance

38« Vous avez entendu qu'il a été dit : "Œil pour œil et dent pour dent." 39Eh bien, moi je vous dis de ne pas vous venger de celui qui vous fait du mal. Si quelqu'un te gifle sur la joue droite, laisse-le te gifler aussi sur la joue gauche. 40Si quelqu'un veut te faire un procès pour te prendre ta chemise, laisse-le prendre aussi ton manteau. 41Si quelqu'un t'oblige à faire mille pas, fais-en deux mille avec lui. 42Donne à celui qui te demande quelque chose ; ne refuse pas de prêter à celui qui veut t'emprunter. »

L'amour pour les ennemis

43« Vous avez entendu qu'il a été dit : "Tu dois aimer ton prochain et haïr ton ennemi." 44Eh bien, moi je vous dis : aimez vos ennemis et priez pour ceux qui vous persécutent. 45Ainsi vous deviendrez les fils de votre Père qui est dans les cieux. Car il fait lever son soleil aussi bien sur les méchants que sur les bons, il fait pleuvoir sur ceux qui lui sont fidèles que sur ceux qui ne le sont pas. 46Si vous aimez seulement ceux qui vous aiment, pourquoi vous attendre à recevoir une récompense de Dieu ? Même les collecteurs d'impôts en font autant ! 47Si vous ne saluez que vos frères, faites-vous là quelque chose d'extraordinaire ? Même les païens en font autant ! 48Soyez donc parfaits, tout comme votre Père qui est au ciel est parfait. »

Enseignement au sujet des dons faits aux pauvres

6 [1] «Gardez-vous d'accomplir vos devoirs religieux en public, pour que tout le monde vous remarque. Sinon, vous ne recevrez pas de récompense de votre Père qui est dans les cieux. [2] Quand donc tu donnes quelque chose à un pauvre, n'attire pas bruyamment l'attention sur toi, comme le font les hypocrites dans les synagogues et dans les rues : ils agissent ainsi pour être loués par les hommes. Je vous le déclare, c'est la vérité : ils ont déjà leur récompense. [3] Mais quand ta main droite donne quelque chose à un pauvre, ta main gauche elle-même ne doit pas le savoir. [4] Ainsi, il faut que ce don reste secret ; et Dieu, ton Père, qui voit ce que tu fais en secret, te récompensera.»

Enseignement au sujet de la prière

[5] «Quand vous priez, ne soyez pas comme les hypocrites : ils aiment à prier debout dans les synagogues et au coin des rues pour que tout le monde les voie. Je vous le déclare, c'est la vérité : ils ont déjà leur récompense. [6] Mais toi, lorsque tu veux prier, entre dans ta chambre, ferme la porte et prie ton Père qui est là, dans cet endroit secret ; et ton Père, qui voit ce que tu fais en secret, te récompensera.

[7] «Quand vous priez, ne répétez pas sans fin les mêmes choses comme les païens : ils s'imaginent que Dieu les exaucera s'ils parlent beaucoup. [8] Ne

les imitez pas, car Dieu, votre Père, sait déjà de quoi vous avez besoin avant que vous le lui demandiez. [9] Voici comment vous devez prier :

"Notre Père qui es dans les cieux,
que chacun reconnaisse
que tu es le Dieu saint,
[10] que ton Règne vienne ;
que chacun, sur la terre,
fasse ta volonté
comme elle est faite dans le ciel.
[11] Donne-nous aujourd'hui
le pain nécessaire.
[12] Pardonne-nous nos torts,
comme nous pardonnons nous aussi
à ceux qui nous ont fait du tort.
[13] Et ne nous expose pas
à la tentation,
mais délivre-nous du Mauvais.
[Car c'est à toi qu'appartiennent
le règne, la puissance et la gloire,
pour toujours. Amen.]"

[14] «En effet, si vous pardonnez aux autres le mal qu'ils vous ont fait, votre Père qui est au ciel vous pardonnera aussi. [15] Mais si vous ne pardonnez pas aux autres, votre Père ne vous pardonnera pas non plus le mal que vous avez fait.»

Enseignement au sujet du jeûne

[16] «Quand vous jeûnez, ne prenez pas un air triste comme font les hypocrites : ils changent de visage pour que tout le monde voie qu'ils jeûnent. Je vous le déclare, c'est la vérité : ils ont déjà leur récompense. [17] Mais toi, quand tu jeûnes, lave-toi le visage et parfume ta tête, [18] afin que les gens ne se rendent pas compte que tu jeûnes. Seul ton Père qui est là, dans le secret,

le saura ; et ton Père, qui voit ce que tu fais en secret, te récompensera.»

Des richesses dans le ciel

19«Ne vous amassez pas de richesses dans ce monde, où les vers et la rouille détruisent, où les cambrioleurs forcent les serrures pour voler. 20Amassez-vous plutôt des richesses dans le ciel, où il n'y a ni vers ni rouille pour détruire, ni cambrioleurs pour forcer les serrures et voler. 21Car ton cœur sera toujours là où sont tes richesses.»

La lumière du corps

22«Les yeux sont la lampe du corps : si tes yeux sont en bon état, tout ton corps est éclairé ; 23mais si tes yeux sont malades, tout ton corps est dans l'obscurité. Si donc la lumière qui est en toi n'est qu'obscurité, comme cette obscurité sera noire !»

Dieu ou l'argent

24«Personne ne peut servir deux maîtres : ou bien il haïra le premier et aimera le second ; ou bien il s'attachera au premier et méprisera le second. Vous ne pouvez pas servir à la fois Dieu et l'argent.»

Avoir confiance en Dieu

25«Voilà pourquoi je vous dis : Ne vous inquiétez pas au sujet de la nourriture et de la boisson dont vous avez besoin pour vivre, ou au sujet des vêtements dont vous avez besoin pour votre corps. La vie est plus importante que la nourriture et le corps plus important que les vêtements, n'est-ce pas ? 26Regardez les oiseaux : ils ne sèment ni ne moissonnent, ils n'amassent pas de récoltes dans des greniers, mais votre Père qui est au ciel les nourrit ! Ne valez-vous pas beaucoup plus que les oiseaux ? 27Qui d'entre vous parvient à prolonger un peu la durée de sa vie par le souci qu'il se fait ?

28«Et pourquoi vous inquiétez-vous au sujet des vêtements ? Observez comment poussent les fleurs des champs : elles ne travaillent pas, elles ne se font pas de vêtements. 29Pourtant, je vous le dis, même Salomon, avec toute sa richesse, n'a pas eu de vêtements aussi beaux qu'une seule de ces fleurs. 30Dieu habille ainsi l'herbe des champs qui est là aujourd'hui et qui demain sera jetée au feu : alors ne vous habillera-t-il pas à bien plus forte raison vous-mêmes ? Comme votre confiance en lui est faible ! 31Ne vous inquiétez donc pas en disant : "Qu'allons-nous manger ? qu'allons-nous boire ? qu'allons-nous mettre pour nous habiller ?" 32Ce sont les païens qui recherchent sans arrêt tout cela. Mais votre Père qui est au ciel sait que vous en avez besoin. 33Préoccupez-vous d'abord du Royaume de Dieu et de la vie juste qu'il demande, et Dieu vous accordera aussi tout le reste. 34Ne vous inquiétez donc pas du lendemain : le lendemain se souciera de lui-même. À chaque jour suffit sa peine.»

Ne pas juger les autres

7 1«Ne portez de jugement contre personne, afin que Dieu ne vous

juge pas non plus. ²Car Dieu vous jugera comme vous jugez les autres ; il vous mesurera avec la mesure que vous employez pour eux. ³Pourquoi regardes-tu le brin de paille qui est dans l'œil de ton frère, alors que tu ne remarques pas la poutre qui est dans ton œil ? ⁴Comment peux-tu dire à ton frère : "Laisse-moi enlever cette paille de ton œil", alors que tu as une poutre dans le tien ? ⁵Hypocrite, enlève d'abord la poutre de ton œil et alors tu verras assez clair pour enlever la paille de l'œil de ton frère.

⁶«Ne donnez pas ce qui est saint aux chiens, de peur qu'ils ne se retournent contre vous et ne vous déchirent ; ne jetez pas vos perles devant les porcs, de peur qu'ils ne les piétinent.»

Demander, chercher et frapper à la porte

⁷«Demandez et vous recevrez ; cherchez et vous trouverez ; frappez et l'on vous ouvrira la porte. ⁸Car quiconque demande reçoit, qui cherche trouve et l'on ouvre la porte à qui frappe. ⁹Y a-t-il quelqu'un parmi vous qui donne à son fils une pierre si celui-ci demande du pain ? ¹⁰ou qui lui donne un serpent s'il demande un poisson ? ¹¹Tout mauvais que vous êtes, vous savez donner de bonnes choses à vos enfants. A combien plus forte raison, donc, votre Père qui est dans les cieux donnera-t-il de bonnes choses à ceux qui les lui demandent !

¹²«Faites pour les autres tout ce que vous voulez qu'ils fassent pour vous :

c'est là ce qu'enseignent les livres de la loi de Moïse et des Prophètes.»

La porte étroite

¹³«Entrez par la porte étroite ! Car large est la porte et facile le chemin qui mènent à la ruine ; nombreux sont ceux qui passent par là. ¹⁴Mais combien étroite est la porte et difficile le chemin qui mènent à la vie ; peu nombreux sont ceux qui les trouvent.»

Les faux prophètes

¹⁵«Gardez-vous des faux prophètes. Ils viennent à vous déguisés en brebis, mais au-dedans ce sont des loups féroces. ¹⁶Vous les reconnaîtrez à leur conduite. On ne cueille pas des raisins sur des buissons d'épines, ni des figues sur des chardons. ¹⁷Un bon arbre produit de bons fruits et un arbre malade de mauvais fruits. ¹⁸Un bon arbre ne peut pas produire de mauvais fruits ni un arbre malade de bons fruits. ¹⁹Tout arbre qui ne produit pas de bons fruits est coupé, puis jeté au feu. ²⁰Ainsi donc, vous reconnaîtrez les faux prophètes à leur conduite.»

Dire et faire

²¹«Ce ne sont pas tous ceux qui me disent : "Seigneur, Seigneur", qui entreront dans le Royaume des cieux, mais seulement ceux qui font la volonté de mon Père qui est dans les cieux. ²²Au jour du Jugement, beaucoup me diront : "Seigneur, Seigneur, c'est en ton nom que nous avons été prophètes ; c'est en ton nom que nous avons chassé des esprits mauvais ; c'est en ton nom que nous

avons accompli de nombreux miracles. Ne le sais-tu pas?» ²³Alors je leur déclarerai: "Je ne vous ai jamais connus; allez-vous-en loin de moi, vous qui commettez le mal!"»

Les deux maisons

²⁴«Ainsi, quiconque écoute ce que je viens de dire et le met en pratique sera comme un homme intelligent qui a bâti sa maison sur le roc. ²⁵La pluie est tombée, les rivières ont débordé, la tempête s'est abattue sur cette maison, mais elle ne s'est pas écroulée, car ses fondations avaient été posées sur le roc. ²⁶Mais quiconque écoute ce que je viens de dire et ne le met pas en pratique sera comme un homme insensé qui a bâti sa maison sur le sable. ²⁷La pluie est tombée, les rivières ont débordé, la tempête s'est abattue sur cette maison et elle s'est écroulée: sa ruine a été complète.»

L'autorité de Jésus

²⁸Quand Jésus eut achevé ces instructions, tous restèrent impressionnés par sa manière d'enseigner; ²⁹car il n'était pas comme leurs maîtres de la loi, mais il les enseignait avec autorité.

Jésus guérit un lépreux

8 ¹Jésus descendit de la montagne et une foule de gens le suivirent. ²Alors un lépreux s'approcha, se mit à genoux devant lui et dit: «Maître, si tu le veux, tu peux me rendre pur.» ³Jésus étendit la main, le toucha et déclara: «Je le veux, sois pur!» Aussitôt, l'homme fut purifié de sa lèpre. ⁴Puis Jésus lui dit: «Écoute bien: ne parle de cela à personne. Mais va te faire examiner par le prêtre, puis offre le sacrifice que Moïse a ordonné, pour prouver à tous que tu es guéri.»

Jésus guérit le serviteur d'un officier romain

⁵Au moment où Jésus entrait dans Capernaüm, un capitaine romain s'approcha et lui demanda son aide ⁶en ces termes: «Maître, mon serviteur est couché à la maison, il est paralysé et souffre terriblement.» ⁷Jésus lui dit: «J'y vais et je le guérirai.» ⁸Mais le capitaine répondit: «Maître, je ne suis pas digne que tu entres dans ma maison. Mais il suffit que tu dises un mot et mon serviteur sera guéri. ⁹Je suis moi-même soumis à mes supérieurs et j'ai des soldats sous mes ordres. Si je dis à l'un: "Va!", il va; si je dis à un autre: "Viens!", il vient; et si je dis à mon serviteur: "Fais ceci!", il le fait.» ¹⁰Quand Jésus entendit ces mots, il fut dans l'admiration et dit à ceux qui le suivaient: «Je vous le déclare, c'est la vérité: je n'ai trouvé une telle foi chez personne en Israël. ¹¹Je vous l'affirme, beaucoup viendront de l'est et de l'ouest et prendront place à table dans le Royaume des cieux avec Abraham, Isaac et Jacob. ¹²Mais ceux qui étaient destinés au Royaume seront jetés dehors, dans le noir, où ils pleureront et grinceront des dents.»

¹³Puis Jésus dit au capitaine: «Retourne chez toi, Dieu t'accorde ce que tu as demandé avec foi!» Et le

serviteur du capitaine fut guéri à ce moment même.

Jésus guérit beaucoup de malades

14Jésus se rend à la maison de Pierre. Il y trouva la belle-mère de Pierre au lit : elle avait de la fièvre. 15Il lui toucha la main et la fièvre la quitta ; elle se leva et se mit à le servir.

16Le soir venu, on amena à Jésus un grand nombre de personnes tourmentées par des esprits mauvais. Par sa parole Jésus chassa ces esprits et il guérit aussi tous les malades. 17Il le fit afin que se réalise cette parole du prophète Ésaïe : «Il a pris nos infirmités et nous a déchargés de nos maladies.»

Ceux qui désirent suivre Jésus

18Quand Jésus vit toute la foule qui l'entourait, il donna l'ordre à ses disciples de passer avec lui de l'autre côté du lac. 19Un maître de la loi s'approcha et lui dit : «Maître, je te suivrai partout où tu iras.» 20Jésus lui répondit : «Les renards ont des terriers et les oiseaux ont des nids, mais le Fils de l'homme n'a pas un endroit où il puisse se coucher et se reposer.» 21Quelqu'un d'autre, un de ses disciples, lui dit : «Maître, permets-moi d'aller d'abord enterrer mon père.» 22Jésus lui répondit : «Suis-moi et laisse les morts enterrer leurs morts.»

Jésus apaise une tempête

23Jésus monta dans la barque et ses disciples l'accompagnèrent. 24Soudain, une grande tempête s'éleva sur le lac, si bien que les vagues recouvraient la barque. Mais Jésus dormait. 25Les disciples s'approchèrent de lui et le réveillèrent en criant : «Seigneur, sauve-nous ! Nous allons mourir!» 26Jésus leur répondit : «Pourquoi avez-vous peur? Comme votre confiance est faible!» Alors il se leva, parla sévèrement au vent et à l'eau du lac, et il se fit un grand calme. 27Tous étaient remplis d'étonnement et disaient : «Quel genre d'homme est-ce pour que même le vent et les flots lui obéissent?»

Jésus guérit deux hommes possédés par des esprits mauvais

28Quand Jésus arriva de l'autre côté du lac, dans le territoire des Gadaréniens, deux hommes sortirent du milieu des tombeaux et vinrent à sa rencontre. Ces hommes étaient possédés par des esprits mauvais ; ils étaient si dangereux que personne n'osait passer par ce chemin. 29Ils se mirent à crier : «Que nous veux-tu, Fils de Dieu? Es-tu venu ici pour nous tourmenter avant le moment fixé?»

30Il y avait, à une certaine distance, un grand troupeau de porcs qui cherchait sa nourriture. 31Les esprits mauvais adressèrent cette prière à Jésus : «Si tu veux nous chasser, envoie-nous dans ce troupeau de porcs.» – 32«Allez», leur dit Jésus. Ils sortirent des deux hommes et s'en allèrent dans les porcs. Aussitôt, tout le troupeau se précipita du haut de la falaise dans le lac et disparut dans l'eau. 33Les hommes qui gardaient les porcs s'enfuirent ; ils se rendirent dans la ville où ils racontèrent toute l'histoire et ce qui s'était passé pour les deux possédés. ³⁴Alors tous les habitants de la ville sortirent à la rencontre de Jésus ; quand ils le virent, ils le supplièrent de quitter leur territoire.

Jésus guérit un homme paralysé

9 ¹Jésus monta dans la barque, refit la traversée du lac et se rendit dans sa ville. ²Quelques personnes lui amenèrent un paralysé couché sur une civière. Quand Jésus vit leur foi, il dit au paralysé : «Courage, mon fils ! Tes péchés sont pardonnés !» ³Alors quelques maîtres de la loi se dirent en eux-mêmes : «Cet homme fait insulte à Dieu !» ⁴Jésus discerna ce qu'ils pensaient et dit : «Pourquoi avez-vous ces mauvaises pensées ? ⁵Est-il plus facile de dire : "Tes péchés sont pardonnés", ou de dire : "Lève-toi et marche"? ⁶Mais je veux que vous le sachiez : le Fils de l'homme a le pouvoir sur la terre de pardonner les péchés.» Il dit alors au paralysé : «Lève-toi, prends ta civière et rentre chez toi !» ⁷L'homme se leva et s'en alla chez lui. ⁸Quand la foule vit cela, elle fut remplie de crainte et loua Dieu d'avoir donné un tel pouvoir aux hommes.

Jésus appelle Matthieu

⁹Jésus partit de là et vit, en passant, un homme appelé Matthieu assis au bureau des impôts. Il lui dit : «Suis-moi !» Matthieu se leva et le suivit. ¹⁰Jésus prenait un repas dans la maison de Matthieu ; beaucoup de collecteurs d'impôts et autres gens de mauvaise réputation vinrent prendre place à table avec lui et ses disciples. ¹¹Les Pharisiens virent cela et dirent à ses disciples : «Pourquoi votre maître mange-t-il avec les collecteurs d'impôts et les gens de mauvaise réputation ?» ¹²Jésus les entendit et déclara : «Les personnes en bonne santé n'ont pas besoin de médecin, ce sont les malades qui en ont besoin. ¹³Allez apprendre ce que signifient ces mots prononcés par Dieu : "Je désire la bonté et non des sacrifices d'animaux." Car je ne suis pas venu appeler ceux qui s'estiment justes, mais ceux qui se savent pécheurs.»

Jésus et le jeûne

¹⁴Les disciples de Jean-Baptiste s'approchèrent alors de Jésus et lui demandèrent : «Pourquoi nous et les Pharisiens jeûnons-nous souvent, tandis que tes disciples ne le font pas ?» ¹⁵Et Jésus leur répondit : «Pensez-vous que les invités d'une noce peuvent être tristes pendant que le marié est avec eux ? Bien sûr que non ! Mais le temps viendra où le marié leur sera enlevé ; alors ils jeûneront.

¹⁶«Personne ne répare un vieux vêtement avec une pièce d'étoffe neuve ; car cette pièce arracherait une partie du vêtement et la déchirure s'agrandirait encore. ¹⁷On ne verse pas non plus du vin nouveau dans de vieilles outres ; sinon les outres éclatent, le vin se répand et les outres sont perdues. On verse au contraire le vin nouveau dans des outres neuves et ainsi le tout se conserve bien.»

La fille d'un chef juif et la femme qui toucha le vêtement de Jésus

18Pendant que Jésus leur parlait ainsi, un chef juif arriva, se mit à genoux devant lui et dit: «Ma fille est morte il y a un instant; mais viens, pose ta main sur elle et elle vivra.» 19Jésus se leva et le suivit avec ses disciples.

20Une femme, qui souffrait de pertes de sang depuis douze ans, s'approcha alors de Jésus par derrière et toucha le bord de son vêtement. 21Car elle se disait: «Si je peux seulement toucher son vêtement, je serai guérie». 22Jésus se retourna, la vit et déclara: «Courage, ma fille! Ta foi t'a guérie.» Et à ce moment même, la femme fut guérie.

23Jésus arriva à la maison du chef. Quand il vit les musiciens prêts pour l'enterrement et la foule qui s'agitait bruyamment, 24il dit: «Sortez d'ici, car la fillette n'est pas morte, elle dort.» Mais ils se moquèrent de lui. 25Quand on eut mis la foule dehors, Jésus entra dans la chambre, il prit la fillette par la main et elle se leva. 26La nouvelle s'en répandit dans toute cette région.

Jésus guérit deux aveugles

27Au moment où Jésus partit de là, deux aveugles se mirent à le suivre en criant: «Aie pitié de nous, Fils de David!»

28Quand Jésus fut arrivé à la maison, les aveugles s'approchèrent de lui et il leur demanda: «Croyez-vous que je peux faire celr?» Ils lui répondirent: «Oui, Maître.» 29Alors Jésus leur toucha les yeux et dit: «Dieu vous accorde ce que vous

attendez avec foi!» 30Et leurs yeux purent voir. Jésus leur parla avec sévérité: «Écoutez bien, leur dit-il, personne ne doit le savoir.» 31Mais ils s'en allèrent parler de Jésus dans toute cette région.

Jésus guérit un homme muet

32Alors qu'ils s'en allaient, on amena à Jésus un homme qui était muet parce qu'il était possédé d'un esprit mauvais. 33Dès que Jésus eut chassé cet esprit, le muet se mit à parler. Dans la foule tous étaient remplis d'étonnement et disaient: «On n'a jamais rien vu de pareil en Israël!» 34Mais les Pharisiens affirmaient: «C'est le chef des esprits mauvais qui lui donne le pouvoir de chasser ces esprits!»

Jésus a pitié des foules

35Jésus parcourait villes et villages; il enseignait dans leurs synagogues, prêchait la Bonne Nouvelle du Royaume et guérissait toutes les maladies et toutes les infirmités. 36Son cœur fut rempli de pitié pour les foules qu'il voyait, car ces gens étaient fatigués et découragés, comme un troupeau qui n'a pas de berger. 37Il dit alors à ses disciples: «La moisson à faire est grande, mais il y a peu d'ouvriers pour cela. 38Priez donc le propriétaire de la moisson d'envoyer davantage d'ouvriers pour la faire.»

Les douze apôtres

10 1Jésus appela ses douze disciples et leur donna le pouvoir de chasser les esprits mauvais et de guérir toutes les maladies et toutes les infirmités. ²Voici les noms de ces douze apôtres : d'abord Simon, surnommé Pierre, et son frère André ; Jacques et son frère Jean, tous deux fils de Zébédée ; ³Philippe et Barthélemy ; Thomas et Matthieu le collecteur d'impôts ; Jacques le fils d'Alphée et Thaddée ; ⁴Simon le nationaliste et Judas Iscariote, qui trahit Jésus.

La mission des douze

⁵Jésus envoya ces douze hommes en mission, avec les instructions suivantes : «Évitez les régions où habitent les non-Juifs et n'entrez dans aucune ville de Samarie. ⁶Allez plutôt vers les brebis perdues du peuple d'Israël. ⁷En chemin, prêchez et dites : "Le Royaume des cieux s'est approché !" ⁸Guérissez les malades, rendez la vie aux morts, purifiez les lépreux, chassez les esprits mauvais. Vous avez reçu gratuitement, donnez aussi gratuitement. ⁹Ne vous procurez ni or, ni argent, ni monnaie de cuivre à mettre dans vos poches ; ¹⁰ne prenez pas de sac pour le voyage, ni une deuxième chemise, ne prenez ni chaussures, ni bâton. En effet, l'ouvrier a droit à sa nourriture.

¹¹«Quand vous arriverez dans une ville ou un village, cherchez qui est prêt à vous recevoir et restez chez cette personne jusqu'à ce que vous quittiez l'endroit. ¹²Quand vous entrerez dans une maison, dites : "La paix soit avec vous." ¹³Si les habitants de cette maison vous reçoivent, que votre souhait de paix repose sur eux ; mais s'ils ne vous reçoivent pas, retirez votre souhait de paix. ¹⁴Si, dans une maison ou dans une ville, on refuse de vous accueillir ou de vous écouter, partez de là et secouez la poussière de vos pieds. ¹⁵Je vous le déclare, c'est la vérité : au jour du Jugement, les habitants de Sodome et Gomorrhe seront traités moins sévèrement que les habitants de cette ville-là.»

Les persécutions à venir

¹⁶«Écoutez ! Je vous envoie comme des moutons au milieu des loups. Soyez donc prudents comme les serpents et innocents comme les colombes. ¹⁷Prenez garde, car des hommes vous feront passer devant les tribunaux et vous frapperont à coups de fouet dans leurs synagogues. ¹⁸On vous fera comparaître devant des gouverneurs et des rois à cause de moi, pour que vous puissiez apporter votre témoignage devant eux et devant les non-Juifs. ¹⁹Lorsqu'on vous conduira devant le tribunal, ne vous inquiétez pas de ce que vous aurez à dire ni de la manière de l'exprimer ; les paroles que vous aurez à prononcer vous seront données à ce moment-là : ²⁰elles ne viendront pas de vous, mais l'Esprit de votre Père parlera en vous. ²¹Des frères livreront leurs propres frères pour qu'on les mette à mort, et des pères agiront de même avec leurs enfants ; des enfants se tourneront contre leurs parents et les feront condamner à mort. ²²Tout le monde vous haïra à cause de moi. Mais celui qui tiendra bon jusqu'à la fin sera sauvé. ²³Quand on vous persécutera dans une ville, fuyez dans une autre. Je

vous le déclare, c'est la vérité : vous n'aurez pas encore fini de parcourir toutes les villes d'Israël avant que vienne le Fils de l'homme.

24 «Aucun élève n'est supérieur à son maître ; aucun serviteur n'est supérieur à son patron. 25 Il suffit que l'élève devienne comme son maître et que le serviteur devienne comme son patron. Si l'on a appelé le chef de famille Béelzébul, à combien plus forte raison insultera-t-on les membres de sa famille ! »

Celui qu'il faut craindre

26 «Ne craignez donc aucun homme. Tout ce qui est caché sera découvert, et tout ce qui est secret sera connu. 27 Ce que je vous dis dans l'obscurité, répétez-le à la lumière du jour ; et ce que l'on chuchote à votre oreille, criez-le du haut des toits. 28 Ne craignez pas ceux qui tuent le corps mais qui ne peuvent pas tuer l'âme ; craignez plutôt Dieu qui peut faire périr à la fois le corps et l'âme dans l'enfer. 29 Ne vend-on pas deux moineaux pour un sou ? Cependant, aucun d'eux ne tombe à terre sans que Dieu votre Père le sache. 30 Quant à vous, même vos cheveux sont tous comptés. 31 N'ayez donc pas peur : vous valez plus que beaucoup de moineaux ! »

Confesser ou renier Jésus-Christ

32 «Quiconque reconnaît publiquement qu'il est mon disciple, je reconnaîtrai moi aussi devant mon Père qui est dans les cieux qu'il est à moi ; 33 mais si quelqu'un affirme publiquement ne pas me connaître, j'affirmerai moi aussi devant mon Père qui est dans les cieux que je ne le connais pas. »

Non la paix, mais le combat

34 «Ne pensez pas que je sois venu apporter la paix sur la terre : je ne suis pas venu apporter la paix, mais le combat. 35 Je suis venu séparer l'homme de son père, la fille de sa mère, la belle-fille de sa belle-mère ; 36 on aura pour ennemis les membres de sa propre famille. 37 Celui qui aime son père ou sa mère plus que moi n'est pas digne de moi ; celui qui aime son fils ou sa fille plus que moi n'est pas digne de moi. 38 Celui qui ne se charge pas de sa croix pour marcher à ma suite n'est pas digne de moi. 39 Celui qui voudra garder sa vie la perdra ; mais celui qui perdra sa vie pour moi la retrouvera. »

Des récompenses

40 «Quiconque vous accueille m'accueille ; quiconque m'accueille accueille celui qui m'a envoyé. 41 Celui qui accueille un prophète de Dieu parce qu'il est prophète, recevra la récompense accordée à un prophète ; et celui qui accueille un homme fidèle à Dieu parce qu'il est fidèle, recevra la récompense accordée à un fidèle. 42 Je vous le déclare, c'est la vérité : celui qui donne même un simple verre d'eau fraîche à l'un de ces petits parmi mes disciples parce qu'il est mon disciple recevra sa récompense. »

Les envoyés de Jean-Baptiste

11 1 Lorsque Jésus eut achevé de donner ces instructions à ses

douze disciples, il partit de là pour aller enseigner et prêcher dans les villes de la région.

²Jean-Baptiste, dans sa prison, entendit parler des œuvres du Christ. Alors il envoya quelques-uns de ses disciples ³demander à Jésus : « Es-tu le Messie qui doit venir ou devons-nous attendre quelqu'un d'autre ? » ⁴Jésus leur répondit : « Allez raconter à Jean ce que vous entendez et voyez : ⁵les aveugles voient, les boiteux marchent, les lépreux sont guéris, les sourds entendent, les morts reviennent à la vie et la Bonne Nouvelle est annoncée aux pauvres. ⁶Heureux celui qui n'abandonnera pas la foi en moi ! »

⁷Quand les disciples de Jean partirent, Jésus se mit à parler de Jean à la foule en disant : « Qu'êtes-vous allés voir au désert ? un roseau agité par le vent ? Non ? ⁸Alors qu'êtes-vous allés voir ? un homme vêtu d'habits magnifiques ? Mais ceux qui portent des habits magnifiques se trouvent dans les palais des rois. ⁹Qu'êtes-vous donc allés voir ? un prophète ? Oui, vous dis-je, et même bien plus qu'un prophète. ¹⁰Car Jean est celui dont l'Écriture déclare : "Je vais envoyer mon messager devant toi, dit Dieu, pour t'ouvrir le chemin." ¹¹Je vous le déclare, c'est la vérité : parmi les humains, il n'a jamais existé personne de plus grand que Jean-Baptiste ; pourtant, celui qui est le plus petit dans le Royaume des cieux est plus grand que lui. ¹²Depuis l'époque où Jean-Baptiste prêchait jusqu'à présent, le Royaume des cieux subit la violence et les violents cherchent à s'en

emparer. ¹³Tous les prophètes et la loi de Moïse ont annoncé le Royaume, jusqu'à l'époque de Jean. ¹⁴Et si vous voulez bien l'admettre, Jean est cet Élie dont la venue a été annoncée. ¹⁵Écoutez bien, si vous avez des oreilles !

¹⁶« À qui puis-je comparer les gens d'aujourd'hui ? Ils ressemblent à des enfants assis sur les places publiques, dont les uns crient aux autres : ¹⁷« Nous vous avons joué un air de danse sur la flûte et vous n'avez pas dansé ! Nous avons chanté des chants de deuil et vous ne vous êtes pas lamentés ! » ¹⁸En effet, Jean est venu, il ne mange ni ne boit, et l'on dit : "Il est possédé d'un esprit mauvais !" ¹⁹Le Fils de l'homme est venu, il mange et boit, et l'on dit : "Voyez cet homme qui ne pense qu'à manger et à boire du vin, qui est ami des collecteurs d'impôts et autres gens de mauvaise réputation !" Mais la sagesse de Dieu se révèle juste par ses effets. »

Les villes qui refusent de croire

²⁰Alors Jésus se mit à faire des reproches aux villes dans lesquelles il avait accompli le plus grand nombre de ses miracles, parce que leurs habitants n'avaient pas changé de comportement. Il dit : ²¹« Malheur à toi, Chorazin ! Malheur à toi, Bethsaïda ! Car si les miracles qui ont été accomplis chez vous l'avaient été à Tyr et à Sidon, il y a longtemps que leurs habitants auraient pris le deuil, se seraient couvert la tête de cendre et auraient changé de comportement. ²²C'est pourquoi, je vous le déclare, au

jour du Jugement Tyr et Sidon seront traitées moins sévèrement que vous. ²³Et toi, Capernaüm, crois-tu que tu t'élèveras jusqu'au ciel? Tu seras abaissée jusqu'au monde des morts. Car si les miracles qui ont été accomplis chez toi l'avaient été à Sodome, cette ville existerait encore aujourd'hui. ²⁴C'est pourquoi, je vous le déclare, au jour du Jugement Sodome sera traitée moins sévèrement que toi.»

Venez à moi
pour trouver le repos

²⁵En ce temps-là, Jésus s'écria: «O Père, Seigneur du ciel et de la terre, je te remercie d'avoir révélé aux petits ce que tu as caché aux sages et aux gens instruits. ²⁶Oui, Père, tu as bien voulu qu'il en soit ainsi.

²⁷«Mon Père m'a remis toutes choses. Personne ne connaît le Fils si ce n'est le Père, et personne ne connaît le Père si ce n'est le Fils et ceux à qui le Fils veut le révéler.

²⁸«Venez à moi vous tous qui êtes fatigués de porter un lourd fardeau et je vous donnerai le repos. ²⁹Prenez sur vous mon joug et laissez-moi vous instruire, car je suis doux et humble de cœur, et vous trouverez le repos pour vous-mêmes. ³⁰Le joug que je vous invite à prendre est facile à porter et le fardeau que je vous propose est léger.»

Jésus et le sabbat

12 ¹Quelque temps après, Jésus traversait des champs de blé un jour de sabbat. Ses disciples avaient faim; ils se mirent à cueillir des épis et à en manger les grains. ²Quand les Pharisiens virent cela, ils dirent à Jésus: «Regarde, tes disciples font ce que notre loi ne permet pas le jour du sabbat!» ³Jésus leur répondit: «N'avez-vous pas lu ce que fit David un jour où lui-même et ses compagnons avaient faim? ⁴Il entra dans la maison de Dieu et lui et ses compagnons mangèrent les pains offerts à Dieu; il ne leur était pourtant pas permis d'en manger: notre loi ne le permet qu'aux seuls prêtres. ⁵Ou bien, n'avez-vous pas lu dans la loi de Moïse que, le jour du sabbat, les prêtres en service dans le temple n'observent pas la loi du sabbat, et cela sans être coupables? ⁶Or, je vous le déclare, il y a ici plus que le temple! ⁷Si vous saviez vraiment ce que signifient ces mots de l'Écriture: "Je désire la bonté et non des sacrifices d'animaux", vous n'auriez pas condamné des innocents. ⁸Car le Fils de l'homme est maître du sabbat.»

L'homme à la main paralysée

⁹Jésus partit de là et se rendit dans leur synagogue. ¹⁰Il y avait là un homme dont la main était paralysée. Les Pharisiens voulaient accuser Jésus; c'est pourquoi ils lui demandèrent: «Notre loi permet-elle de faire une guérison le jour du sabbat?» ¹¹Jésus leur répondit: «Si l'un d'entre vous a un seul mouton et que celui-ci tombe dans un trou profond le jour du sabbat, n'ira-t-il pas le prendre pour le sortir du trou? ¹²Et un homme vaut beaucoup plus qu'un mouton! Donc, notre loi permet de

faire du bien à quelqu'un le jour du sabbat.» [13]Jésus dit alors à l'homme : «Avance ta main.» Il l'avança et elle redevint saine comme l'autre. [14]Les Pharisiens s'en allèrent et tinrent conseil pour décider comment ils pourraient faire mourir Jésus.

Le serviteur que Dieu a choisi

[15]Quand Jésus apprit cela, il quitta cet endroit et un grand nombre de personnes le suivirent. Il guérit tous les malades, [16]mais il leur recommanda sévèrement de ne pas dire qui il était. [17]Il en fut ainsi afin que se réalisent ces paroles du prophète Ésaïe :

[18]«Voici mon serviteur
que j'ai choisi, dit Dieu,
celui que j'aime et en qui je mets
toute ma joie.
Je placerai mon Esprit sur lui
et il annoncera aux nations
le droit que j'instaure.
[19]Il ne se disputera avec personne
et ne criera pas,
on ne l'entendra pas faire
des discours dans les rues.
[20]Il ne cassera pas le roseau déjà plié
et n'éteindra pas la lampe
dont la lumière faiblit.
Il agira ainsi jusqu'à ce qu'il ait fait
triompher le droit ;
[21]et toutes les nations mettront
leur espoir en lui.»

Jésus répond à une accusation portée contre lui

[22]On amena alors à Jésus un homme qui était aveugle et muet parce qu'il était possédé d'un esprit mauvais. Jésus guérit cet homme, de sorte qu'il se mit à parler et à voir. [23]La foule était remplie d'étonnement et tous disaient : «Serait-il le Fils de David ?» [24]Quand les Pharisiens les entendirent, ils déclarèrent : «Cet homme ne chasse les esprits mauvais que parce que Béelzébul, leur chef, lui en donne le pouvoir !» [25]Mais Jésus connaissait leurs pensées ; il leur dit alors : «Tout royaume dont les habitants luttent les uns contre les autres finit par être détruit. Aucune ville ou aucune famille dont les habitants ou les membres luttent les uns contre les autres ne pourra se maintenir. [26]Si Satan chasse ce qui est à Satan, il est en lutte contre lui-même ; comment donc son royaume pourra-t-il se maintenir ? [27]Vous prétendez que je chasse les esprits mauvais parce que Béelzébul m'en donne le pouvoir ; qui donne alors à vos partisans le pouvoir de les chasser ? Vos partisans eux-mêmes démontrent que vous avez tort ! [28]En réalité, c'est par l'Esprit de Dieu que je chasse les esprits mauvais, ce qui signifie que le Royaume de Dieu est déjà venu jusqu'à vous.

[29]«Personne ne peut entrer dans la maison d'un homme fort et s'emparer de ses biens, s'il n'a pas d'abord ligoté cet homme fort ; mais après l'avoir ligoté, il peut s'emparer de tout dans sa maison. [30]Celui qui n'est pas avec moi est contre moi ; et celui qui ne m'aide pas à rassembler disperse. [31]C'est pourquoi, je vous le déclare : les êtres humains pourront être pardonnés pour tout péché et pour

toute insulte qu'ils font à Dieu ; mais celui qui fait insulte au Saint-Esprit ne recevra pas de pardon. 32Celui qui dit une parole contre le Fils de l'homme sera pardonné ; mais celui qui parle contre le Saint-Esprit ne sera pardonné ni dans le monde présent, ni dans le monde à venir.»

L'arbre et ses fruits

33«Pour avoir de bons fruits, vous devez avoir un bon arbre ; si vous avez un arbre malade, vous aurez de mauvais fruits. Car on reconnaît un arbre au genre de fruits qu'il produit. 34Bande de serpents ! Comment pourriez-vous dire de bonnes choses, alors que vous êtes mauvais ? Car la bouche exprime ce dont le cœur est plein. 35L'homme bon tire de bonnes choses de son bon trésor ; l'homme mauvais tire de mauvaises choses de son mauvais trésor. 36Je vous le déclare : au jour du Jugement, les hommes auront à rendre compte de toute parole inutile qu'ils auront prononcée. 37Car c'est d'après tes paroles que tu seras jugé et déclaré soit innocent, soit coupable.»

La demande d'un signe miraculeux

38Alors quelques maîtres de la loi et quelques Pharisiens dirent à Jésus : «Maître, nous voudrions que tu nous fasses voir un signe miraculeux.» 39Jésus leur répondit en ces termes : «Les gens d'aujourd'hui, qui sont mauvais et infidèles à Dieu, réclament un signe miraculeux, mais aucun signe ne leur sera accordé si ce n'est celui du prophète Jonas. 40En effet, de même que Jonas a passé trois jours et trois nuits dans le ventre du grand poisson, ainsi le Fils de l'homme passera trois jours et trois nuits dans la terre. 41Au jour du Jugement, les habitants de Ninive se lèveront en face des gens d'aujourd'hui et les accuseront, car les Ninivites ont changé de comportement quand ils ont entendu prêcher Jonas. Et il y a ici plus que Jonas ! 42Au jour du Jugement, la reine du Sud se lèvera en face des gens d'aujourd'hui et les accusera, car elle est venue des régions les plus lointaines de la terre pour écouter les paroles pleines de sagesse de Salomon. Et il y a ici plus que Salomon !»

Le retour de l'esprit mauvais

43«Lorsqu'un esprit mauvais est sorti d'un homme, il va et vient dans des espaces déserts en cherchant un lieu où s'établir. Comme il n'en trouve pas, 44il se dit : "Je vais retourner dans ma maison, celle que j'ai quittée." Il y retourne et la trouve vide, balayée, bien arrangée. 45Alors il s'en va prendre sept autres esprits encore plus malfaisants que lui ; ils reviennent ensemble dans la maison et s'y installent. Finalement, l'état de cet homme est donc pire qu'au début. Et il en ira de même pour les gens mauvais d'aujourd'hui.»

La mère et les frères de Jésus

46Jésus parlait encore à la foule, lorsque sa mère et ses frères arrivèrent. Ils se tenaient dehors et cherchaient à lui parler. 47Quelqu'un dit à Jésus :

«Écoute, ta mère et tes frères se tiennent dehors et désirent te parler.» [48] Jésus répondit à cette personne: «Qui est ma mère et qui sont mes frères?» [49] Puis il désigna de la main ses disciples et dit: «Voyez: ma mère et mes frères sont ici. [50] Car celui qui fait la volonté de mon Père qui est dans les cieux est mon frère, ma sœur ou ma mère.»

La parabole du semeur

13 [1] Ce jour-là, Jésus sortit de la maison et alla s'asseoir au bord du lac pour enseigner. [2] Une foule nombreuse s'assembla autour de lui, si bien qu'il monta dans une barque et s'y assit. Les gens se tenaient au bord de l'eau. [3] Il leur parlait de beaucoup de choses en utilisant des paraboles et il leur disait: «Un jour, un homme s'en alla dans son champ pour semer. [4] Tandis qu'il lançait la semence, une partie des grains tomba le long du chemin: les oiseaux vinrent et les mangèrent. [5] Une autre partie tomba sur un sol pierreux où il y avait peu de terre. Les grains poussèrent aussitôt parce que la couche de terre n'était pas profonde. [6] Quand le soleil fut haut dans le ciel, il brûla les jeunes plantes: elles se desséchèrent parce que leurs racines étaient insuffisantes. [7] Une autre partie des grains tomba parmi des plantes épineuses. Celles-ci grandirent et étouffèrent les bonnes pousses. [8] Mais d'autres grains tombèrent dans la bonne terre et produisirent des épis: les uns portaient cent grains, d'autres soixante et d'autres trente.» [9] Et Jésus ajouta:

«Écoutez bien, si vous avez des oreilles!»

Pourquoi Jésus utilise des paraboles

[10] Les disciples s'approchèrent alors de Jésus et lui demandèrent: «Pourquoi leur parles-tu en utilisant des paraboles?» [11] Il leur répondit: «Vous avez reçu, vous, la connaissance des secrets du Royaume des cieux, mais eux ne l'ont pas reçue. [12] Car celui qui a quelque chose recevra davantage et il sera dans l'abondance; mais à celui qui n'a rien on enlèvera même le peu qui pourrait lui rester. [13] C'est pourquoi j'utilise des paraboles pour leur parler: parce qu'ils regardent sans voir et qu'ils écoutent sans entendre et sans comprendre. [14] Ainsi s'accomplit pour eux la prophétie exprimée par Ésaïe en ces termes:

"Vous entendrez bien,
  mais vous ne comprendrez pas;
vous regarderez bien,
  mais vous ne verrez pas.
[15] Car ce peuple
  est devenu insensible;
ils se sont bouché les oreilles,
ils ont fermé les yeux,
afin d'empêcher leurs yeux de voir,
  leurs oreilles d'entendre,
  leur intelligence de comprendre,
et ainsi, ils ne reviendront pas
    à moi
pour que je les guérisse, dit Dieu."

[16] «Quant à vous, heureux êtes-vous: vos yeux voient et vos oreilles entendent! [17] Je vous le déclare, c'est la vérité: beaucoup de prophètes et de gens fidèles à Dieu ont désiré voir ce

que vous voyez, mais ne l'ont pas vu, et entendre ce que vous entendez, mais ne l'ont pas entendu. »

Jésus explique la parabole du semeur

18 « Écoutez donc ce que signifie la parabole du semeur. 19 Ceux qui entendent parler du Royaume et ne comprennent pas sont comme le bord du chemin où tombe la semence : le Mauvais arrive et arrache ce qui a été semé dans leur cœur. 20 D'autres sont comme le terrain pierreux où tombe la semence : ils entendent la parole et la reçoivent aussitôt avec joie. 21 Mais ils ne la laissent pas s'enraciner en eux, ils ne s'y attachent qu'un instant. Et alors, quand survient la détresse ou la persécution à cause de la parole de Dieu, ils renoncent bien vite à la foi. 22 D'autres encore reçoivent la semence parmi des plantes épineuses : ils ont entendu la parole, mais les préoccupations de ce monde et l'attrait trompeur de la richesse étouffent la parole, et elle ne produit rien. 23 D'autres, enfin, reçoivent la semence dans de la bonne terre : ils entendent la parole et la comprennent ; ils portent alors des fruits, les uns cent, d'autres soixante et d'autres trente. »

La parabole de la mauvaise herbe

24 Jésus leur raconta une autre parabole : « Voici à quoi ressemble le Royaume des cieux : Un homme avait semé de la bonne semence dans son champ. 25 Une nuit, pendant que tout le monde dormait, un ennemi de cet homme vint semer de la mauvaise herbe parmi le blé et s'en alla. 26 Lorsque les plantes poussèrent et que les épis se formèrent, la mauvaise herbe apparut aussi. 27 Les serviteurs du propriétaire vinrent lui dire : "Maître, tu avais semé de la bonne semence dans ton champ : d'où vient donc cette mauvaise herbe ?" 28 Il leur répondit : "C'est un ennemi qui a fait cela." Les serviteurs lui demandèrent alors : "Veux-tu que nous allions enlever la mauvaise herbe ?" – 29 "Non, répondit-il, car en l'enlevant vous risqueriez d'arracher aussi le blé. 30 Laissez-les pousser ensemble jusqu'à la moisson et, à ce moment-là, je dirai aux moissonneurs : Enlevez d'abord la mauvaise herbe et liez-la en bottes pour la brûler, puis vous rentrerez le blé dans mon grenier." »

La parabole de la graine de moutarde

31 Jésus leur raconta une autre parabole : « Le Royaume des cieux ressemble à une graine de moutarde qu'un homme a prise et semée dans son champ. 32 C'est la plus petite de toutes les graines ; mais quand elle a poussé, c'est la plus grande de toutes les plantes du jardin : elle devient un arbre, de sorte que les oiseaux viennent faire leurs nids dans ses branches. »

La parabole du levain

33 Jésus leur dit une autre parabole : « Le Royaume des cieux ressemble au levain qu'une femme prend et mêle à une grande quantité de farine, si bien que toute la pâte lève. »

Comment Jésus utilisait
des paraboles

34Jésus dit tout cela aux foules en utilisant des paraboles ; il ne leur parlait pas sans utiliser de paraboles. 35Il agissait ainsi afin que se réalise cette parole du prophète :

«Je m'exprimerai par des
    paraboles,
j'annoncerai
    des choses tenues secrètes
    depuis la création du monde.»

Jésus explique
la parabole de la mauvaise herbe

36Alors Jésus quitta la foule et se rendit à la maison. Ses disciples s'approchèrent de lui et dirent : «Explique-nous la parabole de la mauvaise herbe dans le champ.» 37Jésus répondit en ces termes : «Celui qui sème la bonne semence, c'est le Fils de l'homme ; 38le champ, c'est le monde ; la bonne semence représente ceux qui se soumettent au Royaume ; la mauvaise herbe représente ceux qui obéissent au Mauvais ; 39l'ennemi qui sème la mauvaise herbe, c'est le diable ; la moisson, c'est la fin du monde ; et les moissonneurs, ce sont les anges. 40Comme on enlève la mauvaise herbe pour la jeter au feu, ainsi en sera-t-il à la fin du monde : 41le Fils de l'homme enverra ses anges, ils élimineront de son Royaume tous ceux qui détournent de la foi les autres et ceux qui commettent le mal, 42et ils les jetteront dans le feu de la fournaise ; c'est là que beaucoup pleureront et grinceront des dents. 43Mais alors, ceux qui sont fidèles à

Dieu brilleront comme le soleil dans le Royaume de leur Père. Écoutez bien, si vous avez des oreilles !»

Le trésor caché et la perle

44«Le Royaume des cieux ressemble à un trésor caché dans un champ. Un homme découvre ce trésor et le cache de nouveau. Il est si heureux qu'il va vendre tout ce qu'il possède et revient acheter ce champ.

45«Le Royaume des cieux ressemble encore à un marchand qui cherche de belles perles. 46Quand il en a trouvé une de grande valeur, il va vendre tout ce qu'il possède et achète cette perle.»

La parabole du filet

47«Le Royaume des cieux ressemble encore à un filet qu'on a jeté dans le lac et qui attrape toutes sortes de poissons. 48Quand il est plein, les pêcheurs le tirent au bord de l'eau, puis s'asseyent pour trier les poissons : ils mettent les bons dans des paniers et rejettent ceux qui ne valent rien. 49Ainsi en sera-t-il à la fin du monde : les anges viendront séparer les méchants d'avec les bons 50pour les jeter dans le feu de la fournaise ; c'est là que beaucoup pleureront et grinceront des dents.

Des richesses nouvelles
et anciennes

51«Avez-vous compris tout cela ?» leur demanda Jésus. «Oui», répondirent-ils. 52Il leur dit alors : «Ainsi donc, tout maître de la loi qui devient disciple du Royaume des cieux est semblable à un propriétaire qui tire de son trésor des choses nouvelles et des choses anciennes.»

Les gens de Nazareth ne croient pas en Jésus

53Quand Jésus eut fini de raconter ces paraboles, il partit de là 54et se rendit dans la ville où il avait grandi. Il se mit à enseigner dans la synagogue de l'endroit et toutes les personnes présentes furent très étonnées. Elles disaient: «D'où a-t-il cette sagesse? comment peut-il accomplir ces miracles? 55N'est-ce pas lui le fils du charpentier? Marie n'est-elle pas sa mère? Jacques, Joseph, Simon et Jude ne sont-ils pas ses frères? 56Et ses sœurs ne vivent-elles pas toutes parmi nous? D'où a-t-il donc tout ce pouvoir?» 57Et cela les empêchait de croire en lui. Alors Jésus leur dit: «Un prophète est estimé partout, excepté dans sa ville natale et dans sa famille.» 58Jésus n'accomplit là que peu de miracles à cause de leur manque de foi.

La mort de Jean-Baptiste

14 1En ce temps-là, Hérode, qui régnait sur la Galilée, entendit parler de Jésus. 2Il dit à ses serviteurs: «C'est Jean-Baptiste: il est revenu d'entre les morts! Voilà pourquoi il a le pouvoir d'accomplir des miracles.»

3En effet, Hérode avait ordonné d'arrêter Jean, de l'enchaîner et de le jeter en prison. C'était à cause d'Hérodiade, la femme de son frère Philippe. 4Car Jean disait à Hérode: «Il ne t'est pas permis d'avoir Hérodiade pour femme!» 5Hérode voulait faire mourir Jean, mais il craignait le peuple juif, car tous considéraient Jean comme un prophète. 6Cependant, le jour de l'anniversaire d'Hérode, la fille d'Hérodiade dansa devant les invités. Elle plut tellement à Hérode 7qu'il jura de lui donner tout ce qu'elle demanderait. 8Sur le conseil de sa mère, elle lui dit: «Donne-moi ici la tête de Jean-Baptiste sur un plat!» 9Le roi en fut attristé; mais à cause des serments qu'il avait faits devant ses invités, il donna l'ordre de la lui accorder. 10Il envoya donc quelqu'un couper la tête de Jean-Baptiste dans la prison. 11La tête fut apportée sur un plat et donnée à la jeune fille, qui la remit à sa mère. 12Les disciples de Jean vinrent prendre son corps et l'enterrèrent; puis ils allèrent annoncer à Jésus ce qui s'était passé.

Jésus nourrit cinq mille hommes

13Quand Jésus entendit cette nouvelle, il partit de là en barque pour se rendre seul dans un endroit isolé. Mais les foules l'apprirent; elles sortirent des localités voisines et suivirent Jésus en marchant au bord de l'eau. 14Lorsque Jésus sortit de la barque, il vit une grande foule; il eut le cœur rempli de pitié pour ces gens et il se mit à guérir leurs malades. 15Quand le soir fut venu, les disciples de Jésus s'approchèrent de lui et dirent: «Il est déjà tard et cet endroit est isolé. Renvoie tous ces gens pour qu'ils aillent dans les villages s'acheter des vivres.» 16Jésus leur répondit: «Il n'est pas nécessaire qu'ils s'en aillent;

donnez-leur vous-mêmes à manger!»
¹⁷Mais ils lui dirent : «Nous n'avons
ici que cinq pains et deux poissons.» –
¹⁸«Apportez-les-moi», leur dit Jésus.
¹⁹Ensuite, il ordonna à la foule de
s'asseoir sur l'herbe ; puis il prit les
cinq pains et les deux poissons, leva les
yeux vers le ciel et remercia Dieu. Il
rompit les pains et les donna aux
disciples, et ceux-ci les distribuèrent à
la foule. ²⁰Chacun mangea à sa faim.
Les disciples emportèrent douze
corbeilles pleines des morceaux qui
restaient. ²¹Ceux qui avaient mangé
étaient au nombre d'environ cinq
mille hommes, sans compter les
femmes et les enfants.

Jésus marche sur le lac

²²Aussitôt après, Jésus fit monter les
disciples dans la barque pour qu'ils
passent avant lui de l'autre côté du lac,
pendant que lui-même renverrait la
foule. ²³Après l'avoir renvoyée, il
monta sur une colline pour prier.
Quand le soir fut venu, il se tenait là,
seul ; ²⁴la barque était déjà à une
bonne distance de la terre, elle était
battue par les vagues, car le vent
soufflait contre elle. ²⁵Tard dans la
nuit, Jésus se dirigea vers ses disciples
en marchant sur l'eau. ²⁶Quand ils le
virent marcher sur l'eau, ils furent
terrifiés et dirent : «C'est un fantôme!»
Et ils poussèrent des cris de frayeur.
²⁷Mais aussitôt Jésus leur parla :
«Courage, leur dit-il. C'est moi, n'ayez
pas peur!» ²⁸Pierre prit alors la parole
et lui dit : «Seigneur, si c'est bien toi,
ordonne que j'aille vers toi sur l'eau.»
– ²⁹«Viens!» répondit Jésus.

Pierre sortit de la barque et se mit à
marcher sur l'eau pour aller à Jésus.
³⁰Mais quand il remarqua la violence
du vent, il prit peur. Il commença à
s'enfoncer dans l'eau et s'écria :
«Seigneur, sauve-moi!» ³¹Aussitôt,
Jésus étendit la main, le saisit et lui
dit : «Comme ta confiance est faible!
Pourquoi as-tu douté?» ³²Ils
montèrent tous les deux dans la
barque et le vent tomba. ³³Alors les
disciples qui étaient dans la barque se
mirent à genoux devant Jésus et
dirent : «Tu es vraiment le Fils de
Dieu!»

Jésus guérit les malades dans la région de Génésareth

³⁴Ils achevèrent la traversée du lac
et arrivèrent dans la région de
Génésareth. ³⁵Les gens de l'endroit
reconnurent Jésus et répandirent dans
les environs la nouvelle de son arrivée,
et on lui amena tous les malades. ³⁶On
le suppliait de les laisser toucher au
moins le bord de son manteau ; et tous
ceux qui le touchaient étaient guéris.

L'enseignement transmis par les ancêtres

15 ¹Des Pharisiens et des
maîtres de la loi vinrent alors
de Jérusalem trouver Jésus et lui
demandèrent : ²«Pourquoi tes disciples désobéissent-ils aux règles
transmises par nos ancêtres? Car ils
ne se lavent pas les mains selon la
coutume avant de manger.» ³Jésus
leur répondit : «Et vous, pourquoi
désobéissez-vous au commandement
de Dieu pour agir selon votre propre

tradition? ⁴Dieu a dit en effet: "Respecte ton père et ta mère", et aussi "Celui qui maudit son père ou sa mère doit être mis à mort." ⁵Mais vous, vous enseignez que si quelqu'un déclare à son père ou à sa mère: "Ce que je pourrais te donner pour t'aider est une offrande réservée à Dieu", ⁶il n'a pas besoin de marquer pratiquement son respect pour son père. C'est ainsi que vous annulez l'exigence de la parole de Dieu pour agir selon votre propre tradition! ⁷Hypocrites! Ésaïe avait bien raison lorsqu'il prophétisait à votre sujet en ces termes:

⁸ "Ce peuple, dit Dieu, m'honore
    en paroles,
  mais de cœur il est loin de moi.
⁹ Le culte que ces gens me rendent
    est sans valeur
  car les doctrines qu'ils enseignent
    ne sont que
  des prescriptions humaines."»

Les choses qui rendent un homme impur

¹⁰Puis Jésus appela la foule et dit à tous: «Écoutez et comprenez ceci: ¹¹Ce n'est pas ce qui entre dans la bouche d'un homme qui le rend impur. Mais ce qui sort de sa bouche, voilà ce qui le rend impur.» ¹²Les disciples s'approchèrent alors de Jésus et lui dirent: «Sais-tu que les Pharisiens ont été scandalisés de t'entendre parler ainsi?» ¹³Il répondit: «Toute plante que n'a pas plantée mon Père qui est au ciel sera arrachée. ¹⁴Laissez-les: ce sont des aveugles conducteurs d'aveugles! Et si un aveugle conduit un autre aveugle, ils tomberont tous les deux dans un trou.» ¹⁵Pierre prit la parole et lui dit: «Explique-nous le sens de cette image.» ¹⁶Jésus dit: «Êtes-vous encore, vous aussi, sans intelligence? ¹⁷Ne comprenez-vous pas que tout ce qui entre dans la bouche de quelqu'un passe dans son ventre et sort ensuite de son corps? ¹⁸Mais ce qui sort de la bouche vient du cœur, et c'est cela qui rend l'homme impur. ¹⁹Car de son cœur viennent les mauvaises pensées qui le poussent à tuer, commettre l'adultère, vivre dans l'immoralité, voler, prononcer de faux témoignages et dire du mal des autres. ²⁰Voilà ce qui rend l'homme impur! Mais manger sans s'être lavé les mains selon la coutume, cela ne rend pas l'homme impur.»

Une femme étrangère croit en Jésus

²¹Puis Jésus partit de là et s'en alla dans le territoire de Tyr et de Sidon. ²²Une femme cananéenne qui vivait dans cette région vint à lui et s'écria: «Maître, Fils de David, aie pitié de moi! Ma fille est tourmentée par un esprit mauvais, elle va très mal!» ²³Mais Jésus ne répondit pas un mot. Ses disciples s'approchèrent pour lui adresser cette demande: «Renvoie-la, car elle ne cesse de crier en nous suivant.» ²⁴Jésus répondit: «Je n'ai été envoyé qu'aux brebis perdues du peuple d'Israël.»

²⁵Mais la femme vint se mettre à genoux devant lui et dit: «Maître, aide-moi!» ²⁶Jésus répondit: «Il n'est pas bien de prendre le pain des enfants

et de le jeter aux chiens.» — ²⁷«C'est vrai, Maître, dit-elle, pourtant même les chiens mangent les miettes qui tombent de la table de leurs maîtres.» ²⁸Alors Jésus lui répondit: «Oh! que ta foi est grande! Dieu t'accordera ce que tu désires.» Et sa fille fut guérie à ce moment même.

Jésus guérit
de nombreux malades

²⁹Jésus partit de là et se rendit au bord du lac de Galilée. Il monta sur une colline et s'assit. ³⁰Des foules nombreuses vinrent à lui, amenant avec elles des boiteux, des aveugles, des infirmes, des muets et beaucoup d'autres malades. On les déposa aux pieds de Jésus et il les guérit. ³¹Les gens furent remplis d'étonnement quand ils virent les muets parler, les infirmes être guéris, les boiteux marcher et les aveugles voir, et ils se mirent à louer le Dieu d'Israël.

Jésus nourrit
quatre mille hommes

³²Jésus appela ses disciples et dit: «J'ai pitié de ces gens, car voilà trois jours qu'ils sont avec moi et ils n'ont plus rien à manger. Je ne veux pas les renvoyer le ventre vide; ils pourraient se trouver mal en chemin.» ³³Les disciples lui demandèrent: «Où pourrions-nous trouver de quoi faire manger à sa faim une telle foule, dans cet endroit désert?» ³⁴Jésus leur demanda: «Combien avez-vous de pains?» Et ils répondirent: «Sept, et quelques petits poissons.» ³⁵Alors, il ordonna à la foule de s'asseoir par

terre. ³⁶Puis il prit les sept pains et les poissons, remercia Dieu, les rompit et les donna à ses disciples, et les disciples les distribuèrent à tous. ³⁷Chacun mangea à sa faim. Les disciples emportèrent sept corbeilles pleines des morceaux qui restaient. ³⁸Ceux qui avaient mangé étaient au nombre de quatre mille hommes, sans compter les femmes et les enfants. ³⁹Après avoir renvoyé la foule, Jésus monta dans la barque et se rendit dans la région de Magadan.

Les Pharisiens et les Sadducéens
demandent un signe miraculeux

16 ¹Les Pharisiens et les Sadducéens s'approchèrent de Jésus pour lui tendre un piège. Ils lui demandèrent de leur montrer par un signe miraculeux qu'il venait de la part de Dieu. ²Mais Jésus leur répondit en ces termes: «Au coucher du soleil, vous dites: "Il va faire beau temps, car le ciel est rouge." ³Et tôt le matin, vous dites: "Il va pleuvoir aujourd'hui, car le ciel est rouge sombre." Vous savez interpréter les aspects du ciel, mais vous êtes incapables d'interpréter les signes qui concernent ces temps-ci! ⁴Les gens d'aujourd'hui, qui sont mauvais et infidèles à Dieu, réclament un signe miraculeux, mais aucun signe ne leur sera accordé si ce n'est celui de Jonas.» Puis il les laissa et partit.

Le levain des Pharisiens
et des Sadducéens

⁵Quand les disciples passèrent de l'autre côté du lac, ils oublièrent d'emporter du pain. ⁶Jésus leur dit

alors: «Attention! Gardez-vous du levain des Pharisiens et des Sadducéens.» 7Les disciples se mirent à dire entre eux: «Il parle ainsi parce que nous n'avons pas emporté de pain.» 8Jésus s'aperçut de ce qu'ils disaient et leur demanda: «Pourquoi dire entre vous: c'est parce que nous n'avons pas de pain? Comme votre confiance est faible! 9Ne comprenez-vous pas encore? Ne vous rappelez-vous pas les cinq pains distribués aux cinq mille hommes et le nombre de corbeilles que vous avez emportées? 10Et ne vous rappelez-vous pas les sept pains distribués aux quatre mille hommes et le nombre de corbeilles que vous avez emportées? 11Comment ne comprenez-vous pas que je ne vous parlais pas de pain quand je vous disais: Gardez-vous du levain des Pharisiens et des Sadducéens?»

12Alors les disciples comprirent qu'il ne leur avait pas dit de se garder du levain utilisé pour le pain, mais de l'enseignement des Pharisiens et des Sadducéens.

Pierre déclare
que Jésus est le Messie

13Jésus se rend dans le territoire de Césarée de Philippe. Il demanda à ses disciples: «Que disent les gens au sujet du Fils de l'homme?» 14Ils répondirent: «Certains disent que tu es Jean-Baptiste, d'autres que tu es Élie, et d'autres encore que tu es Jérémie ou un autre prophète.» – 15«Et vous, leur demanda Jésus, qui dites-vous que je suis?» 16Simon Pierre répondit: «Tu es le Messie, le Fils du Dieu vivant.» 17Jésus lui dit alors: «Tu es heureux, Simon fils de Jean, car ce n'est pas un être humain qui t'a révélé cette vérité, mais mon Père qui est dans les cieux. 18Eh bien, moi, je te le déclare, tu es Pierre et sur cette pierre je construirai mon Église. La mort elle-même ne pourra rien contre elle. 19Je te donnerai les clés du Royaume des cieux: ce que tu exclusur terre sera exclu dans les cieux; ce que tu accueilleras sur terre sera accueilli dans les cieux.» 20Puis Jésus ordonna sévèrement à ses disciples de ne dire à personne qu'il était le Messie.

Jésus annonce sa mort
et sa résurrection

21A partir de ce moment, Jésus se mit à parler ouvertement à ses disciples en disant: «Il faut que j'aille à Jérusalem et que j'y souffre beaucoup de la part des anciens, des chefs des prêtres et des maîtres de la loi. Je serai mis à mort et, le troisième jour, je reviendrai à la vie.» 22Alors Pierre le prit à part et se mit à lui faire des reproches: «Dieu t'en garde, Seigneur! dit-il. Non, cela ne t'arrivera pas!» 23Mais Jésus se retourna et dit à Pierre: «Va-t'en loin de moi, Satan! Tu es un obstacle sur ma route, car tu ne penses pas comme Dieu, mais comme les êtres humains.»

24Puis Jésus dit à ses disciples: «Si quelqu'un veut venir avec moi, qu'il cesse de penser à lui-même, qu'il porte sa croix et me suive. 25En effet, celui qui veut sauver sa vie la perdra; mais celui qui perdra sa vie pour moi la retrouvera. 26A quoi servirait-il à un homme de gagner le monde entier, si c'est au prix de sa vie? Que pourrait-il donner pour racheter sa vie? 27En effet, le Fils de l'homme va venir dans la gloire de son Père avec ses anges, et alors il traitera chacun selon la façon dont il aura agi. 28Je vous le déclare, c'est la vérité: quelques-uns de ceux qui sont ici ne mourront pas avant d'avoir vu le Fils de l'homme venir comme roi.»

La transfiguration de Jésus

17 1Six jours après, Jésus prit avec lui Pierre, Jacques et Jean, frère de Jacques, et les conduisit sur une haute montagne où ils se trouvèrent seuls. 2Il changea d'aspect devant leurs yeux; son visage se mit à briller comme le soleil et ses vêtements devinrent blancs comme la lumière. 3Soudain les trois disciples virent Moïse et Élie qui parlaient avec Jésus. 4Pierre dit alors à Jésus: «Seigneur, il est bon que nous soyons ici. Si tu le veux, je vais dresser ici trois tentes, une pour toi, une pour Moïse et une pour Élie.» 5Il parlait encore, lorsqu'un nuage brillant vint les couvrir, et du nuage une voix se fit entendre: «Celui-ci est mon Fils bien-aimé en qui je mets toute ma joie. Écoutez-le!» 6Quand les disciples entendirent cette voix, ils eurent tellement peur qu'ils se jetèrent le visage contre terre. 7Jésus s'approcha d'eux, les toucha et dit: «Relevez-vous, n'ayez pas peur.» 8Ils levèrent alors les yeux et ne virent personne

d'autre que Jésus. 9Tandis qu'ils descendaient de la montagne, Jésus leur fit cette recommandation: «Ne parlez à personne de cette vision, jusqu'à ce que le Fils de l'homme revienne d'entre les morts.»

10Puis les disciples interrogèrent Jésus: «Pourquoi les maîtres de la loi disent-ils qu'Élie doit venir d'abord?» 11Il leur répondit: «Élie doit en effet venir et tout remettre en ordre. 12Quant à moi, je vous le déclare: Élie est déjà venu, les gens ne l'ont pas reconnu mais l'ont traité comme ils l'ont voulu. C'est ainsi que le Fils de l'homme lui-même sera maltraité par eux.» 13Les disciples comprirent alors qu'il leur parlait de Jean-Baptiste.

Jésus guérit un enfant épileptique

14Quand ils arrivèrent là où était la foule, un homme s'approcha de Jésus, se mit à genoux devant lui 15et dit: «Maître, aie pitié de mon fils. Il est épileptique et il a de telles crises que, souvent, il tombe dans le feu ou dans l'eau. 16Je l'ai amené à tes disciples, mais ils n'ont pas pu le guérir.» 17Jésus s'écria: «Gens mauvais et sans foi que vous êtes! Combien de temps encore devrai-je rester avec vous? Combien de temps encore devrai-je vous supporter? Amenez-moi l'enfant ici.» 18Jésus menaça l'esprit mauvais; celui-ci sortit de l'enfant qui fut guéri à ce moment même. 19Les disciples s'approchèrent alors de Jésus en particulier et lui demandèrent: «Pourquoi n'avons-nous pas pu chasser cet esprit?» 20Jésus leur répondit: «Parce que vous avez trop peu de foi.

Je vous le déclare, c'est la vérité : si vous aviez de la foi gros comme un grain de moutarde, vous diriez à cette colline : "Déplace-toi d'ici à là-bas", et elle se déplacerait. Rien ne vous serait impossible. [21Mais c'est par la prière et le jeûne seulement qu'on peut faire sortir ce genre d'esprit.]»

Jésus annonce de nouveau sa mort et sa résurrection

22Un jour que les disciples se trouvaient tous ensemble en Galilée, Jésus leur dit : «Le Fils de l'homme va être livré entre les mains des hommes, 23qui le mettront à mort ; mais, le troisième jour, il reviendra à la vie.» Alors les disciples furent profondément attristés.

Le paiement de l'impôt du temple

24Quand Jésus et ses disciples arrivèrent à Capernaüm, ceux qui percevaient l'impôt du temple s'approchèrent de Pierre et lui demandèrent : «Votre maître ne paie-t-il pas l'impôt du temple ?» – 25«Si, répondit Pierre, il le paie.» Au moment où Pierre entrait dans la maison, Jésus prit la parole le premier et dit : «Qu'en penses-tu, Simon ? Qui doit payer les impôts ou les taxes aux rois de ce monde ? Les citoyens de leurs pays ou les étrangers ?» – 26«Les étrangers», répondit Pierre. «Par conséquent, lui dit Jésus, les citoyens n'ont pas à payer. 27Cependant, nous ne voulons pas choquer ces gens. C'est pourquoi, va au lac, lance une ligne à l'eau, tire à toi le premier poisson que tu attraperas et

ouvre-lui la bouche : tu y trouveras une pièce d'argent qui suffira pour payer mon impôt et le tien ; prends-la et paie-leur notre impôt.»

Le plus grand dans le Royaume des cieux

18 1A ce moment, les disciples s'approchèrent de Jésus et lui demandèrent : «Qui est le plus grand dans le Royaume des cieux ?» 2Jésus appela un petit enfant, le plaça au milieu d'eux 3et dit : «Je vous le déclare, c'est la vérité : si vous ne changez pas pour devenir comme des petits enfants, vous n'entrerez pas dans le Royaume des cieux. 4Le plus grand dans le Royaume des cieux est celui qui s'abaisse et devient comme cet enfant. 5Et l'homme qui reçoit un enfant comme celui-ci par amour pour moi, me reçoit moi-même.»

Sérieuse mise en garde

6«Celui qui fait tomber dans le péché un de ces petits qui croient en moi, il vaudrait mieux pour lui qu'on lui attache au cou une grosse pierre et qu'on le noie au fond de la mer. 7Quel malheur pour le monde que tous les faits qui entraînent les hommes à pécher ! Ils se produisent fatalement, mais malheur à l'homme qui en est la cause ! 8Si c'est à cause de ta main ou de ton pied que tu tombes dans le péché, coupe-les et jette-les loin de toi ; il vaut mieux pour toi entrer dans la vraie vie avec une seule main ou un seul pied que de garder les deux mains et les deux pieds et d'être jeté dans le feu éternel. 9Et si c'est à cause de ton œil que tu tombes dans le péché, arrache-le et jette-le loin de toi ; il vaut mieux pour toi entrer dans la vraie vie avec un seul œil que de garder les deux yeux et d'être jeté dans le feu de l'enfer. »

La parabole
du mouton égaré et retrouvé

10 « Gardez-vous de mépriser l'un de ces petits ; je vous l'affirme, en effet, leurs anges se tiennent continuelle-ment en présence de mon Père dans les cieux. [11 Car le Fils de l'homme est venu sauver ceux qui étaient perdus.]

12 « Qu'en pensez-vous ? Supposons qu'un homme possède cent moutons et que l'un d'eux s'égare, ne va-t-il pas laisser les quatre-vingt-dix-neuf autres sur la colline pour partir à la recherche de celui qui s'est égaré ? 13 Je vous l'affirme, s'il le retrouve, il ressent plus de joie pour ce mouton que pour les quatre-vingt-dix-neuf autres qui ne se sont pas égarés. 14 De même, votre Père qui est dans les cieux ne veut pas qu'un seul de ces petits se perde. »

Quand un frère se rend coupable

15 « Si ton frère se rend coupable à ton égard, va le trouver seul à seul et montre-lui sa faute. S'il t'écoute, tu auras gagné ton frère. 16 Mais s'il refuse de t'écouter, prends une ou deux autres personnes avec toi, afin que, comme le dit l'Écriture, "toute affaire soit réglée sur le témoignage de deux ou trois personnes." 17 Mais s'il refuse de les écouter, dis-le à l'Église ; et s'il refuse d'écouter l'Église, considère-le comme un incroyant ou un collecteur d'impôts.

18 « Je vous le déclare, c'est la vérité : tout ce que vous exclurez sur terre sera exclu dans le ciel ; tout ce que vous accueillerez sur terre sera accueilli dans le ciel.

19 « Je vous déclare aussi que si deux d'entre vous, sur la terre, s'accordent pour demander quoi que ce soit dans la prière, mon Père qui est dans les cieux le leur donnera. 20 Car là où deux ou trois s'assemblent en mon nom, je suis au milieu d'eux. »

La parabole du serviteur
qui refuse de pardonner

21 Alors Pierre s'approcha de Jésus et lui demanda : « Seigneur, combien de fois devrai-je pardonner à mon frère s'il se rend coupable envers moi ? jusqu'à sept fois ? » – 22 « Non, répondit Jésus, je ne te dis pas jusqu'à sept fois, mais jusqu'à soixante-dix fois sept fois. 23 C'est pourquoi, voici à quoi ressemble le Royaume des cieux : Un roi décida de régler ses comptes avec ses serviteurs. 24 Il commençait à le faire, quand on lui en amena un qui lui devait une énorme somme d'argent. 25 Cet homme n'avait pas de quoi rendre cet argent ; alors son maître donna l'ordre de le vendre comme esclave et de vendre aussi sa femme, ses enfants et tout ce qu'il possédait, afin de rembourser ainsi la dette. 26 Le serviteur se jeta à genoux devant son maître et lui dit : "Prends patience envers moi et je te paierai tout !" 27 Le maître en eut pitié : il annula sa dette et le laissa partir. 28 Le serviteur sortit et rencontra un de ses compagnons de service qui lui devait une très petite somme d'argent. Il le

saisit à la gorge et le serrait à l'étouffer en disant : "Paie ce que tu me dois !" 29Son compagnon se jeta à ses pieds et le supplia en ces termes : "Prends patience envers moi et je te paierai !" 30Mais l'autre refusa ; bien plus, il le fit jeter en prison en attendant qu'il ait payé sa dette. 31Quand les autres serviteurs virent ce qui était arrivé, ils en furent profondément attristés et allèrent tout raconter à leur maître. 32Alors le maître fit venir ce serviteur et lui dit : "Méchant serviteur ! j'ai annulé toute ta dette parce que tu m'as supplié de le faire. 33Tu devais toi aussi avoir pitié de ton compagnon, comme j'ai eu pitié de toi." 34Le maître était fort en colère et il envoya le serviteur aux travaux forcés en attendant qu'il ait payé toute sa dette.»

35Et Jésus ajouta : «C'est ainsi que mon Père qui est au ciel vous traitera si chacun de vous ne pardonne pas à son frère de tout son cœur.»

L'enseignement de Jésus sur le divorce

19 1Quand Jésus eut achevé ces instructions, il quitta la Galilée et se rendit dans la partie de la Judée qui se trouve de l'autre côté de la rivière, le Jourdain. 2Une foule de gens l'y suivirent et il guérit leurs malades. 3Quelques Pharisiens s'approchèrent de lui pour lui tendre un piège. Ils lui demandèrent : «Notre loi permet-elle à un homme de renvoyer sa femme pour n'importe quelle raison ?» 4Jésus répondit : «N'avez-vous pas lu ce que déclare l'Écriture ? "Au commencement, le Créateur les fit homme et

femme", 5puis il dit : C'est pourquoi, l'homme quittera son père et sa mère pour s'attacher à sa femme, et les deux deviendront un seul être. 6Ainsi, ils ne sont plus deux mais un seul être. Que l'homme ne sépare donc pas ce que Dieu a uni.» 7Les Pharisiens lui demandèrent : «Pourquoi donc Moïse a-t-il commandé à l'homme de donner une attestation de divorce à sa femme quand il la renvoie ?» 8Jésus répondit : «Moïse vous a permis de renvoyer vos femmes parce que vous avez le cœur dur. Mais au commencement, il n'en était pas ainsi. 9Je vous le déclare : si un homme renvoie sa femme, alors qu'elle n'a pas été infidèle, et en épouse une autre, il commet un adultère.»

10Ses disciples lui dirent : «Si telle est la condition de l'homme par rapport à sa femme, il vaut mieux ne pas se marier.» 11Jésus leur répondit : «Tous les hommes ne sont pas capables d'accepter cet enseignement, mais seulement ceux à qui Dieu en donne les moyens. 12Il y a différentes raisons qui empêchent les hommes de se marier : pour certains, c'est une impossibilité dès leur naissance ; d'autres, les eunuques, en ont été rendus incapables par les hommes ; d'autres enfin renoncent à se marier à cause du Royaume des cieux. Que celui qui peut accepter cet enseignement l'accepte !»

Jésus bénit des enfants

13Des gens amenèrent des enfants à Jésus pour qu'il pose les mains sur eux et prie pour eux, mais les disciples leur firent des reproches. 14Jésus dit alors :

«Laissez les enfants venir à moi et ne les en empêchez pas, car le Royaume des cieux appartient à ceux qui sont comme eux.» 15Il posa les mains sur eux, puis partit de là.

Le jeune homme riche

16Un homme s'approcha de Jésus et lui demanda: «Maître, que dois-je faire de bon pour avoir la vie éternelle?» 17Jésus lui dit: «Pourquoi m'interroges-tu au sujet de ce qui est bon? Un seul est bon. Si tu veux entrer dans la vie, obéis aux commandements.» – 18«Auxquels?» demanda-t-il. Jésus répondit: «Ne commets pas de meurtre; ne commets pas d'adultère; ne vole pas; ne prononce pas de faux témoignage contre quelqu'un; 19respecte ton père et ta mère; aime ton prochain comme toi-même.» 20L'homme lui dit: «J'ai obéi à tous ces commandements. Que dois-je faire encore?» – 21«Si tu veux être parfait, lui dit Jésus, va vendre tout ce que tu possèdes et donne l'argent aux pauvres, alors tu auras des richesses dans les cieux; puis viens et suis-moi.» 22Mais quand le jeune homme entendit cela, il s'en alla tout triste, parce qu'il avait de grands biens.

23Jésus dit alors à ses disciples: «Je vous le déclare, c'est la vérité: il est difficile à un homme riche d'entrer dans le Royaume des cieux. 24Et je vous déclare encore ceci: il est difficile à un chameau de passer par le trou d'une aiguille, mais il est encore plus difficile à un riche d'entrer dans le Royaume de Dieu.» 25Quand les disciples entendirent ces mots, ils furent très étonnés et dirent: «Mais qui donc peut être sauvé?» 26Jésus les regarda et leur dit: «C'est impossible aux hommes, mais tout est possible à Dieu.» 27Alors Pierre prit la parole: «Écoute, lui dit-il, nous avons tout quitté pour te suivre. Que se passera-t-il pour nous?» 28Jésus lui dit: «Je vous le déclare, c'est la vérité: quand le Fils de l'homme siégera sur son trône glorieux dans le monde nouveau, vous, les douze qui m'avez suivi, vous siégerez également sur des trônes pour juger les douze tribus d'Israël. 29Et tous ceux qui auront quitté pour moi leurs maisons, ou leurs frères, leurs sœurs, leur père, leur mère, leurs enfants, leurs champs, recevront cent fois plus et auront part à la vie éternelle. 30Mais beaucoup qui sont maintenant les premiers seront les derniers et beaucoup qui sont maintenant les derniers seront les premiers.»

Les ouvriers dans la vigne

20 1«Voici, en effet, à quoi ressemble le Royaume des cieux: Un propriétaire sortit tôt le matin afin d'engager des ouvriers pour sa vigne. 2Il convint avec eux de leur payer le salaire habituel, une pièce d'argent par jour, et les envoya travailler dans sa vigne. 3Il sortit de nouveau à neuf heures du matin et en vit d'autres qui se tenaient sur la place sans rien faire. 4Il leur dit: "Allez, vous aussi, travailler dans ma vigne et je vous donnerai un juste salaire." 5Et ils y allèrent. Le propriétaire sortit encore

à midi, puis à trois heures de l'après-midi et fit de même. ⁶Enfin, vers cinq heures du soir, il sortit et trouva d'autres hommes qui se tenaient encore sur la place. Il leur demanda : "Pourquoi restez-vous ici tout le jour sans rien faire ?" – 7"Parce que personne ne nous a engagés", répondirent-ils. Il leur dit : "Eh bien, allez, vous aussi, travailler dans ma vigne."

⁸«Quand vint le soir, le propriétaire de la vigne dit à son contremaître : "Appelle les ouvriers et paie à chacun son salaire. Tu commenceras par les derniers engagés et tu termineras par les premiers engagés." ⁹Ceux qui s'étaient mis au travail à cinq heures du soir vinrent alors et reçurent chacun une pièce d'argent. ¹⁰Quand ce fut le tour des premiers engagés, ils pensèrent qu'ils recevraient plus ; mais on leur remit aussi à chacun une pièce d'argent. ¹¹En la recevant, ils critiquaient le propriétaire ¹²et disaient : "Ces ouvriers engagés en dernier n'ont travaillé qu'une heure et tu les as payés comme nous qui avons supporté la fatigue d'une journée entière de travail sous un soleil brûlant !" ¹³Mais le propriétaire répondit à l'un d'eux : "Mon ami, je ne te cause aucun tort. Tu as convenu avec moi de travailler pour une pièce d'argent par jour, n'est-ce pas ? ¹⁴Prends donc ton salaire et va-t'en. Je veux donner à ce dernier engagé autant qu'à toi. ¹⁵N'ai-je pas le droit de faire ce que je veux de mon argent ? Ou bien es-tu jaloux parce que je suis bon ?" ¹⁶Ainsi, ajouta Jésus, ceux qui sont les derniers seront les premiers et ceux qui sont les premiers seront les derniers.»

Jésus annonce une troisième fois sa mort et sa résurrection

¹⁷Jésus se rendait à Jérusalem. Il prit les douze disciples à part et leur dit, tout en marchant : ¹⁸«Écoutez, nous montons à Jérusalem, où le Fils de l'homme sera livré aux chefs des prêtres et aux maîtres de la loi. Ils le condamneront à mort ¹⁹et le livreront aux païens, qui se moqueront de lui, le frapperont à coups de fouet et le cloueront sur une croix. Et le troisième jour, il reviendra de la mort à la vie.»

La demande de la mère de Jacques et Jean

²⁰Alors la femme de Zébédée s'approcha de Jésus avec ses deux fils ; elle s'inclina devant lui pour lui demander une faveur. ²¹«Que désires-tu ?» lui dit Jésus. Elle lui répondit : «Promets-moi que mes deux fils que voici siégeront l'un à ta droite et l'autre à ta gauche quand tu seras roi.» – ²²«Vous ne savez pas ce que vous demandez, répondit Jésus. Pouvez-vous boire la coupe de douleur que je vais boire ?» – «Nous le pouvons», lui répondirent-ils. ²³«Vous boirez en effet ma coupe, leur dit Jésus. Mais ce n'est pas à moi de décider qui siégera à ma droite et à ma gauche ; ces places sont à ceux pour qui mon Père les a préparées.»

²⁴Quand les dix autres disciples entendirent cela, ils s'indignèrent contre les deux frères. ²⁵Alors Jésus

les appela tous et dit : «Vous savez que les chefs des peuples les commandent en maîtres et que les grands personnages leur font sentir leur pouvoir. 26Mais cela ne doit pas se passer ainsi parmi vous. Au contraire, si l'un de vous veut être grand, il doit être votre serviteur, 27et si l'un de vous veut être le premier, il doit être votre esclave : 28c'est ainsi que le Fils de l'homme n'est pas venu pour se faire servir, mais il est venu pour servir, et donner sa vie comme rançon pour libérer une multitude de gens.»

Jésus guérit deux aveugles

29Lorsqu'ils sortirent de Jéricho, une grande foule suivit Jésus. 30Deux aveugles qui étaient assis au bord du chemin entendirent que Jésus passait ; ils se mirent alors à crier : «Maître, Fils de David, aie pitié de nous !» 31La foule leur faisait des reproches pour qu'ils se taisent, mais ils criaient encore plus fort : «Maître, Fils de David, aie pitié de nous !» 32Jésus s'arrêta, les appela et leur demanda : «Que voulez-vous que je fasse pour vous ?» 33Ils lui répondirent : «Maître, fais que nous puissions voir.» 34Jésus eut pitié d'eux et toucha leurs yeux ; aussitôt, les deux hommes purent voir, et ils le suivirent.

Jésus entre à Jérusalem

21 1Quand ils approchèrent de Jérusalem et arrivèrent près du village de Bethfagé, sur le mont des Oliviers, Jésus envoya en avant deux des disciples : 2«Allez au village qui est là devant vous, leur dit-il. Vous y trouverez tout de suite une ânesse attachée et son ânon avec elle. Détachez-les et amenez-les-moi. 3Si l'on vous dit quelque chose, répondez : "Le Seigneur en a besoin." Et aussitôt on les laissera partir.»

4Cela arriva afin que se réalisent ces paroles du prophète :
5 «Dites à la population de Sion :
Regarde, ton roi vient à toi,
plein de douceur,
    monté sur une ânesse,
et sur un ânon,
    le petit d'une ânesse.»

6Les disciples partirent donc et firent ce que Jésus leur avait ordonné. 7Ils amenèrent l'ânesse et l'ânon, posèrent leurs manteaux sur eux et Jésus s'assit dessus. 8Une grande foule de gens étendirent leurs manteaux sur le chemin ; d'autres coupaient des branches aux arbres et les mettaient sur le chemin. 9Les gens qui marchaient devant Jésus et ceux qui le suivaient criaient : «Gloire au Fils de David ! Que Dieu bénisse celui qui vient au nom du Seigneur ! Gloire à Dieu dans les cieux !»

10Quand Jésus entra dans Jérusalem, toute la population se mit à s'agiter. «Qui est ce homme ?» demandait-on. 11«C'est le prophète Jésus, de Nazareth en Galilée», répondaient les gens.

Jésus dans le temple

12Jésus entra dans le temple et chassa tous ceux qui vendaient ou qui achetaient à cet endroit ; il renversa les tables des changeurs d'argent et les sièges des vendeurs de pigeons. 13Puis il leur dit : «Dans les Écritures, Dieu déclare : "On appellera ma maison maison de prière." Mais vous, ajouta-t-il, vous en faites une caverne de voleurs!»

¹⁴Des aveugles et des boiteux s'approchèrent de Jésus dans le temple et il les guérit. ¹⁵Les chefs des prêtres et les maîtres de la loi s'indignèrent quand ils virent les actions étonnantes qu'il accomplissait et les enfants qui criaient dans le temple : «Gloire au Fils de David!» ¹⁶Ils dirent alors à Jésus : «Entends-tu ce qu'ils disent?» – «Oui, leur répondit Jésus. N'avez-vous jamais lu ce passage de l'Écriture : "Tu as fait en sorte que même des enfants et des bébés te louent"?» ¹⁷Puis il les quitta et sortit de la ville pour se rendre à Béthanie où il passa la nuit.

Jésus maudit un figuier

¹⁸Le lendemain matin, tandis qu'il revenait en ville, Jésus eut faim. ¹⁹Il vit un figuier au bord du chemin et s'en approcha, mais il n'y trouva que des feuilles. Il dit alors au figuier : «Tu ne porteras plus jamais de fruit!» Aussitôt, le figuier devint tout sec. ²⁰Les disciples virent cela et furent remplis d'étonnement. Ils demandèrent à Jésus : «Comment ce figuier est-il devenu tout sec en un instant?» ²¹Jésus leur répondit : «Je vous le déclare, c'est la vérité : si vous avez de la foi et si vous ne doutez pas, non seulement vous pourrez faire ce que j'ai fait à ce figuier, mais vous pourrez même dire à cette colline : "Ôte-toi de là et jette-toi dans la mer", et cela arrivera. ²²Si vous croyez, vous recevrez tout ce que vous demanderez dans la prière.»

D'où vient l'autorité de Jésus ?

²³Jésus entra dans le temple et se mit à enseigner; les chefs des prêtres et les anciens du peuple juif s'approchèrent alors et lui demandèrent : «De quel droit fais-tu ces choses? Qui t'a donné autorité pour cela?» ²⁴Jésus leur répondit : «Je vais vous poser à mon tour une question, une seule; si vous me donnez une réponse, alors je vous dirai de quel droit je fais ces choses. ²⁵Qui a envoyé Jean baptiser? Est-ce Dieu ou les hommes?» Mais ils se mirent à discuter entre eux et se dirent : «Si nous répondons: "C'est Dieu qui l'a envoyé", il nous demandera : "Pourquoi donc n'avez-vous pas cru Jean?" ²⁶Mais si nous disons : "Ce sont les hommes qui l'ont envoyé", nous avons à craindre la foule, car tous pensent que Jean était un prophète.» ²⁷Alors ils répondirent à Jésus : «Nous ne savons pas.» – «Eh bien, répliqua-t-il, moi non plus, je ne vous dirai pas de quel droit je fais ces choses.»

La parabole des deux fils

²⁸«Que pensez-vous de ceci? ajouta Jésus. Un homme avait deux fils. Il s'adressa au premier et lui dit : "Mon enfant, va travailler aujourd'hui dans la vigne." – ²⁹"Non, je ne veux pas", répondit-il; mais, plus tard, il changea d'idée et se rendit à la vigne. ³⁰Le père adressa la même demande à l'autre fils. Celui-ci lui répondit : "Oui, père, j'y vais", mais il n'y alla pas. ³¹Lequel

des deux a fait la volonté de son père?» – «Le premier», répondirent-ils. Jésus leur dit alors: «Je vous le déclare, c'est la vérité: les collecteurs d'impôts et les prostituées arrivent avant vous dans le Royaume de Dieu. 32Car Jean-Baptiste est venu à vous en vous montrant le juste chemin et vous ne l'avez pas cru; mais les collecteurs d'impôts et les prostituées l'ont cru. Et même après avoir vu cela, vous n'avez pas changé intérieurement pour croire en lui.»

La parabole des méchants vignerons

33«Écoutez une autre parabole: Il y avait un propriétaire qui planta une vigne; il l'entoura d'un mur, y creusa la roche pour le pressoir à raisin et bâtit une tour de garde. Ensuite, il loua la vigne à des ouvriers vignerons et partit en voyage. 34Quand vint le moment de récolter le raisin, il envoya ses serviteurs aux ouvriers vignerons pour recevoir sa récolte. 35Mais les vignerons saisirent ses serviteurs, battirent l'un, assassinèrent l'autre et tuèrent un troisième à coups de pierres. 36Alors le propriétaire envoya d'autres serviteurs, en plus grand nombre que la première fois, mais les vignerons les traitèrent de la même façon. 37Finalement, il leur envoya son fils en pensant: "Ils auront du respect pour mon fils." 38Mais quand les vignerons virent le fils, ils se dirent entre eux: "Voici le futur héritier! Allons, tuons-le et nous aurons sa propriété!" 39Ils se saisirent donc, le jetèrent hors de la vigne et le tuèrent.

40«Eh bien, quand le propriétaire de la vigne viendra, que fera-t-il à ces vignerons?» demanda Jésus. 41Ils lui répondirent: «Il mettra à mort sans pitié ces criminels et louera la vigne à d'autres vignerons, qui lui remettront la récolte au moment voulu.»

42Puis Jésus leur dit: «N'avez-vous jamais lu ce que déclare l'Écriture?

"La pierre que les bâtisseurs
    avaient rejetée
est devenue la pierre principale.
Cela vient du Seigneur,
pour nous, c'est une merveille!"

43«C'est pourquoi, ajouta Jésus, je vous le déclare: le Royaume de Dieu vous sera enlevé pour être confié à un peuple qui en produira les fruits. [44Celui qui tombera sur cette pierre s'y brisera; et si la pierre tombe sur quelqu'un, elle le réduira en poussière.]»

45Les chefs des prêtres et les Pharisiens entendirent les paraboles de Jésus et comprirent qu'il parlait d'eux. 46Ils cherchèrent alors un moyen de l'arrêter, mais ils eurent peur de la foule qui considérait Jésus comme un prophète.

La parabole du grand repas de mariage

22 1Jésus utilisa de nouveau des paraboles pour parler à ses auditeurs. Il leur dit: 2«Voici à quoi ressemble le Royaume des cieux: Un roi organisa un repas pour le mariage de son fils. 3Il envoya ses serviteurs appeler les invités pour ce repas, mais ils ne voulurent pas venir. 4Il envoya alors d'autres serviteurs avec cet ordre:

"Dites aux invités: Mon repas est préparé maintenant, mes taureaux et mes bêtes grasses sont tués, tout est prêt. Venez au repas de mariage!" [5]Mais les invités ne s'en soucièrent pas et s'en allèrent à leurs affaires: l'un à son champ, l'autre à son commerce; [6]les autres saisirent les serviteurs, les maltraitèrent et les tuèrent. [7]Le roi se mit en colère: il envoya ses soldats tuer ces assassins et incendier leur ville. [8]Puis il dit à ses serviteurs: "Le repas de mariage est prêt, mais les invités ne le méritaient pas. [9]Allez donc dans les principales rues et invitez au repas tous ceux que vous pourrez trouver." [10]Les serviteurs s'en allèrent dans les rues et rassemblèrent tous ceux qu'ils trouvèrent, les mauvais comme les bons; et ainsi, la salle de fête se remplit de monde. [11]Le roi entra alors pour voir les invités et il aperçut un homme qui ne portait pas de costume de fête. [12]Il lui demanda: "Mon ami, comment es-tu entré ici sans costume de fête?" Mais l'homme ne répondit rien. [13]Alors le roi dit aux serviteurs: "Liez-lui les pieds et les mains et jetez-le dehors, dans le noir. C'est là qu'il pleurera et grincera des dents." [14]En effet, ajouta Jésus, beaucoup sont invités, mais peu sont admis.»

L'impôt payé à l'empereur

[15]Les Pharisiens allèrent alors tenir conseil pour décider comment ils pourraient prendre Jésus au piège par une question. [16]Ils envoyèrent ensuite quelques-uns de leurs disciples et quelques membres du parti d'Hérode dire à Jésus: «Maître, nous savons que tu dis la vérité: tu enseignes la vérité sur la conduite que Dieu demande; tu n'as pas peur de ce que pensent les autres et tu ne tiens pas compte de l'apparence des gens. [17]Dis-nous donc ce que tu penses de ceci: notre loi permet-elle ou non de payer des impôts à l'empereur romain?» [18]Mais Jésus connaissait leurs mauvaises intentions; il leur dit alors: «Hypocrites, pourquoi me tendez-vous un piège? [19]Montrez-moi l'argent qui sert à payer l'impôt.» Ils lui présentèrent une pièce d'argent, [20]et Jésus leur demanda: «Ce visage et ce nom gravés ici, de qui sont-ils?» – [21]«De l'empereur», répondirent-ils. Alors Jésus leur dit: «Payez donc à l'empereur ce qui lui appartient, et à Dieu ce qui lui appartient.» [22]Quand ils entendirent cette réponse, ils furent remplis d'étonnement. Ils le laissèrent et s'en allèrent.

Une question
sur la résurrection des morts

[23]Le même jour, quelques Sadducéens vinrent auprès de Jésus. – Ce sont eux qui affirment qu'il n'y a pas de résurrection. – Ils l'interrogèrent [24]de la façon suivante: «Maître, voici ce que Moïse a déclaré: "Si un homme meurt sans avoir eu d'enfants, son frère doit épouser la veuve pour donner des descendants à celui qui est mort." [25]Or, il y avait parmi nous sept frères. Le premier se maria, mourut sans avoir eu d'enfants et laissa ainsi sa veuve à son frère. [26]Il en fut de même pour le deuxième frère, puis pour le troisième et pour tous les sept.

27Après eux tous, la femme mourut aussi. 28Au jour où les morts se relèveront, duquel des sept sera-t-elle donc la femme? Car ils l'ont tous eue comme épouse!» 29Jésus leur répondit: «Vous vous trompez parce que vous ne connaissez ni les Écritures, ni la puissance de Dieu. 30En effet, quand les morts se relèveront, les hommes et les femmes ne se marieront pas, mais ils vivront comme les anges dans le ciel. 31Pour ce qui est de se relever d'entre les morts, n'avez-vous jamais lu ce que Dieu vous a déclaré? Il a dit: 32«Je suis le Dieu d'Abraham, le Dieu d'Isaac et le Dieu de Jacob." Dieu, ajouta Jésus, est le Dieu des vivants, et non des morts.» 33Tous ceux qui l'avaient entendu étaient impressionnés par son enseignement.

Le commandement
le plus important

34Quand les Pharisiens apprirent que Jésus avait réduit au silence les Sadducéens, ils se réunirent. 35Et l'un d'eux, un maître de la loi, voulut lui tendre un piège; il lui demanda: 36«Maître, quel est le plus grand commandement de la loi?»

37Jésus lui répondit: «"Tu dois aimer le Seigneur ton Dieu de tout ton cœur, de toute ton âme et de toute ton intelligence." 38C'est là le commandement le plus grand et le plus important. 39Et voici le second commandement, qui est d'une importance semblable: "Tu dois aimer ton prochain comme toi-même." 40Toute la loi de Moïse et tout l'enseignement

des prophètes dépendent de ces deux commandements.»

Le Messie et David

41Les Pharisiens se trouvaient réunis et Jésus leur posa cette question: 42«Que pensez-vous du Messie? De qui est-il le descendant?» – «Il est le descendant de David», lui répondirent-ils. 43Jésus leur dit: «Comment donc David, guidé par le Saint-Esprit, a-t-il pu l'appeler "Seigneur"? Car David a dit: 44«Le Seigneur Dieu a déclaré
    à mon Seigneur:
Viens siéger à ma droite,
je veux contraindre tes ennemis
    à passer sous tes pieds."
45Si donc David l'appelle "Seigneur", comment le Messie peut-il être aussi descendant de David?» 46Aucun d'eux ne put lui répondre un seul mot et, à partir de ce jour, personne n'osa plus lui poser de questions.

Jésus met en garde
contre les maîtres de la loi
et les Pharisiens

23 1Alors Jésus s'adressa à toute la foule, ainsi qu'à ses disciples: 2«Les maîtres de la loi et les Pharisiens, dit-il, sont chargés d'expliquer la loi de Moïse. 3Vous devez donc leur obéir et accomplir tout ce qu'ils vous disent; mais n'imitez pas leur façon d'agir, car ils ne mettent pas en pratique ce qu'ils enseignent. 4Ils attachent de lourds fardeaux, difficiles à porter, et les mettent sur les épaules des hommes; mais eux-mêmes refusent de bouger un doigt pour les aider à remuer ces fardeaux. 5Ils accomplissent toutes leurs

œuvres de façon que les hommes les remarquent. Ainsi, pour les paroles sacrées qu'ils portent au front ou au bras, ils ont des étuis particulièrement grands ; les franges de leurs manteaux sont exceptionnellement larges. ⁶Ils aiment les places d'honneur dans les grands repas et les sièges les plus en vue dans les synagogues ; ⁷ils aiment à recevoir des salutations respectueuses sur les places publiques et à être appelés "Maître" par les gens. ⁸Mais vous, ne vous faites pas appeler "Maître", car vous êtes tous frères et vous n'avez qu'un seul Maître. ⁹N'appelez personne sur la terre votre "Père", car vous n'avez qu'un seul Père, celui qui est au ciel. ¹⁰Ne vous faites pas non plus appeler "Chef", car vous n'avez qu'un seul Chef, le Messie. ¹¹Le plus grand parmi vous doit être votre serviteur. ¹²Celui qui s'élève sera abaissé, mais celui qui s'abaisse sera élevé.»

Jésus dénonce l'hypocrisie des maîtres de la loi et des Pharisiens

¹³«Malheur à vous, maîtres de la loi et Pharisiens, hypocrites ! Vous fermez la porte du Royaume des cieux devant les hommes ; vous n'y entrez pas vous-mêmes et vous ne laissez pas entrer ceux qui le désirent.

[¹⁴«Malheur à vous, maîtres de la loi et Pharisiens, hypocrites ! Vous prenez aux veuves tout ce qu'elles possèdent et, en même temps, vous faites de longues prières pour vous faire remarquer. C'est pourquoi vous serez jugés d'autant plus sévèrement !]

¹⁵«Malheur à vous, maîtres de la loi et Pharisiens, hypocrites ! Vous voyagez partout sur terre et sur mer pour gagner un seul converti, et quand vous l'avez gagné vous le rendez digne de l'enfer deux fois plus que vous.

¹⁶«Malheur à vous, conducteurs aveugles ! Vous dites : "Si quelqu'un jure par le temple, il n'est pas engagé par ce serment ; mais s'il jure par l'or du temple, il est engagé." ¹⁷Insensés, aveugles ! Qu'est-ce qui a le plus d'importance : l'or, ou le temple qui rend cet or sacré ? ¹⁸Vous dites aussi : "Si quelqu'un jure par l'autel, il n'est pas engagé par ce serment ; mais s'il jure par l'offrande qui se trouve sur l'autel, il est engagé." ¹⁹Aveugles ! Qu'est-ce qui a le plus d'importance : l'offrande, ou l'autel qui rend cette offrande sacrée ? ²⁰Celui donc qui jure par l'autel jure par l'autel et par tout ce qui se trouve dessus ; ²¹celui qui jure par le temple jure par le temple et par Dieu qui l'habite ; ²²celui qui jure par le ciel jure par le trône de Dieu et par Dieu qui y siège.

²³«Malheur à vous, maîtres de la loi et Pharisiens, hypocrites ! Vous donnez à Dieu le dixième de plantes comme la menthe, le fenouil et le cumin, mais vous négligez les enseignements les plus importants de la loi, tels que la justice, la bonté et la fidélité : c'est pourtant là ce qu'il fallait pratiquer, sans négliger le reste. ²⁴Conducteurs aveugles ! Vous filtrez une boisson pour en éliminer un moustique, mais vous avalez un chameau !

²⁵«Malheur à vous, maîtres de la loi et Pharisiens, hypocrites ! Vous nettoyez l'extérieur de la coupe et du plat, mais l'intérieur reste rempli du

produit de vos vols et de vos mauvais désirs. 26Pharisien aveugle! Nettoie d'abord l'intérieur de la coupe et alors l'extérieur deviendra également propre.

27«Malheur à vous, maîtres de la loi et Pharisiens, hypocrites! Vous ressemblez à des tombeaux blanchis qui paraissent beaux à l'extérieur mais qui, à l'intérieur, sont pleins d'ossements de morts et de toute sorte de pourriture. 28Vous de même, extérieurement vous donnez à tout le monde l'impression que vous êtes fidèles à Dieu, mais intérieurement vous êtes pleins d'hypocrisie et de mal.

29«Malheur à vous, maîtres de la loi et Pharisiens, hypocrites! Vous construisez de belles tombes pour les prophètes, vous décorez les tombeaux des hommes justes, 30et vous dites: "Si nous avions vécu au temps de nos ancêtres, nous n'aurions pas été leurs complices pour tuer les prophètes." 31Ainsi, vous reconnaissez vous-mêmes que vous êtes les descendants de ceux qui ont assassiné les prophètes. 32Eh bien, continuez, achevez ce que vos ancêtres ont commencé! 33Serpents, bande de vipères! Comment pensez-vous éviter d'être condamnés à l'enfer? 34C'est pourquoi, écoutez: je vais vous envoyer des prophètes, des sages et de vrais maîtres de la loi. Vous tuerez les uns, vous en clouerez d'autres sur des croix, vous en frapperez d'autres encore à coups de fouet dans vos synagogues et vous les poursuivrez de ville en ville. 35Et alors, c'est sur vous que retomberont les conséquences de tous les meurtres commis contre des innocents depuis le meurtre d'Abel le juste jusqu'à celui de Zacharie, fils de Barachie, que vous avez assassiné entre le sanctuaire et l'autel. 36Je vous le déclare, c'est la vérité: les conséquences de tous ces meurtres retomberont sur les gens d'aujourd'hui!»

Jésus et Jérusalem

37«Jérusalem, Jérusalem, toi qui mets à mort les prophètes et tues à coups de pierres ceux que Dieu t'envoie! Combien de fois ai-je désiré rassembler tes habitants auprès de moi comme une poule rassemble ses poussins sous ses ailes, mais vous ne l'avez pas voulu. 38Eh bien, votre maison va être complètement abandonnée. 39En effet, je vous le déclare: dès maintenant vous ne me verrez plus jusqu'à ce que vous disiez: "Que Dieu bénisse celui qui vient au nom du Seigneur!"»

Jésus annonce la destruction du temple

24 1Jésus sortit du temple et, tandis qu'il s'en allait, ses disciples s'approchèrent de lui pour lui faire remarquer les constructions du temple. 2Alors Jésus prit la parole et leur dit: «Vous voyez tout cela? Je vous le déclare, c'est la vérité: il ne restera pas ici une seule pierre posée sur une autre; tout sera renversé.»

Des malheurs et des persécutions

3Jésus s'était assis au mont des Oliviers. Ses disciples s'approchèrent alors de lui en particulier et lui demandèrent : «Dis-nous quand cela se passera, et quel signe indiquera le moment de ta venue et de la fin du monde.» [4]Jésus leur répondit : «Faites attention que personne ne vous trompe. [5]Car beaucoup d'hommes viendront en usant de mon nom et diront : "Je suis le Messie !" Et ils tromperont quantité de gens. [6]Vous allez entendre le bruit de guerres proches et des nouvelles sur des guerres lointaines ; ne vous laissez pas effrayer : il faut que cela arrive, mais ce ne sera pas encore la fin de ce monde. [7]Un peuple combattra contre un autre peuple, et un royaume attaquera un autre royaume ; il y aura des famines et des tremblements de terre dans différentes régions. [8]Tous ces événements seront comme les premières douleurs de l'accouchement. [9]Alors des hommes vous livreront pour qu'on vous tourmente et l'on vous mettra à mort. Tous les peuples vous haïront à cause de moi. [10]En ce temps-là, beaucoup abandonneront la foi ; ils se trahiront et se haïront les uns les autres. [11]De nombreux faux prophètes apparaîtront et tromperont beaucoup de gens. [12]Le mal se répandra à tel point que l'amour d'un grand nombre de personnes se refroidira. [13]Mais celui qui tiendra bon jusqu'à la fin sera sauvé. [14]Cette Bonne Nouvelle du Royaume sera annoncée dans le monde entier pour que le témoignage en soit présenté à tous les peuples. Et alors viendra la fin.»

L'Horreur abominable

[15]«Vous verrez celui qu'on appelle "l'Horreur abominable", dont le prophète Daniel a parlé ; il sera placé dans le lieu saint. – Que celui qui lit comprenne bien cela ! – [16]Alors, ceux qui seront en Judée devront s'enfuir vers les montagnes ; [17]celui qui sera sur la terrasse de sa maison ne devra pas descendre pour prendre ses affaires à l'intérieur ; [18]et celui qui sera dans les champs ne devra pas retourner chez lui pour emporter son manteau. [19]Quel malheur ce sera, en ces jours-là, pour les femmes enceintes et pour celles qui allaiteront ! [20]Priez Dieu pour que vous n'ayez pas à fuir pendant la mauvaise saison ou un jour de sabbat ! [21]Car, en ce temps-là, la détresse sera plus terrible que toutes celles qu'on a 'connues depuis le commencement du monde jusqu'à maintenant, et il n'y en aura plus jamais de pareille. [22]Si Dieu n'avait pas décidé d'abréger cette période, personne ne pourrait survivre. Mais il l'a abrégée à cause de ceux qu'il a choisis. [23]Si quelqu'un vous dit alors : "Regardez, le Messie est ici !" ou bien : "Il est là !", ne le croyez pas. [24]Car de faux messies et de faux prophètes apparaîtront ; ils accompliront de grands miracles et des prodiges pour tromper, si possible, même ceux que Dieu a choisis. [25]Écoutez ! Je vous ai avertis à l'avance.

[26]«Si donc on vous dit : "Regardez, il est dans le désert !", n'y allez pas. Ou si l'on vous dit : "Regardez, il se cache ici !", ne le croyez pas. [27]Comme l'éclair brille à travers le ciel de l'est à l'ouest, ainsi viendra le Fils de l'homme. [28]Où que soit le cadavre, là se rassembleront les vautours.»

La venue du Fils de l'homme

29 «Aussitôt après la détresse de ces jours-là, le soleil s'obscurcira, la lune ne donnera plus sa clarté, les étoiles tomberont du ciel et les puissances des cieux seront ébranlées. 30 Alors, le signe du Fils de l'homme apparaîtra dans le ciel ; alors, tous les peuples de la terre se lamenteront, ils verront le Fils de l'homme arriver sur les nuages du ciel avec beaucoup de puissance et de gloire. 31 La grande trompette sonnera et il enverra ses anges aux quatre coins de la terre : ils rassembleront ceux qu'il a choisis, d'un bout du monde à l'autre.»

L'enseignement donné par le figuier

32 «Comprenez l'enseignement que donne le figuier : dès que la sève circule dans ses branches et que ses feuilles poussent, vous savez que la bonne saison est proche. 33 De même, quand vous verrez tout cela, sachez que l'événement est proche, qu'il va se produire. 34 Je vous le déclare, c'est la vérité : les gens d'aujourd'hui n'auront pas tous disparu avant que tout cela arrive. 35 Le ciel et la terre disparaîtront, tandis que mes paroles ne disparaîtront jamais.»

Dieu seul connaît le moment de la fin

36 «Cependant personne ne sait quand viendra ce jour ou cette heure, pas même les anges dans les cieux, ni même le Fils ; le Père seul le sait. 37 Ce qui s'est passé du temps de Noé se passera de la même façon quand viendra le Fils de l'homme. 38 En effet, à cette époque, avant la grande inondation, les gens mangeaient et buvaient, se mariaient ou donnaient leurs filles en mariage, jusqu'au jour où Noé entra dans l'arche ; 39 ils ne se rendirent compte de rien jusqu'au moment où la grande inondation vint et les emporta tous. Ainsi en sera-t-il quand viendra le Fils de l'homme. 40 Alors, deux hommes seront aux champs : l'un sera emmené et l'autre laissé. 41 Deux femmes moudront du grain au moulin : l'une sera emmenée et l'autre laissée. 42 Veillez donc, car vous ne savez pas quel jour votre Seigneur viendra. 43 Comprenez bien ceci : si le maître de la maison savait à quel moment de la nuit le voleur doit venir, il resterait éveillé et ne le laisserait pas pénétrer dans sa maison. 44 C'est pourquoi, tenez-vous prêts, vous aussi, car le Fils de l'homme viendra à l'heure que vous ne pensez pas.»

Le serviteur fidèle et le serviteur infidèle

45 «Quel est donc le serviteur fidèle et intelligent ? En voici un que son maître a chargé de prendre soin des autres serviteurs pour leur donner leur nourriture au moment voulu. 46 Heureux ce serviteur si le maître, à son retour chez lui, le trouve occupé à ce travail ! 47 Je vous le déclare, c'est la vérité : le maître lui confiera la charge de tous ses biens. 48 Mais si c'est un mauvais serviteur, il se dira : "Mon maître tarde à revenir", 49 et il se

mettra à battre ses compagnons de service, il mangera et boira avec des ivrognes. 50Eh bien, le maître reviendra un jour où le serviteur ne l'attend pas et à une heure qu'il ne connaît pas ; 51il chassera le serviteur et lui fera partager le sort des hypocrites, là où l'on pleure et grince des dents. »

La parabole des dix jeunes filles

25 1«Alors le Royaume des cieux ressemblera à l'histoire de dix jeunes filles qui prirent leurs lampes et sortirent pour aller à la rencontre du marié. 2Cinq d'entre elles étaient imprévoyantes et cinq étaient raisonnables. 3Celles qui étaient imprévoyantes prirent leurs lampes mais sans emporter une réserve d'huile. 4En revanche, celles qui étaient raisonnables emportèrent des flacons d'huile avec leurs lampes. 5Or, le marié tardait à venir ; les jeunes filles eurent toutes sommeil et s'endormirent. 6À minuit, un cri se fit entendre : "Voici le marié ! Sortez à sa rencontre !" 7Alors les dix jeunes filles se réveillèrent et se mirent à préparer leurs lampes. 8Les imprévoyantes demandèrent aux raisonnables : "Donnez-nous un peu de votre huile, car nos lampes s'éteignent." 9Les raisonnables répondirent : "Non, car il n'y en aurait pas assez pour nous et pour vous. Vous feriez mieux d'aller au magasin en acheter pour vous." 10Les imprévoyantes partirent donc acheter de l'huile, mais pendant ce temps, le marié arriva. Les cinq jeunes filles qui étaient prêtes entrèrent avec lui dans la salle de mariage et l'on ferma la porte à clé. 11Plus tard, les autres jeunes filles arrivèrent et s'écrièrent : "Maître, maître, ouvre-nous !" 12Mais le marié répondit : "Je vous le déclare, c'est la vérité : je ne vous connais pas." 13Veillez donc, ajouta Jésus, car vous ne connaissez ni le jour ni l'heure. »

La parabole des trois serviteurs

14«Il en sera comme d'un homme qui allait partir en voyage : il appela ses serviteurs et leur confia ses biens. 15Il remit à l'un cinq cents pièces d'or, à un autre deux cents, à un troisième cent : à chacun selon ses capacités. Puis il partit. 16Le serviteur qui avait reçu les cinq cents pièces d'or s'en alla aussitôt faire du commerce avec cet argent et gagna cinq cents autres pièces d'or. 17Celui qui avait reçu deux cents pièces agit de même et gagna deux cents autres pièces. 18Mais celui qui avait reçu cent pièces s'en alla creuser un trou dans la terre et y cacha l'argent de son maître.

19«Longtemps après, le maître de ces serviteurs revint et se mit à régler ses comptes avec eux. 20Celui qui avait reçu cinq cents pièces d'or s'approcha et présenta les cinq cents autres pièces en disant : "Maître, tu m'avais remis cinq cents pièces d'or. J'en ai gagné cinq cents autres : les voici." 21Son maître lui dit : "C'est bien, bon et fidèle serviteur. Tu as été fidèle dans les choses qui ont peu de valeur, je te confierai donc celles qui ont beaucoup de valeur. Viens te réjouir avec moi." 22Le serviteur qui avait reçu les deux cents pièces s'approcha ensuite et dit :

"Maître, tu m'avais remis deux cents pièces d'or. J'en ai gagné deux cents autres : les voici." 23Son maître lui dit : "C'est bien, bon et fidèle serviteur. Tu as été fidèle dans des choses qui ont peu de valeur, je te confierai donc celles qui ont beaucoup de valeur. Viens te réjouir avec moi." 24Enfin, le serviteur qui avait reçu les cent pièces s'approcha et dit : "Maître, je te connaissais comme un homme dur : tu moissonnes où tu n'as pas semé, tu récoltes où tu n'as rien planté. 25J'ai eu peur et je suis allé cacher ton argent dans la terre. Eh bien, voici ce qui t'appartient." 26Son maître lui répondit : "Mauvais serviteur, paresseux ! Tu savais que je moissonne où je n'ai pas semé, que je récolte où je n'ai rien planté ? 27Eh bien, tu aurais dû placer mon argent à la banque et, à mon retour, j'aurais retiré mon bien avec les intérêts. 28Enlevez-lui donc les cent pièces d'or et remettez-les à celui qui en a mille. 29Car quiconque a quelque chose recevra davantage et il sera dans l'abondance ; mais à celui qui n'a rien, on enlèvera même le peu qui pourrait lui rester. 30Quant à ce serviteur bon à rien, jetez-le dehors, dans le noir, là où l'on pleure et grince des dents."»

Le jugement dernier

31«Quand le Fils de l'homme viendra dans sa gloire avec tous les anges, il siégera sur son trône royal. 32Tous les peuples de la terre seront assemblés devant lui et il séparera les gens les uns des autres comme le berger sépare les moutons des chèvres ; 33il placera les moutons à sa droite et les chèvres à sa gauche.

34Alors le roi dira à ceux qui seront à sa droite : "Venez, vous qui êtes bénis par mon Père, et recevez le Royaume qui a été préparé pour vous depuis la création du monde. 35Car j'ai eu faim et vous m'avez donné à manger ; j'ai eu soif et vous m'avez donné à boire ; j'étais étranger et vous m'avez accueilli chez vous ; 36j'étais nu et vous m'avez habillé ; j'étais malade et vous avez pris soin de moi ; j'étais en prison et vous êtes venus me voir." 37Ceux qui ont fait la volonté de Dieu lui répondront alors : "Seigneur, quand t'avons-nous vu affamé et t'avons-nous donné à manger, ou assoiffé et t'avons-nous donné à boire ? 38Quand t'avons-nous vu étranger et t'avons-nous accueilli chez nous, ou nu et t'avons-nous habillé ? 39Quand t'avons-nous vu malade ou en prison et sommes-nous allés te voir ?" 40Le roi leur répondra : "Je vous le déclare, c'est la vérité : toutes les fois que vous l'avez fait à l'un de ces plus petits de mes frères, c'est à moi que vous l'avez fait.

41«Ensuite, le roi dira à ceux qui seront à sa gauche : "Allez-vous-en loin de moi, maudits ! Allez dans le feu éternel qui a été préparé pour le diable et ses anges ! 42Car j'ai eu faim et vous ne m'avez pas donné à manger ; j'ai eu soif et vous ne m'avez pas donné à boire ; 43j'étais étranger et vous ne m'avez pas accueilli ; j'étais nu et vous ne m'avez pas habillé ; j'étais malade et en prison et vous n'avez pas pris soin de moi." 44Ils lui répondront alors : "Seigneur, quand t'avons-nous vu affamé, ou assoiffé, ou étranger, ou nu, ou malade, ou en prison et ne t'avons-nous pas secouru ?" 45Le roi leur répondra : "Je vous le déclare, c'est la vérité : toutes les fois que vous ne l'avez pas fait à l'un de ces plus petits, vous ne l'avez pas fait à moi non plus." 46Et ils iront subir la peine éternelle, tandis que ceux qui ont fait la volonté de Dieu iront à la vie éternelle.»

Les chefs complotent contre Jésus

26 1Quand Jésus eut achevé toutes ces instructions, il dit à ses disciples : 2«Vous savez que la fête de la Pâque aura lieu dans deux jours : le Fils de l'homme va être livré pour être cloué sur une croix.»

3Alors les chefs des prêtres et les anciens du peuple juif se réunirent dans le palais de Caïphe, le grand-prêtre ; 4ils prirent ensemble la décision d'arrêter Jésus en cachette et de le mettre à mort. 5Ils disaient : «Nous ne devons pas l'arrêter pendant la fête, sinon le peuple va se soulever.»

Une femme met du parfum sur la tête de Jésus

6Jésus était à Béthanie, dans la maison de Simon le lépreux. 7Une femme s'approcha de lui avec un flacon d'albâtre plein d'un parfum de grande valeur : elle versa ce parfum sur la tête de Jésus pendant qu'il était à table. 8Quand les disciples virent cela, ils furent indignés et dirent : «Pourquoi ce gaspillage ? 9On aurait pu vendre ce parfum très cher et donner l'argent aux pauvres !»

10Jésus se rendit compte qu'ils parlaient ainsi et leur dit : «Pourquoi faites-vous de la peine à cette femme ? Ce qu'elle a accompli pour moi est beau. 11Car vous aurez toujours des pauvres avec vous ; mais moi, vous ne m'aurez pas toujours avec vous. 12Elle a répandu ce parfum sur mon corps afin de me préparer pour le tombeau. 13Je vous le déclare, c'est la vérité : partout où l'on annoncera cette Bonne Nouvelle, dans le monde entier, on racontera ce que cette femme a fait, et l'on se souviendra d'elle.»

Judas veut livrer Jésus aux chefs des prêtres

14Alors l'un des douze disciples, appelé Judas Iscariote, alla trouver les chefs des prêtres 15et leur dit : «Que me donnerez-vous si je vous livre Jésus ?» Ceux-ci comptèrent trente pièces d'argent qu'ils lui remirent. 16À partir de ce moment, Judas se mit à chercher une occasion favorable pour leur livrer Jésus.

Jésus prend le repas de la Pâque avec ses disciples

17Le premier jour de la fête des pains sans levain, les disciples vinrent demander à Jésus : «Où veux-tu que nous te préparions le repas de la Pâque ?» 18Jésus leur dit alors : «Allez à la ville chez un tel et dites-lui : "Le Maître déclare : Mon heure est arrivée ; c'est chez toi que je célébrerai la Pâque avec mes disciples."» 19Les disciples firent ce que Jésus leur avait ordonné et préparèrent le repas de la Pâque.

20Quand le soir fut venu, Jésus se mit à table avec les douze disciples. 21Pendant qu'ils mangeaient, Jésus dit : «Je vous le déclare, c'est la vérité : l'un de vous me trahira.» 22Les disciples en furent profondément attristés et se mirent à lui demander l'un après l'autre : «Ce n'est pas moi, n'est-ce pas, Seigneur?» 23Jésus répondit : «Celui qui a trempé avec moi son pain dans le plat, c'est lui qui me trahira. 24Le Fils de l'homme va mourir comme les Écritures l'annoncent à son sujet ; mais quel malheur pour celui qui trahit le Fils de l'homme ! Il aurait mieux valu pour cet homme-là ne pas naître !» 25Judas, celui qui le trahissait, prit la parole et demanda : «Ce n'est pas moi, n'est-ce pas, Maître ?» Jésus lui répondit : «C'est toi qui le dis.»

La sainte cène

26Pendant le repas, Jésus prit du pain et, après avoir remercié Dieu, il le rompit et le donna à ses disciples ; il leur dit : «Prenez et mangez ceci, c'est mon corps.» 27Il prit ensuite une coupe de vin et, après avoir remercié Dieu, il la leur donna en disant : «Buvez-en tous, 28car ceci est mon sang, le sang qui garantit l'alliance de Dieu et qui est versé pour une multitude de gens, pour le pardon des péchés. 29Je vous le déclare : dès maintenant, je ne boirai plus de ce vin jusqu'au jour où je boirai avec vous le vin nouveau dans le Royaume de mon Père.» 30Ils chantèrent les psaumes de la fête, puis ils s'en allèrent au mont des Oliviers.

Jésus annonce que Pierre le reniera

31Alors Jésus dit à ses disciples : «Cette nuit même, vous allez tous m'abandonner, car on lit dans les Écritures : "Je tuerai le berger, et les moutons du troupeau partiront de tous côtés." 32Mais, ajouta Jésus, quand je serai de nouveau vivant, j'irai vous attendre en Galilée.» 33Pierre prit la parole et lui dit : «Même si tous les autres t'abandonnent, moi je ne t'abandonnerai jamais.» 34Jésus lui répondit : «Je te le déclare, c'est la vérité : cette nuit même, avant que le coq chante, tu auras prétendu trois fois ne pas me connaître.» 35Pierre lui dit : «Je ne prétendrai jamais que je ne te connais pas, même si je dois mourir avec toi.» Et tous les autres disciples dirent la même chose.

Jésus prie à Gethsémané

36Alors Jésus arriva avec ses disciples à un endroit appelé Gethsémané et il leur dit : «Asseyez-vous ici, pendant que je vais là-bas pour prier.» 37Puis il emmena avec lui Pierre et les deux fils de Zébédée. Il commença à ressentir de la tristesse et de l'angoisse. 38Il leur dit alors : «Mon cœur est plein d'une tristesse mortelle ; restez ici et veillez avec moi.» 39Il alla un peu plus loin, se jeta le visage contre terre et pria en ces termes : «Mon Père, si c'est possible, éloigne de moi cette coupe de douleur. Toutefois, non pas comme je veux, mais comme tu veux.» 40Il revint ensuite vers les trois disciples et les trouva endormis. Il dit à Pierre : «Ainsi vous n'avez pas été capables de veiller avec moi même une heure ? ⁴¹Restez éveillés et priez pour ne pas tomber dans la tentation. L'être humain est plein de bonne volonté, mais il est faible.»

⁴²Il s'éloigna une deuxième fois et pria en ces termes : «Mon Père, si cette coupe ne peut pas être enlevée sans que je la boive, que ta volonté soit faite!» ⁴³Il revint encore auprès de ses disciples et les trouva endormis ; ils ne pouvaient pas garder les yeux ouverts. ⁴⁴Jésus les quitta de nouveau, s'éloigna et pria pour la troisième fois en répétant les mêmes paroles. ⁴⁵Puis il revint auprès des disciples et leur dit : «Vous dormez encore et vous vous reposez ? Maintenant, l'heure est arrivée et le Fils de l'homme va être livré entre les mains des pécheurs. ⁴⁶Levez-vous, allons-y! Voyez, l'homme qui me livre à eux est ici!»

L'arrestation de Jésus

⁴⁷Jésus parlait encore quand arriva Judas, l'un des douze disciples. Il y avait avec lui une foule nombreuse de gens armés d'épées et de bâtons. Ils étaient envoyés par les chefs des prêtres et les anciens du peuple juif. ⁴⁸Judas, celui qui leur livrait Jésus, avait indiqué à cette foule le signe qu'il utiliserait : «L'homme que j'embrasserai, c'est lui. Saisissez-le.» ⁴⁹Judas s'approcha immédiatement de Jésus et lui dit : «Salut, Maître!» Puis il l'embrassa. ⁵⁰Jésus lui répondit : «Mon ami, ce que tu es venu faire, fais-le vite.» Alors les autres s'approchèrent, mirent la main sur Jésus et l'arrêtèrent.

⁵¹Un de ceux qui étaient avec Jésus tira son épée, frappa le serviteur du grand-prêtre et lui coupa l'oreille. ⁵²Jésus lui dit alors : «Remets ton épée à sa place, car tous ceux qui prennent l'épée périront par l'épée. ⁵³Ne sais-tu pas que je pourrais appeler mon Père à l'aide et qu'aussitôt il m'enverrait plus de douze armées d'anges ? ⁵⁴Mais, en ce cas, comment se réaliseraient les Écritures ? Elles déclarent, en effet, que cela doit se passer ainsi.»

⁵⁵Puis Jésus dit à la foule : «Deviez-vous venir armés d'épées et de bâtons pour me prendre, comme si j'étais un brigand ? Tous les jours, j'étais assis dans le temple pour y enseigner, et vous ne m'avez pas arrêté. ⁵⁶Mais tout cela est arrivé pour que se réalisent les paroles des prophètes contenues dans les Écritures.» Alors tous les disciples l'abandonnèrent et s'enfuirent.

Jésus devant le Conseil supérieur

⁵⁷Ceux qui avaient arrêté Jésus l'emmenèrent chez Caïphe, le grand-prêtre, où les maîtres de la loi et les anciens étaient assemblés. ⁵⁸Pierre suivit Jésus de loin, jusqu'à la cour de la maison du grand-prêtre. Il entra dans la cour et s'assit avec les gardes pour voir comment cela finirait.

⁵⁹Les chefs des prêtres et tout le Conseil supérieur cherchaient une accusation, même fausse, contre Jésus pour le condamner à mort; ⁶⁰mais ils n'en trouvèrent pas, quoique beaucoup de gens fussent venus déposer de fausses accusations contre lui. Finalement, deux hommes se présentèrent ⁶¹et dirent : «Cet homme

a déclaré : "Je peux détruire le temple de Dieu et le rebâtir en trois jours."» 62Le grand-prêtre se leva et dit à Jésus : «Ne réponds-tu rien à ce que ces gens disent contre toi ?» 63Mais Jésus se taisait. Le grand-prêtre lui dit alors : «Au nom du Dieu vivant, je te demande de nous répondre sous serment : es-tu le Messie, le Fils de Dieu ?» 64Jésus lui répondit : «C'est toi qui le dis. Mais je vous le déclare : dès maintenant vous verrez le Fils de l'homme siégeant à la droite du Dieu puissant ; vous le verrez aussi venir sur les nuages du ciel.» 65Alors le grand-prêtre déchira ses vêtements et dit : «Il a fait insulte à Dieu ! Nous n'avons plus besoin de témoins ! Vous venez d'entendre cette insulte faite à Dieu. 66Qu'en pensez-vous ?» Ils répondirent : «Il est coupable et mérite la mort.» 67Puis ils lui crachèrent au visage et le frappèrent à coups de poing ; certains lui donnèrent des gifles 68en disant : «Devine, toi le Messie, dis-nous qui t'a frappé !»

Pierre renie Jésus

69Pierre était assis dehors, dans la cour. Une servante s'approcha de lui et lui dit : «Toi aussi, tu étais avec Jésus, cet homme de Galilée.» 70Mais il le nia devant tout le monde en déclarant : «Je ne sais pas ce que tu veux dire.» 71Puis il s'en alla vers la porte de la cour. Une autre servante le vit et dit à ceux qui étaient là : «Celui-ci était avec Jésus de Nazareth.» 72Et Pierre le nia de nouveau en déclarant : «Je jure que je ne connais pas cet homme.»

73Peu après, ceux qui étaient là s'approchèrent de Pierre et lui dirent : «Certainement, tu es l'un d'eux : ton accent révèle d'où tu viens.» 74Alors Pierre s'écria : «Que Dieu me punisse si je mens ! Je le jure, je ne connais pas cet homme !» A ce moment même, un coq chanta, 75et Pierre se rappela ce que Jésus lui avait dit : «Avant que le coq chante, tu auras prétendu trois fois ne pas me connaître.» Il sortit et pleura amèrement.

Jésus est amené à Pilate

27 1Tôt le matin, tous les chefs des prêtres et les anciens du peuple juif prirent ensemble la décision de faire mourir Jésus. 2Ils le firent ligoter, l'emmenèrent et le livrèrent à Pilate, le gouverneur romain.

La mort de Judas

3Judas, celui qui l'avait trahi, apprit que Jésus avait été condamné. Il fut alors pris de remords et rapporta les trente pièces d'argent aux chefs des prêtres et aux anciens. 4Il leur dit : «Je suis coupable, j'ai livré un innocent à la mort !» Mais ils lui répondirent : «Cela nous est égal ! C'est ton affaire !» 5Judas jeta l'argent dans le temple et partit ; puis il alla se pendre. 6Les chefs des prêtres ramassèrent l'argent et dirent : «Notre loi ne permet pas de verser cet argent dans le trésor du temple, car c'est le prix du sang.» 7Après s'être mis d'accord, ils achetèrent avec cette somme le champ du potier pour y établir un cimetière d'étrangers. 8C'est pourquoi ce champ s'est appelé «champ du sang» jusqu'à ce jour. 9Alors se réalisèrent ces paroles du prophète Jérémie: «Ils prirent les trente pièces d'argent – le prix auquel les Israélites l'avaient estimé – 10et les employèrent pour acheter le champ du potier, comme le Seigneur me l'avait ordonné.»

Pilate interroge Jésus

11Jésus comparut devant le gouverneur qui l'interrogea: «Es-tu le roi des Juifs?» Jésus répondit: «Tu le dis.» 12Ensuite, lorsque les chefs des prêtres et les anciens l'accusèrent, il ne répondit rien. 13 Pilate lui dit alors: «N'entends-tu pas toutes les accusations qu'ils portent contre toi?» 14Mais Jésus ne lui répondit sur aucun point, de sorte que le gouverneur était profondément étonné.

Jésus est condamné à mort

15A chaque fête de la Pâque, le gouverneur avait l'habitude de libérer un prisonnier, celui que la foule voulait. 16Or, il y avait à ce moment-là un prisonnier célèbre appelé Jésus Barabbas. 17 Pilate demanda donc à la foule assemblée: «Qui voulez-vous que je vous libère: Jésus Barabbas ou Jésus appelé Christ?» 18Pilate savait bien, en effet, qu'ils lui avaient livré Jésus par jalousie. 19Pendant que Pilate siégeait au tribunal, sa femme lui envoya ce message: «N'aie rien à faire avec cet homme innocent car, cette nuit, j'ai beaucoup souffert en rêve à cause de lui.»

20Les chefs des prêtres et les anciens persuadèrent la foule de demander la libération de Barabbas et la mise à mort de Jésus. 21Le gouverneur reprit la parole pour leur demander: «Lequel des deux voulez-vous que je vous libère?» – «Barabbas!» lui répondirent-ils. 22«Que ferai-je donc de Jésus appelé Christ?» leur demanda Pilate. Tous répondirent: «Cloue-le sur une croix!» – 23«Quel mal a-t-il donc commis?» demanda Pilate. Mais ils se mirent à crier de toutes leurs forces: «Cloue-le sur une croix!» 24Quand Pilate vit qu'il n'arrivait à rien, mais que l'agitation augmentait, il prit de l'eau, se lava les mains devant la foule et dit: «Je ne suis pas responsable de la mort de cet homme! C'est votre affaire!» 25Toute la foule répondit: «Que les conséquences de sa mort retombent sur nous et sur nos enfants!» 26Alors Pilate leur libéra Barabbas; il fit frapper Jésus à coups de fouet et le livra pour qu'on le cloue sur une croix.

Les soldats» se moquent de Jésus

27Les soldats de Pilate emmenèrent Jésus dans le palais du gouverneur et toute la troupe se rassembla autour de lui. 28Ils lui enlevèrent ses vêtements et le revêtirent d'un manteau rouge. 29Puis ils tressèrent une couronne avec des branches épineuses, la posèrent sur sa tête et placèrent un roseau dans sa main droite. Ils se mirent ensuite à genoux devant lui et se moquèrent de lui en disant: «Salut, roi des Juifs!» 30Ils crachaient sur lui et prenaient le roseau pour le frapper sur la tête. 31Quand ils se furent bien moqués de lui, ils lui enlevèrent le manteau, lui remirent ses vêtements et l'emmenèrent pour le clouer sur une croix.

Jésus est cloué sur la croix

32 En sortant de la ville, ils rencontrèrent un homme de Cyrène, appelé Simon ; les soldats l'obligèrent à porter la croix de Jésus. 33 Ils arrivèrent à un endroit appelé Golgotha, ce qui signifie «le lieu du Crâne». 34 Et là, ils donnèrent à boire à Jésus du vin mélangé avec une drogue amère ; après l'avoir goûté, il ne voulut pas en boire. 35 Ils le clouèrent sur la croix et se partagèrent ses vêtements en tirant au sort. 36 Puis ils s'assirent là pour le garder. 37 Au-dessus de sa tête, ils placèrent une inscription qui indiquait la raison de sa condamnation : «Celui-ci est Jésus, le roi des Juifs.» 38 Deux brigands furent alors cloués sur des croix à côté de Jésus, l'un à sa droite et l'autre à sa gauche.

39 Les passants l'insultaient en hochant la tête ; 40 ils lui disaient : «Toi qui voulais détruire le temple et en bâtir un autre en trois jours, sauve-toi toi-même, si tu es le Fils de Dieu, et descends de la croix !» 41 De même, les chefs des prêtres, les maîtres de la loi et les anciens se moquaient de lui et disaient : 42 «Il a sauvé d'autres gens, mais il ne peut pas se sauver lui-même ! Il est le roi d'Israël ? Qu'il descende maintenant de la croix et nous croirons en lui. 43 Il a mis sa confiance en Dieu et a déclaré : "Je suis le Fils de Dieu." Eh bien, si Dieu l'aime, qu'il le sauve maintenant !» 44 Et les brigands qui avaient été mis en croix à côté de lui l'insultaient de la même manière.

La mort de Jésus

45 A midi, l'obscurité se fit sur tout le pays et dura jusqu'à trois heures de l'après-midi. 46 Vers trois heures, Jésus cria avec force : *«Éli, Éli, lema sabactani ?»* – ce qui signifie «Mon Dieu, mon Dieu, pourquoi m'as-tu abandonné ?» – 47 Quelques-uns de ceux qui se tenaient là l'entendirent et s'écrièrent : «Il appelle Élie !» 48 L'un d'eux courut aussitôt prendre une éponge, la remplit de vinaigre et la fixa au bout d'un roseau, puis il la tendit à Jésus pour qu'il boive. 49 Mais les autres dirent : «Attends, nous allons voir si Élie vient le sauver !»

50 Jésus poussa de nouveau un grand cri et mourut. 51 A ce moment, le rideau suspendu dans le temple se déchira depuis le haut jusqu'en bas. La terre trembla, les rochers se fendirent, 52 les tombeaux s'ouvrirent et de nombreux croyants qui étaient morts revinrent à la vie. 53 Ils sortirent des tombeaux et, après la résurrection de Jésus, ils entrèrent dans Jérusalem, la ville sainte, où beaucoup de personnes les virent. 54 Le capitaine romain et les soldats qui gardaient Jésus avec lui virent le tremblement de terre et tout ce qui arrivait ; ils eurent alors très peur et dirent : «Il était vraiment le Fils de Dieu !» 55 De nombreuses femmes étaient là et regardaient de loin : elles avaient suivi Jésus depuis la Galilée pour le servir. 56 Parmi elles, il y avait Marie du village de Magdala, Marie la mère de Jacques et de Joseph, et la mère des fils de Zébédée.

Jésus est mis dans un tombeau

⁵⁷Quand le soir fut venu, un homme riche, qui était d'Arimathée, arriva. Il s'appelait Joseph et était lui aussi disciple de Jésus. ⁵⁸Il alla trouver Pilate et lui demanda le corps de Jésus. Alors Pilate ordonna de le remettre à Joseph. ⁵⁹Celui-ci prit le corps, l'enveloppa dans un drap de lin neuf ⁶⁰et le déposa dans son propre tombeau qu'il venait de faire creuser dans le rocher. Puis il roula une grosse pierre pour fermer l'entrée du tombeau et s'en alla. ⁶¹Marie de Magdala et l'autre Marie étaient là, assises en face du tombeau.

La garde du tombeau

⁶²Le lendemain, c'est-à-dire le jour qui suivit la préparation du sabbat, les chefs des prêtres et les Pharisiens allèrent ensemble chez Pilate ⁶³et dirent : «Excellence, nous nous souvenons que cet imposteur, quand il était encore vivant, a dit : "Au bout de trois jours, je reviendrai de la mort à la vie." ⁶⁴Veuillez donc ordonner que le tombeau soit gardé jusqu'au troisième jour, sinon ses disciples pourraient venir voler le corps et diraient ensuite au peuple : "Il est revenu d'entre les morts." Cette dernière imposture serait encore pire que la première.» ⁶⁵Pilate leur dit : «Voici des soldats pour monter la garde. Allez et faites surveiller le tombeau comme vous le jugez bon.» ⁶⁶Ils allèrent donc organiser la surveillance du tombeau : ils scellèrent la pierre qui le fermait et placèrent les gardes.

La résurrection de Jésus

28 ¹Après le sabbat, dimanche au lever du jour, Marie de Magdala et l'autre Marie vinrent voir le tombeau. ²Soudain, il y eut un fort tremblement de terre ; un ange du Seigneur descendit du ciel, vint rouler la grosse pierre et s'assit dessus. ³Il avait l'aspect d'un éclair et ses vêtements étaient blancs comme la neige. ⁴Les gardes en eurent une telle peur qu'ils se mirent à trembler et devinrent comme morts. ⁵L'ange prit la parole et dit aux femmes : «N'ayez pas peur. Je sais que vous cherchez Jésus, celui qu'on a cloué sur la croix ; ⁶il n'est pas ici, il est revenu de la mort à la vie comme il l'avait dit. Venez, voyez l'endroit où il était couché. ⁷Allez vite dire à ses disciples : "Il est revenu d'entre les morts et il va maintenant vous attendre en Galilée, c'est là que vous le verrez." Voilà ce que j'avais à vous dire.» ⁸Elles quittèrent rapidement le tombeau, remplies tout à la fois de crainte et d'une grande joie, et coururent porter la nouvelle aux disciples de Jésus. ⁹Tout à coup, Jésus vint à leur rencontre et dit : «Je vous salue !» Elles s'approchèrent de lui, saisirent ses pieds et l'adorèrent. ¹⁰Jésus leur dit alors : «N'ayez pas peur. Allez dire à mes frères de se rendre en Galilée : c'est là qu'ils me verront.»

Le récit des gardes

¹¹Pendant qu'elles étaient en chemin, quelques-uns des soldats qui devaient garder le tombeau revinrent

en ville et racontèrent aux chefs des prêtres tout ce qui était arrivé. ¹²Les chefs des prêtres se réunirent avec les anciens : après s'être mis d'accord, ils donnèrent une forte somme d'argent aux soldats ¹³et leur dirent : «Vous déclarerez que les disciples de cet homme sont venus voler son corps durant la nuit, pendant que vous dormiez. ¹⁴Et si le gouverneur l'apprend, nous saurons le convaincre et vous éviter toute difficulté.» ¹⁵Les gardes prirent l'argent et agirent conformément aux instructions reçues. Ainsi, cette histoire s'est répandue parmi les Juifs jusqu'à ce jour.

Jésus se montre à ses disciples

¹⁶Les onze disciples se rendirent en Galilée, sur la colline que Jésus leur avait indiquée. ¹⁷Quand ils le virent, ils l'adorèrent ; certains d'entre eux, pourtant, eurent des doutes. ¹⁸Jésus s'approcha et leur dit : «Tout pouvoir m'a été donné dans le ciel et sur la terre. ¹⁹Allez donc auprès des gens de toutes les nations et faites d'eux mes disciples ; baptisez-les au nom du Père, du Fils et du Saint-Esprit, ²⁰et enseignez-leur à pratiquer tout ce que je vous ai commandé. Et sachez-le : je vais être avec vous tous les jours, jusqu'à la fin du monde.»

el Evangelio según
MATEO

Dios, Padre nuestro,
Tu Hijo Jesús nos llama a ser sal de la tierra y luz del mundo. Permite que la luz de tu justicia brille en nuestras vidas, para que nuestras palabras sazonen el mundo con el sabor de tu Evangelio, y que nuestras vidas sean ejemplos brillantes de Jesús quien es la Verdadera Luz. Te lo pedimos por Jesucristo Nuestro Señor, tu Hijo, Quien vive y reina contigo en la unidad del Espíritu Santo, Dios por los siglos de los siglos. Amén.

El Evangelio según San Mateo
Texto en español de la Biblia 'Dios Habla Hoy'
© Sociedades Bíblicas Unidas, 1994

INTRODUCCIÓN

Jesús llamó a sus discípulos a seguirlo y vivió con ellos enseñando a las multitudes, haciendo milagros, ayudándoles a entender su misión y la oposición a la que se enfrentaría. Dios respondió a la vergüenza de la cruz al resucitar a Jesús y glorificarlo como el Cristo y Señor.

El misterio de la muerte que se convierte en vida tenía que ser proclamado a todo el mundo en forma de "evangelio"; es decir, de "buenas noticias". Los discípulos de Jesús habían presenciado y puesto en memorias los milagros, actos de misericordia, el amor y la experiencia de la pasión de Jesús.

Era importante hacer significativas estas palabras y eventos a las diferentes comunidades que escucharon las enseñanzas de Jesús y los evangelistas (autores de los evangelios) escribieron de acuerdo a las tradiciones orales y escritas de estas comunidades. Así nacieron los cuatro evangelios que la Iglesia reconoce como testigos fieles de la vida de Jesucristo y de la fe que hay en él: los Evangelios según Mateo, Marcos, Lucas y Juan.

EL EVANGELIO DE MATEO

UNA IGLESIA DIFERENTE A LA SINAGOGA

Mateo probablemente escribió su evangelio en Antioquia, entre los años 80 y 90 AD. Los judíos cristianos habían fundado la iglesia a finales de la década de los treinta. La iglesia de Antioquia se caracterizaba por su abierta disposición y mentalidad.

Esta comunidad no solamente estaba separada de la sinagoga, sino que se encontraba involucrada en un debate con los líderes judíos. Las siete exclamaciones que se encuentran en Mt 23:13-36 "¡Ay de ustedes, maestros de la ley y fariseos, hipócritas!" muestra la profunda división entre estos dos grupos.

UNA IGLESIA EN BUSCA DE SU IDENTIDAD

Hay dos problemas que compiten entre sí y que llevan en direcciones opuestas a la iglesia primitiva. ¿Cómo se puede ser fiel a la herencia judía del Antiguo Testamento y aceptar una salvación proclamada por el Cristo resucitado que es para toda clase de personas?

Antes que se escribiera el Evangelio de Mateo, la iglesia en Antioquia estaba experimentando ya tensiones entre los fundadores liberales y los "hermanos" conservadores de Jerusalén. ¿Debe la iglesia, con raíces en el judaísmo y, a la vez, guardián del Antiguo Testamento, abrirse al vasto mundo gentil? ¿Sobre qué bases?

El evangelio de Mateo representa un intento de reconciliación de las tradiciones heredadas por los primeros cristianos. Mateo afirma que las buenas noticias de la salvación son para todos y no es necesario que la gente se circuncide u observe una dieta judía.

Mateo intenta preservar la herencia antigua y, al mismo tiempo, presentar el nuevo mensaje del evangelio. Trata de encontrar un terreno neutral -- donde la tradición judía se intersecte con el futuro global. También resalta el perfil de Pedro, el líder de la iglesia (16:18-19). Para Mateo, Pedro representa la posición moderada – más conservadora que la de San Pablo en sus cartas a los gálatas y romanos; pero más abierto hacia los gentiles que la carta de Santiago. Entonces, no es de sorprenderse, que el evangelio de Mateo, el cual establece el marco para favorecer la unidad cristiana al enlazar las posiciones doctrinales más importantes de esa época, llegara a ser tan popular en un período de tiempo tan corto.

CONCLUSIÓN

Hoy en día, el tema de la globalización es un asunto candente para los cristianos. Todas las barreras entre las naciones, culturas y aún entre religiones se están derrumbando. Es claro que esta señal de los tiempos, de la cual el Día Mundial de la Juventud es un ejemplo, nos obliga abrirnos a otros. Pero, ¿cómo podemos preservar nuestra identidad cristiana y, al mismo tiempo, respetar la identidad y valores de otros? Los primeros cristianos discutieron un problema similar – el balance entre un sentido de identidad en particular que los judíos gozaban y la característica acogedora sin barreras del evangelio. Su búsqueda por una solución, a instancias de Mateo, es la que debe inspirarnos hoy.

MATEO

Los antepasados de Jesucristo

1 ¹Esta es una lista de los antepasados de Jesucristo, que fue descendiente de David y de Abraham.

²Abraham fue padre de Isaac, este lo fue de Jacob y este de Judá y sus hermanos. ³Judá fue padre de Fares y de Zérah, y su madre fue Tamar. Fares fue padre de Hesrón y este de Aram. ⁴Aram fue padre de Aminadab, este lo fue de Nahasón y este de Salmón. ⁵Salmón fue padre de Booz, cuya madre fue Rahab. Booz fue padre de Obed, cuya madre fue Rut. Obed fue padre de Jesé, ⁶y Jesé fue padre del rey David.

El rey David fue padre de Salomón, cuya madre fue la que había sido esposa de Urías. ⁷Salomón fue padre de Roboam, este lo fue de Abías y este de Asá. ⁸Asá fue padre de Josafat, este lo fue de Joram y este de Ozías. ⁹Ozías fue padre de Jotam, este lo fue de Acaz y este de Ezequías. ¹⁰Ezequías fue padre de Manasés, este lo fue de Amón y este de Josías. ¹¹Josías fue padre de Jeconías y de sus hermanos, en el tiempo en que los israelitas fueron llevados cautivos a Babilonia.

¹²Después de la cautividad, Jeconías fue padre de Salatiel y este de Zorobabel. ¹³Zorobabel fue padre de Abihud, este lo fue de Eliaquim y este de Azor. ¹⁴Azor fue padre de Sadoc, este lo fue de Aquim y este de Eliud. ¹⁵Eliud fue padre de Eleazar, este lo fue de Matán y este de Jacob. ¹⁶Jacob fue padre de José, el marido de María, y ella fue madre de Jesús, al que llamamos el Mesías.

¹⁷De modo que hubo catorce generaciones desde Abraham hasta David, catorce desde David hasta la cautividad de los israelitas en Babilonia, y otras catorce desde la cautividad hasta el Mesías.

Origen de Jesucristo

¹⁸El origen de Jesucristo fue este: María, su madre, estaba comprometida para casarse con José; pero antes que vivieran juntos, se encontró encinta por el poder del Espíritu Santo. ¹⁹José, su marido, que era un hombre justo y no quería denunciar públicamente a María, decidió separarse de ella en secreto. ²⁰Ya había pensado hacerlo así, cuando un ángel del Señor se le apareció en sueños y le dijo: "José, descendiente de David, no tengas miedo de tomar a María por esposa, porque su hijo lo ha concebido por el poder del Espíritu Santo. ²¹María tendrá un hijo, y le pondrás por nombre Jesús. Se llamará así porque salvará a su pueblo de sus pecados."

²²Todo esto sucedió para que se cumpliera lo que el Señor había dicho por medio del profeta:

²³"La virgen quedará encinta
y tendrá un hijo,
al que pondrán por nombre
Emanuel"

(que significa: "Dios con nosotros").

²⁴Cuando José despertó del sueño, hizo lo que el ángel del Señor le había mandado, y tomó a María por esposa. ²⁵Y sin haber tenido relaciones conyugales, ella dio a luz a su hijo, al que José puso por nombre Jesús.

La visita de los sabios del Oriente

2 ¹Jesús nació en Belén, un pueblo de la región de Judea, en el tiempo en que Herodes era rey del país. Llegaron por entonces a Jerusalén unos sabios del Oriente que se dedicaban al estudio de las estrellas, ²y preguntaron:

—¿Dónde está el rey de los judíos que ha nacido? Pues vimos salir su estrella y hemos venido a adorarlo.

³El rey Herodes se inquietó mucho al oír esto, y lo mismo les pasó a todos los habitantes de Jerusalén. ⁴Mandó el rey llamar a todos los jefes de los sacerdotes y a los maestros de la ley, y les preguntó dónde había de nacer el Mesías. ⁵Ellos le dijeron:

—En Belén de Judea; porque así lo escribió el profeta:

⁶ "En cuanto a ti, Belén,
de la tierra de Judá,
no eres la más pequeña
entre las principales ciudades
de esa tierra;

porque de ti saldrá un gobernante que guiará a mi pueblo Israel.'

⁷Entonces Herodes llamó en secreto a los sabios, y se informó por ellos del tiempo exacto en que había aparecido la estrella. ⁸Luego los mandó a Belén, y les dijo:

—Vayan allá, y averigüen todo lo que puedan acerca de ese niño; y cuando lo encuentren, avísenme, para que yo también vaya a rendirle homenaje.

⁹Con estas indicaciones del rey, los sabios se fueron. Y la estrella que habían visto salir iba delante de ellos, hasta por fin se detuvo sobre el lugar donde estaba el niño. ¹⁰Cuando los sabios vieron la estrella, se alegraron mucho. ¹¹Luego entraron en la casa, y vieron al niño con María, su madre; y arrodillándose le rindieron homenaje. Abrieron sus cofres y le ofrecieron oro, incienso y mirra. ¹²Después, advertidos en sueños de que no debían volver a donde estaba Herodes, regresaron a su tierra por otro camino.

La huida a Egipto

¹³Cuando ya los sabios se habían ido, un ángel del Señor se le apareció en sueños a José, y le dijo: "Levántate, toma al niño y a su madre, y huye a Egipto. Quédate allí hasta que yo te avise, porque Herodes va a buscar al niño para matarlo."

¹⁴José se levantó, tomó al niño y a su madre, y salió con ellos de noche camino de Egipto, ¹⁵donde estuvieron hasta que murió Herodes. Esto sucedió para que se cumpliera lo que el Señor había dicho por medio del profeta: "De Egipto llamé a mi Hijo."

Herodes manda matar a los niños

¹⁶Al darse cuenta Herodes de que aquellos sabios lo habían engañado, se llenó de ira y mandó matar a todos los niños de dos años para abajo que vivían en Belén y sus alrededores, de acuerdo con el tiempo que le habían dicho los sabios. ¹⁷Así se cumplió lo escrito por el profeta Jeremías:

¹⁸ "Se oyó una voz en Ramá,
llantos y grandes lamentos.
Era Raquel, que lloraba
    por sus hijos
y no quería ser consolada
porque ya estaban muertos."

La familia
se establece en Nazaret

¹⁹Pero después que murió Herodes, un ángel del Señor se le apareció en sueños a José, en Egipto, y le dijo: ²⁰"Levántate, toma contigo al niño y a su madre, y regresa a Israel, porque ya han muerto los que querían matar al niño."

²¹Entonces José se levantó y llevó al niño y a su madre a Israel. ²²Pero cuando supo que Arquelao estaba gobernando en Judea en lugar de su padre Herodes, tuvo miedo de ir allá; y habiendo sido advertido en sueños por Dios, se dirigió a la región de Galilea. ²³Al llegar, se fue a vivir al pueblo de Nazaret. Esto sucedió para que se cumpliera lo que dijeron los profetas: que Jesús sería llamado nazareno.

Juan el Bautista en el desierto

3 ¹Por aquel tiempo se presentó Juan el Bautista en el desierto de Judea. ²En su proclamación decía: "¡Vuélvanse a Dios, porque el reino de los cielos está cerca!"

³Juan era aquel de quien Dios había dicho por medio del profeta Isaías:

"Una voz grita en el desierto:
'Preparen el camino del Señor;
ábranle un camino recto.'"

⁴La ropa de Juan estaba hecha de pelo de camello, y se la sujetaba al cuerpo con un cinturón de cuero; su comida era langostas y miel del monte. ⁵La gente de Jerusalén y todos los de la región de Judea y de la región cercana al Jordán salían a oírle. ⁶Confesaban sus pecados y Juan los bautizaba en el río Jordán.

⁷Pero cuando Juan vio que muchos fariseos y saduceos iban a que los bautizara, les dijo: "¡Raza de víboras! ¿Quién les ha dicho a ustedes que van a librarse del terrible castigo que se acerca? ⁸Pórtense de tal modo que se vea claramente que se han vuelto al Señor, ⁹y no presuman diciéndose a sí mismos: 'Nosotros somos descendientes de Abraham'; porque les aseguro que incluso a estas piedras Dios puede convertirlas en descendientes de Abraham. ¹⁰El hacha ya está lista para cortar los árboles de raíz. Todo árbol que no da buen fruto, se corta y se echa al fuego. ¹¹Yo, en verdad, los bautizo con agua para invitarlos a que se vuelvan a Dios; pero el que viene después de mí los bautizará con el Espíritu Santo y con fuego. Él es más poderoso que yo, que ni siquiera merezco llevarle sus sandalias. ¹²Trae su pala en la mano y limpiará el trigo y lo separará de la

paja. Guardará su trigo en el granero, pero quemará la paja en un fuego que nunca se apagará."

Jesús es bautizado

¹³Jesús fue de Galilea al río Jordán, donde estaba Juan, para que este lo bautizara. ¹⁴Al principio Juan quería impedírselo, y le dijo:

—Yo debería ser bautizado por ti, ¿y tú vienes a mí?

¹⁵Jesús le contestó:

—Déjalo así por ahora, pues es conveniente que cumplamos todo lo que es justo ante Dios.

Entonces Juan consintió. ¹⁶En cuanto Jesús fue bautizado y salió del agua, el cielo se le abrió y vio que el Espíritu de Dios bajaba sobre él como una paloma. ¹⁷Se oyó entonces una voz del cielo, que decía: "Este es mi Hijo amado, a quien he elegido."

El diablo pone a prueba a Jesús

4 ¹Luego el Espíritu llevó a Jesús al desierto, para que el diablo lo pusiera a prueba.

²Estuvo cuarenta días y cuarenta noches sin comer, y después sintió hambre. ³El diablo se acercó entonces a Jesús para ponerlo a prueba, y le dijo:

—Si de veras eres Hijo de Dios, ordena que estas piedras se conviertan en panes.

⁴Pero Jesús le contestó:

—La Escritura dice: 'No solo de pan vivirá el hombre, sino también de toda palabra que salga de los labios de Dios.'

⁵Luego el diablo lo llevó a la santa ciudad de Jerusalén, lo subió a la parte más alta del templo ⁶y le dijo:

—Si de veras eres Hijo de Dios, tírate abajo; porque la Escritura dice:

'Dios mandará
que sus ángeles te cuiden.
Te levantarán con sus manos,
para que no tropieces
con piedra alguna.'

⁷Jesús le contestó:

—También dice la Escritura: 'No pongas a prueba al Señor tu Dios.'

⁸Finalmente el diablo lo llevó a un cerro muy alto, y mostrándole todos los países del mundo y la grandeza de ellos, ⁹le dijo:

—Yo te daré todo esto, si te arrodillas y me adoras.

¹⁰Jesús le contestó:

—Vete, Satanás, porque la Escritura dice: 'Adora al Señor tu Dios, y sírvele solo a él.'

¹¹Entonces el diablo se apartó de Jesús, y unos ángeles acudieron a servirle.

Jesús comienza su actividad en Galilea

¹²Cuando Jesús oyó que habían metido a Juan en la cárcel, se dirigió a Galilea. ¹³Pero no se quedó en Nazaret, sino que se fue a vivir a Cafarnaúm, a orillas del lago, en la región de las tribus de Zabulón y Neftalí. ¹⁴Esto sucedió para que se cumpliera lo que había escrito el profeta Isaías:

¹⁵ "Tierra de Zabulón y de Neftalí,
al otro lado del Jordán,
a la orilla del mar:
Galilea, donde viven los paganos.
¹⁶ El pueblo que andaba
en la oscuridad

vio una gran luz;
una luz ha brillado
para los que vivían en sombras
de muerte."

¹⁷Desde entonces Jesús comenzó a proclamar: "Vuélvanse a Dios, porque el reino de los cielos está cerca."

Jesús llama a cuatro pescadores

¹⁸Jesús iba caminando por la orilla del Lago de Galilea, cuando vio a dos hermanos: uno era Simón, también llamado Pedro, y el otro Andrés. Eran pescadores, y estaban echando la red al agua. ¹⁹Jesús les dijo:

—Síganme, y yo los haré pescadores de hombres.

²⁰Al momento dejaron sus redes y se fueron con él.

²¹Un poco más adelante, Jesús vio a otros dos hermanos: Santiago y Juan, hijos de Zebedeo, que estaban con su padre en una barca arreglando las redes. Jesús los llamó, ²²y en seguida ellos dejaron la barca y a su padre, y lo siguieron.

Jesús enseña a mucha gente

²³Jesús recorría toda Galilea, enseñando en la sinagoga de cada lugar. Anunciaba la buena noticia del reino y curaba a la gente de todas sus enfermedades y dolencias. ²⁴Se hablaba de Jesús en toda la región de Siria, y le traían a cuantos sufrían de diferentes males, enfermedades y dolores, y a los endemoniados, a los epilépticos y a los paralíticos. Y Jesús los sanaba.

²⁵Mucha gente de Galilea, de los pueblos de Decápolis, de Jerusalén, de

Judea y de la región al oriente del Jordán seguía a Jesús.

Sermón del monte

5 ¹Al ver la multitud, Jesús subió al monte y se sentó. Sus discípulos se le acercaron, ²y él tomó la palabra y comenzó a enseñarles, diciendo:

Lo que realmente cuenta ante Dios

³ "Dichosos los que tienen espíritu de pobres,
porque de ellos es el reino de los cielos.
⁴ "Dichosos los que sufren,
porque serán consolados.
⁵ "Dichosos los humildes,
porque heredarán la tierra prometida.
⁶ "Dichosos los que tienen hambre y sed de la justicia,
porque serán satisfechos.
⁷ "Dichosos los compasivos,
porque Dios tendrá compasión de ellos.
⁸ "Dichosos los de corazón limpio,
porque verán a Dios.
⁹ "Dichosos los que trabajan por la paz,
porque Dios los llamará hijos suyos.
¹⁰ "Dichosos los perseguidos por hacer lo que es justo,
porque de ellos es el reino de los cielos.
¹¹ "Dichosos ustedes, cuando la gente los insulte y los maltrate, y cuando por causa mía los ataquen con toda clase de mentiras. ¹²Alégrense,

están contentos, porque van a recibir un gran premio en el cielo; pues así también persiguieron a los profetas que vivieron antes que ustedes.

Sal y luz del mundo

13 "Ustedes son la sal de este mundo. Pero si la sal deja de estar salada, ¿cómo podrá recobrar su sabor? Ya no sirve para nada, así que se la tira a la calle y la gente la pisotea.

14 "Ustedes son la luz de este mundo. Una ciudad en lo alto de un cerro no puede esconderse. 15 Ni se enciende una lámpara para ponerla bajo un cajón; antes bien, se la pone en alto para que alumbre a todos los que están en la casa. 16 Del mismo modo, procuren ustedes que su luz brille delante de la gente, para que, viendo el bien que ustedes hacen, todos alaben a su Padre que está en el cielo.

Jesús enseña sobre la ley

17 "No crean ustedes que yo he venido a suprimir la ley o los profetas; no he venido a ponerles fin, sino a darles su pleno valor. 18 Pues les aseguro que mientras existan el cielo y la tierra, no se le quitará a la ley ni un punto ni una letra, hasta que todo llegue a su cumplimiento. 19 Por eso, el que no obedece uno de los mandatos de la ley, aunque sea el más pequeño, ni enseña a la gente a obedecerlo, será considerado el más pequeño en el reino de los cielos. Pero el que los obedece y enseña a otros a hacer lo mismo, será considerado grande en el reino de los cielos.

Jesús enseña una justicia superior

20 "Porque les digo a ustedes que, si no superan a los maestros de la ley y a los fariseos en hacer lo que es justo ante Dios, nunca entrarán en el reino de los cielos.

Jesús enseña sobre el enojo

21 "Ustedes han oído que a sus antepasados se les dijo: 'No mates, pues el que mate será condenado.' 22 Pero yo les digo que cualquiera que se enoje con su hermano, será condenado. Al que insulte a su hermano, lo juzgará la Junta Suprema; y el que injurie gravemente a su hermano, se hará merecedor del fuego del infierno.

23 "Así que, si al llevar tu ofrenda al altar te acuerdas de que tu hermano tiene algo contra ti, 24 deja tu ofrenda allí mismo delante del altar y ve primero a ponerte en paz con tu hermano. Entonces podrás volver al altar y presentar tu ofrenda.

25 "Si alguien te lleva a juicio, ponte de acuerdo con él mientras todavía estés a tiempo, para que no te entregue al juez; porque si no, el juez te entregará a los guardias y te meterán en la cárcel. 26 Te aseguro que no saldrás de allí hasta que pagues el último centavo.

Jesús enseña sobre el adulterio

27 "Ustedes han oído que se dijo: 'No cometas adulterio.' 28 Pero yo les digo que cualquiera que mira con deseo a una mujer, ya cometió adulterio con ella en su corazón.

²⁹"Así pues, si tu ojo derecho te hace caer en pecado, sácatelo y échalo lejos de ti; es mejor que pierdas una sola parte de tu cuerpo, y no que todo tu cuerpo sea arrojado al infierno. ³⁰Y si tu mano derecha te hace caer en pecado, córtatela y échala lejos de ti; es mejor que pierdas una sola parte de tu cuerpo, y no que todo tu cuerpo vaya a parar al infierno.

Jesús enseña sobre el divorcio

³¹"También se dijo: 'Cualquiera que se divorcia de su esposa, debe darle un certificado de divorcio.' ³²Pero yo les digo que si un hombre se divorcia de su esposa, a no ser en el caso de una unión ilegal, la pone en peligro de cometer adulterio. Y el que se casa con una divorciada, comete adulterio.

Jesús enseña sobre los juramentos

³³"También han oído ustedes que se dijo a los antepasados: 'No dejes de cumplir lo que hayas ofrecido al Señor bajo juramento.' ³⁴Pero yo les digo: simplemente, no juren. No juren por el cielo, porque es el trono de Dios; ³⁵ni por la tierra, porque es el estrado de sus pies; ni por Jerusalén, porque es la ciudad del gran Rey. ³⁶Ni juren ustedes tampoco por su propia cabeza, porque no pueden hacer blanco o negro ni un solo cabello. ³⁷Baste con decir claramente 'sí' o 'no'. Pues lo que se aparta de esto, es malo.

Jesús enseña sobre la venganza

³⁸"Ustedes han oído que se dijo: 'Ojo por ojo y diente por diente.' ³⁹Pero yo les digo: No resistas al que te haga algún mal; al contrario, si alguien te pega en la mejilla derecha, ofrécele también la otra. ⁴⁰Si alguien te demanda y te quiere quitar la camisa, déjale que se lleve también tu capa. ⁴¹Si te obligan a llevar carga una milla, llévala dos. ⁴²A cualquiera que te pida algo, dáselo; y no te vuelvas la espalda al que te pida prestado.

El amor a los enemigos

⁴³"También han oído que se dijo: 'Ama a tu prójimo y odia a tu enemigo.' ⁴⁴Pero yo les digo: Amen a sus enemigos, y oren por quienes los persiguen. ⁴⁵Así ustedes serán hijos de su Padre que está en el cielo; pues él hace que su sol salga sobre malos y buenos, y manda la lluvia sobre justos e injustos. ⁴⁶Porque si ustedes aman solamente a quienes los aman, ¿qué premio recibirán? Hasta los que cobran impuestos para Roma se portan así. ⁴⁷Y si saludan solamente a sus hermanos, ¿qué hacen de extraordinario? Hasta los paganos se portan así. ⁴⁸Sean ustedes perfectos, como su Padre que está en el cielo es perfecto.

Jesús enseña sobre prácticas de piedad

6 ¹"No hagan sus buenas obras delante de la gente solo para que los demás los vean. Si lo hacen así, su Padre que está en el cielo no les dará ningún premio.

²"Por eso, cuando ayudes a los necesitados, no lo publiques a los cuatro vientos, como hacen los

hipócritas en las sinagogas y en las calles para que la gente hable bien de ellos. Les aseguro que con eso ya tienen su premio. 3Cuando tú ayudes a los necesitados, no se lo cuentes ni siquiera a tu amigo más íntimo; 4hazlo en secreto. Y tu Padre, que ve lo que haces en secreto, te dará tu premio.

Jesús enseña a orar

5"Cuando ustedes oren, no sean como los hipócritas, a quienes les gusta orar de pie en las sinagogas y en las esquinas de las plazas para que la gente los vea. Les aseguro que con eso ya tienen su premio. 6Pero tú, cuando ores, entra en tu cuarto, cierra la puerta y ora a tu Padre en secreto. Y tu Padre, que ve lo que haces en secreto, te dará tu premio.

7"Y al orar no repitan ustedes palabras inútiles, como hacen los paganos, que se imaginan que cuanto más hablen más caso les hará Dios. 8No sean como ellos, porque su Padre ya sabe lo que ustedes necesitan, antes que se lo pidan. 9Ustedes deben orar así:

'Padre nuestro que estás
   en el cielo,
santificado sea tu nombre.
10Venga tu reino.
   Hágase tu voluntad en la tierra,
   así como se hace en el cielo.
11Danos hoy el pan que necesitamos.
12Perdónanos el mal
   que hemos hecho,
   así como nosotros
   hemos perdonado
a los que nos han hecho mal.

13No nos expongas a la tentación,
   sino líbranos del maligno.'

14"Porque si ustedes perdonan a otros el mal que les han hecho, su Padre que está en el cielo los perdonará también a ustedes; 15pero si no perdonan a otros, tampoco su Padre les perdonará a ustedes sus pecados.

Jesús enseña sobre el ayuno

16"Cuando ustedes ayunen, no pongan cara triste, como los hipócritas, que aparentan tristeza para que la gente vea que están ayunando. Les aseguro que con eso ya tienen su premio. 17Tú, cuando ayunes, lávate la cara y arréglate bien, 18para que la gente no note que estás ayunando. Solamente lo notará tu Padre, que está en lo oculto, y tu Padre que ve en lo oculto te dará tu recompensa.

Riquezas en el cielo

19"No amontonen riquezas aquí en la tierra, donde la polilla destruye y las cosas se echan a perder, y donde los ladrones entran a robar. 20Más bien amontonen riquezas en el cielo, donde la polilla no destruye ni las cosas se echan a perder ni los ladrones entran a robar. 21Pues donde esté tu riqueza, allí estará también tu corazón.

La lámpara del cuerpo

22"Los ojos son la lámpara del cuerpo; así que, si tus ojos son buenos, todo tu cuerpo tendrá luz; 23pero si tus ojos son malos, todo tu cuerpo estará en oscuridad. Y si la luz que hay en ti resulta ser oscuridad, ¡qué negra será la oscuridad misma!

Dios y las riquezas

24 "Nadie puede servir a dos amos, porque odiará a uno y querrá al otro, o será fiel a uno y despreciará al otro. No se puede servir a Dios y a las riquezas.

Dios cuida de sus hijos

25 "Por lo tanto, yo les digo: No se preocupen por lo que han de comer o beber para vivir, ni por la ropa que necesitan para el cuerpo. ¿No vale la vida más que la comida y el cuerpo más que la ropa? 26 Miren las aves que vuelan por el aire: no siembran ni cosechan ni guardan la cosecha en graneros; sin embargo, el Padre de ustedes que está en el cielo les da de comer. ¡Y ustedes valen más que las aves! 27 En todo caso, por mucho que uno se preocupe, ¿cómo podrá prolongar su vida ni siquiera una hora? 28 ¿Y por qué se preocupan ustedes por la ropa? Fíjense cómo crecen los lirios del campo: no trabajan ni hilan. 29 Sin embargo, les digo que ni siquiera el rey Salomón, con todo su lujo, se vestía como uno de ellos. 30 Pues si Dios viste así a la hierba, que hoy está en el campo y mañana se quema en el horno, ¡con mayor razón los vestirá a ustedes, gente falta de fe! 31 Así que no se preocupen, preguntándose: '¿Qué vamos a comer?' o '¿Qué vamos a beber?' o '¿Con qué vamos a vestirnos?' 32 Todas estas cosas son las que preocupan a los paganos, pero ustedes tienen un Padre celestial que ya sabe que las necesitan. 33 Por lo

tanto, pongan toda su atención en el reino de los cielos y en hacer lo que es justo ante Dios, y recibirán también todas estas cosas. 34 No se preocupen por el día de mañana, porque mañana habrá tiempo para preocuparse. Cada día tiene bastante con sus propios problemas.

No juzgar a otros

7 1 "No juzguen a otros, para que Dios no los juzgue a ustedes. 2 Pues Dios los juzgará a ustedes de la misma manera que ustedes juzguen a otros; y con la misma medida con que ustedes den a otros, Dios les dará a ustedes. 3 ¿Por qué te pones a mirar la astilla que tiene tu hermano en el ojo, y no te fijas en el tronco que tú tienes en el tuyo? 4 Y si tú tienes un tronco en tu propio ojo, ¿cómo puedes decirle a tu hermano: 'Déjame sacarte la astilla que tienes en el ojo'? 5 ¡Hipócrita!, saca primero el tronco de tu propio ojo, y así podrás ver bien para sacar la astilla que tiene tu hermano en el suyo.

6 "No den las cosas sagradas a los perros, no sea que se vuelvan contra ustedes y los hagan pedazos. Y no echen sus perlas a los cerdos, no sea que las pisoteen.

Pedir, buscar y llamar a la puerta

7 "Pidan, y Dios les dará; busquen, y encontrarán; llamen a la puerta, y se les abrirá. 8 Porque el que pide, recibe; y el que busca, encuentra; y al que llama a la puerta, se le abre.

9 "¿Acaso alguno de ustedes sería capaz de darle a su hijo una piedra cuando le pide pan? 10 O de darle una

culebra cuando le pide un pescado? [11]Pues si ustedes, que son malos, saben dar cosas buenas a sus hijos, ¡cuánto más su Padre que está en el cielo dará cosas buenas a quienes se las pidan!

[12]"Así pues, hagan ustedes con los demás como quieran que los demás hagan con ustedes; porque en eso se resumen la ley y los profetas.

La puerta angosta

[13]"Entren por la puerta angosta. Porque la puerta y el camino que llevan a la perdición son anchos y espaciosos, y muchos entran por ellos; [14]pero la puerta y el camino que llevan a la vida son angostos y difíciles, y pocos los encuentran.

Los reconocerán por sus acciones

[15]"Cuídense de esos mentirosos que pretenden hablar de parte de Dios. Vienen a ustedes disfrazados de ovejas, pero por dentro son lobos feroces. [16]Ustedes pueden reconocer por sus acciones, pues no se cosechan uvas de los espinos ni higos de los cardos. [17]Así, todo árbol bueno da fruto bueno, pero el árbol malo da fruto malo. [18]El árbol bueno no puede dar fruto malo, ni el árbol malo dar fruto bueno. [19]Todo árbol que no da buen fruto, se corta y se echa al fuego. [20]De modo que ustedes los reconocerán por sus acciones.

Para entrar en el reino de los cielos

[21]"No todos los que me dicen: 'Señor, Señor', entrarán en el reino de los cielos, sino solamente los que hacen la voluntad de mi Padre celestial. [22]Aquel día muchos me dirán: 'Señor, Señor, nosotros comunicamos mensajes en tu nombre, y en tu nombre expulsamos demonios, y en tu nombre hicimos muchos milagros.' [23]Pero entonces les contestaré: 'Nunca los conocí; ¡aléjense de mí, malhechores!'

La casa bien o mal fundada

[24]"Por tanto, el que me oye y hace lo que yo digo, es como un hombre prudente que construyó su casa sobre la roca. [25]Vino la lluvia, crecieron los ríos y soplaron los vientos contra la casa; pero no cayó, porque tenía su base sobre la roca. [26]Pero el que me oye y no hace lo que yo digo, es como un tonto que construyó su casa sobre la arena. [27]Vino la lluvia, crecieron los ríos, soplaron los vientos y la casa se vino abajo. ¡Fue un gran desastre!"

[28]Cuando Jesús terminó de hablar, toda la gente estaba admirada de cómo les enseñaba, [29]porque lo hacía con plena autoridad, y no como sus maestros de la ley.

Jesús sana a un leproso

8 [1]Cuando Jesús bajó del monte, mucha gente lo siguió. [2]En esto se le acercó un hombre enfermo de lepra, el cual se puso de rodillas delante de él y le dijo:

—Señor, si quieres, puedes limpiarme de mi enfermedad.

[3]Jesús lo tocó con la mano, y dijo:

—Quiero. ¡Queda limpio!

Al momento, el leproso quedó limpio de su enfermedad. [4]Jesús añadió:

—Mira, no se lo digas a nadie; solamente ve y preséntate al sacerdote, y lleva la ofrenda que ordenó Moisés, para que conste ante los sacerdotes.

Jesús sana al criado de un capitán romano

5 Al entrar Jesús en Cafarnaúm, un capitán romano se le acercó para hacerle un ruego. 6 Le dijo:

—Señor, mi criado está en casa enfermo, paralizado y sufriendo terribles dolores.

7 Jesús le respondió:

—Iré a sanarlo.

8 El capitán contestó:

—Señor, yo no merezco que entres en mi casa; solamente da la orden, y mi criado quedará sano. 9 Porque yo mismo estoy bajo órdenes superiores, y a la vez tengo soldados bajo mi mando. Cuando le digo a uno de ellos que vaya, va; cuando le digo a otro que venga, viene; y cuando mando a mi criado que haga algo, lo hace.

10 Jesús se quedó admirado al oír esto, y dijo a los que le seguían:

—Les aseguro que no he encontrado a nadie en Israel con tanta fe como este hombre. 11 Y les digo que muchos vendrán de oriente y de occidente, y se sentarán a comer con Abraham, Isaac y Jacob en el reino de los cielos, 12 pero los que deberían estar en el reino, serán echados a la oscuridad de afuera. Entonces vendrán el llanto y la desesperación.

13 Luego Jesús dijo al capitán:

—Vete a tu casa, y que se haga tal como has creído.

En ese mismo momento el criado quedó sano.

Jesús sana a la suegra de Pedro

14 Jesús fue a casa de Pedro, donde encontró a la suegra de este en cama y con fiebre. 15 Jesús tocó entonces la mano de ella, y la fiebre se le quitó, así que ella se levantó y comenzó a atenderlo.

Jesús sana a muchos enfermos

16 Al anochecer llevaron a Jesús muchas personas endemoniadas; y con una orden expulsó a los espíritus malos, y también sanó a todos los enfermos. 17 Esto sucedió para que se cumpliera lo que anunció el profeta Isaías, cuando dijo: "Él tomó nuestras debilidades y cargó con nuestras enfermedades."

Para seguir a Jesús

18 Jesús, al verse rodeado por la multitud, dio orden de pasar al otro lado del lago. 19 Entonces se le acercó un maestro de la ley, y le dijo:

—Maestro, deseo seguirte a dondequiera que vayas.

20 Jesús le contestó:

—Las zorras tienen cuevas y las aves tienen nidos, pero el Hijo del hombre no tiene donde recostar la cabeza.

21 Otro, que era uno de sus discípulos, le dijo:

—Señor, déjame ir primero a enterrar a mi padre.

22 Jesús le contestó:

—Sígueme, y deja que los muertos entierren a sus muertos.

Jesús calma la tormenta

²³Jesús subió a la barca, y sus discípulos lo acompañaron. ²⁴En esto se desató sobre el lago una tormenta tan fuerte que las olas cubrían la barca. Pero Jesús se había dormido. ²⁵Entonces sus discípulos fueron a despertarlo, diciéndole:

—¡Señor, sálvanos! ¡Nos estamos hundiendo!

²⁶Él les contestó:

—¿Por qué tanto miedo? ¡Qué poca fe tienen ustedes!

Dicho esto, se levantó y dio una orden al viento y al mar, y todo quedó completamente tranquilo. ²⁷Ellos, admirados, se preguntaban:

—¿Pues quién será este, que hasta los vientos y el mar lo obedecen?

Los endemoniados de Gadara

²⁸Cuando Jesús llegó al otro lado del lago, a la tierra de Gadara, dos endemoniados salieron de entre las tumbas y se acercaron a él. Eran tan feroces que nadie podía pasar por aquel camino; ²⁹y se pusieron a gritar:

—¡No te metas con nosotros, Hijo de Dios! ¿Viniste acá para atormentarnos antes de tiempo?

³⁰A cierta distancia de allí había muchos cerdos comiendo, ³¹y los demonios le rogaron a Jesús:

—Si nos expulsas, déjanos entrar en esos cerdos.

³²Jesús les dijo:

—Vayan.

Los demonios salieron de los hombres y entraron en los cerdos; y al momento todos los cerdos echaron a correr pendiente abajo hasta el lago, y allí se ahogaron.

³³Los que cuidaban de los cerdos salieron huyendo, y al llegar al pueblo comenzaron a contar lo sucedido, todo lo que había pasado con los endemoniados. ³⁴Entonces todos los del pueblo salieron a donde estaba Jesús, y al verlo le rogaron que se fuera de aquellos lugares.

Jesús perdona y sana a un paralítico

9 ¹Después de esto, Jesús subió a una barca, pasó al otro lado del lago y llegó a su propio pueblo. ²Allí le llevaron un paralítico, acostado en una camilla; y cuando Jesús vio la fe que tenían, le dijo al enfermo:

—Ánimo, hijo; tus pecados quedan perdonados.

³Algunos maestros de la ley pensaron: "Lo que este ha dicho es una ofensa contra Dios." ⁴Pero como Jesús se dio cuenta de lo que estaban pensando, les preguntó:

—¿Por qué tienen ustedes tan malos pensamientos? ⁵¿Qué es más fácil, decir: 'Tus pecados quedan perdonados', o decir: 'Levántate y anda'? ⁶Pues voy a demostrarles que el Hijo del hombre tiene autoridad en la tierra para perdonar pecados.

Entonces le dijo al paralítico:

—Levántate, toma tu camilla y vete a tu casa.

⁷El paralítico se levantó y se fue a su casa. ⁸Al ver esto, la gente tuvo miedo y alabó a Dios por haber dado tal poder a los hombres.

Jesús llama a Mateo

9 Jesús se fue de allí y vio a un hombre llamado Mateo, que estaba sentado en el lugar donde cobraba los impuestos para Roma. Jesús le dijo:

—Sígueme.

Entonces Mateo se levantó y lo siguió.

10 Sucedió que Jesús estaba comiendo en la casa, y muchos de los que cobraban impuestos para Roma, y otra gente de mala fama, llegaron y se sentaron también a la mesa junto con Jesús y sus discípulos. 11 Al ver esto, los fariseos preguntaron a los discípulos:

—¿Cómo es que su maestro come con cobradores de impuestos y pecadores?

12 Jesús lo oyó y les dijo:

—Los que están buenos y sanos no necesitan médico, sino los enfermos. 13 Vayan y aprendan el significado de estas palabras: 'Lo que quiero es que sean compasivos, y no que ofrezcan sacrificios.' Pues yo no he venido a llamar a los justos, sino a los pecadores.

La pregunta sobre el ayuno

14 Los seguidores de Juan el Bautista se acercaron a Jesús y le preguntaron:

—Nosotros y los fariseos ayunamos mucho, ¿por qué tus discípulos no ayunan?

15 Jesús les contestó:

—¿Acaso pueden estar tristes los invitados a una boda, mientras el novio está con ellos? Pero llegará el momento en que se lleven al novio; entonces sí ayunarán.

16 "Nadie arregla un vestido viejo con un remiendo de tela nueva, porque el remiendo nuevo se encoge y rompe el vestido viejo, y el desgarrón se hace mayor. 17 Ni tampoco se echa vino nuevo en cueros viejos, porque los cueros se revientan, y tanto el vino como los cueros se pierden. Por eso hay que echar el vino nuevo en cueros nuevos, para que así se conserven las dos cosas."

La mujer enferma y la hija de Jairo

18 Mientras Jesús les estaba hablando, un jefe de los judíos llegó, se arrodilló ante él y le dijo:

—Mi hija acaba de morir; pero si tú vienes y pones tu mano sobre ella, volverá a la vida.

19 Jesús se levantó, y acompañado de sus discípulos se fue con él. 20 Entonces una mujer que desde hacía doce años estaba enferma, con derrames de sangre, se acercó a Jesús por detrás y le tocó el borde de la capa. 21 Porque pensaba: "Tan solo con que llegue a tocar su capa, quedaré sana." 22 Pero Jesús se dio la vuelta, vio a la mujer y le dijo:

—Ánimo, hija, por tu fe has sido sanada.

Y desde aquel mismo momento quedó sana.

23 Cuando Jesús llegó a casa del jefe de los judíos, y vio que los músicos estaban preparados ya para el entierro y que la gente lloraba a gritos, 24 les dijo:

—Sálganse de aquí, pues la muchacha no está muerta, sino dormida.

La gente se rió de Jesús, 25pero él los hizo salir; luego entró y tomó de la mano a la muchacha, y ella se levantó. 26Y por toda aquella región corrió la noticia de lo que había pasado.

Jesús sana a dos ciegos

27Al salir Jesús de allí, dos ciegos lo siguieron, gritando:

—¡Ten compasión de nosotros, Hijo de David!

28Cuando Jesús entró en la casa, los ciegos se le acercaron, y él les preguntó:

—¿Creen ustedes que puedo hacer esto?

—Sí, Señor —le contestaron.

29Entonces Jesús les tocó los ojos, y les dijo:

—Que se haga conforme a la fe que ustedes tienen.

30Y recobraron la vista. Jesús les advirtió mucho:

—Procuren que no lo sepa nadie.

31Pero, apenas salieron, contaron por toda aquella región lo que Jesús había hecho.

Jesús sana a un mudo

32Mientras los ciegos salían, algunas personas trajeron a Jesús un mudo que estaba endemoniado. 33En cuanto Jesús expulsó al demonio, el mudo comenzó a hablar. La gente, admirada, decía:

—¡Nunca se ha visto en Israel una cosa igual!

34Pero los fariseos decían:

—Es el propio jefe de los demonios quien le ha dado a este el poder de expulsarlos.

La cosecha es mucha

35Jesús recorría todos los pueblos y aldeas, enseñando en las sinagogas de cada lugar. Anunciaba la buena noticia del reino, y curaba toda clase de enfermedades y dolencias. 36Al ver a la gente, sintió compasión de ellos, porque estaban cansados y abatidos, como ovejas que no tienen pastor. 37Dijo entonces a sus discípulos:

—Ciertamente la cosecha es mucha, pero los trabajadores son pocos. 38Por eso, pidan ustedes al Dueño de la cosecha que mande trabajadores a recogerla.

Jesús escoge a los doce apóstoles

10 1Jesús llamó a sus doce discípulos, y les dio autoridad para expulsar a los espíritus impuros y para curar toda clase de enfermedades y dolencias.

2Estos son los nombres de los doce apóstoles: primero Simón, llamado también Pedro, y su hermano Andrés; Santiago y su hermano Juan, hijos de Zebedeo; 3Felipe y Bartolomé; Tomás y Mateo, el que cobraba impuestos para Roma; Santiago, hijo de Alfeo, y Tadeo; 4Simón el cananeo, y Judas Iscariote, que después traicionó a Jesús.

Jesús instruye y envía a los apóstoles

5Jesús envió a estos doce con las siguientes instrucciones: "No vayan a las regiones de los paganos ni entren en los pueblos de Samaria; 6vayan más bien a las ovejas perdidas del pueblo de

Israel. 7Vayan y anuncien que el reino de los cielos se ha acercado. 8Sanen a los enfermos, resuciten a los muertos, limpien de su enfermedad a los leprosos y expulsen a los demonios. Ustedes recibieron gratis este poder; no cobren tampoco por emplearlo.

9"No lleven oro ni plata ni cobre 10ni provisiones para el camino. No lleven ropa de repuesto ni sandalias ni bastón, pues el trabajador tiene derecho a su alimento.

11"Cuando lleguen ustedes a un pueblo o aldea, busquen alguna persona de confianza y quédense en su casa hasta que se vayan de allí. 12Al entrar en la casa, saluden a los que viven en ella. 13Si la gente de la casa lo merece, su deseo de paz se cumplirá; pero si no lo merece, ustedes nada perderán. 14Y si no los reciben ni los quieren oír, salgan de la casa o del pueblo y sacúdanse el polvo de los pies. 15Les aseguro que en el día del juicio el castigo para ese pueblo será peor que para la gente de la región de Sodoma y Gomorra.

Persecuciones

16"¡Miren! Yo los envío a ustedes como ovejas en medio de lobos. Sean, pues, astutos como serpientes, aunque también sencillos como palomas. 17Tengan cuidado, porque los entregarán a las autoridades, los golpearán en las sinagogas 18y hasta los presentarán ante gobernadores y reyes por causa mía; así podrán dar testimonio de mí delante de ellos y de los paganos. 19Pero cuando los entreguen a las autoridades, no se preocupen ustedes por lo que han de decir o cómo han de decirlo, porque cuando les llegue el momento de hablar, Dios les dará las palabras. 20Pues no serán ustedes quienes hablen, sino que el Espíritu de su Padre hablará por ustedes.

21"Los hermanos entregarán a la muerte a sus hermanos, y los padres a sus hijos; y los hijos se volverán contra sus padres y los matarán. 22Todo el mundo los odiará a ustedes por causa mía; pero el que se mantenga firme hasta el fin, se salvará. 23Cuando los persigan en una ciudad, huyan a otra; pues les aseguro que el Hijo del hombre vendrá antes que ustedes hayan recorrido todas las ciudades de Israel.

24"Ningún discípulo es más que su maestro, y ningún criado es más que su amo. 25El discípulo debe conformarse con llegar a ser como su maestro, y el criado como su amo. Si al jefe de la casa lo llaman Beelzebú, ¿qué dirán de los de su familia?

Hablar sin temor

26"No tengan, pues, miedo de la gente. Porque no hay nada secreto que no llegue a descubrirse, ni nada escondido que no llegue a saberse. 27Lo que les digo en la oscuridad, díganlo ustedes a la luz del día; y lo que les digo en secreto, grítenlo desde las azoteas de las casas. 28No tengan miedo de los que matan el cuerpo pero no pueden matar el alma; teman más bien al que puede hacer perecer alma y cuerpo en el infierno.

29"¿No se venden dos pajarillos por una monedita? Sin embargo, ni uno de ellos cae a tierra sin que el Padre de ustedes lo permita. ³⁰En cuanto a ustedes mismos, hasta los cabellos de la cabeza él los tiene contados uno por uno. ³¹Así que no tengan miedo: ustedes valen más que muchos pajarillos.

Reconocer a Jesucristo delante de los hombres

³²"Si alguien se declara a mi favor delante de los hombres, yo también me declararé a favor de él delante de mi Padre que está en el cielo; ³³pero al que me niegue delante de los hombres, yo también lo negaré delante de mi Padre que está en el cielo.

Jesús, causa de división

³⁴"No crean que yo he venido a traer paz al mundo; no he venido a traer paz, sino guerra. ³⁵He venido a poner al hombre contra su padre, a la hija contra su madre y a la nuera contra su suegra; ³⁶de modo que los enemigos de cada cual serán sus propios parientes.

³⁷"El que quiere a su padre o a su madre más que a mí, no merece ser mío; el que quiere a su hijo o a su hija más que a mí, no merece ser mío; ³⁸y el que no toma su cruz y me sigue, no merece ser mío. ³⁹El que trate de salvar su vida, la perderá, pero el que pierda su vida por causa mía, la salvará.

Premios

⁴⁰"El que los recibe a ustedes, me recibe a mí; y el que me recibe a mí, recibe al que me envió. ⁴¹El que recibe a un profeta por ser profeta, recibirá igual premio que el profeta; y el que recibe a

un justo por ser justo, recibirá el mismo premio que el justo. ⁴²Y cualquiera que le da siquiera un vaso de agua fresca a uno de estos pequeños por ser seguidor mío, les aseguro que tendrá su premio."

11 ¹Cuando Jesús terminó de dar instrucciones a sus doce discípulos, se fue de allí a enseñar y anunciar el mensaje en los pueblos de aquella región.

Los enviados de Juan el Bautista

²Juan, que estaba en la cárcel, tuvo noticias de lo que Cristo estaba haciendo. Entonces envió algunos de sus seguidores ³a que le preguntaran si él era de veras el que había de venir, o si debían esperar a otro.

⁴Jesús les contestó: "Vayan y díganle a Juan lo que están viendo y oyendo. ⁵Cuéntenle que los ciegos ven, los cojos andan, los leprosos quedan limpios de su enfermedad, los sordos oyen, los muertos vuelven a la vida y a los pobres se les anuncia la buena noticia. ⁶¡Y dichoso aquel que no encuentre en mí motivo de tropiezo!"

⁷Cuando ellos se fueron, Jesús comenzó a hablar a la gente acerca de Juan, diciendo: "¿Qué salieron ustedes a ver al desierto? ¿Una caña sacudida por el viento? ⁸Y si no, ¿qué salieron a ver? ¿Un hombre vestido lujosamente? Ustedes saben que los que se visten lujosamente están en las casas de los reyes. ⁹En fin, ¿a qué salieron? ¿A ver a un profeta? Sí, de veras, y a uno que es mucho más que profeta. ¹⁰Juan es aquel de quien dice la Escritura:

'Yo envío mi mensajero delante de ti, para que te prepare el camino.'

11 Les aseguro que, entre todos los hombres, ninguno ha sido más grande que Juan el Bautista; y, sin embargo, el más pequeño en el reino de los cielos es más grande que él.

12 "Desde que vino Juan el Bautista hasta ahora, el reino de los cielos sufre violencia, y los que usan la fuerza pretenden acabar con él. 13 Todos los profetas y la ley fueron solo un anuncio del reino, hasta que vino Juan; 14 y, si ustedes quieren aceptar esto, Juan es el profeta Elías que había de venir. 15 Los que tienen oídos, oigan.

16 "¿A qué compararé la gente de este tiempo? Se parece a los niños que se sientan a jugar en las plazas y gritan a sus compañeros: 17 'Tocamos la flauta, pero ustedes no bailaron; cantamos canciones tristes, pero ustedes no lloraron.' 18 Porque vino Juan, que ni come ni bebe, y dicen que tiene un demonio. 19 Luego ha venido el Hijo del hombre, que come y bebe, y dicen que es glotón y bebedor, amigo de gente de mala fama y de los que cobran impuestos para Roma. Pero la sabiduría de Dios se demuestra por sus resultados."

Reproches contra las ciudades incrédulas

20 Entonces Jesús comenzó a reprender a los pueblos donde había hecho la mayor parte de sus milagros, porque no se habían vuelto a Dios. Decía Jesús: 21 "¡Ay de ti, Corazín! ¡Ay de ti, Betsaida! Porque si en Tiro y Sidón se hubieran hecho los milagros que se han hecho en ustedes, ya hace tiempo que se habrían vuelto a Dios, cubiertos de ropas ásperas y ceniza. 22 Pero les digo que en el día del juicio el castigo para ustedes será peor que para la gente de Tiro y Sidón. 23 Y tú, Cafarnaúm, ¿crees que serás levantado hasta el cielo? ¡Bajarás hasta lo más hondo del abismo! Porque si en Sodoma se hubieran hecho los milagros que se han hecho en ti, esa ciudad habría permanecido hasta el día de hoy. 24 Pero les digo que en el día del juicio el castigo para ti será peor que para la región de Sodoma."

Solo el Hijo sabe quién es el Padre

25 En aquel tiempo, Jesús dijo: "Te alabo, Padre, Señor del cielo y de la tierra, porque has mostrado a los sencillos las cosas que escondiste de los sabios y entendidos. 26 Sí, Padre, porque así lo has querido.

27 "Mi Padre me ha entregado todas las cosas. Nadie conoce realmente al Hijo, sino el Padre; y nadie conoce realmente al Padre, sino el Hijo y aquellos a quienes el Hijo quiera darlo a conocer. 28 Vengan a mí todos ustedes que están cansados de sus trabajos y cargas, y yo los haré descansar. 29 Acepten el yugo que les pongo, y aprendan de mí, que soy paciente y de corazón humilde; así encontrarán descanso. 30 Porque el yugo que les pongo y la carga que les doy a llevar son ligeros.

Los discípulos arrancan espigas en sábado

12 1 Por aquel tiempo, Jesús caminaba un sábado entre los sembrados. Sus discípulos sintieron

hambre, y comenzaron a arrancar espigas de trigo y a comer los granos. [2] Los fariseos lo vieron, y dijeron a Jesús:

—Mira, tus discípulos están haciendo algo que no está permitido hacer en sábado.

[3] Él les contestó:

—¿No han leído ustedes lo que hizo David en una ocasión en que él y sus compañeros tuvieron hambre? [4] Pues entró en la casa de Dios y comieron los panes consagrados a Dios, los cuales no les estaba permitido comer ni a él ni a sus compañeros, sino solamente a los sacerdotes. [5] ¿O no han leído en la ley de Moisés que los sacerdotes en el templo no cometen pecado aunque no descansen el sábado? [6] Pues les digo que aquí hay algo más importante que el templo. [7] Ustedes no han entendido el significado de estas palabras: 'Lo que quiero es que sean compasivos, y no que ofrezcan sacrificios.' Si lo hubieran entendido, no condenarían a quienes no han cometido ninguna falta. [8] Pues bien, el Hijo del hombre tiene autoridad sobre el sábado.

Jesús sana a un enfermo en sábado

[9] Jesús se fue de allí y entró en la sinagoga del lugar. [10] Había en ella un hombre que tenía una mano tullida; y como buscaban algún pretexto para acusar a Jesús, le preguntaron:

—¿Está permitido sanar a un enfermo en sábado?

[11] Jesús les contestó:

—¿Quién de ustedes, si tiene una oveja y se le cae a un pozo en sábado, no va y la saca? [12] Pues ¡cuánto más vale un hombre que una oveja! Por lo tanto, sí está permitido hacer el bien los sábados.

[13] Entonces le dijo a aquel hombre:

—Extiende la mano.

El hombre la extendió, y le quedó tan sana como la otra. [14] Pero cuando los fariseos salieron, comenzaron a hacer planes para matar a Jesús.

Cumplimiento de la profecía

[15] Jesús, al saberlo, se fue de allí, y mucha gente lo siguió. Jesús sanaba a todos los enfermos, [16] y les ordenaba que no hablaran de él en público. [17] Esto fue para que se cumpliera lo que anunció el profeta Isaías, cuando dijo:

[18] "Aquí está mi siervo,
a quien he escogido,
mi amado, en quien me deleito.
Pondré sobre él mi Espíritu,
y proclamará justicia a las naciones.
[19] No protestará ni gritará;
nadie oirá su voz en las calles.
[20] No romperá la caña quebrada
ni apagará la mecha
que apenas humea,
hasta que haga triunfar la justicia.
[21] Y las naciones pondrán su esperanza
en él."

Acusación contra Jesús

[22] Llevaron a Jesús un hombre ciego y mudo, que estaba endemoniado, y Jesús le devolvió la vista y el habla. [23] Todos se preguntaban admirados: "¿Será este el Hijo de David?"

[24] Al oír esto, los fariseos dijeron: "Beelzebú, el jefe de los demonios, es quien le ha dado a este hombre el poder de expulsarlos."

25 Jesús, que sabía lo que estaban pensando, les dijo: "Todo país dividido en bandos enemigos, se destruye a sí mismo; y una ciudad o una familia dividida en bandos, no puede mantenerse. 26 Así también, si Satanás expulsa al propio Satanás, contra sí mismo está dividido; ¿cómo, pues, mantendrá su poder? 27 Ustedes dicen que yo expulso a los demonios por el poder de Beelzebú; pero si es así, ¿quién da a los seguidores de ustedes el poder para expulsarlos? Por eso, ellos mismos demuestran que ustedes están equivocados. 28 Porque si yo expulso a los demonios por medio del Espíritu de Dios, eso significa que el reino de los cielos ya ha llegado a ustedes.

29 "¿Cómo podrá entrar alguien en la casa de un hombre fuerte y robarle sus cosas, si primero no lo ata? Solamente así podrá robárselas.

30 "El que no está a mi favor, está en contra mía; y el que conmigo no recoge, desparrama.

31 "Por eso les digo que Dios perdonará a los hombres todos los pecados y todo lo malo que digan, pero no les perdonará que con sus palabras ofendan al Espíritu Santo. 32 Dios perdonará incluso a aquel que diga algo contra el Hijo del hombre; pero al que hable contra el Espíritu Santo, no lo perdonará ni en el mundo presente ni en el venidero.

El árbol se conoce por su fruto

33 "Si el árbol es bueno, dará buen fruto; si el árbol es malo, dará mal fruto; pues el árbol se conoce por su fruto. 34 ¡Raza de víboras! ¿Cómo pueden decir cosas buenas, si ustedes mismos son malos? De lo que abunda en el corazón, habla la boca. 35 El hombre bueno dice cosas buenas porque el bien está en él, y el hombre malo dice cosas malas porque el mal está en él. 36 Y yo les digo que en el día del juicio todos tendrán que dar cuenta de cualquier palabra inútil que hayan pronunciado. 37 Pues por tus propias palabras serás juzgado, y declarado inocente o culpable."

Algunos piden una señal milagrosa

38 Algunos de los fariseos y maestros de la ley dijeron entonces a Jesús:

—Maestro, queremos verte hacer alguna señal milagrosa.

39 Jesús les contestó:

—Esta gente malvada e infiel pide una señal milagrosa; pero no va a dársele más señal que la del profeta Jonás. 40 Pues así como Jonás estuvo tres días y tres noches dentro del gran pez, así también el Hijo del hombre estará tres días y tres noches dentro de la tierra. 41 Los de Nínive se levantarán en el día del juicio, cuando se juzgue a la gente de este tiempo, y la condenarán; porque los de Nínive se volvieron a Dios cuando oyeron el mensaje de Jonás, y lo que hay aquí es mayor que Jonás. 42 También la reina del Sur se levantará en el día del juicio, cuando se juzgue a la gente de este tiempo, y la condenará; porque ella vino de lo más lejano de la tierra para escuchar la sabiduría de Salomón, y lo que hay aquí es mayor que Salomón.

El espíritu impuro que regresa

43 "Cuando un espíritu impuro sale de un hombre, anda por lugares secos buscando descanso; y si no lo encuentra, piensa: 44 'Regresaré a mi casa, de donde salí.' Cuando regresa, encuentra a ese hombre como una casa desocupada, barrida y arreglada. 45 Entonces va y reúne otros siete espíritus peores que él, y todos juntos se meten a vivir en aquel hombre, que al final queda peor que al principio. Eso mismo le va a suceder a esta gente malvada."

La madre y los hermanos de Jesús

46 Todavía estaba Jesús hablando a la gente, cuando acudieron su madre y sus hermanos, que deseaban hablar con él. Como se quedaron fuera, 47 alguien avisó a Jesús:

—Tu madre y tus hermanos están ahí fuera, y quieren hablar contigo.

48 Pero él contestó al que le llevó el aviso:

—¿Quién es mi madre, y quiénes son mis hermanos?

49 Entonces, señalando a sus discípulos, dijo:

—Estos son mi madre y mis hermanos. 50 Porque cualquiera que hace la voluntad de mi Padre que está en el cielo, ese es mi hermano, mi hermana y mi madre.

La parábola del sembrador

13 1 Aquel mismo día salió Jesús de casa y se sentó a la orilla del lago. 2 Como se reunió mucha gente, Jesús subió a una barca y se sentó, mientras la gente se quedaba en la playa. 3 Entonces se puso a hablarles de muchas cosas por medio de parábolas.

Les dijo: "Un sembrador salió a sembrar. 4 Y al sembrar, una parte de la semilla cayó en el camino, y llegaron las aves y se la comieron. 5 Otra parte cayó entre las piedras, donde no había mucha tierra; esa semilla brotó pronto, porque la tierra no era muy honda; 6 pero el sol, al salir, la quemó, y como no tenía raíz, se secó. 7 Otra parte de la semilla cayó entre espinos, y los espinos crecieron y la ahogaron. 8 Pero otra parte cayó en buena tierra, y dio buena cosecha; algunas espigas dieron cien granos por semilla, otras sesenta granos, y otras treinta. 9 Los que tienen oídos, oigan."

El porqué de las parábolas

10 Los discípulos se acercaron a Jesús y le preguntaron por qué hablaba a la gente por medio de parábolas. 11 Jesús les contestó: "A ustedes, Dios les da a conocer los secretos del reino de los cielos; pero a ellos no. 12 Pues al que tiene, se le dará más, y tendrá bastante; pero al que no tiene, hasta lo poco que tiene se le quitará. 13 Por eso les hablo por medio de parábolas; porque ellos miran, pero no ven; escuchan, pero no oyen ni entienden. 14 Así, en el caso de ellos se cumple lo que dijo el profeta Isaías:

'Por más que escuchen,
　　no entenderán,
por más que miren, no verán.
15 Pues la mente de este pueblo
　　está entorpecida,
tienen tapados los oídos
y han cerrado sus ojos,

para no ver ni oír,
para no entender ni volverse a mí,
para que yo no los sane.'

¹⁶"Pero dichosos ustedes, porque tienen ojos que ven y oídos que oyen. ¹⁷Les aseguro que muchos profetas y personas justas quisieron ver esto que ustedes ven, y no lo vieron; quisieron oír esto que ustedes oyen, y no lo oyeron.

Jesús explica
la parábola del sembrador

¹⁸"Escuchen, pues, lo que quiere decir la parábola del sembrador: ¹⁹Los que oyen el mensaje del reino y no lo entienden, son como la semilla que cayó en el camino; viene el maligno y les quita el mensaje sembrado en su corazón. ²⁰La semilla que cayó entre las piedras representa a los que oyen el mensaje y lo reciben con gusto, ²¹pero como no tienen suficiente raíz, no se mantienen firmes; cuando por causa del mensaje sufren pruebas o persecución, fallan. ²²La semilla sembrada entre espinos representa a los que oyen el mensaje, pero los negocios de esta vida les preocupan demasiado y el amor por las riquezas los engaña. Todo esto ahoga el mensaje y no le deja dar fruto en ellos. ²³Pero la semilla sembrada en buena tierra representa a los que oyen el mensaje y lo entienden y dan una buena cosecha, como las espigas que dieron cien, sesenta o treinta granos por semilla."

La parábola de la mala hierba
entre el trigo

²⁴Jesús les contó esta otra parábola: "Sucede con el reino de los cielos como con un hombre que sembró buena semilla en su campo; ²⁵pero cuando todos estaban durmiendo, llegó un enemigo, sembró mala hierba entre el trigo y se fue. ²⁶Cuando el trigo creció y se formó la espiga, apareció también la mala hierba. ²⁷Entonces los trabajadores fueron a decirle al dueño: 'Señor, si la semilla que sembró usted en el campo era buena, ¿de dónde ha salido la mala hierba?' ²⁸El dueño les dijo: 'Algún enemigo ha hecho esto.' Los trabajadores le preguntaron: '¿Quiere usted que vayamos a arrancar la mala hierba?' ²⁹Pero él les dijo: 'No, porque al arrancar la mala hierba pueden arrancar también el trigo. ³⁰Lo mejor es dejarlos crecer juntos hasta la cosecha; entonces mandaré a los que han de recogerla que recojan primero la mala hierba y la aten en manojos, para quemarla, y que después guarden el trigo en mi granero.'"

La parábola
de la semilla de mostaza

³¹Jesús también les contó esta parábola: "El reino de los cielos es como una semilla de mostaza que un hombre siembra en su campo. ³²Es, por cierto, la más pequeña de todas las semillas; pero cuando crece, se hace más grande que las otras plantas del huerto, y llega a ser como un árbol, tan grande que las aves van y se posan en sus ramas."

La parábola de la levadura

³³También les contó esta parábola: "El reino de los cielos es como la

levadura que una mujer mezcla con tres medidas de harina para hacer fermentar toda la masa."

Cumplimiento de la Escritura

³⁴Jesús habló de todo esto a la gente por medio de parábolas, y sin parábolas no les hablaba. ³⁵Esto fue para que se cumpliera lo que había dicho el profeta:

"Hablaré por medio de parábolas; diré cosas que han estado en secreto desde que Dios hizo el mundo."

Jesús explica la parábola de la mala hierba

³⁶Jesús despidió entonces a la gente y entró en la casa, donde sus discípulos se le acercaron y le pidieron que les explicara la parábola de la mala hierba en el campo. ³⁷Jesús les respondió: "El que siembra la buena semilla es el Hijo del hombre, ³⁸y el campo es el mundo. La buena semilla representa a los que son del reino, y la mala hierba representa a los que son del maligno, ³⁹y el enemigo que sembró la mala hierba es el diablo. La cosecha representa el fin del mundo, y los que recogen la cosecha son los ángeles. ⁴⁰Así como la mala hierba se recoge y se echa al fuego para quemarla, así sucederá también al fin del mundo. ⁴¹El Hijo del hombre mandará a sus ángeles a recoger de su reino a todos los que hacen pecar a otros, y a los que practican el mal. ⁴²Los echarán en el horno encendido, y vendrán el llanto y la desesperación. ⁴³Entonces los justos brillarán como el sol en el reino de su Padre. Los que tienen oídos, oigan.

La parábola del tesoro escondido

⁴⁴"El reino de los cielos es como un tesoro escondido en un terreno. Un hombre encuentra el tesoro, y lo vuelve a esconder allí mismo; lleno de alegría, va y vende todo lo que tiene, y compra ese terreno.

La parábola de la perla de mucho valor

⁴⁵"Sucede también con el reino de los cielos como con un comerciante que andaba buscando perlas finas; ⁴⁶cuando encontró una de mucho valor, fue y vendió todo lo que tenía, y compró esa perla.

La parábola de la red

⁴⁷"Sucede también con el reino de los cielos como con la red que se echa al mar y recoge toda clase de pescado. ⁴⁸Cuando la red se llena, los pescadores la sacan a la playa, donde se sientan a escoger el pescado; guardan el bueno en canastas y tiran el malo. ⁴⁹Así también sucederá al fin del mundo: saldrán los ángeles para separar a los malos de los buenos, ⁵⁰y echarán a los malos en el horno de fuego. Entonces vendrán el llanto y la desesperación."

Lo nuevo y lo viejo

⁵¹Jesús preguntó:

—¿Entienden ustedes todo esto?

—Sí —contestaron ellos.

⁵²Entonces Jesús les dijo:

—Cuando un maestro de la ley se instruye acerca del reino de los cielos, se parece al dueño de una casa, que de lo que tiene guardado sabe sacar cosas nuevas y cosas viejas.

Jesús en Nazaret

53 Cuando Jesús terminó de contar estas parábolas, se fue de allí 54y llegó a su propia tierra, donde comenzó a enseñar en la sinagoga del lugar. La gente, admirada, decía:

— ¿Dónde aprendió este todo lo que sabe? ¿Cómo puede hacer esos milagros? 55¿No es este el hijo del carpintero, y no es María su madre? ¿No es el hermano de Santiago, José, Simón y Judas, 56y no viven sus hermanas también aquí entre nosotros? ¿De dónde le viene todo esto?

57 Y se resistían a creer en él. Pero Jesús les dijo:

— En todas partes se honra a un profeta, menos en su propia tierra y en su propia casa.

58 Y no hizo allí muchos milagros porque aquella gente no tenía fe en él.

La muerte de Juan el Bautista

14 1 Por aquel mismo tiempo, Herodes, el que gobernaba en Galilea, oyó hablar de Jesús, 2y dijo a los que estaban a su servicio: "Ese es Juan el Bautista, que ha resucitado. Por eso tiene este poder milagroso."

3 Es que Herodes había hecho arrestar y encarcelar a Juan. Lo hizo por causa de Herodías, esposa de su hermano Filipo, 4pues Juan había dicho a Herodes: "No debes tenerla como tu mujer."

5 Herodes, que quería matar a Juan, tenía miedo de la gente, porque todos creían que Juan era un profeta. 6Pero en el cumpleaños de Herodes, la hija de Herodías salió a bailar delante de los invitados, y le gustó tanto a Herodes 7que le prometió bajo juramento darle cualquier cosa que pidiera. 8Ella entonces, aconsejada por su madre, dijo a Herodes:

— Dame en un plato la cabeza de Juan el Bautista.

9 Esto entristeció al rey Herodes; pero como había hecho un juramento en presencia de sus invitados, mandó que se la dieran. 10Ordenó, pues, cortarle la cabeza a Juan en la cárcel; 11luego la llevaron en un plato y se la dieron a la muchacha, y ella se la entregó a su madre.

12 Llegaron los seguidores de Juan, se llevaron el cuerpo y lo enterraron; después fueron y avisaron a Jesús.

Jesús da de comer a una multitud

13 Cuando Jesús recibió la noticia, se fue de allí él solo, en una barca, a un lugar apartado. Pero la gente lo supo y salió de los pueblos para seguirlo por tierra. 14Al bajar Jesús de la barca, vio la multitud; sintió compasión de ellos y sanó a los enfermos que llevaban. 15Como ya se hacía de noche, los discípulos se le acercaron y le dijeron:

— Ya es tarde, y este es un lugar solitario. Despide a la gente, para que vayan a las aldeas y se compren comida.

16 Jesús les contestó:

— No es necesario que se vayan; denles ustedes de comer.

17 Ellos respondieron:

— No tenemos aquí más que cinco panes y dos pescados.

18Jesús les dijo:

—Tráiganmelos aquí.

19Entonces mandó a la multitud que se sentara sobre la hierba. Luego tomó en sus manos los cinco panes y los dos pescados y, mirando al cielo, pronunció la bendición y partió los panes, los dio a los discípulos y ellos los repartieron entre la gente. 20Todos comieron hasta quedar satisfechos; recogieron los pedazos sobrantes, y con ellos llenaron doce canastas. 21Los que comieron fueron unos cinco mil hombres, sin contar las mujeres y los niños.

Jesús camina sobre el agua

22Después de esto, Jesús hizo que sus discípulos subieran a la barca, para que cruzaran el lago antes que él y llegaran al otro lado mientras él se despedía a la gente. 23Cuando la hubo despedido, Jesús subió a un cerro, para orar a solas. Al llegar la noche, estaba allí él solo, 24mientras la barca ya iba bastante lejos de tierra firme. Las olas azotaban la barca, porque tenían el viento en contra. 25A la madrugada, Jesús fue hacia ellos caminando sobre el agua. 26Cuando los discípulos lo vieron andar sobre el agua, se asustaron, y gritaron llenos de miedo:

—¡Es un fantasma!

27Pero Jesús les habló, diciéndoles:

—¡Calma! ¡Soy yo: no tengan miedo!

28Entonces Pedro le respondió:

—Señor, si eres tú, ordena que yo vaya hasta ti sobre el agua.

29— Ven —dijo Jesús.

Pedro entonces bajó de la barca y comenzó a caminar sobre el agua en dirección a Jesús. 30Pero al notar la fuerza del viento, tuvo miedo; y como comenzaba a hundirse, gritó:

—¡Sálvame, Señor!

31Al momento, Jesús lo tomó de la mano y le dijo:

—¡Qué poca fe tienes! ¿Por qué dudaste?

32En cuanto subieron a la barca, se calmó el viento. 33Entonces los que estaban en la barca se pusieron de rodillas delante de Jesús, y le dijeron:

—¡En verdad tú eres el Hijo de Dios!

Jesús sana a los enfermos en Genesaret

34Cruzaron el lago y llegaron a tierra en Genesaret. 35La gente del lugar reconoció a Jesús, y la noticia se extendió por toda la región. Le llevaban los enfermos, 36y le rogaban que les dejara tocar siquiera el borde de su capa; y todos los que la tocaban, quedaban sanos.

Lo que hace impuro al hombre

15 1Se acercaron a Jesús algunos fariseos y maestros de la ley, que habían llegado de Jerusalén, y le preguntaron:

2—¿Por qué tus discípulos desobedecen la tradición de nuestros antepasados? ¿Por qué no cumplen con la ceremonia de lavarse las manos antes de comer?

3Jesús les preguntó:

—¿Y por qué también ustedes desobedecen el mandato de Dios para seguir sus propias tradiciones? 4Porque Dios dijo: 'Honra a tu padre y a tu madre', y 'El que maldiga a su padre o a su madre será condenado a muerte.' ⁵Pero ustedes afirman que un hombre puede decirle a su padre o a su madre: 'No puedo ayudarte, porque todo lo que tengo lo he ofrecido a Dios'; ⁶y que cualquiera que diga esto, ya no está obligado a ayudar a su padre o a su madre. Así pues, ustedes han anulado la palabra de Dios para seguir sus propias tradiciones. ⁷¡Hipócritas! Bien habló el profeta Isaías acerca de ustedes, cuando dijo:

⁸ 'Este pueblo me honra con la boca,
pero su corazón está lejos de mí.
⁹ De nada sirve que me rinda culto;
sus enseñanzas son mandatos
de hombres.'

¹⁰Luego Jesús llamó a la gente y dijo:

—Escuchen y entiendan: ¹¹Lo que entra por la boca del hombre no es lo que lo hace impuro. Al contrario, lo que hace impuro al hombre es lo que sale de su boca.

¹²Entonces los discípulos se acercaron a Jesús y le preguntaron:

—¿Sabes que los fariseos se ofendieron al oír lo que dijiste?

¹³Él les contestó:

—Cualquier planta que mi Padre celestial no haya plantado, será arrancada de raíz. ¹⁴Déjenlos, pues son ciegos que guían a otros ciegos. Y si un ciego guía a otro, los dos caerán en algún hoyo.

¹⁵Pedro entonces le dijo a Jesús:

—Explícanos lo que dijiste.

¹⁶Jesús respondió:

—¿Ni siquiera ustedes son todavía capaces de comprender? ¹⁷¿No entienden que todo lo que entra por la boca va al vientre, para después salir del cuerpo? ¹⁸Pero lo que sale de la boca viene del interior del hombre; y eso es lo que lo hace impuro. ¹⁹Porque del interior del hombre salen los malos pensamientos, los asesinatos, el adulterio, la inmoralidad sexual, los robos, las mentiras y los insultos. ²⁰Estas cosas son las que hacen impuro al hombre; pero el comer sin cumplir con la ceremonia de lavarse las manos, no lo hace impuro.

La fe de una mujer no judía

²¹Jesús se dirigió de allí a la región de Tiro y Sidón. ²²Y una mujer cananea, de aquella región, se le acercó, gritando:

—¡Señor, Hijo de David, ten compasión de mí! ¡Mi hija tiene un demonio que la hace sufrir mucho!

²³Jesús no le contestó nada. Entonces sus discípulos se acercaron a él y le rogaron:

—Dile a esa mujer que se vaya, porque viene gritando detrás de nosotros.

²⁴Jesús dijo:

—Dios me ha enviado solamente a las ovejas perdidas del pueblo de Israel.

²⁵Pero la mujer fue a arrodillarse delante de él, diciendo:

—¡Señor, ayúdame!

²⁶Jesús le contestó:

—No está bien quitarles el pan a los hijos y dárselo a los perros.

²⁷Ella le dijo:

—Sí, Señor; pero hasta los perros comen las migajas que caen de la mesa de sus amos.

28Entonces le dijo Jesús:

—¡Mujer, qué grande es tu fe! Hágase como quieres.

Y desde ese mismo momento su hija quedó sana.

Jesús sana a muchos enfermos

29Jesús salió de allí y llegó a la orilla del Lago de Galilea; luego subió a un cerro y se sentó. 30Mucha gente se reunió donde él estaba. Llevaban cojos, ciegos, mancos, mudos y otros muchos enfermos, que pusieron a los pies de Jesús, y él los sanó. 31De modo que la gente estaba admirada al ver que los mudos hablaban, los mancos quedaban sanos, los cojos andaban y los ciegos podían ver. Y comenzaron a alabar al Dios de Israel.

Jesús da de comer a una multitud

32Jesús llamó a sus discípulos, y les dijo:

—Siento compasión de esta gente, porque ya hace tres días que están aquí conmigo y no tienen nada que comer. No quiero mandarlos sin comer a sus casas, porque pueden desmayarse por el camino.

33Sus discípulos le dijeron:

—Pero ¿cómo podremos encontrar comida para tanta gente, en un lugar como este, donde no vive nadie?

34Jesús les preguntó:

—¿Cuántos panes tienen ustedes?

—Siete, y unos pocos pescaditos —contestaron ellos.

35Entonces mandó que la gente se sentara en el suelo, 36tomó en sus manos los siete panes y los pescados y, habiendo dado gracias a Dios, los partió y los dio a sus discípulos, y ellos los repartieron entre la gente. 37Todos comieron hasta quedar satisfechos, y aun llenaron siete canastas con los pedazos sobrantes. 38Los que comieron eran cuatro mil hombres, sin contar las mujeres y los niños. 39Después Jesús despidió a la gente, subió a la barca y se fue a la región de Magadán.

La señal de Jonás

16 1Los fariseos y los saduceos fueron a ver a Jesús y, para tenderle una trampa, le pidieron que hiciera alguna señal milagrosa que probara que él venía de parte de Dios.

2Pero Jesús les contestó: "Por la tarde dicen ustedes: 'Va a hacer buen tiempo, porque el cielo está rojo'; 3y por la mañana dicen: 'Hoy va a hacer mal tiempo, porque el cielo está rojo y nublado.' Pues si ustedes saben interpretar tan bien el aspecto del cielo, ¿cómo es que no saben interpretar las señales de estos tiempos? 4Esta gente malvada e infiel pide una señal milagrosa; pero no va a dársele más señal que la de Jonás."

Y los dejó, y se fue.

La levadura de los fariseos

5Cuando los discípulos pasaron al otro lado del lago, se olvidaron de llevar pan. 6Entonces Jesús les dijo:

—Miren, cuídense de la levadura de los fariseos y de los saduceos.

7Los discípulos comentaban unos con otros:

—¡No trajimos pan!

8Jesús se dio cuenta, y les dijo:

—¿Por qué dicen que no tienen pan? ¡Qué poca fe tienen ustedes! 9¿Todavía no entienden, ni se acuerdan de los cinco panes que repartí entre cinco mil hombres, y cuántas canastas recogieron? 10¿Ni se acuerdan tampoco de los siete panes que repartí entre cuatro mil, y cuántas canastas recogieron? 11¿Cómo no se dan cuenta ustedes de que yo no estaba hablando del pan? Cuídense de la levadura de los fariseos y de los saduceos.

12Entonces comprendieron que Jesús no les había dicho que se cuidaran de la levadura del pan, sino de la enseñanza de los fariseos y de los saduceos.

Pedro declara
que Jesús es el Mesías

13Cuando Jesús llegó a la región de Cesarea de Filipo, preguntó a sus discípulos:

—¿Quién dice la gente que es el Hijo del hombre?

14Ellos contestaron:

—Algunos dicen que Juan el Bautista; otros dicen que Elías, y otros dicen que Jeremías o algún otro profeta.

15 —Y ustedes, ¿quién dicen que soy? —les preguntó.

16Simón Pedro le respondió:

—Tú eres el Mesías, el Hijo del Dios viviente.

17Entonces Jesús le dijo:

—Dichoso tú, Simón, hijo de Jonás, porque esto no lo conociste por medios humanos, sino porque te lo reveló mi Padre que está en el cielo.

18Y yo te digo que tú eres Pedro, y sobre esta piedra voy a construir mi iglesia; y ni siquiera el poder de la muerte podrá vencerla. 19Te daré las llaves del reino de los cielos; lo que tú ates aquí en la tierra, quedará atado en el cielo, y lo que tú desates aquí en la tierra, también quedará desatado en el cielo.

20Luego Jesús ordenó a sus discípulos que no dijeran a nadie que él era el Mesías.

Jesús anuncia su muerte

21A partir de entonces Jesús comenzó a explicar a sus discípulos que él tendría que ir a Jerusalén, y que los ancianos, los jefes de los sacerdotes y los maestros de la ley lo harían sufrir mucho. Les dijo que lo iban a matar, pero que al tercer día resucitaría. 22Entonces Pedro lo llevó aparte y comenzó a reprenderlo, diciendo:

—¡Dios no lo quiera, Señor! ¡Esto no te puede pasar!

23Pero Jesús se volvió y le dijo a Pedro:

—¡Apártate de mí, Satanás, pues eres un tropiezo para mí! Tú no ves las cosas como las ve Dios, sino como las ven los hombres.

24Luego Jesús dijo a sus discípulos:

—Si alguno quiere ser discípulo mío, olvídese de sí mismo, cargue con su cruz y sígame. 25Porque el que quiera salvar su vida, la perderá; pero el que pierda la vida por causa mía, la encontrará. 26¿De qué le sirve al hombre ganar el mundo entero, si pierde la vida? ¿O cuánto podrá pagar el hombre por su vida? 27Porque el

Hijo del hombre va a venir con la gloria de su Padre y con sus ángeles, y entonces recompensará a cada uno conforme a lo que haya hecho. ²⁸Les aseguro que algunos de los que están aquí presentes no morirán hasta que vean al Hijo del hombre venir a reinar.

La transfiguración de Jesús

17 ¹Seis días después, Jesús tomó a Pedro, a Santiago y a Juan, el hermano de Santiago, y se fue aparte con ellos a un cerro muy alto. ²Allí, delante de ellos, cambió la apariencia de Jesús. Su cara brillaba como el sol, y su ropa se volvió blanca como la luz. ³En esto vieron a Moisés y a Elías conversando con Jesús. ⁴Pedro le dijo a Jesús:

—Señor, ¡qué bien que estemos aquí! Si quieres, haré tres chozas: una para ti, otra para Moisés y otra para Elías.

⁵Mientras Pedro estaba hablando, una nube luminosa se posó sobre ellos, y de la nube salió una voz, que dijo: "Este es mi Hijo amado, a quien he elegido: escúchenlo."

⁶Al oír esto, los discípulos se postraron con la cara en tierra, llenos de miedo. ⁷Jesús se acercó a ellos, los tocó y les dijo:

—Levántense; no tengan miedo.

⁸Y cuando miraron, ya no vieron a nadie, sino a Jesús solo.

⁹Mientras bajaban del cerro, Jesús les ordenó:

—No cuenten a nadie esta visión, hasta que el Hijo del hombre haya resucitado.

¹⁰Los discípulos preguntaron entonces a Jesús:

—¿Por qué dicen los maestros de la ley que Elías ha de venir primero?

¹¹Y Jesús contestó:

—Es cierto que Elías viene primero, y que él lo arreglará todo. ¹²Pero yo les digo que Elías ya vino, y que ellos no lo reconocieron, sino que hicieron con él todo lo que quisieron. Del mismo modo, el Hijo del hombre va a sufrir a manos de ellos.

¹³Entonces los discípulos se dieron cuenta de que Jesús les estaba hablando de Juan el Bautista.

Jesús sana a un muchacho que tenía un demonio

¹⁴Cuando llegaron a donde estaba la gente, se acercó un hombre a Jesús, y arrodillándose delante de él le dijo:

¹⁵—Señor, ten compasión de mi hijo, porque le dan ataques y sufre terriblemente; muchas veces cae en el fuego o en el agua. ¹⁶Aquí se lo traje a tus discípulos, pero no han podido sanarlo.

¹⁷Jesús contestó:

—¡Oh gente sin fe y perversa! ¿Hasta cuándo tendré que estar con ustedes? ¿Hasta cuándo tendré que soportarlos? Traigan acá al muchacho.

¹⁸Entonces Jesús reprendió al demonio y lo hizo salir del muchacho, que quedó sano desde aquel momento.

¹⁹Después los discípulos hablaron aparte con Jesús, y le preguntaron:

—¿Por qué no pudimos nosotros expulsar el demonio?

²⁰Jesús les dijo:

—Porque ustedes tienen muy poca fe. Les aseguro que si tuvieran fe, aunque solo fuera del tamaño de una semilla de mostaza, le dirían a este cerro: 'Quítate de aquí y vete a otro lugar', y el cerro se quitaría. Nada les sería imposible.

Jesús anuncia por segunda vez su muerte

22 Mientras andaban juntos por la región de Galilea, Jesús les dijo:

—El Hijo del hombre va a ser entregado en manos de los hombres, 23 y lo matarán; pero al tercer día resucitará.

Esta noticia los llenó de tristeza.

El pago del impuesto para el templo

24 Cuando Jesús y sus discípulos llegaron a Cafarnaúm, los que cobraban el impuesto para el templo fueron a ver a Pedro, y le preguntaron:

—¿Tu maestro no paga el impuesto para el templo?

25 —Sí, lo paga —contestó Pedro.

Luego, al entrar Pedro en la casa, Jesús le habló primero, diciendo:

—¿Tú qué opinas, Simón? ¿A quiénes cobran impuestos y contribuciones los reyes de este mundo: a sus propios súbditos o a los extranjeros?

26 Pedro le contestó:

—A los extranjeros.

Jesús añadió:

—Así pues, los propios súbditos no tienen que pagar nada. 27 Pero, para no servir de tropiezo a nadie, vete al lago, echa el anzuelo y saca el primer pez que pique. En su boca encontrarás una moneda, que será suficiente para pagar mi impuesto y el tuyo; llévala y págalos.

¿Quién es el más importante?

18 1 En aquella misma ocasión los discípulos se acercaron a Jesús y le preguntaron:

—¿Quién es el más importante en el reino de los cielos?

2 Jesús llamó entonces a un niño, lo puso en medio de ellos 3 y dijo:

—Les aseguro que si ustedes no cambian y se vuelven como niños, no entrarán en el reino de los cielos. 4 El más importante en el reino de los cielos es el que se humilla y se vuelve como este niño. 5 Y el que recibe en mi nombre a un niño como este, me recibe a mí.

El peligro de caer en pecado

6 "A cualquiera que haga caer en pecado a uno de estos pequeños que creen en mí, más le valdría que lo hundieran en lo profundo del mar con una gran piedra de molino atada al cuello. 7 ¡Qué malo es para el mundo que haya tantas incitaciones al pecado! Tiene que haberlas, pero ¡ay del hombre que haga pecar a los demás!

8 "Por eso, si tu mano o tu pie te hacen caer en pecado, córtatelos y échalos lejos de ti; es mejor que entres en la vida manco o cojo, y no que con tus dos manos y tus dos pies seas arrojado al fuego eterno. 9 Y si tu ojo te hace caer en pecado, sácatelo y échalo lejos de ti; es mejor que entres en la vida con un solo ojo, y no que con tus dos ojos seas arrojado al fuego del infierno.

La parábola de la oveja perdida

10 "No desprecien a ninguno de estos pequeños. Pues les digo que en el cielo los ángeles de ellos están mirando siempre el rostro de mi Padre celestial.

12 "¿Qué les parece? Si un hombre tiene cien ovejas y se le extravía una de ellas, ¿acaso no dejará las otras noventa y nueve en el monte, para ir a buscar la oveja extraviada? 13 Y si logra encontrarla, de seguro se alegrará más por esa oveja que por las noventa y nueve que no se extraviaron. 14 Así también, el Padre de ustedes que está en el cielo no quiere que se pierda ninguno de estos pequeños.

Cómo se debe perdonar al hermano

15 "Si tu hermano te hace algo malo, habla con él a solas y hazle reconocer su falta. Si te hace caso, ya has ganado a tu hermano. 16 Si no te hace caso, llama a una o dos personas más, para que toda acusación se base en el testimonio de dos o tres testigos. 17 Si tampoco les hace caso a ellos, díselo a la comunidad; y si tampoco hace caso a la comunidad, entonces habrás de considerarlo como un pagano o como uno de esos que cobran impuestos para Roma.

18 "Les aseguro que lo que ustedes aten aquí en la tierra, también quedará atado en el cielo, y lo que ustedes desaten aquí en la tierra, también quedará desatado en el cielo.

19 "Esto les digo: Si dos de ustedes se ponen de acuerdo aquí en la tierra para pedir algo en oración, mi Padre que está en el cielo se lo dará.

20 Porque donde dos o tres se reúnen en mi nombre, allí estoy yo en medio de ellos."

21 Entonces Pedro fue y preguntó a Jesús:

—Señor, ¿cuántas veces deberé perdonar a mi hermano, si me hace algo malo? ¿Hasta siete?

22 Jesús le contestó:

—No te digo hasta siete veces, sino hasta setenta veces siete.

La parábola del funcionario que no quiso perdonar

23 "Por esto, sucede con el reino de los cielos como con un rey que quiso hacer cuentas con sus funcionarios. 24 Estaba comenzando a hacerlas cuando le presentaron a uno que le debía muchos millones. 25 Como aquel funcionario no tenía con qué pagar, el rey ordenó que lo vendieran como esclavo, junto con su esposa, sus hijos y todo lo que tenía, para que quedara pagada la deuda. 26 El funcionario se arrodilló delante del rey, y le rogó: 'Tenga usted paciencia conmigo y se lo pagaré todo.' 27 Y el rey tuvo compasión de él; así que le perdonó la deuda y lo puso en libertad.

28 "Pero al salir, aquel funcionario se encontró con un compañero suyo que le debía una pequeña cantidad. Lo agarró del cuello y comenzó a estrangularlo, diciéndole: '¡Págame lo que me debes!' 29 El compañero, arrodillándose delante de él, le rogó: 'Ten paciencia conmigo y te lo pagaré todo.' 30 Pero el otro no quiso, sino que lo hizo meter en la cárcel hasta que le pagara la deuda. 31 Esto dolió mucho a los otros

funcionarios, que fueron a contarle al rey todo lo sucedido. ³²Entonces el rey lo mandó llamar, y le dijo: '¡Malvado! Yo te perdoné toda aquella deuda porque me lo rogaste. ³³Pues tú también debiste tener compasión de tu compañero, del mismo modo que yo tuve compasión de ti.' ³⁴Y tanto se enojó el rey, que ordenó castigarlo hasta que pagara todo lo que debía."

³⁵Jesús añadió:

—Así hará también con ustedes mi Padre celestial, si cada uno de ustedes no perdona de corazón a su hermano.

Jesús enseña sobre el divorcio

19 ¹Después de decir estas cosas, Jesús se fue de Galilea y llegó a la región de Judea que está al oriente del Jordán. ²Mucha gente lo siguió, y allí sanó a los enfermos.

³Algunos fariseos se acercaron a Jesús y, para tenderle una trampa, le preguntaron:

—¿Le está permitido a uno divorciarse de su esposa por un motivo cualquiera?

⁴Jesús les contestó:

—¿No han leído ustedes en la Escritura que el que los creó en el principio, 'hombre y mujer los creó'? ⁵Y dijo: 'Por eso, el hombre dejará a su padre y a su madre para unirse a su esposa, y los dos serán como una sola persona.' ⁶Así que ya no son dos, sino uno solo. De modo que el hombre no debe separar lo que Dios ha unido.

⁷Ellos le preguntaron:

—¿Por qué, pues, mandó Moisés darle a la esposa un certificado de divorcio, y despedirla así?

⁸Jesús les dijo:

—Precisamente por lo tercos que son ustedes, Moisés les permitió divorciarse de su esposa; pero al principio no fue de esa manera. ⁹Yo les digo que el que se divorcia de su esposa, a no ser en el caso de una unión ilegal, y se casa con otra, comete adulterio.

¹⁰Le dijeron sus discípulos:

—Si este es el caso del hombre en relación con su esposa, no conviene casarse.

¹¹Jesús les contestó:

—No todos pueden comprender esto, sino únicamente aquellos a quienes Dios les ha dado que lo comprendan. ¹²Hay diferentes razones que impiden a los hombres casarse: unos ya nacen incapacitados para el matrimonio, a otros los incapacitan los hombres, y otros viven como incapacitados por causa del reino de los cielos. El que pueda entender esto, que lo entienda.

Jesús bendice a los niños

¹³Llevaron unos niños a Jesús, para que pusiera sobre ellos las manos y orara por ellos; pero los discípulos comenzaron a reprender a quienes los llevaban. ¹⁴Entonces Jesús dijo:

—Dejen que los niños vengan a mí, y no se lo impidan, porque el reino de los cielos es de quienes son como ellos.

¹⁵Puso las manos sobre los niños, y se fue de aquel lugar.

Un joven rico habla con Jesús

¹⁶Un joven fue a ver a Jesús, y le preguntó:

—Maestro, ¿qué cosa buena debo hacer para tener vida eterna?

17 Jesús le contestó:

—¿Por qué me preguntas acerca de lo que es bueno? Bueno solamente hay uno. Pero si quieres entrar en la vida, obedece los mandamientos.

18 —¿Cuáles? —preguntó el joven.

Y Jesús le dijo:

—'No mates, no cometas adulterio, no robes, no digas mentiras en perjuicio de nadie; 19 honra a tu padre y a tu madre, y ama a tu prójimo como a ti mismo.'

20 —Todo eso ya lo he cumplido —dijo el joven—. ¿Qué más me falta?

21 Jesús le contestó:

—Si quieres ser perfecto, anda, vende lo que tienes y dáselo a los pobres. Así tendrás riqueza en el cielo. Luego ven y sígueme.

22 Cuando el joven oyó esto, se fue triste, porque era muy rico.

23 Jesús dijo entonces a sus discípulos:

—Les aseguro que difícilmente entrará un rico en el reino de los cielos. 24 Les repito que es más fácil para un camello pasar por el ojo de una aguja, que para un rico entrar en el reino de Dios.

25 Al oírlo, sus discípulos se asombraron más aún, y decían:

—Entonces, ¿quién podrá salvarse?

26 Jesús los miró y les contestó:

—Para los hombres esto es imposible, pero para Dios todo es posible.

27 Pedro le dijo entonces:

—Nosotros hemos dejado todo lo que teníamos y te hemos seguido. ¿Qué vamos a recibir?

28 Jesús les respondió:

—Les aseguro que cuando llegue el tiempo en que todo sea renovado, cuando el Hijo del hombre se siente en su trono glorioso, ustedes que me han seguido se sentarán también en doce tronos para juzgar a las doce tribus de Israel. 29 Y todos los que por causa mía hayan dejado casa, o hermanos, o hermanas, o padre, o madre, o hijos, o terrenos, recibirán cien veces más, y también recibirán la vida eterna. 30 Pero muchos que ahora son los primeros, serán los últimos; y muchos que ahora son los últimos, serán los primeros.

La parábola de los trabajadores del viñedo

20 1 "Sucede con el reino de los cielos como con el dueño de una finca, que salió muy de mañana a contratar trabajadores para su viñedo. 2 Se arregló con ellos para pagarles el salario de un día, y los mandó a trabajar a su viñedo. 3 Volvió a salir como a las nueve de la mañana, y vio a otros que estaban en la plaza desocupados. 4 Les dijo: 'Vayan también ustedes a trabajar a mi viñedo, y les daré lo que sea justo.' Y ellos fueron. 5 Después salió de nuevo a eso del mediodía, y otra vez a las tres de la tarde, e hizo lo mismo. 6 Alrededor de las cinco de la tarde volvió a la plaza, y encontró en ella a otros que estaban desocupados. Les preguntó: '¿Por qué están ustedes aquí todo el día sin trabajar?' 7 Le contestaron: 'Porque nadie nos ha contratado.' Entonces les dijo: 'Vayan también ustedes a trabajar a mi viñedo.'

8 "Cuando llegó la noche, el dueño dijo al encargado del trabajo: 'Llama a los trabajadores, y págales comenzando por los últimos que entraron y terminando por los que entraron primero.' 9 Se presentaron, pues, los que habían entrado a trabajar alrededor de las cinco de la tarde, y cada uno recibió el salario completo de un día. 10 Después, cuando les tocó el turno a los que habían entrado primero, pensaron que iban a recibir más; pero cada uno de ellos recibió también el salario de un día. 11 Al cobrarlo, comenzaron a murmurar contra el dueño, 12 diciendo: 'Estos, que llegaron al final, trabajaron solamente una hora, y usted les ha pagado igual que a nosotros, que hemos aguantado el trabajo y el calor de todo el día.' 13 Pero el dueño contestó a uno de ellos: 'Amigo, no te estoy haciendo ninguna injusticia. ¿Acaso no te arreglaste conmigo por el salario de un día? 14 Pues toma tu paga y vete. Si yo quiero darle a este que entró a trabajar al final lo mismo que te doy a ti, 15 es porque tengo el derecho de hacer lo que quiera con mi dinero. ¿O es que te da envidia que yo sea bondadoso?

16 "De modo que los que ahora son los últimos, serán los primeros; y los que ahora son los primeros, serán los últimos."

Jesús anuncia por tercera vez su muerte

17 Jesús, yendo ya de camino a Jerusalén, llamó aparte a sus doce discípulos y les dijo:

18 —Como ustedes ven, ahora vamos a Jerusalén, donde el Hijo del hombre va a ser entregado a los jefes de los sacerdotes y a los maestros de la ley, que lo condenarán a muerte 19 y lo entregarán a los extranjeros para que se burlen de él, lo golpeen y lo crucifiquen; pero al tercer día resucitará.

Jesús responde a la madre de Santiago y Juan

20 La madre de los hijos de Zebedeo, junto con sus hijos, se acercó a Jesús y se arrodilló delante de él para pedirle un favor. 21 Jesús le preguntó:

—¿Qué quieres?

Ella le dijo:

—Manda que en tu reino uno de mis hijos se siente a tu derecha y el otro a tu izquierda.

22 Jesús contestó:

—Ustedes no saben lo que piden. ¿Pueden beber el trago amargo que voy a beber yo?

Ellos dijeron:

—Podemos.

23 Jesús les respondió:

—Ustedes beberán este trago amargo, pero el sentarse a mi derecha o a mi izquierda no me corresponde a mí darlo, sino que se les dará a aquellos para quienes mi Padre lo ha preparado.

24 Cuando los otros diez discípulos oyeron esto, se enojaron con los dos hermanos. 25 Pero Jesús los llamó, y les dijo:

—Como ustedes saben, entre los paganos los jefes gobiernan con tiranía a sus súbditos, y los grandes hacen sentir su autoridad sobre ellos. 26Pero entre ustedes no debe ser así. Al contrario, el que entre ustedes quiera ser grande, deberá servir a los demás; 27y el que entre ustedes quiera ser el primero, deberá ser su esclavo. 28Porque, del mismo modo, el Hijo del hombre no vino para que le sirvan, sino para servir y para dar su vida en rescate por una multitud.

Jesús sana a dos ciegos

29Al salir ellos de Jericó, mucha gente siguió a Jesús. 30Dos ciegos que estaban sentados junto al camino, al oír que Jesús pasaba, gritaron:

—¡Señor, Hijo de David, ten compasión de nosotros!

31La gente los reprendía para que se callaran, pero ellos gritaban más todavía:

—¡Señor, Hijo de David, ten compasión de nosotros!

32Entonces Jesús se detuvo, llamó a los ciegos y les preguntó:

—¿Qué quieren que haga por ustedes?

33Ellos le contestaron:

—Señor, que recobremos la vista.

34Jesús tuvo compasión de ellos, y les tocó los ojos. En el mismo momento los ciegos recobraron la vista, y siguieron a Jesús.

Jesús entra en Jerusalén

21 1Cuando ya estaban cerca de Jerusalén y habían llegado a Betfagé, al Monte de los Olivos, Jesús envió a dos de sus discípulos, 2diciéndoles:

—Vayan a la aldea que está enfrente. Allí encontrarán una burra atada, y un burrito con ella. Desátenla y tráiganmelos. 3Y si alguien les dice algo, díganle que el Señor los necesita y que en seguida los devolverá.

4Esto sucedió para que se cumpliera lo que dijo el profeta, cuando escribió:

5 "Digan a la ciudad de Sión:
  'Mira, tu Rey viene a ti,
   humilde, montado en un burro,
   en un burrito,
     cría de una bestia de carga.'"

6Los discípulos fueron e hicieron lo que Jesús les había mandado. 7Llevaron la burra y su cría, echaron sus capas encima de ellos, y Jesús montó. 8Había mucha gente. Unos tendían sus capas por el camino, y otros tendían ramas que cortaban de los árboles. 9Y tanto los que iban delante como los que iban detrás, gritaban:

—¡Hosana al Hijo del rey David! ¡Bendito el que viene en el nombre del Señor! ¡Hosana en las alturas!

10Cuando Jesús entró en Jerusalén, toda la ciudad se alborotó, y muchos preguntaban:

—¿Quién es este?

11Y la gente contestaba:

—Es el profeta Jesús, el de Nazaret de Galilea.

Jesús purifica el templo

12Jesús entró en el templo y echó de allí a todos los que estaban vendiendo y comprando. Volcó las mesas de los que cambiaban dinero a la gente, y los puestos de los que vendían palomas; 13y les dijo:

—En las Escrituras se dice: 'Mi casa será declarada casa de oración', pero ustedes están haciendo de ella una cueva de ladrones.

¹⁴Se acercaron a Jesús en el templo los ciegos y los cojos, y él los sanó. ¹⁵Pero cuando los jefes de los sacerdotes y los maestros de la ley vieron los milagros que hacía, y oyeron que los niños gritaban en el templo: "¡Hosana al Hijo del rey David!", se enojaron ¹⁶y dijeron a Jesús:

—¿Oyes lo que esos están diciendo?

Jesús les contestó:

—Sí, lo oigo. Pero ¿no han leído ustedes la Escritura que habla de esto? Dice:

'Con los cantos de los pequeños,
de los niñitos de pecho,
has dispuesto tu alabanza.'

¹⁷Entonces los dejó, y se fue de la ciudad a Betania, donde pasó la noche.

Jesús maldice la higuera sin fruto

¹⁸Por la mañana, cuando volvía a la ciudad, Jesús sintió hambre. ¹⁹Vio una higuera junto al camino y se acercó a ella, pero no encontró más que hojas. Entonces le dijo a la higuera:

—¡Nunca más vuelvas a dar fruto!

Y al instante la higuera se secó. ²⁰Al ver lo ocurrido, los discípulos se maravillaron y preguntaron a Jesús:

—¿Cómo es que la higuera se secó al instante?

²¹Jesús les contestó:

—Les aseguro que si tienen fe y no dudan, no solamente podrán hacer esto que le hice a la higuera, sino que aun si a este cerro le dicen: 'Quítate de ahí y arrójate al mar', así sucederá. ²²Y todo lo que ustedes, al orar, pidan con fe, lo recibirán.

La autoridad de Jesús

²³Después de esto, Jesús entró en el templo. Mientras estaba allí, enseñando, se le acercaron los jefes de los sacerdotes y los ancianos de los judíos, y le preguntaron:

—¿Con qué autoridad haces esto? ¿Quién te dio esta autoridad?

²⁴⁻²⁵Jesús les dijo:

—Yo también les voy a hacer una pregunta: ¿Quién envió a Juan a bautizar, Dios o los hombres? Si ustedes me responden, yo les diré con qué autoridad hago esto.

Comenzaron a discutir unos con otros: "Si respondemos que Dios lo envió, nos dirá: 'Entonces, ¿por qué no le creyeron?' ²⁶Y no podemos decir que fueron los hombres, porque tenemos miedo de la gente, ya que todos creen que Juan era un profeta." ²⁷Así que respondieron a Jesús:

—No lo sabemos.

Entonces él les contestó:

—Pues yo tampoco les digo con qué autoridad hago esto.

La parábola de los dos hijos

²⁸Jesús les preguntó:

—¿Qué opinan ustedes de esto? Un hombre tenía dos hijos, y le dijo a uno de ellos: 'Hijo, ve hoy a trabajar a mi viñedo.' ²⁹El hijo le contestó: '¡No quiero ir!' Pero después cambió de parecer, y fue. ³⁰Luego el padre se dirigió al otro, y le dijo lo mismo. Este contestó: 'Sí, señor, yo iré.' Pero no fue. ³¹¿Cuál de los dos hizo lo que su padre quería?

—El primero —contestaron ellos.

Y Jesús les dijo:

—Les aseguro que los que cobran impuestos para Roma, y las prostitutas, entrarán antes que ustedes en el reino de los cielos. ³²Porque Juan el Bautista vino a enseñarles el camino de la justicia, y ustedes no le creyeron; en cambio, esos cobradores de impuestos y esas prostitutas sí le creyeron. Pero ustedes, aunque vieron todo esto, no cambiaron de actitud para creerle.

La parábola de los labradores malvados

³³"Escuchen otra parábola: El dueño de una finca plantó un viñedo y le puso un cerco; preparó un lugar donde hacer el vino y levantó una torre para vigilarlo todo. Luego alquiló el terreno a unos labradores y se fue de viaje. ³⁴Cuando llegó el tiempo de la cosecha, mandó unos criados a pedir a los labradores la parte que le correspondía. ³⁵Pero los labradores echaron mano a los criados: golpearon a uno, mataron a otro y apedrearon a otro. ³⁶El dueño volvió a mandar más criados que al principio; pero los labradores los trataron a todos de la misma manera.

³⁷"Por fin mandó a su propio hijo, pensando: 'Sin duda, respetarán a mi hijo.' ³⁸Pero cuando vieron al hijo, los labradores se dijeron unos a otros: 'Este es el que ha de recibir la herencia; matémoslo y nos quedaremos con su propiedad.' ³⁹Así que lo agarraron, lo sacaron del viñedo y lo mataron.

⁴⁰"Y ahora, cuando venga el dueño del viñedo, ¿qué creen ustedes que hará con esos labradores?"

⁴¹Le contestaron:

—Matará sin compasión a esos malvados, y alquilará el viñedo a otros labradores que le entreguen a su debido tiempo la parte de la cosecha que le corresponde.

⁴²Jesús entonces les dijo:

—¿Nunca han leído ustedes las Escrituras? Dicen:

'La piedra
que los constructores despreciaron
se ha convertido
   en la piedra principal.
Esto lo hizo el Señor,
y estamos maravillados.'

⁴³Por eso les digo que a ustedes se les quitará el reino, y que se le dará a un pueblo que produzca la debida cosecha. ⁴⁴En cuanto a la piedra, cualquiera que caiga sobre ella quedará hecho pedazos; y si la piedra cae sobre alguien, lo hará polvo.

⁴⁵Los jefes de los sacerdotes y los fariseos, al oír las parábolas que Jesús contaba, se dieron cuenta de que hablaba de ellos. ⁴⁶Quisieron entonces arrestarlo, pero tenían miedo, porque la gente creía que Jesús era un profeta.

La parábola del banquete de bodas

22 ¹Jesús comenzó a hablarles otra vez por medio de parábolas. Les dijo:

²"Sucede con el reino de los cielos como con un rey que hizo un banquete para la boda de su hijo. ³Mandó a sus criados que fueran a llamar a los invitados, pero estos no quisieron asistir. ⁴Volvió a mandar

otros criados, encargándoles: 'Digan a los invitados que ya tengo preparada la comida. Mandé matar mis reses y animales engordados, y todo está listo; que vengan al banquete.' [5]Pero los invitados no hicieron caso. Uno de ellos se fue a sus terrenos, otro se fue a sus negocios, [6]y los otros agarraron a los criados del rey y los maltrataron hasta matarlos. [7]Entonces el rey se enojó mucho, y ordenó a sus soldados que mataran a aquellos asesinos y quemaran su pueblo. [8]Luego dijo a sus criados: 'El banquete está listo, pero aquellos invitados no merecían venir. [9]Vayan, pues, ustedes a las calles principales, e inviten al banquete a todos los que encuentren.' [10]Los criados salieron a las calles y reunieron a todos los que encontraron, malos y buenos; y así la sala se llenó de gente.

[11] "Cuando el rey entró a ver a los invitados, se fijó en un hombre que no iba vestido con traje de boda. [12]Le dijo: 'Amigo, ¿cómo has entrado aquí, si no traes traje de boda?' Pero el otro se quedó callado. [13]Entonces el rey dijo a los que atendían las mesas: 'Átenlo de pies y manos y échenlo a la oscuridad de afuera. Entonces vendrán el llanto y la desesperación.' [14]Porque muchos son llamados, pero pocos escogidos."

La pregunta sobre los impuestos

[15]Después de esto, los fariseos fueron y se pusieron de acuerdo para hacerle decir a Jesús algo que les diera motivo para acusarlo. [16]Así que mandaron a algunos de sus partidarios, junto con otros del partido de Herodes, a decirle:

—Maestro, sabemos que tú dices la verdad, y que enseñas de veras el camino de Dios, sin dejarte llevar por lo que diga la gente, porque no hablas para darles gusto. [17]Danos, pues, tu opinión: ¿Está bien que paguemos impuestos al emperador romano, o no?

[18]Jesús, dándose cuenta de la mala intención que llevaban, les dijo:

—Hipócritas, ¿por qué me tienden trampas? [19]Enséñenme la moneda con que se paga el impuesto.

Le trajeron un denario, [20]y Jesús les preguntó:

—¿De quién es esta cara y el nombre que aquí está escrito?

[21]Le contestaron:

—Del emperador.

Jesús les dijo entonces:

—Pues den al emperador lo que es del emperador, y a Dios lo que es de Dios.

[22]Cuando oyeron esto, se quedaron admirados; y dejándolo, se fueron.

La pregunta sobre la resurrección

[23]Aquel mismo día, algunos saduceos fueron a ver a Jesús. Alegaban que no hay resurrección de los muertos, así que le presentaron este caso:

[24] —Maestro, Moisés dijo que si alguien muere sin dejar hijos, su hermano deberá tomar por esposa a la viuda, para darle hijos al hermano que murió. [25]Pues bien, aquí, entre nosotros, había una vez siete hermanos. El primero se casó, y murió. Como no tuvo hijos, dejó su viuda al segundo hermano. [26]Lo mismo le pasó al segundo, y después al tercero, y así hasta el séptimo

hermano. 27 Después de todos murió también la mujer. 28 Pues bien, en la resurrección, ¿de cuál de los siete hermanos será esposa esta mujer, si todos estuvieron casados con ella?

29 Jesús les contestó:

—¡Qué equivocados están, por no conocer las Escrituras ni el poder de Dios! 30 Cuando los muertos resuciten, los hombres y las mujeres no se casarán, pues serán como los ángeles que están en el cielo. 31 Y en cuanto a que los muertos resucitan, ¿no han leído ustedes que Dios mismo dijo: 32 'Yo soy el Dios de Abraham, de Isaac y de Jacob'? ¡Y él no es Dios de muertos, sino de vivos!

33 Al oír esto, la gente se quedó admirada de las enseñanzas de Jesús.

El mandamiento más importante

34 Los fariseos se reunieron al saber que Jesús había hecho callar a los saduceos, 35 y uno, que era maestro de la ley, para tenderle una trampa, le preguntó:

36 —Maestro, ¿cuál es el mandamiento más importante de la ley?

37 Jesús le dijo:

—'Ama al Señor tu Dios con todo tu corazón, con toda tu alma y con toda tu mente.' 38 Este es el más importante y el primero de los mandamientos. 39 Pero hay un segundo, parecido a este; dice: 'Ama a tu prójimo como a ti mismo.' 40 En estos dos mandamientos se basan toda la ley y los profetas.

¿De quién desciende el Mesías?

41 Mientras los fariseos todavía estaban reunidos, 42 Jesús les preguntó:

—¿Qué piensan ustedes del Mesías? ¿De quién desciende?

Le contestaron:

—Desciende de David.

43 Entonces les dijo Jesús:

—¿Pues cómo es que David, inspirado por el Espíritu, lo llama Señor? Porque David dijo:

44 'El Señor dijo a mi Señor:
Siéntate a mi derecha,
hasta que yo ponga a tus enemigos
debajo de tus pies.'

45 ¿Cómo puede el Mesías descender de David, si David mismo lo llama Señor?

46 Nadie pudo responderle ni una sola palabra, y desde ese día ninguno se atrevió a hacerle más preguntas.

Jesús denuncia a los fariseos y a los maestros de la ley

23 1 Después de esto, Jesús dijo a la gente y a sus discípulos: 2 "Los maestros de la ley y los fariseos enseñan con la autoridad que viene de Moisés. 3 Por lo tanto, obedézcanlos ustedes y hagan todo lo que les digan; pero no sigan su ejemplo, porque ellos dicen una cosa y hacen otra. 4 Atan cargas tan pesadas que es imposible soportarlas, y las echan sobre los hombros de los demás, mientras que ellos mismos no quieren tocarlas ni siquiera con un dedo. 5 Todo lo hacen para que la gente los vea. Les gusta llevar en la frente y en los brazos porciones de las Escrituras escritas en anchas tiras, y ponerse ropas con grandes borlas. 6 Quieren tener los mejores lugares en las comidas y los asientos de honor en las sinagogas,

7y desean que la gente los salude con todo respeto en la calle y que los llame maestros.

8"Pero ustedes no deben pretender que la gente los llame maestros, porque todos ustedes son hermanos y tienen solamente un Maestro. 9Y no llamen ustedes padre a nadie en la tierra, porque tienen solamente un Padre: el que está en el cielo. 10Ni deben pretender que los llamen guías, porque Cristo es su único Guía. 11El más grande entre ustedes debe servir a los demás. 12Porque el que a sí mismo se engrandece, será humillado; y el que se humilla, será engrandecido.

13"¡Ay de ustedes, maestros de la ley y fariseos, hipócritas!, que cierran la puerta del reino de los cielos para que otros no entren. Y ni ustedes mismos entran, ni dejan entrar a los que quieren hacerlo.

15"¡Ay de ustedes, maestros de la ley y fariseos, hipócritas!, que recorren tierra y mar para ganar un adepto, y cuando lo han logrado, hacen de él una persona dos veces más merecedora del infierno que ustedes mismos.

16"¡Ay de ustedes, guías ciegos!, que dicen: 'Quien hace una promesa jurando por el templo, no se compromete a nada; pero si jura por el oro del templo, entonces sí queda comprometido.' 17¡Tontos y ciegos! ¿Qué es más importante: el oro, o el templo por cuya causa el oro queda consagrado? 18También dicen ustedes: 'Quien hace una promesa jurando por el altar, no se compromete a nada; pero si jura por la ofrenda que está sobre el altar, entonces sí queda comprometido.' 19¡Ciegos! ¿Qué es más importante: la ofrenda, o el altar por cuya causa la ofrenda queda consagrada? 20El que jura por el altar, no está jurando solamente por el altar, sino también por todo lo que hay encima; 21y el que jura por el templo, no está jurando solamente por el templo, sino también por Dios, que vive allí. 22Y el que jura por el cielo, está jurando por el trono de Dios, y a la vez por Dios, que se sienta en él.

23"¡Ay de ustedes, maestros de la ley y fariseos, hipócritas!, que separan para Dios la décima parte de la menta, del anís y del comino, pero no hacen caso de las enseñanzas más importantes de la ley, que son la justicia, la misericordia y la fidelidad. Esto es lo que deben hacer, sin dejar de hacer lo otro. 24¡Ustedes, guías ciegos, cuelan el mosquito, pero se tragan el camello!

25"¡Ay de ustedes, maestros de la ley y fariseos, hipócritas!, que limpian por fuera el vaso y el plato, pero no les importa llenarlos con el robo y la avaricia. 26¡Fariseo ciego: primero limpia por dentro el vaso, y así quedará limpio también por fuera!

27"¡Ay de ustedes, maestros de la ley y fariseos, hipócritas!, que son como sepulcros blanqueados, bien arreglados por fuera, pero llenos por dentro de huesos de muertos y de toda clase de impureza. 28Así son ustedes: por fuera aparentan ser gente honrada, pero por dentro están llenos de hipocresía y de maldad.

29"¡Ay de ustedes, maestros de la ley y fariseos, hipócritas!, qué construyen los sepulcros de los profetas y adornan los monumentos de los justos, 30y luego dicen: 'Si nosotros hubiéramos vivido en tiempos de nuestros antepasados, no habríamos tomado parte en la muerte de los profetas.' 31Ya con esto, ustedes mismos reconocen que son descendientes de los que mataron a los profetas. 32¡Terminen de hacer, pues, lo que sus antepasados comenzaron!

33"¡Serpientes! ¡Raza de víboras! ¿Cómo van a escapar del castigo del infierno? 34Por eso yo les voy a enviar profetas, sabios y maestros. Pero ustedes matarán y crucificarán a algunos de ellos, y a otros los golpearán en las sinagogas y los perseguirán de pueblo en pueblo. 35Así que sobre ustedes caerá el castigo por toda la sangre inocente que ha sido derramada desde Abel el justo hasta Zacarías, hijo de Berequías, a quien ustedes mataron entre el santuario y el altar. 36Les aseguro que el castigo por todo esto caerá sobre la gente de hoy.

Jesús llora por Jerusalén

37"¡Jerusalén, Jerusalén, que matas a los profetas y apedreas a los mensajeros que Dios te envía! ¡Cuántas veces quise juntar a tus hijos, como la gallina junta sus pollitos bajo las alas, pero no quisiste! 38Pues miren, el hogar de ustedes va a quedar abandonado! 39y les digo que, a partir de este momento, no volverán a verme hasta que digan: ¡Bendito el que viene en el nombre del Señor!'"

Jesús anuncia que el templo será destruido

24 1Jesús salió del templo, y ya se iba, cuando sus discípulos se acercaron y comenzaron a atraer su atención a los edificios del templo. 2Jesús les dijo:

—¿Ven ustedes todo esto? Pues les aseguro que aquí no va a quedar ni una piedra sobre otra. Todo será destruido.

Señales antes del fin

3Luego se fueron al Monte de los Olivos. Jesús se sentó, y los discípulos se le acercaron para preguntarle aparte:

—Queremos que nos digas cuándo va a ocurrir esto. ¿Cuál será la señal de tu regreso y del fin del mundo?

4Jesús les contestó:

—Tengan cuidado de que nadie los engañe. 5Porque vendrán muchos haciéndose pasar por mí. Dirán: 'Yo soy el Mesías', y engañarán a mucha gente. 6Ustedes tendrán noticias de que hay guerras aquí y allá; pero no se asusten, pues así tiene que ocurrir; sin embargo, aún no será el fin. 7Porque una nación peleará contra otra y un país hará guerra contra otro; y habrá hambres y terremotos en muchos lugares. 8Pero todo eso apenas será el comienzo de los dolores.

9"Entonces los entregarán a ustedes para que los maltraten; y los matarán, y todo el mundo los odiará por causa mía. 10En aquel tiempo muchos renegarán de su fe, y se odiarán y se traicionarán unos a otros. [11] Aparecerán muchos falsos profetas, y engañarán a mucha gente. [12] Habrá tanta maldad, que la mayoría dejará de tener amor hacia los demás. [13] Pero el que siga firme hasta el fin, se salvará. [14] Y esta buena noticia del reino será anunciada en todo el mundo, para que todas las naciones la conozcan; entonces vendrá el fin.

[15] "El profeta Daniel escribió acerca del horrible sacrilegio. Cuando ustedes lo vean en el Lugar Santo —el que lee, entienda,— [16] entonces los que estén en Judea, que huyan a las montañas; [17] y el que esté en la azotea de su casa, que no baje a sacar nada; [18] y el que esté en el campo, que no regrese ni aun a recoger su ropa. [19] ¡Pobres mujeres aquellas que en tales días estén embarazadas o tengan niños de pecho! [20] Pidan ustedes a Dios que no hayan de huir en el invierno ni en sábado; [21] porque habrá entonces un sufrimiento tan grande como nunca lo ha habido desde el comienzo del mundo ni lo habrá después. [22] Y si Dios no acortara ese tiempo, no se salvaría nadie; pero lo acortará por amor a los que ha escogido.

[23] "Si entonces alguien les dice a ustedes: 'Miren, aquí está el Mesías', o 'Miren, allí está', no lo crean. [24] Porque vendrán falsos mesías y falsos profetas; y harán grandes señales y milagros, para engañar, a ser posible, hasta a los que Dios mismo ha escogido. [25] Ya se lo he advertido a ustedes de antemano. [26] Por eso, si les dicen: 'Miren, allí está, en el desierto', no vayan; o si les dicen: 'Miren, aquí está escondido', no lo crean. [27] Porque como un relámpago que se ve brillar de oriente a occidente, así será cuando regrese el Hijo del hombre. [28] Donde esté el cadáver, allí se juntarán los buitres.

El regreso del Hijo del hombre

[29] "Tan pronto como pasen aquellos días de sufrimiento, el sol se oscurecerá, la luna dejará de dar su luz, las estrellas caerán del cielo y las fuerzas celestiales temblarán. [30] Entonces se verá en el cielo la señal del Hijo del hombre, y llenos de terror todos los pueblos del mundo llorarán, y verán al Hijo del hombre que viene en las nubes del cielo con gran poder y gloria. [31] Y él mandará a sus ángeles con una gran trompeta, para que reúnan a sus escogidos de los cuatro puntos cardinales, desde un extremo del cielo hasta el otro.

[32] "Aprendan esta enseñanza de la higuera: Cuando sus ramas se ponen tiernas, y brotan sus hojas, se dan cuenta ustedes de que ya el verano está cerca. [33] De la misma manera, cuando vean todo esto, sepan que el Hijo del hombre ya está a la puerta. [34] Les aseguro que todo esto sucederá antes que muera la gente de este tiempo. [35] El cielo y la tierra dejarán de existir, pero mis palabras no dejarán de cumplirse.

[36] "En cuanto al día y la hora, nadie lo sabe, ni aun los ángeles del cielo, ni el Hijo. Solamente lo sabe el Padre.

[37] "Como sucedió en tiempos de Noé, así sucederá también cuando

regrese el Hijo del hombre. **38**En aquellos tiempos antes del diluvio, y hasta el día en que Noé entró en el arca, la gente comía y bebía y se casaba. **39**Pero cuando menos lo esperaban, vino el diluvio y se los llevó a todos. Así sucederá también cuando regrese el Hijo del hombre. **40**En aquel momento, de dos hombres que estén en el campo, uno será llevado y el otro será dejado. **41**De dos mujeres que estén moliendo, una será llevada y la otra será dejada.

42"Manténganse ustedes despiertos, porque no saben qué día va a venir su Señor. **43**Pero sepan esto, que si el dueño de una casa supiera a qué hora de la noche va a llegar el ladrón, se mantendría despierto y no dejaría que nadie se metiera en su casa a robar. **44**Por eso, ustedes también estén preparados; porque el Hijo del hombre vendrá cuando menos lo esperen.

El criado fiel y el criado infiel

45"¿Quién es el criado fiel y atento, a quien su amo deja encargado de los de su casa, para darles de comer a su debido tiempo? **46**Dichoso el criado a quien su amo, cuando llega, lo encuentra cumpliendo con deber. **47**Les aseguro que el amo lo pondrá como encargado de todos sus bienes. **48**Pero si ese criado es un malvado, y pensando que su amo va a tardar **49**comienza a maltratar a los otros criados, y se junta con borrachos a comer y beber, **50**el día que menos lo espere y a una hora que no lo sabe, llegará su amo **51**y lo castigará, condenándolo a correr la misma suerte

que los hipócritas. Entonces vendrán el llanto y la desesperación.

La parábola de las diez muchachas

25 **1**"Sucederá entonces con el reino de los cielos como lo que sucedió en una boda: diez muchachas tomaron sus lámparas de aceite y salieron a recibir al novio. **2**Cinco de ellas eran despreocupadas y cinco previsoras. **3**Las despreocupadas llevaron sus lámparas, pero no llenaron aceite para llenarlas de nuevo; **4**en cambio, las previsoras llevaron sus botellas de aceite, además de sus lámparas. **5**Como el novio tardaba en llegar, les dio sueño a todas, y por fin se durmieron. **6**Cerca de la medianoche, se oyó gritar: '¡Ya viene el novio! ¡Salgan a recibirlo!' **7**Todas las muchachas se levantaron y comenzaron a preparar sus lámparas. **8**Entonces las cinco despreocupadas dijeron a las cinco previsoras: 'Dennos un poco de su aceite, porque nuestras lámparas se están apagando.' **9**Pero las muchachas previsoras contestaron: 'No, porque así no alcanzará ni para nosotras ni para ustedes. Más vale que vayan a donde lo venden, y compren para ustedes mismas.' **10**Pero mientras aquellas cinco muchachas fueron a comprar aceite, llegó el novio, y las que habían sido previsoras entraron con él en la boda, y se cerró la puerta. **11**Después llegaron las otras muchachas, diciendo: '¡Señor, señor, ábrenos!' **12**Pero él les contestó: 'Les aseguro que no las conozco.'

13 "Manténganse ustedes despiertos —añadió Jesús—, porque no saben ni el día ni la hora.

La parábola del dinero

14 "Sucederá también con el reino de los cielos como con un hombre que, estando a punto de irse a otro país, llamó a sus empleados y les encargó que le cuidaran su dinero. 15 A uno de ellos le entregó cinco mil monedas, a otro dos mil y a otro mil: a cada uno según su capacidad. Entonces se fue de viaje. 16 El empleado que recibió las cinco mil monedas hizo negocio con el dinero y ganó otras cinco mil monedas. 17 Del mismo modo, el que recibió dos mil ganó otras dos mil. 18 Pero el que recibió mil fue y escondió el dinero de su jefe en un hoyo que hizo en la tierra.

19 "Mucho tiempo después volvió el jefe de aquellos empleados, y se puso a hacer cuentas con ellos. 20 Primero llegó el que había recibido las cinco mil monedas, y entregó a su jefe otras cinco mil, diciéndole: 'Señor, usted me dio cinco mil, y aquí tiene otras cinco mil que gané.' 21 El jefe le dijo: 'Muy bien, eres un empleado bueno y fiel; ya que fuiste fiel en lo poco, te pondré a cargo de mucho más. Entra y alégrate conmigo.' 22 Después llegó el empleado que había recibido las dos mil monedas, y dijo: 'Señor, usted me dio dos mil, y aquí tiene otras dos mil que gané.' 23 El jefe le dijo: 'Muy bien, eres un empleado bueno y fiel; ya que fuiste fiel en lo poco, te pondré a cargo de mucho más. Entra y alégrate conmigo.'

24 "Pero cuando llegó el empleado que había recibido las mil monedas, le dijo a su jefe: 'Señor, yo sabía que usted es un hombre duro, que cosecha donde no sembró y recoge donde no esparció. 25 Por eso tuve miedo, y fui y escondí su dinero en la tierra. Pero aquí tiene lo que es suyo.' 26 El jefe le contestó: 'Tú eres un empleado malo y perezoso, pues si sabías que yo cosecho donde no sembré y que recojo donde no esparcí, 27 deberías haber llevado mi dinero al banco, y yo, al volver, habría recibido mi dinero más los intereses.' 28 Y dijo a los que estaban allí: 'Quítenle las mil monedas, y dénselas al que tiene diez mil. 29 Porque al que tiene, se le dará más, y tendrá de sobra; pero al que no tiene, hasta lo poco que tiene se le quitará. 30 Y a este empleado inútil, échenlo fuera, a la oscuridad. Entonces vendrán el llanto y la desesperación.'

El juicio de las naciones

31 "Cuando el Hijo del hombre venga, rodeado de esplendor y de todos sus ángeles, se sentará en su trono glorioso. 32 La gente de todas las naciones se reunirá delante de él, y él separará unos de otros, como el pastor separa las ovejas de las cabras. 33 Pondrá las ovejas a su derecha y las cabras a su izquierda. 34 Y dirá el Rey a los que estén a su derecha: 'Vengan ustedes, los que han sido bendecidos por mi Padre; reciban el reino que está preparado para ustedes desde que Dios hizo el mundo. 35 Pues tuve hambre, y ustedes me dieron de comer; tuve sed, y me dieron de beber; anduve como forastero, y me dieron

alojamiento. ³⁶Estuve sin ropa, y ustedes me la dieron; estuve enfermo, y me visitaron; estuve en la cárcel, y vinieron a verme.' ³⁷Entonces los justos preguntarán: 'Señor, ¿cuándo te vimos con hambre, y te dimos de comer? ¿O cuándo te vimos con sed, y te dimos de beber? ³⁸¿O cuándo te vimos como forastero, y te dimos alojamiento, o sin ropa, y te la dimos? ³⁹¿O cuándo te vimos enfermo o en la cárcel, y fuimos a verte?' ⁴⁰El Rey les contestará: 'Les aseguro que todo lo que hicieron por uno de estos hermanos míos más humildes, por mí mismo lo hicieron.'

⁴¹"Luego el Rey dirá a los que estén a su izquierda: 'Apártense de mí, los que merecieron la condenación; váyanse al fuego eterno preparado para el diablo y sus ángeles. ⁴²Pues tuve hambre, y ustedes no me dieron de comer; tuve sed, y no me dieron de beber; ⁴³anduve como forastero, y no me dieron alojamiento; sin ropa, y no me la dieron; estuve enfermo, y en la cárcel, y no vinieron a visitarme.' ⁴⁴Entonces ellos le preguntarán: 'Señor, ¿cuándo te vimos con hambre o con sed, o como forastero, o falto de ropa, o enfermo, o en la cárcel, y no te ayudamos?' ⁴⁵El Rey les contestará: 'Les aseguro que todo lo que no hicieron por una de estas personas más humildes, tampoco por mí lo hicieron.' ⁴⁶Esos irán al castigo eterno, y los justos a la vida eterna."

Conspiración para arrestar a Jesús

26 ¹Cuando Jesús terminó toda su enseñanza, dijo a sus discípulos:

² —Como ustedes saben, dentro de dos días es la fiesta de la Pascua, y el Hijo del hombre será entregado para que lo crucifiquen.

³Por aquel tiempo, los jefes de los sacerdotes y los ancianos de los judíos se reunieron en el palacio de Caifás, el sumo sacerdote, ⁴e hicieron planes para arrestar a Jesús mediante algún engaño, y matarlo. ⁵Pero decían:

—No durante la fiesta, para que no se alborote la gente.

Una mujer derrama perfume sobre Jesús

⁶Jesús estaba en Betania, en casa de Simón, al que llamaban el leproso; ⁷en esto se le acercó una mujer que llevaba un frasco de alabastro lleno de un perfume muy caro. Mientras Jesús estaba a la mesa, ella le derramó el perfume sobre la cabeza. ⁸Los discípulos, al verlo, se enojaron y comenzaron a decir:

—¿Por qué se desperdicia esto? ⁹Pudo haberse vendido por mucho dinero, para ayudar a los pobres.

¹⁰Jesús lo oyó, y les dijo:

—¿Por qué molestan a esta mujer? Ha hecho una obra buena conmigo. ¹¹Pues a los pobres los tendrán siempre entre ustedes; pero a mí no siempre me van a tener. ¹²Lo que ha hecho esta mujer, al derramar el perfume sobre mi cuerpo, es prepararme para mi entierro. ¹³Les aseguro que en cualquier lugar del mundo donde se anuncie esta buena noticia, se hablará también de lo que hizo esta mujer, y así será recordada.

Judas traiciona a Jesús

¹⁴Uno de los doce discípulos, el que se llamaba Judas Iscariote, fue a ver a los jefes de los sacerdotes ¹⁵y les dijo:

—¿Cuánto me quieren dar, y yo les entrego a Jesús?

Ellos le pagaron treinta monedas de plata. ¹⁶Y desde entonces Judas anduvo buscando el momento más oportuno para entregarles a Jesús.

La Cena del Señor

¹⁷El primer día de la fiesta en que se comía el pan sin levadura, los discípulos se acercaron a Jesús y le preguntaron:

—¿Dónde quieres que te preparemos la cena de Pascua?

¹⁸Él les contestó:

—Vayan a la ciudad, a casa de Fulano, y díganle: 'El Maestro dice: Mi hora está cerca, y voy a tu casa a celebrar la Pascua con mis discípulos.'

¹⁹Los discípulos hicieron como Jesús les había mandado, y prepararon la cena de Pascua.

²⁰Cuando llegó la noche, Jesús estaba a la mesa con los doce discípulos; ²¹y mientras comían, les dijo:

—Les aseguro que uno de ustedes me va a traicionar.

²²Ellos se pusieron muy tristes, y comenzaron a preguntarle uno tras otro:

—Señor, ¿acaso seré yo?

²³Jesús les contestó:

—Uno que moja el pan en el mismo plato que yo, va a traicionarme. ²⁴El Hijo del hombre ha de recorrer el camino que dicen las Escrituras; pero ¡ay de aquel que lo traiciona! Hubiera sido mejor para él no haber nacido.

²⁵Entonces Judas, el que lo estaba traicionando, le preguntó:

—Maestro, ¿acaso seré yo?

—Tú lo has dicho —contestó Jesús.

²⁶Mientras comían, Jesús tomó en sus manos el pan y, habiendo dado gracias a Dios, lo partió y se lo dio a los discípulos, diciendo:

—Tomen y coman, esto es mi cuerpo.

²⁷Luego tomó en sus manos una copa y, habiendo dado gracias a Dios, se la pasó a ellos, diciendo:

—Beban todos ustedes de esta copa, ²⁸porque esto es mi sangre, con la que se confirma la alianza, sangre que es derramada en favor de muchos para perdón de sus pecados. ²⁹Pero les digo que no volveré a beber de este producto de la vid, hasta el día en que beba con ustedes el vino nuevo en el reino de mi Padre.

Jesús anuncia
que Pedro lo negará

³⁰Después de cantar los salmos, se fueron al Monte de los Olivos. ³¹Y Jesús les dijo:

—Todos ustedes van a perder su fe en mí esta noche. Así lo dicen las Escrituras: 'Mataré al pastor, y las ovejas se dispersarán.' ³²Pero cuando yo resucite, los volveré a reunir en Galilea.

³³Pedro le contestó:

—Aunque todos pierdan su fe en ti, yo no la perderé.

34 Jesús le dijo:

—Te aseguro que esta misma noche, antes que cante el gallo, me negarás tres veces.

35 Pedro afirmó:

—Aunque tenga que morir contigo, no te negaré.

Y todos los discípulos decían lo mismo.

Jesús ora en Getsemaní

36 Luego fue Jesús con sus discípulos a un lugar llamado Getsemaní, y les dijo:

—Siéntense aquí, mientras yo voy allí a orar.

37 Y se llevó a Pedro y a los dos hijos de Zebedeo, y comenzó a sentirse muy triste y angustiado. 38 Les dijo:

—Siento en mi alma una tristeza de muerte. Quédense ustedes aquí, y permanezcan despiertos conmigo.

39 En seguida se fue un poco más adelante, se inclinó hasta tocar el suelo con la frente, y oró diciendo: "Padre mío, si es posible, líbrame de este trago amargo; pero que no se haga lo que yo quiero, sino lo que quieres tú."

40 Luego volvió a donde estaban los discípulos, y los encontró dormidos. Le dijo a Pedro:

—¿Ni siquiera una hora pudieron ustedes mantenerse despiertos conmigo? 41 Manténganse despiertos y oren, para que no caigan en tentación. Ustedes tienen buena voluntad, pero son débiles.

42 Por segunda vez se fue, y oró así: "Padre mío, si no es posible evitar que yo sufra esta prueba, hágase tu voluntad."

43 Cuando volvió, encontró otra vez dormidos a los discípulos, porque sus ojos se les cerraban de sueño. 44 Los dejó y se fue a orar por tercera vez, repitiendo las mismas palabras. 45 Entonces regresó a donde estaban los discípulos, y les dijo:

—¿Siguen ustedes durmiendo y descansando? Ha llegado la hora en que el Hijo del hombre va a ser entregado en manos de los pecadores. 46 Levántense, vámonos; ya se acerca el que me traiciona.

Arrestan a Jesús

47 Todavía estaba hablando Jesús, cuando Judas, uno de los doce discípulos, llegó acompañado de mucha gente armada con espadas y con palos. Iban de parte de los jefes de los sacerdotes y de los ancianos del pueblo. 48 Judas, el traidor, les había dado una contraseña, diciendo: "Al que yo bese, ese es; arréstenlo." 49 Así que, acercándose a Jesús, dijo:

—¡Buenas noches, Maestro!

Y lo besó. 50 Jesús le contestó:

—Amigo, adelante con tus planes.

Entonces los otros se acercaron, echaron mano a Jesús y lo arrestaron.

51 En eso, uno de los que estaban con Jesús sacó su espada y le cortó una oreja al criado del sumo sacerdote. 52 Jesús le dijo:

—Guarda tu espada en su lugar. Porque todos los que pelean con la espada, también a espada morirán. 53 ¿No sabes que yo podría rogarle a mi Padre, y él me mandaría ahora mismo más de doce ejércitos de ángeles? 54 Pero en ese caso, ¿cómo se cumplirían las Escrituras, que dicen que debe suceder así?

55En seguida Jesús preguntó a la gente:

—¿Por qué han venido ustedes con espadas y con palos a arrestarme, como si yo fuera un bandido? Todos los días he estado enseñando en el templo, y nunca me arrestaron. 56Pero todo esto sucede para que se cumpla lo que dijeron los profetas en las Escrituras.

En aquel momento, todos los discípulos dejaron solo a Jesús y huyeron.

Jesús ante la Junta Suprema

57Los que habían arrestado a Jesús lo llevaron a la casa de Caifás, el sumo sacerdote, donde los maestros de la ley y los ancianos estaban reunidos. 58Pedro lo siguió de lejos hasta el patio de la casa del sumo sacerdote. Entró, y se quedó sentado con los guardianes del templo, para ver en qué terminaría todo aquello.

59Los jefes de los sacerdotes y toda la Junta Suprema buscaban alguna prueba falsa para condenar a muerte a Jesús, 60pero no la encontraron, a pesar de que muchas personas se presentaron y lo acusaron falsamente. Por fin se presentaron dos más, 61que afirmaron:

—Este hombre dijo: 'Yo puedo destruir el templo de Dios y volver a levantarlo en tres días.'

62Entonces el sumo sacerdote se levantó y preguntó a Jesús:

—¿No contestas nada? ¿Qué es esto que están diciendo contra ti?

63Pero Jesús se quedó callado. El sumo sacerdote le dijo:

—En el nombre del Dios viviente te ordeno que digas la verdad. Dinos si tú eres el Mesías, el Hijo de Dios.

64Jesús le contestó:

—Tú lo has dicho. Y yo les digo también que ustedes van a ver al Hijo del hombre sentado a la derecha del Todopoderoso, y viniendo en las nubes del cielo.

65Entonces el sumo sacerdote se rasgó las ropas en señal de indignación, y dijo:

—¡Las palabras de este hombre son una ofensa contra Dios! ¿Qué necesidad tenemos de más testigos? Ustedes han oído sus palabras ofensivas; 66¿qué les parece?

Ellos contestaron:

—Es culpable, y debe morir.

67Entonces le escupieron en la cara y lo golpearon. Otros le pegaron en la cara, 68diciéndole:

—Tú que eres el Mesías, ¡adivina quién te pegó!

Pedro niega conocer a Jesús

69Pedro, entre tanto, estaba sentado afuera, en el patio. En esto, una sirvienta se le acercó y le dijo:

—Tú también andabas con Jesús, el de Galilea.

70Pero Pedro lo negó delante de todos, diciendo:

—No sé de qué estás hablando.

71Luego se fue a la puerta, donde otra lo vio y dijo a los demás:

—Ese andaba con Jesús, el de Nazaret.

72De nuevo Pedro lo negó, jurando:

—¡No conozco a ese hombre!

73 Poco después, los que estaban allí se acercaron a Pedro y le dijeron:

—Seguro que tú también eres uno de ellos. Hasta en tu manera de hablar se te nota.

74 Entonces él comenzó a jurar y perjurar, diciendo:

—¡No conozco a ese hombre!

En aquel mismo momento cantó un gallo, 75 y Pedro se acordó de que Jesús le había dicho: 'Antes que cante el gallo, me negarás tres veces.' Y salió Pedro de allí, y lloró amargamente.

Jesús es entregado a Pilato

27 1 Cuando amaneció, todos los jefes de los sacerdotes y los ancianos de los judíos se pusieron de acuerdo en un plan para matar a Jesús. 2 Lo llevaron atado y se lo entregaron a Pilato, el gobernador romano.

La muerte de Judas

3 Judas, el que había traicionado a Jesús, al ver que lo habían condenado, tuvo remordimientos y devolvió las treinta monedas de plata a los jefes de los sacerdotes y a los ancianos, 4 diciéndoles:

—He pecado entregando a la muerte a un hombre inocente.

Pero ellos le contestaron:

—¿Y eso qué nos importa a nosotros? ¡Eso es cosa tuya!

5 Entonces Judas arrojó las monedas en el templo, y fue y se ahorcó.

6 Los jefes de los sacerdotes recogieron aquel dinero, y dijeron:

—Este dinero está manchado de sangre; no podemos ponerlo en el cofre de las ofrendas.

7 Así que tomaron el acuerdo de comprar con él un terreno llamado el Campo del Alfarero, para tener un lugar donde enterrar a los extranjeros. 8 Por eso, aquel terreno se llama hasta el día de hoy Campo de Sangre. 9 Así se cumplió lo que había dicho el profeta Jeremías: "Tomaron las treinta monedas de plata, el precio que los israelitas le habían puesto, 10 y con ellas compraron el campo del alfarero, tal como me lo ordenó el Señor."

Jesús ante Pilato

11 Jesús fue llevado ante el gobernador, que le preguntó:

—¿Eres tú el Rey de los judíos?

—Tú lo has dicho —contestó Jesús.

12 Mientras los jefes de los sacerdotes y los ancianos lo acusaban, Jesús no respondía nada. 13 Por eso Pilato le preguntó:

—¿No oyes todo lo que están diciendo contra ti?

14 Pero Jesús no le contestó ni una sola palabra; de manera que el gobernador se quedó muy extrañado.

Jesús es sentenciado a muerte

15 Durante la fiesta, el gobernador acostumbraba dejar libre un preso, el que la gente escogiera. 16 Había entonces un preso famoso llamado Jesús Barrabás. 17 y estando ellos reunidos, Pilato les preguntó:

—¿A quién quieren ustedes que les ponga en libertad: a Jesús Barrabás, o a Jesús, el que llaman el Mesías?

18 Porque se había dado cuenta de que lo habían entregado por envidia.

19 Mientras Pilato estaba sentado en el tribunal, su esposa mandó a decirle: "No te metas con ese hombre justo, porque anoche tuve un sueño horrible por causa suya."

20 Pero los jefes de los sacerdotes y los ancianos convencieron a la multitud de que pidiera la libertad de Barrabás y la muerte de Jesús. 21 El gobernador les preguntó otra vez:

— ¿A cuál de los dos quieren ustedes que les ponga en libertad?

Ellos dijeron:

— ¡A Barrabás!

22 Pilato les preguntó:

— ¿Y qué voy a hacer con Jesús, el que llaman el Mesías?

Todos contestaron:

— ¡Crucifícalo!

23 Pilato les dijo:

— Pues ¿qué mal ha hecho?

Pero ellos volvieron a gritar:

— ¡Crucifícalo!

24 Cuando Pilato vio que no conseguía nada, sino que el alboroto era cada vez mayor, mandó traer agua y se lavó las manos delante de todos, diciendo:

— Yo no soy responsable de la muerte de este hombre; es cosa de ustedes.

25 Toda la gente contestó:

— ¡Nosotros y nuestros hijos nos hacemos responsables de su muerte!

26 Entonces Pilato dejó libre a Barrabás; luego mandó azotar a Jesús y lo entregó para que lo crucificaran.

27 Los soldados del gobernador llevaron a Jesús al palacio y reunieron toda la tropa alrededor de él. 28 Le quitaron su ropa, lo vistieron con una capa roja 29 y le pusieron en la cabeza una corona tejida de espinas y una vara en la mano derecha. Luego se arrodillaron delante de él, y burlándose le decían:

— ¡Viva el Rey de los judíos!

30 También lo escupían, y con la misma vara le golpeaban la cabeza. 31 Después de burlarse así de él, le quitaron la capa roja, le pusieron su propia ropa y se lo llevaron para crucificarlo.

Jesús es crucificado

32 Al salir de allí, encontraron a un hombre llamado Simón, natural de Cirene, a quien obligaron a cargar con la cruz de Jesús.

33 Cuando llegaron a un sitio llamado Gólgota, (es decir, "Lugar de la Calavera"), 34 le dieron a beber vino mezclado con hiel; pero Jesús, después de probarlo, no lo quiso beber.

35 Cuando ya lo habían crucificado, los soldados echaron suertes para repartirse entre sí la ropa de Jesús. 36 Luego se sentaron allí para vigilarlo. 37 Y por encima de su cabeza pusieron un letrero, donde estaba escrita a causa de su condena. El letrero decía: "Este es Jesús, el Rey de los judíos."

38 También fueron crucificados con él dos bandidos, uno a su derecha y otro a su izquierda. 39 Los que pasaban lo insultaban, meneando la cabeza 40 y diciendo:

— ¡Tú ibas a derribar el templo y a reconstruirlo en tres días! ¡Si eres Hijo de Dios, sálvate a ti mismo y bájate de la cruz!

⁴¹De la misma manera se burlaban de él los jefes de los sacerdotes y los maestros de la ley, junto con los ancianos. Decían:

⁴² —Salvó a otros, pero a sí mismo no puede salvarse. Es el Rey de Israel: ¡pues que baje de la cruz, y creeremos en él! ⁴³Ha puesto su confianza en Dios: ¡pues que Dios lo salve ahora, si de veras lo quiere! ¿No nos ha dicho que es Hijo de Dios?

⁴⁴Y hasta los bandidos que estaban crucificados con él, lo insultaban.

Muerte de Jesús

⁴⁵Desde el mediodía y hasta las tres de la tarde, toda la tierra quedó en oscuridad. ⁴⁶A esa misma hora, Jesús gritó con fuerza: "Elí, Elí, ¿lemá sabactani?" (es decir: "Dios mío, Dios mío, ¿por qué me has abandonado?")

⁴⁷Algunos de los que estaban allí, lo oyeron y dijeron:

—Este está llamando al profeta Elías.

⁴⁸Al momento, uno de ellos fue corriendo en busca de una esponja, la empapó en vino agrio, la ató a una caña y se la acercó para que bebiera. ⁴⁹Pero los otros dijeron:

—Déjalo, a ver si Elías viene a salvarlo.

⁵⁰Jesús dio otra vez un fuerte grito, y murió. ⁵¹En aquel momento el velo del templo se rasgó en dos, de arriba abajo. La tierra tembló, las rocas se partieron ⁵²y los sepulcros se abrieron; y hasta muchas personas santas, que habían muerto, volvieron a la vida. ⁵³Entonces salieron de sus tumbas, después de la resurrección de Jesús, y

entraron en la santa ciudad de Jerusalén, donde mucha gente los vio.

⁵⁴Cuando el capitán y los que estaban con él vigilando a Jesús vieron el terremoto y todo lo que estaba pasando, se llenaron de miedo y dijeron:

—¡De veras este hombre era Hijo de Dios!

⁵⁵Estaban allí, mirando de lejos, muchas mujeres que habían seguido a Jesús desde Galilea y que lo habían ayudado. ⁵⁶Entre ellas se encontraban María Magdalena, María la madre de Santiago y de José, y la madre de los hijos de Zebedeo.

Jesús es sepultado

⁵⁷Cuando ya anochecía, llegó un hombre rico llamado José, natural de Arimatea, que también se había hecho seguidor de Jesús. ⁵⁸José fue a ver a Pilato y le pidió el cuerpo de Jesús. Pilato ordenó que se lo dieran, ⁵⁹y José tomó el cuerpo, lo envolvió en una sábana de lino limpia ⁶⁰y lo puso en un sepulcro nuevo, de su propiedad, que había hecho cavar en la roca. Después de tapar la entrada del sepulcro con una gran piedra, se fue. ⁶¹Pero María Magdalena y la otra María se quedaron sentadas frente al sepulcro.

La guardia ante el sepulcro de Jesús

⁶²Al día siguiente, es decir, el sábado, los jefes de los sacerdotes y los fariseos fueron juntos a ver a Pilato, ⁶³y le dijeron:

—Señor, recordamos que aquel mentiroso, cuando aún vivía, dijo que

después de tres días iba a resucitar.
64Por eso, mande usted asegurar el
sepulcro hasta el tercer día, no sea que
vengan sus discípulos y roben el
cuerpo, y después digan a la gente que
ha resucitado. En tal caso, la última
mentira sería peor que la primera.

65Pilato les dijo:

—Ahí tienen ustedes soldados de
guardia. Vayan y aseguren el sepulcro
lo mejor que puedan.

66Fueron, pues, y aseguraron el
sepulcro poniendo un sello sobre la
piedra que lo tapaba; y dejaron allí los
soldados de guardia.

Anuncio
de la resurrección de Jesús

28 1Pasado el sábado, cuando al
anochecer comenzaba el
primer día de la semana, María
Magdalena y la otra María fueron a ver
el sepulcro. 2De pronto hubo un fuerte
temblor de tierra, porque un ángel del
Señor bajó del cielo y, acercándose al
sepulcro, quitó la piedra que lo tapaba
y se sentó sobre ella. 3El ángel brillaba
como un relámpago, y su ropa era
blanca como la nieve. 4Al verlo, los
soldados temblaron de miedo y
quedaron como muertos. 5El ángel
dijo a las mujeres:

—No tengan miedo. Yo sé que están
buscando a Jesús, el que fue
crucificado. 6No está aquí, sino que ha
resucitado, como dijo. Vengan a ver el
lugar donde lo pusieron. 7Vayan
pronto y digan a los discípulos: 'Ha
resucitado, y va a Galilea para
reunirlos de nuevo; allí lo verán.' Esto
es lo que yo tenía que decirles.

Jesús se aparece a las mujeres

8Las mujeres se fueron rápidamente
del sepulcro, con miedo y mucha
alegría a la vez, y corrieron a llevar la
noticia a los discípulos. 9En eso, Jesús
se presentó ante ellas y las saludó.
Ellas se acercaron a Jesús y lo
adoraron, abrazándole los pies, 10y él
les dijo:

—No tengan miedo. Vayan a decir a
mis hermanos que se dirijan a Galilea,
y que allá me verán.

Los soldados son sobornados

11Mientras iban las mujeres, algunos
soldados de la guardia llegaron a la
ciudad y contaron a los jefes de los
sacerdotes todo lo que había pasado.
12Estos jefes fueron a hablar con los
ancianos, para ponerse de acuerdo con
ellos. Y dieron mucho dinero a los
soldados, 13a quienes advirtieron:

—Ustedes digan que durante la
noche, mientras ustedes dormían, los
discípulos de Jesús vinieron y roba-
ron el cuerpo. 14Y si el gobernador
se entera de esto, nosotros lo con-
venceremos, y a ustedes les evita-
remos dificultades.

15Los soldados recibieron el dinero e
hicieron lo que se les había dicho. Y
esta es la explicación que hasta el día
de hoy circula entre los judíos.

El encargo de Jesús
a sus discípulos

16Así pues, los once discípulos se
fueron a Galilea, al cerro que Jesús les
había indicado. 17Y cuando vieron a
Jesús, lo adoraron, aunque algunos

dudaban. ¹⁸Jesús se acercó a ellos y les dijo:

—Dios me ha dado toda autoridad en el cielo y en la tierra. ¹⁹Vayan, pues, a las gentes de todas las naciones, y háganlas mis discípulos; bautícenlas en el nombre del Padre, del Hijo y del Espíritu Santo, ²⁰y enséñenles a obedecer todo lo que les he mandado a ustedes. Por mi parte, yo estaré con ustedes todos los días, hasta el fin del mundo.

il Vangelo secondo

MATTEO

Dio nostro Padre,
Tuo Figlio Gesù ci ha chiamati ad essere sale della terra e
luce per il mondo. Fai che la luce della tua giustizia
risplenda nelle nostre vite, così che le nostre parole possano
dare sapore al mondo con il gusto del Vangelo e le nostre
vite possano essere esempi splendenti di Gesù che è Vera
Luce. Per nostro Signore Gesù Cristo, tuo Figlio, che è Dio,
e vive e regna con te, ell'unità dello Spirito Santo, per tutti
i secoli dei secoli. Amen.

Il Vangelo secondo Matteo
Testo italiano da
        'Parola del Signore, il Nuovo Testamento'
© Società Biblica Britannica e Forestiera,
        Roma, 2000

INTRODUZIONE

Gesù invitò i discepoli a seguirlo. Viveva con loro, predicando alla folla e compiendo miracoli, aiutando i discepoli a capire la sua missione e l'opposizione che avrebbe incontrato. Dio ha risposto alla vergogna della croce resuscitando Gesù e innalzandolo alla gloria come Cristo e Signore.

Il mistero della morte trasfigurata in resurrezione doveva essere proclamato al mondo intero come "Vangelo" cioè "Buona Notizia". I discepoli di Gesù, suoi testimoni oculari, conservarono la memoria dei suoi insegnamenti, dei suoi miracoli, dei suoi gesti di misericordia, della sua passione e della sua resurrezione. Gli Evangelisti (scrittori dei Vangeli) si sono ispirati alle tradizioni orali e scritte delle prime comunità cristiane. La Chiesa riconosce quattro libri come testimonianze autentiche della vita e della persona di Gesù Cristo: i Vangeli di Matteo, Marco, Luca e Giovanni.

IL VANGELO DI MATTEO

UNA CHIESA DIVERSA DALLA SINAGOGA

Matteo scrisse probabilmente il suo Vangelo ad Antiochia, tra gli anni 80 e 90 d.C. Gli Ebrei cristiani avevano fondato qui una Chiesa alla fine degli anni 30. Questa chiesa di Antiochia era caratterizzata da una mentalità molto aperta. La comunità non era però solamente separata dalla Sinagoga, ma era anche coinvolta in un acceso dibattito con i capi Ebrei. La serie delle sette dichiarazioni *Guai a voi ipocriti, maestri della Legge e farisei!* (Mt. 23,13-36) mostra chiaramente quanto profondamente fossero divisi questi gruppi.

UNA CHIESA ALLA RICERCA DELLA SUA IDENTITÀ

Due poli attiravano i primi Cristiani verso direzioni opposte. Come potevano rimanere fedeli all'eredità ebraica dell'Antico Testamento accettando allo stesso tempo la salvezza universale proclamata dal Cristo Risorto?

Prima che il Vangelo di Matteo venisse scritto, la chiesa di Antiochia aveva già vissuto tensioni tra i suoi fondatori "liberali" e i fratelli "conservatori" di Gerusalemme. La Chiesa, radicata nel Giudaismo, guardiano dell'Antico Testamento, doveva aprirsi al vasto mondo pagano? Su che basi?

Il Vangelo di Matteo rappresenta un tentativo di riconciliazione tra le tradizioni divergenti ereditate dai primi Cristiani. Matteo sostiene che la Buona Notizia della salvezza è rivolta a tutti, come anche Paolo, che afferma che non è necessaria la circoncisione né l'osservanza delle prescrizioni alimentari ebraiche.

Matteo cerca, infatti, di preservare le antiche tradizioni presentando allo stesso tempo la novità del Vangelo. Egli tenta di trovare un punto d'incontro tra la tradizione ebraica e l'avvenire universale. Esalta anche la figura di Pietro, capo della Chiesa (16,18-19). Per lui Pietro rappresenta una posizione moderata – più conservatrice di quella di Paolo nelle sue lettere ai Galati e ai Romani, ma più aperta ai pagani rispetto a quella presa da Giacomo nella sua lettera. Quindi non sorprende che il Vangelo di Matteo, che armonizza le principali tendenze per favorire l'unità cristiana, sia diventato noto in breve tempo.

CONCLUSIONE

Ai nostri giorni il fenomeno della globalizzazione è un tema molto sentito dai cristiani. Le barriere tra nazioni, culture e persino religioni stanno crollando. I mezzi di comunicazione favoriscono la mutua comprensione e gli scambi. È evidente che questo segno dei tempi, dei quale la GMG (giornata Mondiale della Gioventù) è un forte esempio, ci porta ad essere più aperti verso gli altri. Ma come possiamo preservare la nostra identità cristiana nel rispetto dell'identità e dei valori degli altri?

I primi cristiani hanno vissuto un problema simile – l'equilibrio tra il senso d'identità particolare degli Ebrei e il carattere universale del Vangelo. La loro ricerca di una soluzione, che Matteo riflette, può ispirare noi oggi.

MATTEO

Gli antenati di Gesù

1 [1]Gesù Cristo è discendente di Davide, il quale a sua volta è discendente di Abramo. Ecco l'elenco degli antenati della sua famiglia:

[2]Abramo fu il padre di Isacco;
Isacco di Giacobbe;
Giacobbe di Giuda
    e dei suoi fratelli;
[3]Giuda fu il padre di Fares e Zara
    (loro madre fu Tamar);
Fares di Esròm;
Esròm di Aram;
[4]Aram fu il padre di Aminadàb;
Aminadàb di Naassòn;
Naassòn di Salmòn;
[5]Salmòn fu il padre di Booz
    (la madre di Booz fu Racab);
Booz fu il padre di Obed
    (la madre di Obed fu Rut);
Obed fu il padre di Iesse;
[6]Iesse fu il padre di Davide.
Davide fu il padre di Salomone
    (la madre era stata moglie
    di Urìa);
[7]Salomone fu il padre di Roboamo;
Roboamo di Abìa;
Abìa di Asàf;
[8]Asàf fu il padre di Giòsafat;
Giòsafat di Ioram;
Ioram di Ozia;
[9]Ozia fu il padre di Ioatam;
Ioatam di Acaz;
Acaz di Ezechia;
[10]Ezechia fu il padre di Manasse;
Manasse di Amos;
Amos di Giosia;
[11]Giosia fu il padre di Ieconia e dei suoi fratelli, al tempo in cui il popolo d'Israele fu deportato in esilio a Babilonia.
[12]Dopo l'esilio a Babilonia,
Ieconia fu il padre di Salatiel;
Salatiel fu il padre di Zorobabèle;
[13]Zorobabèle fu il padre di Abiùd;
Abiùd di Elìacim;
Elìacim di Azor;
[14]Azor fu il padre di Sadoc;
Sadoc di Achim;
Achim di Eliùd;
[15]Eliùd fu il padre di Eleàzar;
Eleàzar di Mattan;
Mattan di Giacobbe;
[16]Giacobbe fu il padre di Giuseppe;
Giuseppe sposò Maria
    e Maria fu la madre di Gesù,
    chiamato Cristo.

[17]Dunque da Abramo a Davide ci sono quattordici generazioni; dal tempo di Davide fino all'esilio di Babilonia ce ne sono altre quattordici; infine, dall'esilio in Babilonia fino a Cristo ci sono ancora quattordici generazioni.

Come nacque Gesù

[18]Ecco come è nato Gesù Cristo. Maria, sua madre, era fidanzata con Giuseppe; essi non vivevano ancora

insieme, ma lo Spirito Santo agì in Maria ed ella si trovò incinta. ¹⁹Ormai Giuseppe stava per sposarla. Egli voleva fare ciò che era giusto, ma non voleva denunziarla di fronte a tutti. Allora decise di rompere il fidanzamento, senza dire niente a nessuno.

²⁰Ci stava ancora pensando, quando una notte in sogno gli apparve un angelo del Signore e gli disse: «Giuseppe, discendente di Davide, non devi aver paura di sposare Maria, la tua fidanzata: il bambino che lei aspetta è opera dello Spirito Santo. ²¹Essa partorirà un figlio e tu gli metterai nome Gesù, perché lui salverà il suo popolo da tutti i suoi peccati».

²²E così si realizzò quel che il Signore aveva detto per mezzo del profeta Isaia:

²³*Ecco, la vergine sarà incinta,*
partorirà un figlio ed egli sarà
chiamato Emmanuele.

Questo nome significa: *«Dio è con noi».*

²⁴Quando Giuseppe si svegliò, fece come l'angelo di Dio gli aveva ordinato e prese Maria in casa sua. ²⁵E senza che avessero avuto fin allora rapporti matrimoniali, Maria partorì il bambino e Giuseppe gli mise nome Gesù.

Alcuni uomini sapienti vengono dall'oriente

2 ¹Gesù nacque a Betlemme, una città nella regione della Giudea, al tempo del re Erode. Dopo la sua nascita, arrivarono a Gerusalemme alcuni uomini sapienti che venivano dall'oriente ²e domandarono: «Dove si trova quel bambino, nato da poco, il re dei Giudei? In oriente abbiamo visto apparire la sua stella e siamo venuti qui per onorarlo».

³Queste parole misero in agitazione tutti gli abitanti di Gerusalemme, e specialmente il re Erode. Egli, appena lo seppe, ⁴radunò tutti i capi dei sacerdoti e i maestri della Legge e domandò loro:
– In quale luogo deve nascere il Messia?

⁵Essi risposero:
– A Betlemme, nella regione della Giudea, perché il profeta ha scritto:

⁶ *Tu Betlemme,*
del paese di Giudea,
non sei certo la meno importante
tra le città della Giudea,
perché da te uscirà un capo
che guiderà il mio popolo, Israele.

⁷Allora il re Erode chiamò in segreto quei sapienti e si fece dire con esattezza quando era apparsa la stella. ⁸Poi li mandò a Betlemme dicendo: «Andate e cercate con ogni cura il bambino. Quando l'avrete trovato, fatemelo sapere, così anch'io andrò a onorarlo».

⁹⁻¹⁰Ricevute queste istruzioni da parte del re, essi partirono. In viaggio, apparve ancora a quei sapienti la stella che avevano visto in oriente, ed essi furono pieni di grande gioia. La stella si muoveva davanti a loro fino a quando non arrivò sopra la casa dove si trovava il bambino. Là si fermò.

¹¹Essi entrarono in quella casa e videro il bambino e sua madre, Maria. Si inginocchiarono e lo adorarono. Poi

aprirono i bagagli e gli offrirono regali: oro, incenso e mirra.

¹²Più tardi, in sogno, Dio lo avvertì di non tornare dal re Erode. Essi presero allora un'altra strada e ritornarono al loro paese.

Giuseppe e Maria fuggono in Egitto

¹³Dopo la partenza dei sapienti, Giuseppe fece un sogno. L'angelo di Dio gli apparve e gli disse: «Alzati, prendi con te il bambino e sua madre e fuggi in Egitto. Erode sta·cercando il bambino per ucciderlo. Tu devi rimanere lì, fino a quando io non ti avvertirò».

¹⁴Giuseppe si alzò, di notte prese con sé il bambino e sua madre e si rifugiò in Egitto. ¹⁵E vi rimase fino a quando non morì il re Erode. Così si realizzò quel che il Signore aveva detto per mezzo del profeta Osea: *Ho chiamato mio figlio dall'Egitto.*

Erode fa uccidere i bambini di Betlemme

¹⁶Il re Erode si accorse che i sapienti dell'oriente lo avevano ingannato e allora si infuriò. Ricordando quel che si era fatto dire da loro, calcolò il tempo; e quindi fece uccidere tutti i bambini di Betlemme e dei dintorni, dai due anni in giù. ¹⁷Allora si realizzò quel che Dio aveva detto per mezzo del profeta Geremia:

¹⁸ *Una voce si è sentita nella regione di Rama,*
pianti e lunghi lamenti.
Rachele piange i suoi figli
e non vuole essere consolata,
perché essi non ci sono più.

Giuseppe e Maria tornano dall'Egitto

¹⁹Dopo la morte di Erode, un angelo del Signore apparve in sogno a Giuseppe, in Egitto. ²⁰L'angelo gli disse: «Alzati, prendi il bambino e sua madre e torna nella terra d'Israele: perché ormai sono morti quelli che cercavano di far morire il bambino». ²¹Giuseppe si alzò, prese con sé il bambino e sua madre e ritornò nella terra d'Israele. ²²Ma venuto a sapere che al posto di Erode era diventato re della Giudea suo figlio Archelao, ebbe paura di fermarsi in quella regione. Informato da un sogno, partì verso la Galilea ²³e andò ad abitare in un villaggio che si chiamava Nàzaret. Così si realizzò quel che Dio aveva detto per mezzo dei profeti: «Egli sarà chiamato Nazareno».

Giovanni il Battezzatore predica nel deserto

3 ¹In quei giorni Giovanni il Battezzatore venne a predicare nel deserto della Giudea. ²Egli diceva: «Cambiate vita, perché il regno di Dio è vicino!».

³A lui si riferiva il profeta Isaia quando scriveva queste parole:
Una voce grida nel deserto:
preparate la via per il Signore,
spianate i suoi sentieri!

⁴Giovanni aveva un vestito fatto di peli di cammello e attorno ai fianchi portava una cintura di cuoio; mangiava cavallette e miele selvatico. ⁵La gente veniva a lui da Gerusalemme, da tutta la regione della

Giudea e da tutti i territori lungo il fiume Giordano. 6Essi confessavano pubblicamente i loro peccati ed egli li battezzava nel fiume.

7Venivano a farsi battezzare anche molti che appartenevano ai gruppi dei farisei e dei sadducei. Giovanni se ne accorse e disse: «Razza di vipere! Chi vi ha fatto credere di poter sfuggire al castigo, che ormai è vicino? 8Fate vedere con i fatti che avete cambiato vita 9e non fatevi illusioni dicendo dentro di voi: "Noi siamo discendenti di Abramo!". Perché vi assicuro: Dio è capace di far sorgere veri figli di Abramo da queste pietre. 10La scure è già alla radice degli alberi, pronta per tagliare: ogni albero che non dà frutti buoni sarà tagliato e gettato nel fuoco. 11Io vi battezzo soltanto con l'acqua perché cambiate vita; ma dopo di me viene uno che vi battezzerà con lo Spirito Santo e con il fuoco. Egli è più potente di me, e io non sono degno neppure di portargli i sandali. 12Egli tiene in mano la pala per separare il grano dalla paglia. Il grano lo raccoglierà nel suo granaio, ma la paglia la brucerà con fuoco senza fine».

Gesù viene a farsi battezzare

13In quel tempo, Gesù dalla Galilea venne fino al fiume Giordano e si avvicinò a Giovanni per farsi battezzare da lui. 14Ma Giovanni non voleva e cercava di convincerlo dicendo:
–Sono io che avrei bisogno di essere battezzato da te; e tu invece vieni da me?
15Ma Gesù rispose:
–Lascia fare, per ora. Perché è bene

che noi facciamo così la volontà di Dio sino in fondo.

Allora Giovanni accettò.

16Appena battezzato, Gesù uscì dall'acqua. All'improvviso il cielo si aprì, ed egli vide lo Spirito di Dio il quale, come una colomba, scendeva su di lui. 17E dal cielo venne una voce: «Questo è il Figlio mio, che io amo. Io l'ho mandato».

Le tentazioni di Gesù

4 1Poi lo Spirito di Dio fece andare Gesù nel deserto, per essere tentato dal diavolo. 2Per quaranta giorni e quaranta notti Gesù rimase là, e non mangiava né beveva. Alla fine ebbe fame.

3Allora il diavolo tentatore si avvicinò a lui e gli disse:
–Se tu sei il Figlio di Dio, comanda a queste pietre di diventare pane!
4Ma Gesù rispose:
–Nella Bibbia è scritto:
Non di solo pane vive l'uomo,
ma di ogni parola che viene da Dio.
5Allora il diavolo lo portò a Gerusalemme, la città santa; lo mise su punto più alto del Tempio, 6e gli disse:
–Se tu sei il Figlio di Dio, bùttati giù; perché nella Bibbia è scritto:
Dio comanderà ai suoi angeli.
Essi ti sorreggeranno con le loro
mani
e così tu non inciamperai contro
alcuna pietra.
7Gesù gli rispose:
–Ma nella Bibbia c'è scritto anche:
Non sfidare il Signore, tuo Dio.
8Il diavolo lo portò ancora su una montagna molto alta, gli fece vedere

tutti i regni del mondo e il loro splendore, 9e gli disse:
– Io ti darò tutto questo, se in ginocchio mi adorerai.

10Ma Gesù disse a lui:
– Vattene via, Satana! Perché nella Bibbia è scritto:

Adora il Signore, tuo Dio;
a lui solo rivolgi la tua preghiera.

11Allora il diavolo si allontanò da lui, e subito alcuni angeli vennero a servire Gesù.

Gesù incomincia la sua missione in Galilea

12Quando Gesù seppe che Giovanni il Battezzatore era stato arrestato e messo in prigione, si recò in Galilea. 13Non rimase a Nàzaret, ma andò ad abitare nella città di Cafàrnao, sulla riva del lago di Galilea, nei territori di Zàbulon e di Nèftali.

14Così si realizzò quel che Dio aveva detto per mezzo del profeta Isaia:

15 Terra di Zàbulon e terra di Nèftali,
strada che va dal mare al Giordano,
Galilea abitata da gente pagana:
16 il popolo che vive nelle tenebre
vedrà una grande luce.
Per chi abita il buio paese della
morte
è venuta una luce.

17Da quel momento Gesù cominciò a predicare il suo messaggio. Egli diceva: «Cambiate vita, perché il regno di Dio è vicino!».

Gesù chiama i primi discepoli: quattro pescatori

18Un giorno, mentre camminava lungo la riva del lago di Galilea, Gesù vide due pescatori che stavano gettando le reti nel lago: erano Simone (che poi sarà chiamato Pietro) e suo fratello Andrea. 19Disse loro: «Seguitemi, vi farò diventare pescatori di uomini». 20E quelli, subito, abbandonarono le reti e lo seguirono.

21Poco più avanti, Gesù vide altri due fratelli: erano Giacomo e Giovanni, i figli di Zebedèo. Essi stavano nella barca con il padre e riparavano le reti. Quando li vide, Gesù li chiamò. 22Essi lasciarono subito la barca e il padre, e seguirono Gesù.

Gesù predica e guarisce

23Gesù percorreva tutta la regione della Galilea: insegnava nelle sinagoghe, annunziava il regno di Dio e guariva tutte le malattie e le infermità della gente. 24Si parlava di lui anche in tutto il territorio della Siria.
Gli portavano allora malati di ogni genere, anche indemoniati, epilettici e paralitici; ed egli li guariva. 25Grandi folle lo seguivano: venivano dalla Galilea, dalla regione delle Dieci Città, da Gerusalemme, dalla Giudea e dai territori al di là del fiume Giordano.

Il discorso della montagna

5 1Vedendo che c'era tanta gente Gesù salì verso il monte. Si sedette, i suoi discepoli si avvicinarono a lui 2ed egli cominciò a istruirli con queste parole:

Le beatitudini

3 «Beati quelli che sono poveri di
fronte a Dio:
Dio dona loro il suo regno.

⁴ Beati quelli che sono nella tristezza:
    Dio li consolerà.

⁵ Beati quelli che non sono violenti:
    Dio darà loro la terra promessa.

⁶ Beati quelli che hanno fame e sete
        della giustizia:
    Dio esaudirà i loro desideri.

⁷ Beati quelli che hanno
        compassione degli altri:
    Dio avrà compassione di loro.

⁸ Beati quelli che sono puri di cuore:
    essi vedranno Dio.

⁹ Beati quelli che diffondono la pace:
    Dio li accoglierà come suoi figli.

¹⁰ Beati quelli che sono perseguitati
        perché fanno la volontà di Dio:
    Dio dona loro il suo regno.

¹¹ Beati siete voi quando vi insultano e vi perseguitano, quando dicono falsità e calunnie contro di voi perché avete creduto in me. ¹² Siate lieti e contenti, perché Dio vi ha preparato in cielo una grande ricompensa: infatti, prima di voi, anche i profeti furono perseguitati.

I discepoli di Cristo sono sale e luce del mondo

¹³ «Siete voi il sale del mondo. Ma se il sale perde il suo sapore, come si potrà ridarglielo? Ormai non serve più a nulla; non resta che buttarlo via, e la gente lo calpesta. ¹⁴ Siete voi la luce del mondo. Una città costruita sopra una montagna non può rimanere nascosta. ¹⁵ Non si accende una lampada per metterla sotto un secchio, ma piuttosto per metterla in alto, perché faccia luce a tutti quelli che sono nella casa. ¹⁶ Così deve risplendere la vostra luce davanti agli uomini, perché vedano il bene che voi fate e ringrazino il Padre vostro che è in cielo.

La Legge di Dio

¹⁷ «Non dovete pensare che io sia venuto ad abolire la Legge di Mosè e l'insegnamento dei profeti. Io non sono venuto per abolirla ma per compierla in modo perfetto. ¹⁸ Perché vi assicuro che fino a quando ci saranno il cielo e la terra, nemmeno la più piccola parola, anzi nemmeno una virgola, sarà cancellata dalla Legge di Dio; e così fino a quando tutto non sarà compiuto.

¹⁹ «Perciò, chi disubbidisce al più piccolo dei comandamenti e insegna agli altri a fare come lui, sarà il più piccolo nel regno di Dio. Chi invece mette in pratica i comandamenti e li insegna agli altri, sarà grande nel regno di Dio. ²⁰ Una cosa è certa: se non fate la volontà di Dio più seriamente di come fanno i farisei e i maestri della Legge, non entrerete nel regno di Dio.

La collera e la pace

²¹ «Sapete che nella Bibbia è stato detto ai nostri padri: *Non uccidere.* Chi ucciderà sarà portato davanti al giudice. ²² Ma io vi dico: anche se uno va in collera contro suo fratello sarà portato davanti al giudice. E chi dice a suo fratello: "Sei un cretino" sarà portato di fronte al tribunale superiore. Chi gli dice: "Traditore" sarà condannato al fuoco dell'inferno.

²³ «Perciò, se stai portando la tua offerta all'altare di Dio e ti ricordi che tuo fratello ha qualcosa contro di te, ²⁴ lascia lì l'offerta davanti all'altare e vai a far pace con tuo fratello; poi torna e presenta la tua offerta.

25 «Così, se stai andando con il tuo avversario in tribunale, fa' presto a metterti d'accordo con lui, perché può consegnarti alle guardie per farti mettere in prigione. 26 Ti assicuro che non uscirai di là, fino a quando non avrai pagato anche l'ultimo centesimo.

Adulterio e scandalo

27 «Sapete che nella Bibbia è stato detto: *Non commettere adulterio*. 28 Ma io vi dico: se uno guarda la donna di un altro perché la vuole, nel suo cuore egli ha già peccato di adulterio con lei.

29 «Se il tuo occhio destro ti fa compiere il male, strappalo e gettalo via: ti conviene perdere soltanto una parte del tuo corpo, piuttosto che essere gettato tutto intero all'inferno. 30 Se la tua mano destra ti fa compiere il male, tagliala e gettala via: ti conviene perdere soltanto una parte del tuo corpo, piuttosto che andare tutto intero all'inferno.

Il divorzio

31 «Nella Bibbia è stato detto: *Chi vuole abbandonare la propria moglie deve darle una dichiarazione scritta di divorzio*. 32 Ma io vi dico: chi manda via la propria donna – salvo il caso di relazione illegale – la mette in pericolo di diventare adultera. E chi sposa una donna abbandonata dal marito commette adulterio anche lui.

Il giuramento

33 «Voi sapete pure che nella Bibbia è stato detto ai nostri padri: *Non giurare il falso, ma fa' quel che hai promesso con giuramento di fronte a Dio*. 34 Ma io vi dico: non giurate mai né per il cielo, che è il trono di Dio; 35 né per la terra, che è lo sgabello dei suoi piedi; né per Gerusalemme, che è la città del Signore. 36 Non giurare nemmeno sulla tua testa, perché tu non hai neppure il potere di far diventare bianco o nero uno dei tuoi capelli.

37 «Semplicemente, dite "sì" quando è "sì" e "no" quando è "no": tutto il resto viene dal diavolo.

Vendetta e perdono

38 «Sapete che nella Bibbia è stato detto: *Occhio per occhio, dente per dente*. 39 Ma io vi dico: non vendicatevi contro chi vi fa del male. Se uno ti dà uno schiaffo sulla guancia destra, tu presentagli anche l'altra. 40 Se uno vuol farti un processo per prenderti la camicia, tu lasciagli anche il mantello.

41 «Se uno ti costringe ad accompagnarlo per un chilometro, tu va' con lui per due chilometri. 42 Se qualcuno ti chiede qualcosa, daglierla. Non voltare le spalle a chi ti chiede un prestito.

L'amore verso i nemici

43 «Sapete che è stato detto: *Ama i tuoi amici* e odia i tuoi nemici. 44 Ma io vi dico: amate anche i vostri nemici, pregate per quelli che vi perseguitano. 45 Facendo così, diventerete veri figli di Dio, vostro Padre, che è in cielo. Perché egli fa sorgere il suo sole sui cattivi e sui buoni e fa piovere per quelli che fanno il bene e per quelli che fanno il male.

⁴⁶«Se voi amate soltanto quelli che vi amano, che merito avete? Anche i malvagi si comportano così!

⁴⁷«Se salutate solamente i vostri amici, fate qualcosa di meglio degli altri? Anche quelli che non conoscono Dio si comportano così! ⁴⁸Siate dunque perfetti, così com'è perfetto il Padre vostro che è in cielo.

Elemosina e ipocrisia

6 ¹«State attenti a non fare il bene in pubblico per il desiderio di essere ammirati dalla gente; altrimenti non avrete nessuna ricompensa dal Padre vostro che è in cielo.

²«Quando dai qualcosa ai poveri, non fare come gli ipocriti, non farlo sapere a tutti. Essi fanno così nelle sinagoghe e per le strade, perché cercano di essere lodati dalla gente. Ma io vi assicuro che questa è l'unica loro ricompensa.

³«Invece, quando fai l'elemosina, non farlo sapere a nessuno, neanche ai tuoi amici. ⁴La tua elemosina rimarrà segreta; ma Dio, tuo Padre, vede anche ciò che è nascosto, e ti ricompenserà.

Preghiera e ipocrisia

⁵«E quando pregate, non fate come gli ipocriti che si mettono a pregare nelle sinagoghe o agli angoli delle piazze per farsi vedere dalla gente. Vi assicuro che questa è l'unica loro ricompensa.

⁶«Tu invece, quando preghi, entra in camera tua e chiudi la porta. Poi, prega Dio, presente anche in quel luogo nascosto. E Dio tuo Padre, che vede anche ciò che è nascosto, ti darà la ricompensa.

Gesù insegna come pregare

⁷«Quando pregate, non usate tante parole come fanno i pagani: essi pensano che a furia di parlare Dio finirà per ascoltarli. ⁸Voi non fate come loro, perché Dio, vostro Padre, sa di che cosa avete bisogno, prima ancora che voi glielo chiediate.

⁹«Dunque, pregate così:
Padre nostro che sei in cielo,
fa' che tutti riconoscano te come Padre,
¹⁰che il tuo regno venga,
che la tua volontà si compia
anche in terra come in cielo.
¹¹Dacci oggi il nostro pane necessario.
¹²Perdona le nostre offese
come anche noi perdoniamo a chi ci ha offeso.
¹³Fa' che non cadiamo nella tentazione,
ma liberaci dal Male.

¹⁴«Perché, se voi perdonerete agli altri le loro colpe, il Padre vostro che è in cielo perdonerà anche a voi. ¹⁵Ma se non perdonerete agli altri il male che hanno fatto, neppure il Padre vostro perdonerà le vostre colpe.

Digiuno e ipocrisia

¹⁶«E quando fate un digiuno religioso, non agite come gli ipocriti. Essi mostrano la faccia triste, perché tutti vedano che stanno digiunando. Ma io vi assicuro che questa è l'unica loro ricompensa.

17 «Tu invece, quando fai un digiuno, lavati la faccia e profumati i capelli, 18perché la gente non si accorga che tu stai digiunando. E Dio tuo Padre, che vede anche ciò che è nascosto, ti ricompenserà.

Le vere ricchezze

19 «Non accumulate ricchezze in questo mondo. Qui i tarli e la ruggine distruggono ogni cosa e i ladri vengono e portano via. 20Accumulate piuttosto le vostre ricchezze in cielo. Là, i tarli e la ruggine non le distruggono e i ladri non vanno a rubare. 21Perché, dove sono le tue ricchezze, là c'è anche il tuo cuore.

Gli occhi e la luce

22 «Gli occhi sono come lampada per il corpo: se i tuoi occhi sono buoni, tu sarai totalmente nella luce, 23ma se i tuoi occhi sono cattivi, tu sarai totalmente nelle tenebre. Se dunque la luce in te è tenebra, come sarà nera quella tenebra!

Dio e i soldi

24 «Nessuno può servire due padroni: perché, o amerà l'uno e odierà l'altro; oppure preferirà il primo e disprezzerà il secondo. Non potete servire Dio e i soldi.

La vita e le vere preoccupazioni

25 «Perciò io vi dico: non preoccupatevi troppo del mangiare e del bere che vi servono per vivere, o dei vestiti che vi servono per coprirvi. Non è forse vero che la vita è più importante del cibo e il corpo è più importante del vestito?

26 «Guardate gli uccelli del cielo: essi non seminano, non raccolgono e non mettono il raccolto nei granai. Eppure il Padre vostro che è in cielo li nutre! Ebbene, voi non valete forse più di loro?

27 «E chi di voi con tutte le sue preoccupazioni può vivere un giorno più di quel che è stabilito?

28 «Anche per i vestiti, perché vi preoccupate tanto? Guardate come crescono i fiori dei campi: non lavorano, non si fanno vestiti? 29Eppure vi assicuro che nemmeno Salomone, con tutta la sua ricchezza, ha mai avuto un vestito così bello! 30Se dunque Dio rende così belli i fiori dei campi che oggi ci sono e il giorno dopo vengono bruciati, a maggior ragione procurerà un vestito a voi, gente di poca fede!

31 «Dunque, non state a preoccuparvi troppo, dicendo: "Che cosa mangeremo?, che cosa berremo?, come ci vestiremo?". 32Sono gli altri, quelli che non conoscono Dio, a cercare sempre tutte queste cose. Il Padre vostro che è in cielo sa che avete bisogno di tutte queste cose.

33 «Voi invece cercate prima il regno di Dio e fate la sua volontà: tutto il resto Dio ve lo darà in più. 34Perciò, non preoccupatevi troppo per il domani: ci pensa lui, il domani, a portare altre pena. Per ogni giorno basta la sua pena.

Non giudicare

7 1 «Non giudicate e Dio non vi giudicherà. 2Egli infatti vi giudicherà con lo stesso criterio che

usate voi per giudicare gli altri. Con la stessa misura con la quale voi trattate gli altri, Dio tratterà voi.

³«Perché stai a guardare la pagliuzza che è nell'occhio di un tuo fratello, e non ti accorgi della trave che è nel tuo occhio? ⁴Come puoi dire al tuo fratello: "Lascia che tolga la pagliuzza dal tuo occhio, mentre nel tuo occhio hai una trave? ⁵Ipocrita! Togli prima la trave dal tuo occhio; allora tu ci vedrai bene e potrai togliere la pagliuzza dall'occhio di tuo fratello.

Il valore del Vangelo

⁶«Non date ai cani ciò che è santo, perché non si rivoltino contro di voi per sbranarvi. Non gettate le vostre perle ai porci, perché non le calpestino con le zampe.

Preghiera e risposta

⁷«Chiedete e riceverete. Cercate e troverete. Bussate e la porta vi sarà aperta. ⁸Perché, chiunque chiede riceve, chi cerca trova, a chi bussa sarà aperto.

⁹«Chi di voi darebbe una pietra al figlio che gli chiede un pane? ¹⁰Chi gli darebbe un serpente se chiede un pesce? ¹¹Se voi che siete cattivi sapete dare cose buone ai vostri figli, a maggior ragione il Padre vostro che è in cielo darà cose buone a quelli che gliele chiedono!

Una regola pratica

¹²«Fate anche agli altri tutto quel che volete che essi facciano a voi: così comanda la Legge di Mosè e così hanno insegnato i profeti.

La porta piccola

¹³«Entrate per la porta piccola! Perché grande è la porta e larga è la strada che conduce alla morte, e sono molti quelli che ci entrano. ¹⁴Al contrario, piccola è la porta e stretta è la strada che conduce alla vita, e sono pochi quelli che la trovano.

I falsi profeti.
L'albero e i suoi frutti

¹⁵«Attenti ai falsi profeti! Quando vi vengono incontro, all'apparenza sembrano pecorelle, ma sotto sotto, essi sono lupi feroci. ¹⁶Li riconoscerete dalle loro azioni.

«Si può forse raccogliere uva dalle spine o fichi da un cespuglio? ¹⁷Se un albero è buono, fa frutti buoni; ma se un albero è cattivo, fa frutti cattivi. ¹⁸Un albero buono non può fare frutti cattivi, così come un albero cattivo non può fare frutti buoni. ¹⁹Ma un albero che non fa frutti buoni si taglia e si butta nel fuoco.

²⁰«Dunque, è dalle loro azioni che riconoscerete i falsi profeti.

Condizioni per entrare
nel regno di Dio

²¹«Non tutti quelli che dicono: "Signore, Signore!" entreranno nel regno di Dio. Vi entreranno soltanto quelli che fanno la volontà del Padre mio che è in cielo. ²²Quando verrà il giorno del giudizio, molti mi diranno: "Signore, Signore! Tu sai che noi abbiamo parlato a tuo nome, e invocando il tuo nome abbiamo scacciato demòni e abbiamo fatto molti miracoli".

6Ebbene, io vi assicuro che qui c'è qualcuno che è più importante del Tempio! 7Se voi sapeste veramente il significato di queste parole della Bibbia:

Misericordia io voglio, non sacrifici non avreste condannato uomini senza colpa. 8Infatti, il Figlio dell'uomo è padrone del sabato.

Gesù guarisce un uomo in giorno di sabato

9Gesù andò via di là ed entrò nella sinagoga. 10Tra la gente c'era un uomo che aveva una mano paralizzata. Alcuni farisei, che cercavano il modo di accusare Gesù, gli fecero questa domanda:
– La nostra Legge permette di guarire un uomo in giorno di sabato?

11Gesù rispose:
– Se uno di voi ha soltanto una pecora e questa, in giorno di sabato, va a cadere in una fossa, certo la afferra e là tira fuori. 12E un uomo non vale molto più di una pecora? Perciò la Legge permette di fare del bene a qualcuno anche se è sabato.

13Poi Gesù disse all'uomo malato: «Dammi la tua mano».

Gliela diede e la sua mano ritornò perfettamente sana come l'altra.

14Allora quei farisei uscirono dalla sinagoga e si radunarono per decidere come far morire Gesù.

Gesù è il «servo di Dio» descritto dalla Bibbia

15Quando Gesù venne a sapere queste cose, andò in un altro luogo. Molta gente lo seguì; ed egli guarì tutti i malati, 16ma raccomandò severamente di non dirlo a nessuno. 17Così si realizzò quel che Dio aveva detto per mezzo del profeta Isaia:

18*Ecco il mio servo, quello che io ho*
scelto,

– dice il Signore; –

È lui che io amo, lui ho mandato.

A lui darò il mio Spirito,

e dirà a tutti i popoli che io li
giudicherò.

19*Non farà discussioni, non griderà,*

non terrà discorsi nelle piazze.

20*Se una canna è incrinata, non la*
spezzerà;

se una lampada è debole, non la
spegnerà.

Farà sempre così, fino a quando
non avrà fatto trionfare la
giustizia;

21*per tutti i popoli egli sarà una*
speranza.

Gesù ha potere sui demòni

22Portarono a Gesù un uomo che era cieco e muto, perché uno spirito maligno era dentro di lui. Gesù lo guarì, e quello si mise a parlare e incominciò a vedere. 23Le folle erano piene di meraviglia e dicevano: «Non sarà lui il Figlio di Davide che aspettiamo?».

24Ma i farisei, quando ne furono informati, dissero: «È soltanto con l'aiuto di Beelzebùl, il capo dei demòni, che egli ha il potere di scacciare i demòni».

25Gesù, conoscendo i loro pensieri, disse: «Se gli abitanti di una nazione si dividono e si combattono tra loro, quella nazione va in rovina. Se una città o una famiglia si divide e le persone litigano tra loro, non potranno più durare. ²⁶Se dunque Satana scaccia Satana ed è in lotta contro se stesso, come potrà durare il suo regno? ²⁷Ora se io scaccio i demòni con l'aiuto di Beelzebùl, il capo dei demòni, con l'aiuto di chi li scacciano i vostri discepoli? Perciò saranno proprio loro a mostrare che avete torto. ²⁸Se invece è con lo Spirito di Dio che io scaccio i demòni, allora vuoi dire che è giunto per voi il regno di Dio.

²⁹«Come si può entrare nella casa di un uomo forte e portar via i suoi beni? Prima si deve legare quell'uomo forte e poi si potrà vuotargli la casa.

³⁰«Chi non è con me è contro di me; e chi non raccoglie insieme con me spreca il raccolto.

³¹«Perciò vi dico: tutti i peccati e tutte le bestemmie degli uomini potranno essere perdonati, ma chi avrà detto una bestemmia contro lo Spirito Santo non potrà essere perdonato. ³²Se uno avrà detto una parola contro il Figlio dell'uomo potrà essere perdonato; ma chi avrà detto una parola contro lo Spirito Santo non sarà perdonato, né ora né mai.

L'albero e i frutti

³³«Se prendete un albero buono, anche i suoi frutti saranno buoni; se prendete un albero cattivo, anche i suoi frutti saranno cattivi: perché è dai frutti che si conosce la qualità dell'albero. ³⁴E voi, razza di vipere, come potete dire cose buone se siete cattivi? Ciascuno infatti esprime con

la bocca quel che ha nel cuore. ³⁵L'uomo buono ha con sé un tesoro di bene, dal quale tira fuori cose buone; l'uomo cattivo ha in sé un tesoro di male, dal quale tira fuori cose cattive.

³⁶«Vi assicuro che nel giorno del giudizio tutti dovranno render conto di ogni parola inutile che hanno detto: ³⁷perché saranno le vostre parole che vi porteranno a essere condannati o a essere riconosciuti innocenti».

Alcuni chiedono a Gesù un miracolo

³⁸Alcuni maestri della Legge e alcuni farisei dissero a Gesù: «Maestro, vorremmo che tu ci facessi vedere un segno miracoloso». ³⁹Gesù rispose: «Questa gente malvagia e infedele a Dio vuole vedere un segno miracoloso! Ma non riceverà nessun segno, eccetto il segno del profeta Giona. ⁴⁰Come Giona *rimase nel ventre del grande pesce tre giorni e tre notti*, così il Figlio dell'uomo rimarrà sepolto nella terra tre giorni e tre notti.

⁴¹«Nel giorno del giudizio gli abitanti di Ninive si alzeranno a condannare questa gente, perché essi cambiarono vita quando ascoltarono la predicazione di Giona. Eppure, di fronte a voi c'è uno che è più grande di Giona!

⁴²«Nel giorno del giudizio la regina del sud si alzerà a condannare questa gente: essa infatti venne da molto lontano per ascoltare le sagge parole del re Salomone. Eppure, di fronte a voi c'è uno che è più grande di Salomone!

23 «Ma allora io dirò: Non vi ho mai conosciuti. Andate via da me, gente malvagia!

Le due case

24 «Chi ascolta queste mie parole e le mette in pratica sarà simile a un uomo intelligente che ha costruito la sua casa sulla roccia. 25 È venuta la pioggia, i fiumi sono straripati, i venti hanno soffiato con violenza contro quella casa, ma essa non è crollata, perché le sue fondamenta erano sulla roccia.
26 «Al contrario, chi ascolta queste mie parole e non le mette in pratica sarà simile a un uomo sciocco che ha costruito la sua casa sulla sabbia. 27 È venuta la pioggia, i fiumi sono straripati, i venti hanno soffiato con violenza contro quella casa, e la casa è crollata. E la sua rovina fu grande».

Gesù insegna con autorità

28 Quando Gesù ebbe finito di dire queste cose, la folla era molto meravigliata per i suoi insegnamenti. 29 Infatti egli era diverso dai loro maestri della Legge, perché insegnava come uno che ha piena autorità.

Gesù guarisce un lebbroso

8 ¹Poi Gesù scese dal monte e molta gente lo seguì. ²Allora un lebbroso si avvicinò, si mise in ginocchio davanti a lui e disse:
– Signore, se vuoi, tu puoi guarirmi.
³Gesù lo toccò con la mano e gli disse:
– Sì, lo voglio: guarisci!

E subito fu guarito dalla lebbra. ⁴Poi Gesù gli disse:
– Ascolta! Non dire a nessuno quel che ti è capitato. Va' invece dal sacerdote e fatti vedere da lui: poi fa' l'offerta che Mosè ha stabilito nella Legge. Così avranno una prova della tua guarigione.

Gesù guarisce il servo di un ufficiale romano

⁵Quando Gesù entrò nella città di Cafàrnao, gli si avvicinò un ufficiale dell'esercito romano e si mise a chiedergli aiuto:
⁶– Signore, il mio servitore è a casa paralizzato e soffre terribilmente.
⁷Gesù gli disse:
– Verrò e lo guarirò.
⁸Ma l'ufficiale rispose:
– No, Signore, io non sono degno che tu entri in casa mia. Basta che tu dica soltanto una parola e il mio servo sarà guarito. ⁹Perché anch'io ho i miei superiori e ho dei soldati ai miei ordini. Se dico a uno: Va', egli va; se dico a un altro: Vieni, quello viene; se dico al mio servitore: Fa' questo!, egli lo fa.
¹⁰Quando Gesù lo sentì, rimase ammirato e disse a quelli che lo seguivano: «Vi assicuro che non ho trovato nessuno, tra quelli che appartengono al popolo d'Israele, con una fede così grande! ¹¹E io vi dico che molti verranno da ogni parte, da oriente e da occidente, e si metteranno a tavola con Abramo, Isacco e Giacobbe nel regno di Dio. ¹²Invece, i cittadini del regno saranno gettati fuori, nelle tenebre: là piangeranno come disperati».

¹³Poi disse all'ufficiale:

– Torna a casa tua. Hai creduto, e così sarà.

E in quello stesso momento il servo fu guarito.

Gesù guarisce la suocera di Pietro e molti altri

¹⁴Poi Gesù entrò nella casa di Pietro. La suocera di Pietro era a letto con la febbre. Gesù la vide, ¹⁵toccò la sua mano e la febbre sparì. Allora la donna si alzò e si mise a servirlo.

¹⁶Quando fu sera, portarono a Gesù molte persone indemoniate. Con la sua parola, egli scacciò gli spiriti maligni e guarì tutti i malati.

¹⁷Così si realizzò quel che Dio aveva detto per mezzo del profeta Isaia:

Egli ha preso su di sé le nostre debolezze,
si è caricato di tutte le nostre sofferenze.

Gesù risponde a due che vogliono seguirlo

¹⁸C'era molta gente attorno a Gesù. Allora egli ordinò ai discepoli di andare all'altra riva del lago.

¹⁹Un maestro della Legge gli si avvicinò e disse:

– Maestro, io verrò con te dovunque andrai.

²⁰Gesù gli rispose:

– Le volpi hanno una tana e gli uccelli hanno un nido, ma il Figlio dell'uomo non ha un posto dove poter riposare.

²¹Un altro dei discepoli disse a Gesù:

– Signore, permettimi di andare prima a seppellire mio padre.

²²Ma Gesù gli rispose:

– Seguimi! e lascia che i morti seppelliscano i loro morti.

Gesù calma una tempesta

²³Gesù salì in barca e i suoi discepoli lo accompagnarono. ²⁴Improvvisamente sul lago si scatenò una grande tempesta e le onde erano tanto alte che coprivano la barca. Ma Gesù dormiva. ²⁵I discepoli si avvicinarono a lui e lo svegliarono gridando:

– Signore, salvaci! Affondiamo!

²⁶Gesù rispose:

– Perché avete paura, uomini di poca fede?

Poi si alzò in piedi, sgridò il vento e l'acqua del lago, e ci fu una grande calma.

²⁷La gente rimase piena di stupore, e diceva: «Chi è mai costui? Anche il vento e le onde del lago gli ubbidiscono!».

Gesù guarisce gli indemoniati di Gadara

²⁸Quando Gesù arrivò sull'altra riva del lago, nella regione dei Gadarèni, due uomini uscirono da un cimitero e gli vennero incontro. Erano indemoniati, ma tanto furiosi che nessuno poteva più passare per quella strada. ²⁹Si misero a urlare:

– Che cosa vuoi da noi, Figlio di Dio? Sei venuto qui a tormentarci prima del tempo?

³⁰In quel luogo, a una certa distanza, c'era un grosso branco di maiali al pascolo. ³¹I demòni chiesero con insistenza:

– Se ci vuoi scacciare, mandaci nel branco dei maiali.

Gesù disse loro:

– Andate!

³²Essi uscirono, ed entrarono nei maiali. Subito tutto il branco si mise a correre giù per la discesa, si precipitò nel lago e gli animali morirono annegati.

³³I guardiani dei maiali fuggirono e andarono in città a raccontare quel che era successo, anche il fatto degli indemoniati.

³⁴Così tutta la gente della città venne a cercare Gesù; e quando lo videro, lo pregarono di andare via dal loro territorio.

Gesù guarisce e può perdonare i peccati

9 ¹Gesù salì in barca, rifece la traversata del lago e tornò nella sua città. ²Qui, gli portarono un uomo paralizzato steso su una barella. Quando Gesù vide la fede di quelle persone disse al paralitico:

– Coraggio, figlio mio, i tuoi peccati sono perdonati.

³Allora alcuni maestri della Legge pensarono:

– Costui bestemmia!

⁴Ma Gesù capì i loro pensieri e disse:

– Perché pensate cose cattive dentro di voi? ⁵È più facile dire: I tuoi peccati sono perdonati, o dire: Alzati e cammina? ⁶Ebbene, io vi farò vedere che il Figlio dell'uomo ha il potere sulla terra di perdonare i peccati.

Si voltò quindi verso il paralitico e gli disse:

– Alzati, prendi la tua barella e va' a casa tua.

⁷L'uomo si alzò e andò a casa sua.

⁸Vedendo queste cose, la folla fu presa da timore e lodava Dio perché aveva dato un tale potere agli uomini.

Gesù chiama Matteo

⁹Passando per la via, Gesù vide un uomo, un certo Matteo, il quale stava seduto dietro al banco dove si pagavano le tasse. Gesù disse: «Seguimi!». Quello si alzò e cominciò a seguirlo.

¹⁰Più tardi, Gesù si trovava in casa di Matteo a mangiare. Erano venuti anche molti agenti delle tasse e altre persone di cattiva reputazione e si erano messi a tavola insieme con Gesù e i suoi discepoli. ¹¹Vedendo questo fatto, i farisei dicevano ai suoi discepoli:

– Perché il vostro maestro mangia con quelli delle tasse e con gente di cattiva reputazione?

¹²Gesù sentì e rispose:

– Le persone sane non hanno bisogno del medico; ne hanno bisogno invece i malati. ¹³Andate a imparare che cosa significa quel che Dio dice nella Bibbia: *Misericordia io voglio, non sacrifici*. Perché io non sono venuto a chiamare quelli che si credono giusti, ma quelli che si sentono peccatori.

La questione del digiuno. Il nuovo e il vecchio

¹⁴Un giorno si avvicinarono a Gesù i discepoli di Giovanni il Battezzatore e gli domandarono:

– Perché noi e i farisei facciamo digiuno, i tuoi discepoli invece non lo fanno?

¹⁵Gesù rispose:

– Vi pare possibile che gli invitati a un

banchetto di nozze se ne stiano tristi mentre lo sposo è con loro? Ma verrà il tempo in cui lo sposo gli sarà portato via, e allora faranno digiuno.

¹⁶Nessuno mette una pezza di stoffa nuova sopra un vestito vecchio: perché il tessuto nuovo strappa il vecchio, e il danno diventa peggiore. ¹⁷E ancora: il vino nuovo non si mette in otri vecchi: altrimenti gli otri scoppiano, il vino si rovescia e gli otri sono rovinati. Invece, il vino nuovo si mette in otri nuovi, così si conservano sia l'uno che gli altri.

La figlia del capo-sinagoga e la donna che tocca il mantello di Gesù

¹⁸Mentre Gesù diceva loro queste cose, arrivò un tale, un capo-sinagoga. Si avvicinò, si mise in ginocchio e disse: «Poco fa è morta mia figlia. Ti prego, vieni, metti la tua mano su di lei e vivrà di nuovo». ¹⁹Gesù si alzò e lo seguì insieme con i discepoli.

²⁰Intanto, da dietro, una donna si accostò a Gesù e toccò l'orlo del suo mantello. Da dodici anni questa donna perdeva sangue; ²¹ma aveva pensato: «Se riesco anche solo a toccare il suo mantello sarò guarita».

²²Gesù si voltò, la vide e le disse: «Coraggio, figlia mia, la tua fede ti ha salvata». E da quel momento la donna fu guarita.

²³Poi arrivarono alla casa del capo-sinagoga. Gesù vide la folla che faceva lamenti funebri e i suonatori di flauto. ²⁴Disse: «Andate via! La ragazza non è morta, dorme».

Ma quelli ridevano di lui. ²⁵Quando la folla fu mandata fuori, Gesù entrò,

prese la ragazza per mano e quella si alzò. ²⁶E in tutto quel territorio la gente parlò di Gesù.

Gesù guarisce due ciechi

²⁷Gesù passava di là, e due ciechi si misero a seguirlo gridando: «Pietà di noi, Figlio di Davide!». ²⁸Quando arrivò a casa, i ciechi gli andarono vicino e Gesù domandò:

– Credete che io possa fare quello che mi chiedete?

Essi risposero:

– Sì, Signore.

²⁹Allora egli toccò i loro occhi e disse:

– Come avete creduto, così avvenga!

³⁰E i loro occhi cominciarono a vedere. Poi Gesù, parlando severamente, disse loro:

– Ascoltatemi bene: fate in modo che nessuno lo sappia!

³¹Ma quelli, appena usciti, parlarono di lui in tutta la regione.

Gesù guarisce un muto

³²Dopo che i due ciechi furono usciti, portarono a Gesù un uomo che non poteva parlare a causa di uno spirito maligno. ³³Quando Gesù scacciò questo spirito, il muto si mise a parlare. La gente era piena di meraviglia e diceva: «Non si è mai visto niente di simile in Israele!». ³⁴I farisei invece dicevano: «È il capo degli spiriti maligni che gli dà il potere di scacciare gli spiriti».

Gesù si commuove vedendo la folla

³⁵Gesù percorreva città e villaggi, insegnava nelle sinagoghe e annunziava

Quando lo spirito maligno ritorna

43«Quando uno spirito maligno è uscito da un uomo se ne va per luoghi deserti in cerca di riposo. Se però non lo trova, 44allora dice: "Tornerò nella mia casa, quella che ho lasciato". Egli ci va e la trova vuota, pulita e bene ordinata. 45Allora va a chiamare altri sette spiriti, più maligni di lui; poi, tutti insieme, entrano in quella persona e vi rimangono come a casa loro. Così, alla fine, quell'uomo si trova in condizioni peggiori di prima. E così sarà anche per voi, gente malvagia».

I veri parenti di Gesù

46Gesù stava parlando alla folla. Sua madre e i suoi fratelli volevano parlare con lui, ma erano rimasti fuori. 47Un tale disse a Gesù:

– Qui fuori ci sono tua madre e i tuoi fratelli che vogliono parlare con te.

48Gesù a chi gli parlava rispose:

– Chi è mia madre? e chi sono i miei fratelli?

49Poi, con la mano indicò i suoi discepoli e disse:

– Guarda: sono questi mia madre e i miei fratelli; 50perché se uno fa la volontà del Padre mio che è in cielo, egli è mio fratello, mia sorella e mia madre.

Il discorso delle parabole
La parabola del seminatore

13 1Quel giorno, Gesù uscì di casa e andò a sedersi in riva al lago di Galilea. 2Attorno a lui si radunò una folla tanto grande che egli salì su una barca e si sedette.

Tutta la gente rimase sulla riva.

3Gesù parlava di molte cose servendosi di parabole. Egli diceva: «Un contadino andò a seminare, 4e mentre seminava alcuni semi andarono a cadere sulla strada: vennero allora gli uccelli e li mangiarono. 5Altri semi invece andarono a finire su un terreno dove c'erano molte pietre e poca terra: questi germogliarono subito perché la terra non era profonda, 6ma il sole, quando si levò, bruciò le pianticelle che seccarono perché non avevano radici robuste. 7Altri semi caddero in mezzo alle spine e le spine, crescendo, soffocarono i germogli. 8Ma alcuni semi caddero in un terreno buono e diedero un frutto abbondante: cento o sessanta o trenta volte di più. 9Chi ha orecchi, cerchi di capire!».

Perché Gesù usa le parabole

10Allora i discepoli di Gesù si avvicinarono a lui e gli domandarono:

– Perché, quando parli alla gente, usi le parabole?

11Gesù rispose:

– A voi Dio fa conoscere apertamente i misteri del suo regno, ma agli altri no. 12Perché, chi ha molto riceverà ancor di più e sarà nell'abbondanza; a chi ha poco, invece, porteranno via anche quel poco che ha. 13Per questo parlo in parabole: perché guardano e non vedono, ascoltano e non capiscono, 14e si realizza per loro la profezia che è scritta nel libro del profeta Isaia:

Ascolterete e non capirete, dice il Signore, *guarderete e non vedrete*.

15 *Perché il cuore di questo popolo è
     diventato insensibile:*
sono diventati duri d'orecchi,
hanno chiuso gli occhi:
per non vedere con gli occhi,
per non sentire con gli orecchi,
per non comprendere con il
     cuore,
per non tornare verso di me,
per non lasciarsi guarire da me.

16 Voi invece siete beati, perché i vostri
occhi vedono e i vostri orecchi ascoltano. 17 Vi assicuro che molti profeti
e molti uomini giusti avrebbero
desiderato vedere quel che voi vedete,
ma non l'hanno visto; molti avrebbero
desiderato udire quel che voi udite,
ma non l'hanno udito.

Gesù spiega
la parabola del seminatore

18 «Ascoltate il significato della
parabola del seminatore: 19 Il seme
caduto sulla strada indica chi sente
parlare del regno di Dio, ma non
capisce. Viene il maligno e ruba quel
che è stato seminato nel suo cuore.

20 «Il seme caduto dove c'erano
molte pietre indica chi ascolta la parola
di Dio e l'accoglie con entusiasmo,
21 ma non ha radici e non è costante;
appena incontra difficoltà o persecuzione, subito si lascia andare.

22 «Il seme caduto tra le spine indica
chi ascolta la parola, ma poi si lascia
prendere dalle preoccupazioni di questo
mondo e dai piaceri della ricchezza;
tutto questo soffoca la parola di Dio ed
essa rimane senza frutto.

23 «Infine, il seme caduto nel buon
terreno indica chi ascolta la parola di

Dio e la capisce. Egli la fa fruttificare
ed essa produce cento o sessanta o
trenta volte di più».

Parabola dell'erba cattiva

24 Poi Gesù raccontò un'altra parabola: «Il regno di Dio è come la buona
semente che un uomo fece seminare
nel suo campo. 25 Ma una notte,
mentre i contadini dormivano, un suo
nemico venne a seminare erba cattiva
in mezzo al grano e poi se ne andò.
26 Quando il grano cominciò a
spuntare e a formare le spighe, si vide
che era cresciuta in mezzo al grano
anche erba cattiva. 27 I contadini allora
dissero al padrone:

– Signore, tu avevi fatto seminare del
buon grano nel tuo campo. Da dove
viene l'erba cattiva?

28 «Egli rispose:

– È stato un nemico a far questo!

«I contadini gli domandarono:

– Vuoi che andiamo a strapparla via?

29 «Ma egli rispose:

– No! Perché, così, rischiate di
strappare anche il grano insieme con
l'erba cattiva. 30 Lasciate che crescano
insieme fino al giorno del raccolto. A
quel momento io dirò ai mietitori:
raccogliete prima l'erba cattiva e
legatela in fasci per bruciarla; il grano
invece mettetelo nel mio granaio».

Parabola del granello di senape
e del lievito

31 Poi Gesù raccontò un'altra
parabola: «Il regno di Dio è simile a un
granello di senape che un uomo prese
e seminò nel suo campo. 32 Esso è il
più piccolo di tutti i semi ma, quando

è cresciuto, è più grande di tutte le piante dell'orto: diventa un albero tanto grande che gli uccelli vengono a fare il nido tra i suoi rami».

³³Gesù disse ancora una parabola: «Il regno di Dio è simile a un po' di lievito che una donna ha preso e ha mescolato in una grande quantità di farina, e a un certo punto tutta la pasta è lievitata!».

Perché Gesù parla in parabole

³⁴Gesù raccontava alla folla tutte queste cose usando parabole: e non parlava mai senza parabole. ³⁵Così si realizzò quel che Dio aveva detto per mezzo del profeta:

Io parlerò loro in parabole,
annunzierò cose nascoste
fin dalla creazione del mondo.

Gesù spiega la parabola dell'erba cattiva

³⁶Poi Gesù si allontanò dalla folla e andò a casa. Allora i discepoli si avvicinarono a lui e gli dissero: «Spiegaci la parabola dell'erba cattiva cresciuta nel campo».

³⁷Gesù rispose: «Quello che semina la buona semente è il Figlio dell'uomo. ³⁸Il campo è il mondo. La buona semente rappresenta quelli che appartengono al regno di Dio; l'erba cattiva rappresenta quelli che appartengono al diavolo. ³⁹Il nemico che l'ha seminata è il diavolo stesso, e il giorno del raccolto è la fine di questo mondo. I mietitori infine sono gli angeli.

⁴⁰«Come l'erba cattiva è raccolta e bruciata nel fuoco, così si farà alla fine del mondo. ⁴¹Il Figlio dell'uomo manderà i suoi angeli, ed essi porteranno via dal suo regno tutti quelli che sono di ostacolo agli altri e quelli che fanno il male. ⁴²Li getteranno nel grande forno di fuoco. Là piangeranno come disperati. ⁴³Invece, quelli che fanno la volontà di Dio, quel giorno saranno splendenti come il sole nel regno di Dio Padre. Chi ha orecchi, cerchi di capire».

Tre parabole

⁴⁴«Il regno di Dio è simile a un tesoro nascosto in un campo. Un uomo lo trova, lo nasconde di nuovo, poi, pieno di gioia corre a vendere tutto quello che ha e compera quel campo.

⁴⁵«Il regno di Dio è simile a un mercante che va in cerca di perle preziose. ⁴⁶Quando ha trovato una perla di grande valore, egli va a vendere tutto quel che ha e compera quella perla.

⁴⁷«E ancora: il regno di Dio è simile a una rete gettata nel mare, la quale ha raccolto pesci di ogni genere. ⁴⁸Quando è piena, i pescatori la tirano a riva, si siedono e mettono nei cesti i pesci buoni; i pesci cattivi, invece, li buttano via. ⁴⁹Così sarà alla fine del mondo: verranno gli angeli e separeranno i malvagi dai buoni, ⁵⁰per gettarli nel grande forno di fuoco. Là, essi piangeranno come disperati».

Conclusione sulle parabole

⁵¹Poi Gesù disse ai discepoli:
– Avete capito tutte queste cose?
Risposero:
– Sì, abbiamo capito.
⁵²Ed egli disse:
– Perciò, un maestro della Legge che

diventa discepolo del regno di Dio è come un capofamiglia che dal suo tesoro tira fuori cose vecchie e cose nuove.

La gente di Nàzaret non ha fiducia in Gesù

⁵³Quando Gesù ebbe finito di raccontare queste parabole partì da quel luogo. ⁵⁴Andò nella sua città e si mise a insegnare nella sinagoga. I suoi compaesani, ascoltandolo, erano molto meravigliati e dicevano: «Ma chi gli ha dato questa sapienza e il potere di fare miracoli? ⁵⁵Non è il figlio del falegname? Non è Maria sua madre? I suoi fratelli non sono forse Giacomo, Giuseppe, Simone e Giuda? ⁵⁶E le sue sorelle non vivono, qui in mezzo a noi? Ma allora, dove ha imparato a fare e dire tutte queste cose?». ⁵⁷Per questo non volevano più saperne di lui. Ma Gesù disse loro: «Un profeta è disprezzato soprattutto nella sua patria e nella sua famiglia».

⁵⁸E in quel l'ambiente non fece molti miracoli perché la gente non aveva fede.

Opinioni su Gesù

14 ¹In quel tempo governava in Galilea il re Erode. Egli venne a sapere che Gesù era diventato famoso. ²Disse allora ai suoi servi: «Questi è Giovanni il Battezzatore, che è tornato dal mondo dei morti! Perciò ha il potere di fare i miracoli».

Morte di Giovanni il Battezzatore

³In realtà, qualche tempo prima, Erode aveva fatto arrestare Giovanni, l'aveva incatenato e messo in prigione. Il motivo di tutto ciò era stata la faccenda di Erodìade (la moglie di suo fratello Filippo); ⁴perché Giovanni aveva detto a Erode: «Non è giusto che tu la tenga con te!».

⁵Allora Erode voleva farlo ammazzare, ma aveva paura della gente, perché tutti pensavano che Giovanni era un profeta di Dio.

⁶Un giorno però ci fu la festa del suo compleanno, e la giovane figlia di Erodìade si mise a danzare davanti agli invitati. La sua danza piacque talmente a Erode ⁷che egli le fece una promessa e un giuramento: «Chiedimi quello che vuoi e io te lo darò».

⁸La madre le consigliò che cosa chiedere, e la ragazza disse: «Fammi portare qui, su un piatto, la testa di Giovanni il Battezzatore!».

⁹Il re fu molto dispiaciuto, ma siccome aveva giurato e c'erano lì presenti gli altri invitati, ordinò di dare quel che aveva chiesto. ¹⁰Perciò mandò uno alla prigione a far tagliare la testa a Giovanni. ¹¹La testa fu portata su un piatto e consegnata alla ragazza, ed essa la diede a sua madre.

¹²I discepoli di Giovanni andarono a prendere il corpo e lo seppellirono. Poi raccontarono il fatto a Gesù.

Gesù dà da mangiare a cinquemila uomini

¹³Quando sentì questa notizia, Gesù partì in barca per recarsi in un luogo isolato, lontano da tutti, ma la gente venne a saperlo e seguirono Gesù a piedi, venendo da varie città.

¹⁴Quando Gesù scese dalla barca e vide tutta quella folla, ebbe compassione di loro e si mise a guarire i malati.

¹⁵Verso sera, i discepoli si avvicinarono a Gesù e gli dissero:

– È già tardi e questo luogo è isolato. Lascia andare la gente in modo che possa comprarsi da mangiare nei villaggi.

¹⁶Ma Gesù disse loro:

– Non hanno bisogno di andar via: dategli voi qualcosa da mangiare.

¹⁷Essi gli risposero:

– Ma noi abbiamo soltanto cinque pani e due pesci.

¹⁸E Gesù disse:

– Portateli qui a me.

¹⁹Allora Gesù ordinò di far sedere la folla sull'erba. Prese i cinque pani e i due pesci, alzò gli occhi al cielo e disse la preghiera di benedizione. Poi spezzò i pani e li diede ai discepoli; e i discepoli alla folla.

²⁰Tutti mangiarono e ne ebbero abbastanza. Alla fine raccolsero i pezzi avanzati e ne riempirono dodici ceste. ²¹Quelli che avevano mangiato erano circa cinquemila uomini, senza contare le donne e i bambini.

Gesù cammina sul lago

²²Subito dopo Gesù ordinò ai discepoli di salire in barca e di andare sull'altra riva del lago. Egli intanto avrebbe rimandato a casa la gente. ²³Dopo averla rimandata salì da solo sul monte a pregare.

Venne la notte, e Gesù era ancora là, solo. ²⁴La barca era già molto lontana dalla spiaggia, ma aveva il vento contrario ed era sbattuta dalle onde.

²⁵Sul finire della notte, Gesù andò verso i suoi discepoli camminando sul lago. ²⁶Quando essi lo videro camminare sull'acqua si spaventarono. Dicevano:

– È un fantasma! – e gridavano di paura.

²⁷Ma subito Gesù parlò:

– Coraggio, sono io! Non abbiate paura!

²⁸Pietro rispose:

– Signore, se sei tu, dimmi di venire verso di te, sull'acqua.

²⁹E Gesù gli disse:

– Vieni!

Pietro allora scese dalla barca e cominciò a camminare sull'acqua verso Gesù.

³⁰Ma vedendo la forza del vento, ebbe paura, cominciò ad affondare e gridò:

– Signore! Salvami!

³¹Gesù lo afferrò con la mano e gli disse:

– Uomo di poca fede, perché hai dubitato?

³²Quando salirono insieme nella barca il vento cessò. ³³Allora gli altri che erano nella barca si misero in ginocchio di fronte a Gesù e dissero: «Tu sei veramente il Figlio di Dio!».

Gesù guarisce i malati nella regione di Genèsaret

³⁴Attraversato il lago arrivarono nella regione di Genèsaret. ³⁵La gente del posto riconobbe Gesù e tutto intorno si sparse la voce che egli era arrivato. Allora gli portarono i loro malati, ³⁶e lo supplicarono di permettere che gli toccassero almeno l'orlo del mantello. E tutti quelli che lo toccavano erano guariti.

La tradizione degli uomini e i comandamenti di Dio

15 ¹Alcuni farisei e alcuni maestri della Legge giunti da Gerusalemme si avvicinarono a Gesù e gli dissero:

2 – Prima di mangiare, i tuoi discepoli non fanno il rito di lavarsi le mani. Perché non rispettano la tradizione religiosa dei nostri padri?

3 Gesù rispose loro:

– E voi, perché non rispettate i comandamenti di Dio, per seguire la vostra tradizione? 4 Dio ha detto: *Onora il padre e la madre*. E poi: *Chi parla male di suo padre o di sua madre deve essere condannato a morte*. 5-6 Voi invece insegnate che uno non ha più il dovere di onorare suo padre e sua madre se dice ad essi che ha offerto a Dio quei beni che doveva usare per loro.

Così, per mezzo della vostra tradizione, voi fate diventare inutile la parola di Dio. 7 Ipocriti! Il profeta Isaia aveva ragione quando, parlando di voi, diceva:

8 *Questo popolo,* – dice il Signore – *mi onora a parole,*
  ma il suo cuore è lontano da me.
9 *Il modo con cui mi onorano non ha valore,*
  perché insegnano come dottrina di Dio
  comandamenti che son fatti da uomini.

Le cose che rendono impuro un uomo

10 Poi Gesù chiamò la folla e disse: «Ascoltate e cercate di capire. 11 Non è ciò che entra nella bocca dell'uomo che può farlo diventare impuro. Piuttosto è ciò che esce dalla bocca: questo può far diventare impuro l'uomo!».

12 I discepoli si avvicinarono e gli dissero:

– Sai che i farisei si sono scandalizzati ascoltando le tue parole?

13 Ma Gesù rispose:

– Tutti gli alberi che non sono stati piantati dal Padre mio, che è in cielo, saranno strappati. 14 Lasciateli dire! Sono ciechi, e vogliono far da guida ad altri ciechi. E quando un cieco guida un altro cieco, tutti e due andranno a cadere in una fossa.

15 Allora Pietro disse:

– Spiegaci questa parabola.

16 Ma Gesù rispose:

– Anche voi non riuscite ancora a capire? 17 Non capite che quello che entra in bocca va allo stomaco e quindi va a finire in una fogna? 18 Ciò che invece esce dalla bocca viene dal cuore dell'uomo ed è questo che può renderlo impuro. 19 Perché, è dal cuore che vengono tutti i pensieri malvagi che portano al male: gli assassinii, i tradimenti tra marito e moglie, i peccati sessuali, i furti, le menzogne, gli insulti. 20 Sono queste le cose che fanno diventare impuro l'uomo. Invece, mangiare senza purificarsi prima le mani, questo non fa diventare impuri.

La fede di una donna straniera

21 Poi Gesù andò via di là e si ritirò dalle parti di Tiro e di Sidone. Una donna pagana che veniva da quella regione si presentò a Gesù gridando:

– Signore, Figlio di Davide, abbi pietà di me! Mia figlia sta molto male, uno spirito maligno la tormenta.

23 Ma Gesù non rispondeva nulla. Si avvicinarono allora i suoi discepoli e gli dissero:

– Mandala a casa, perché continua a venirci dietro e a gridare.

²⁴Gesù disse:

– Io sono stato mandato soltanto per le pecore sperdute del popolo d'Israele.

²⁵Ma quella donna si metteva in ginocchio davanti a lui e diceva:

– Signore, aiutami!

²⁶Allora Gesù rispose:

– Non è giusto prendere il pane dei figli e buttarlo ai cagnolini.

²⁷E la donna disse:

– È vero, Signore. Però, sotto la tavola, i cagnolini possono mangiare le briciole che cadono ai loro padroni.

²⁸Allora Gesù le disse:

– O donna, davvero la tua fede è grande! Accada come tu vuoi.

E in quel momento sua figlia guarì.

Gesù guarisce molti malati

²⁹Poi Gesù andò verso il lago di Galilea, salì sopra una collina e si sedette. ³⁰Molta gente venne da lui portando zoppi, storpi, ciechi, muti e molti altri malati. Li mettevano a terra, vicino ai suoi piedi, ed egli li guariva. ³¹La gente era piena di meraviglia perché vedeva che i muti incominciavano a parlare, gli storpi erano guariti, gli zoppi camminavano bene e i ciechi riacquistavano la vista.

Allora tutti lodavano il Dio d'Israele.

Gesù dà da mangiare a quattromila uomini

³²Gesù chiamò i suoi discepoli e disse:

– Questa gente mi fa pena. Già da tre giorni stanno con me e non hanno più niente da mangiare. Non voglio mandarli a casa digiuni, perché potrebbero sentirsi male lungo la strada.

³³I discepoli gli dissero:

– Come potremo qui, in un luogo deserto, trovare tanto pane per una folla così grande?

³⁴E Gesù domandò:

– Quanti pani avete?

Risposero:

– Sette, e pochi pesciolini.

³⁵E Gesù ordinò alla folla di sedersi per terra. ³⁶Prese i sette pani e i pesci, fece la preghiera di ringraziamento, spezzò i pani e li diede ai discepoli, e i discepoli alla folla.

³⁷Tutti mangiarono e ne ebbero abbastanza. Quando poi si raccolsero gli avanzi, se ne riempirono sette ceste.

³⁸Quelli che avevano mangiato erano quattromila uomini, senza contare le donne e i bambini. ³⁹Dopo aver rimandato a casa la folla, Gesù salì in barca e andò nel territorio di Magadàn.

Farisei e sadducei vogliono vedere un miracolo

16 ¹Alcuni farisei e alcuni sadducei andarono da Gesù. Volevano metterlo in difficoltà, perciò gli domandarono di far loro vedere un segno miracoloso come prova che veniva da Dio. ²Ma Gesù rispose così: «Quando si fa sera voi dite: Il tempo sarà bello, perché il cielo è rosso. ³E al mattino presto dite: Oggi avremo un temporale perché il cielo è rosso scuro. Dunque, sapete interpretare l'aspetto del cielo e non sapete capire il significato di ciò che accade in questi tempi? 4Questa gente malvagia e infedele a Dio vuol vedere un segno miracoloso! Ma non riceverà nessun segno eccetto il segno del profeta Giona».

Poi li lasciò e se ne andò.

I discepoli stentano a capire

5Prima di andare all'altra riva, i discepoli si erano dimenticati di prendere il pane. 6Gesù disse loro: «State attenti! Tenetevi lontani dal lievito dei farisei e dei sadducei!».

7E i discepoli si misero a discutere tra loro: «Parla così perché ci siamo dimenticati di prendere il pane».

8Ma Gesù se ne accorse e disse: «Uomini di poca fede, perché state a discutere che non avete pane? 9Non capite ancora? Non ricordate i cinque pani distribuiti a cinquemila uomini e le ceste avanzate? 10Avete dimenticato i sette pani distribuiti ai quattromila uomini e le ceste riempite con gli avanzi raccolti? 11Perché non capite che non stavo parlando di pane? Ho detto soltanto: state lontani dal lievito dei farisei e dei sadducei!».

12Allora i discepoli capirono che non aveva parlato del lievito del pane, ma voleva dire di non fidarsi dell'insegnamento dei farisei e dei sadducei.

Pietro dichiara che Gesù è il Messia e il figlio di Dio

13Quando Gesù giunse dalle parti di Cesarèa di Filippo domandò ai suoi discepoli:

– Chi è il Figlio dell'uomo, secondo la gente?

14Risposero:

– Alcuni dicono che è Giovanni il Battezzatore; altri che è il profeta Elia; altri ancora che è Geremia, o uno degli antichi profeti.

15Gesù riprese:

– E voi, che dite? Chi sono io?

16Simon Pietro rispose:

– Tu sei il Messia, il Cristo; il Figlio del Dio vivente.

17Allora Gesù gli disse:

– Beato te, Simone figlio di Giona, perché non hai scoperto questa verità con forze umane, ma essa ti è stata rivelata dal Padre mio che è in cielo. 18Per questo io ti dico che tu sei Pietro e su di te, come su una pietra, io costruirò la mia comunità. Nemmeno la potenza della morte potrà distruggerla. 19Io ti darò le chiavi del regno di Dio: tutto ciò che tu sulla terra proibirai, sarà proibito anche in cielo; tutto ciò che tu permetterai sulla terra, sarà permesso anche in cielo.

20Poi Gesù ordinò ai suoi discepoli di non dire a nessuno che egli era il Messia.

Gesù annunzia la sua morte e risurrezione. Il rimprovero di Pietro

21Da quel momento Gesù cominciò a spiegare ai discepoli ciò che gli doveva capitare. Diceva: «Io devo andare a Gerusalemme. È necessario. Gli anziani del popolo, i capi dei sacerdoti e i maestri della Legge mi faranno soffrire molto, poi sarò ucciso, ma al terzo giorno risusciterò».

22Allora Pietro prese da parte Gesù e si mise a rimproverarlo:

−Dio non voglia, Signore! No, questo non ti accada mai!

²³Gesù si voltò verso Pietro e disse: −Va' via, Satana! Tu sei un ostacolo per me, perché tu ragioni come gli uomini, ma non pensi come Dio.

Condizioni per seguire Gesù

²⁴Poi Gesù disse ai suoi discepoli: «Se qualcuno vuol venire dietro a me, smetta di pensare a se stesso, prenda la sua croce e mi segua. ²⁵Chi pensa soltanto a salvare la propria vita la perderà; chi invece è pronto a sacrificare la propria vita per me la ritroverà. ²⁶Se un uomo riesce a guadagnare anche il mondo intero, ma perde la vita, che vantaggio ne avrà? Oppure, c'è qualcosa che un uomo potrà dare per riavere, in cambio, la propria vita?

²⁷Il Figlio dell'uomo ritornerà glorioso come Dio suo Padre, insieme con i suoi angeli. Allora egli darà a ciascuno la ricompensa in base a quel che ciascuno avrà fatto. ²⁸Io vi assicuro che alcuni tra quelli che sono qui presenti non moriranno prima di aver visto venire il Figlio dell'uomo e il suo regno».

La trasfigurazione: Gesù manifesta la sua gloria a tre discepoli

17 ¹Sei giorni dopo, Gesù prese con sé tre discepoli: Pietro, Giacomo e Giovanni fratello di Giacomo, e li condusse su un alto monte, in un luogo solitario. ²Là, di fronte a loro, Gesù cambiò aspetto: il suo volto si fece splendente come il sole e i suoi abiti diventarono bian-

chissimi, come di luce. ³Poi i discepoli videro anche Mosè e il profeta Elia: essi stavano accanto a Gesù e parlavano con lui. ⁴Allora Pietro disse a Gesù: «Signore, è bello per noi stare qui. Se vuoi, preparerò tre tende: una per te, una per Mosè e una per Elia».

⁵Stava ancora parlando, quando apparve una nuvola luminosa che li avvolse con la sua ombra. Poi, dalla nuvola venne una voce che diceva: «Questo è il Figlio mio, che io amo. Io l'ho mandato. Ascoltatelo!».

⁶A queste parole, i discepoli furono talmente spaventati che si buttarono con la faccia a terra. ⁷Ma Gesù si avvicinò, li toccò e disse: «Alzatevi! Non abbiate paura!». ⁸Alzarono gli occhi e non videro più nessuno: c'era infatti Gesù solo.

⁹Mentre scendevano dal monte, Gesù diede quest'ordine ai discepoli: «Non dite a nessuno quel che avete visto, fino a quando il Figlio dell'uomo sarà risuscitato dai morti».

¹⁰Poi i discepoli fecero una domanda a Gesù:

−Perché dunque i maestri della Legge dicono che prima di tutto deve tornare il profeta Elia?

¹¹Egli rispose:

−È vero, prima deve venire Elia per mettere in ordine ogni cosa. ¹²Vi assicuro però che Elia è già venuto, ma non l'hanno riconosciuto e gli hanno fatto quel che hanno voluto. Allo stesso modo faranno soffrire anche il Figlio dell'uomo.

¹³Allora i discepoli capirono che aveva parlato di Giovanni il Battezzatore.

Gesù guarisce
un ragazzo tormentato
da uno spirito maligno

[14]Quando arrivarono in mezzo alla gente, un uomo si avvicinò a Gesù, si mise in ginocchio davanti a lui [15]e gli disse:

– Signore, abbi pietà di mio figlio. È epilettico, e quando ha una crisi spesso cade nel fuoco o nell'acqua. [16]L'ho fatto vedere ai tuoi discepoli, ma non sono riusciti a guarirlo.

[17]Allora Gesù rispose:

– Gente malvagia e senza fede! Fino a quando resterò ancora con voi? Per quanto tempo dovrò sopportarvi? Portatemi qui il ragazzo.

[18]Gesù allora minacciò il demonio: quello uscì dal ragazzo, e da quel momento il ragazzo fu guarito.

[19]Allora i discepoli si avvicinarono a Gesù, lo presero da parte e gli domandarono:

– Perché non non siamo stati capaci di scacciare quel demonio?

[20]Gesù rispose:

– Perché non avete fede. Se aveste almeno una fede piccola come un granello di senape, potreste dire a questo monte: «Spostati da qui a là» e il monte si sposterà. Niente sarà impossibile per voi. [21]

Per la seconda volta
Gesù annunzia la sua morte
e risurrezione

[22]Un giorno che i discepoli erano tutti assieme in Galilea, Gesù disse: «Il Figlio dell'uomo sta per essere consegnato nelle mani degli uomini [23]ed essi lo uccideranno; ma al terzo giorno risusciterà». Allora i discepoli diventarono molto tristi.

Gesù e Pietro pagano
la tassa per il Tempio

[24]Poi andarono a Cafàrnao. Là, alcuni esattori della tassa del Tempio si avvicinarono a Pietro e gli domandarono:

– Il vostro maestro paga la tassa?

[25]Pietro rispose:

– Sì, la paga.

Quando entrarono in casa, Gesù parlò per primo e disse a Pietro:

– Simone, dimmi il tuo parere: chi deve pagare le tasse ai re di questo mondo: gli estranei o i figli dei re?

[26]Pietro rispose:

– Gli estranei.

Gesù continuò:

– Dunque i figli non sono obbligati a pagare le tasse. [27]Ma non dobbiamo dare scandalo: vai perciò in riva al lago, getta l'amo per pescare, e il primo pesce che abbocca tiralo fuori; aprigli la bocca e ci troverai una grossa moneta d'argento. Prendi allora la moneta e paga la tassa per me e per te.

Discorso
sulla vita comunitaria

Chi è il più importante?

18 [1]In quel momento i discepoli si avvicinarono a Gesù e gli domandarono: «Chi è il più importante nel regno di Dio?».

[2]Gesù chiamò un bambino, lo mise in mezzo a loro [3]e disse: «Vi assicuro che se non cambiate e non diventate

come bambini non entrerete nel regno di Dio. ⁴Chi si fa piccolo come questo bambino, quello è il più importante nel regno di Dio. ⁵E chi per amor mio accoglie un bambino come questo, accoglie me.

Contro ogni occasione di male

⁶«Ma se qualcuno farà perdere la fede a una di queste persone semplici che credono in me, sarebbe più conveniente per lui che lo buttassero in fondo al mare, con una grossa pietra legata al collo.

⁷«È triste che nel mondo ci siano scandali. Ce ne saranno sempre, ma guai a quelli che li provocano.

⁸«Se la tua mano e il tuo piede ti fanno compiere il male, tagliali e gettali via: è meglio per te entrare nella vera vita senza una mano o senza un piede, piuttosto che essere gettato nel fuoco eterno con due mani e due piedi.

⁹«Se il tuo occhio ti fa compiere il male, strappalo e gettalo via: è meglio per te entrare nella vera vita con un occhio solo, piuttosto che essere gettato nel fuoco dell'inferno con tutti e due gli occhi.

Parabola della pecora perduta e ritrovata

¹⁰«State attenti! Non disprezzate nessuna di queste persone semplici, perché vi dico che in cielo i loro angeli vedono continuamente il Padre mio che è in cielo. [¹¹]

¹²«Provate a pensare: se un tale possiede cento pecore e gli accade che una si perde, che cosa farà? Non lascerà le altre novantanove sui monti per andare a cercare quella pecora che si è perduta? ¹³E se poi la trova, vi assicuro che sarà più contento per questa pecora, che non per le altre novantanove che non si erano perdute. ¹⁴Allo stesso modo, il Padre vostro che è in cielo vuole che nessuna di queste persone semplici vada perduta.

Come si corregge un fratello che sbaglia

¹⁵«Se un tuo fratello ti fa del male, va' da lui e mostragli il suo errore, ma senza farlo sentire ad altri. Se ti ascolta, avrai recuperato tuo fratello.

¹⁶«Se invece non vuole ascoltarti, fatti accompagnare da una o due persone, perché sia fatto come dice la Bibbia: *Ogni questione sia risolta mediante due o tre testimoni.*

¹⁷«Se non vuole ascoltare nemmeno loro, va' a riferire il fatto alla comunità dei credenti. Se poi non ascolterà neppure la comunità, consideralo come un pagano o un estraneo.

Valore della preghiera comunitaria

¹⁸«Vi assicuro che tutto quel che voi avrete proibito sulla terra sarà proibito anche in cielo; e tutto quel che voi permetterete sulla terra sarà permesso anche in cielo. ¹⁹E ancora vi assicuro che se due di voi, in terra, si troveranno d'accordo su quel che devono fare e chiederanno aiuto nella preghiera, il Padre mio che è in cielo glielo concederà. ²⁰Perché, se due o tre si riuniscono per invocare il mio nome, io sono in mezzo a loro».

Il perdono.
Parabola del servo crudele

[21] Allora Pietro si avvicinò a Gesù e gli domandò:

– Signore, quante volte dovrò perdonare a un mio fratello che mi fa del male? Fino a sette volte?

[22] Rispose Gesù:

– No, non dico fino a sette volte, ma fino a settanta volta sette!

[23] «Perché il regno di Dio è così.

«Un re decise di controllare i servi che avevano amministrato i suoi beni. [24] Stava facendo i suoi conti, quando gli portarono un servitore che doveva pagargli un'enorme somma di denaro.

[25] «Ma costui non poteva pagare, e per questo il re ordinò di venderlo come schiavo e di vendere anche sua moglie, i suoi figli e tutto ciò che possedeva, per fargli pagare il debito.

[26] «Allora il servitore si inginocchiò davanti al re e si mise a pregarlo: "Abbi pazienza con me e ti pagherò tutto!"

[27] «Il re ebbe pietà di lui: cancellò il suo debito e lo lasciò andare.

[28] «Appena uscito, quel servitore incontrò un suo compagno che doveva pagargli una piccola somma di denaro. Lo prese per il collo e lo stringeva fino a soffocarlo mentre diceva:

– Paga quel che mi devi!

[29] «L'altro cadde ai suoi piedi e si mise a supplicarlo:

– Abbi pazienza con me e ti pagherò.

[30] «Ma costui non volle saperne, anzi lo fece mettere in prigione fino a quando non avesse pagato tutto il debito.

[31] «Gli altri servitori videro queste cose e rimasero molto dispiaciuti. Andarono dal re e gli raccontarono tutto quel che era accaduto. [32] Allora il re chiamò di nuovo quel servitore e gli disse: "Servo crudele! Io ti ho perdonato quel debito enorme perché tu mi hai supplicato. [33] Dovevi anche tu aver pietà del tuo compagno, così come io ho avuto pietà di te".

[34] «Poi, pieno di collera, lo fece mettere in prigione fino a quando non avesse pagato tutto il debito.

[35] E Gesù aggiunse: «Così il Padre mio che è in cielo farà con ciascuno di voi, se non perdonerete di cuore al vostro fratello».

Matrimonio e divorzio

19 [1] Quando Gesù ebbe finito di parlare lasciò la Galilea e andò verso i confini della Giudea, al di là del fiume Giordano. [2] Grandi folle lo seguivano ed egli guariva i malati.

[3] Si avvicinarono a lui alcuni che erano del gruppo dei farisei. Essi volevano metterlo in difficoltà, perciò gli domandarono:

– Un uomo può divorziare dalla propria moglie per un motivo qualsiasi?

[4] Gesù rispose:

– Non avete letto ciò che dice la Bibbia? Dice che Dio fin dal principio *maschio e femmina li creò.* [5] *Perciò l'uomo lascerà suo padre e sua madre e si unirà alla sua donna e i due saranno una cosa sola.* [6] Così essi non sono più due ma un unico essere. Perciò l'uomo non separi ciò che Dio ha unito.

7I farisei gli domandarono:

– Perché dunque Mosè ha comandato di *mandar via la moglie dopo averle dato una dichiarazione scritta di divorzio?*

8Gesù rispose:

– Mosè vi ha permesso di mandar via le vostre donne perché voi avete il cuore duro; ma al principio non era così. 9Ora io vi dico: se uno manda via la propria donna – salvo il caso di una relazione illegale – e poi ne sposa un'altra, costui commette adulterio.

Matrimonio e celibato

10Allora i suoi discepoli gli dissero:

– Se questa è la condizione dell'uomo che si sposa, è meglio non sposarsi.

11Gesù rispose:

– Non tutti capiscono questo insegnamento; lo accolgono soltanto quelli ai quali Dio dà la capacità di farlo.

12Vi sono diversi motivi per cui certe persone non si sposano: per alcuni vi è un'impossibilità fisica, fin dalla nascita; altri sono incapaci di sposarsi perché gli uomini li hanno fatti diventare così; altri poi non si sposano per servire meglio il regno di Dio. Chi può capire, cerchi di capire.

Gesù benedice i bambini

13Alcune persone portarono i propri bambini a Gesù e gli domandarono di posare le sue mani su di loro e di pregare per loro. Ma i discepoli li sgridavano. 14Gesù invece disse: «Lasciate stare i bambini e non impedite che vengano a me, perché Dio dà il suo regno a quelli che sono come loro». 15E posò le mani sui bambini.

Poi se ne andò da quel luogo.

Gesù incontra un giovane ricco

16Un tale si avvicinò a Gesù e gli domandò:

– Maestro, che cosa devo fare di buono per avere la vita eterna?

17Ma Gesù gli disse:

– Perché mi fai una domanda su ciò che è buono? Dio solo è buono. Ma se vuoi entrare nella vita eterna ubbidisci ai comandamenti.

18Quello chiese ancora:

– Quali comandamenti?

Gesù rispose:

– *Non uccidere;*

Non commettere adulterio;

Non rubare;

Non dire il falso contro nessuno;

19*Rispetta tuo padre e tua madre;*

Ama il prossimo tuo come te stesso.

20Quel giovane disse:

– Io ho sempre ubbidito a tutti questi comandamenti: che cosa mi manca ancora?

21E Gesù gli rispose:

– Per essere perfetto, vai a vendere tutto quello che hai, e i soldi che ricavi dalli ai poveri. Allora avrai un tesoro in cielo. Poi, vieni e seguimi.

22Ma dopo aver ascoltato queste parole, il giovane se ne andò triste, perché era molto ricco.

23Allora Gesù disse ai suoi discepoli: «Vi assicuro che difficilmente un ricco entrerà nel regno di Dio. 24Anzi, vi assicuro che se è difficile per un cammello passare attraverso la cruna di un ago, è ancor più difficile che un ricco possa entrare nel regno di Dio».

²⁵I discepoli rimasero molto meravigliati di quel che avevano sentito e dissero:

– Ma allora chi potrà mai salvarsi?

²⁶Gesù li guardò e rispose:

– Per gli uomini è una cosa impossibile, ma per Dio tutto è possibile.

²⁷Allora parlò Pietro e disse:

– E noi? Noi abbiamo abbandonato tutto per venire con te. Che cosa dobbiamo aspettarci?

²⁸Gesù rispose:

– Io vi assicuro che nel nuovo mondo, quando il Figlio dell'uomo starà sul suo trono glorioso, anche voi che mi avete seguito starete su dodici troni per giudicare le dodici tribù d'Israele. ²⁹E tutti quelli che, per causa mia, hanno abbandonato fratelli e sorelle, padre e madre, case o campi... riceveranno cento volte di più e avranno in eredità la vita eterna. ³⁰Molti che ora sono i primi saranno gli ultimi; e molti che ora sono gli ultimi saranno i primi.

Parabola degli operai nella vigna

20 ¹«Così infatti è il regno di Dio. «Un tale aveva una grande vigna e una mattina, molto presto, uscì in piazza per prendere a giornata uomini da mandare a lavorare nella sua vigna. ²Fissò con loro la paga normale: una moneta d'argento al giorno e li mandò al lavoro.

³«Verso le nove del mattino tornò in piazza e vide che c'erano altri uomini disoccupati. ⁴Gli disse:

"Andate anche voi nella mia vigna; vi pagherò quel che è giusto". ⁵E quelli andarono.

«Anche verso mezzogiorno e poi verso le tre del pomeriggio fece la stessa cosa. ⁶Verso le cinque di sera uscì ancora una volta e trovò altri uomini. Disse:

– Perché state qui tutto il giorno senza far niente?

⁷«E quelli risposero:

– Perché nessuno ci ha preso a giornata.

«Allora disse:

– Andate anche voi nella mia vigna.

⁸«Quando fu sera, il padrone della vigna disse al suo fattore: "Chiama gli uomini e da' loro la paga, cominciando da quelli che son venuti per ultimi".

⁹«Il fattore chiamò dunque quelli che eran venuti alle cinque di sera e diede una moneta d'argento a ciascuno. ¹⁰Gli uomini che avevano cominciato per primi credevano di prendere di più. Invece, anch'essi ricevettero una moneta d'argento ciascuno.

¹¹«Allora cominciarono a brontolare contro il padrone. ¹²Dicevano:

– Questi sono venuti per ultimi, hanno lavorato soltanto un'ora, e tu li hai pagati come noi che abbiamo faticato tutto il giorno sotto il sole.

¹³«Rispondendo a uno di loro, il padrone disse:

– Amico, io non ti ho imbrogliato: l'accordo era che ti avrei pagato una moneta d'argento, o no? ¹⁴Allora prendi la tua paga e sta' zitto. Io voglio dare a questo, che è venuto per ultimo, quel che ho dato a te. ¹⁵Non posso fare quel che voglio con i miei soldi? O forse sei invidioso perché io sono generoso?».

16 Poi Gesù disse: «Così, quelli che sono gli ultimi saranno i primi, e quelli che sono i primi saranno gli ultimi».

Per la terza volta Gesù annunzia la sua morte e risurrezione

17 Gesù stava camminando verso Gerusalemme. Lungo la via egli prese da parte i dodici discepoli e disse loro: 18 «Ecco, noi stiamo salendo verso Gerusalemme. Là il Figlio dell'uomo sarà dato nelle mani dei capi dei sacerdoti e dei maestri della Legge. Essi lo condanneranno a morte 19 e poi lo consegneranno ai pagani. I pagani gli rideranno in faccia, lo prenderanno a frustate e lo inchioderanno su una croce. Ma il terzo giorno egli risusciterà».

Una madre chiede i primi posti per i figli

20 Allora la moglie di Zebedèo insieme con i suoi due figli si avvicinò a Gesù e si gettò ai suoi piedi per chiedergli qualcosa.

21 Gesù le disse:

– Che cosa vuoi?

E la donna:

– Promettimi che questi miei figli staranno uno alla tua destra e uno alla tua sinistra quando tu sarai nel tuo regno.

22 Gesù rispose:

– Voi non sapete quel che chiedete! Siete pronti a bere quel calice di dolore che io sto per bere?

I due fratelli risposero:

– Siamo pronti!

23 E Gesù:

– Sì, certamente anche voi berrete il mio calice. Ma non posso decidere io chi sarà seduto alla mia destra e alla mia sinistra. Quei posti sono per quelli ai quali il Padre mio li ha preparati.

24 Gli altri dieci discepoli avevano sentito tutto e si indignarono contro i due fratelli. 25 Ma Gesù li chiamò vicino a sé e disse: «Come voi sapete, i capi dei popoli comandano come duri padroni; le persone potenti fanno sentire con la forza il peso della loro autorità. 26 Ma tra voi non deve essere così! Anzi, se uno tra voi vuole essere grande, si faccia servitore degli altri. 27 Se uno vuole essere il primo, si faccia servo degli altri.

28 «Perché anche il Figlio dell'uomo è venuto non per farsi servire, ma per servire e per dare la sua vita come riscatto per la liberazione degli uomini».

Gesù guarisce due ciechi

29 Mentre uscivano dalla città di Gèrico una grande folla seguiva Gesù. 30 Sul bordo della strada stavano seduti due ciechi. Quando sentirono che passava Gesù si misero a gridare: «Signore, Figlio di Davide, abbi pietà di noi!». 31 La gente li sgridava per farli tacere, ma quelli gridavano ancora più forte: «Signore, Figlio di Davide, abbi pietà di noi!».

32 Gesù si fermò, li fece chiamare e disse:

– Che cosa volete che io faccia per voi?

33 Quelli risposero:

– Signore, fa' che i nostri occhi possano vedere!

³⁴Gesù ebbe compassione di loro: toccò i loro occhi e subito i ciechi ricuperarono la vista e seguirono Gesù.

Gesù entra in Gerusalemme: entusiasmo della folla

21 ¹Gesù e i discepoli stavano avvicinandosi a Gerusalemme. Quando arrivarono al villaggio di Bètfage, vicino al monte degli Ulivi, Gesù mandò avanti due discepoli. ²Disse loro: «Andate nel villaggio che è qui di fronte a voi, e subito troverete un'asina e il suo puledro, legati. Slegateli e portateli a me. ³E se qualcuno vi domanda qualcosa, dite così: È il Signore che ne ha bisogno, ma poi li rimanda indietro subito».

⁴E così si realizzò quel che Dio aveva detto per mezzo del profeta:

5 *Dite a Gerusalemme:*
guarda, il tuo re viene a te.
Egli è umile,
e viene seduto su un asino
un asinello, puledro d'asina.

⁶I due discepoli partirono e fecero come Gesù aveva comandato. ⁷Portarono l'asina e il puledro, gli misero addosso i mantelli e Gesù vi montò sopra.

⁸La folla era numerosissima. Alcuni stendevano sulla strada i loro mantelli, altri invece stendevano ramoscelli tagliati dagli alberi e facevano come un tappeto. ⁹La gente che camminava davanti a Gesù e quella che veniva dietro gridava:

«*Osanna!* Gloria al Figlio di Davide!
Benedetto colui che viene nel nome del Signore!
Gloria a Dio nell'alto dei cieli!».

¹⁰Quando Gesù entrò in Gerusalemme, tutta la città fu in agitazione. Dicevano: «Ma chi è costui?». ¹¹La folla rispondeva: «È il profeta! È Gesù, quello che viene da Nàzaret di Galilea».

Gesù scaccia i mercanti dal Tempio

¹²Poi Gesù entrò nel cortile del Tempio. Cacciò via tutti quelli che stavano là a vendere e a comprare, buttò all'aria i tavoli di quelli che cambiavano i soldi e rovesciò le sedie dei venditori di colombe. ¹³E disse loro: «Nella Bibbia Dio dice:

La mia casa sarà casa di preghiera.

«*Voi invece ne avete fatto*
un covo di briganti».

¹⁴Nel Tempio si avvicinarono a Gesù alcuni ciechi e zoppi, ed egli li guarì. ¹⁵I capi dei sacerdoti e i maestri della Legge videro le cose straordinarie che aveva fatto e sentirono i bambini che gridavano: «Gloria al Figlio di Davide!» e si sdegnarono. ¹⁶Dissero a Gesù:

– Ma non senti che cosa dicono?

Gesù rispose:

– Sì, sento. Ma voi non avete mai letto nella Bibbia queste parole: *Dalla bocca dei fanciulli e dei bambini ti sei procurata una lode?*

¹⁷Poi li lasciò e se ne andò via; uscì dalla città e passò la notte a Betània.

Gesù e l'albero senza frutti. Fede e preghiera

¹⁸Il mattino dopo Gesù tornò a Gerusalemme. Lungo la via ebbe fame. ¹⁹e poiché aveva visto una pianta di

fichi, si avvicinò per cogliere i frutti; ma non trovò niente, soltanto foglie. Allora disse all'albero: «Mai più in eterno nascano frutti da te!». E l'albero immediatamente diventò secco.

20 I discepoli rimasero pieni di stupore. Perciò domandarono:

– Perché l'albero di fico è seccato immediatamente?

21 Gesù rispose:

– Io vi assicuro che se avete fede e non dubitate, anche voi potrete fare ciò che è capitato a questo albero. Anzi, potrete anche dire a questa montagna: Sollévati e bùttati nel mare! e avverrà così. 22 Tutto quel che chiederete nella preghiera, se avete fede, lo riceverete.

Discussione sull'autorità di Gesù

23 Gesù venne di nuovo nel Tempio. Mentre se ne stava là a insegnare, i capi dei sacerdoti e le altre autorità del popolo si avvicinarono a lui e gli domandarono:

– Che diritto hai di fare quel che fai? Chi ti ha dato l'autorità di agire così?

24 Gesù rispose loro:

– Voglio farvi anch'io una domanda; se mi rispondete, anch'io vi dirò con quale autorità faccio queste cose. 25 Dunque, Giovanni, chi lo ha mandato a battezzare? Dio o gli uomini?

Essi cominciarono a discutere tra loro: «Se diciamo che Giovanni è stato mandato da Dio, ci chiederà: "Perché allora non avete creduto in lui?". 26 Se invece diciamo che è stato mandato dagli uomini, c'è da aver paura della folla, perché tutti considerano Giovanni come un profeta». 27 Perciò risposero:

– Non lo sappiamo.

Allora anche Gesù dichiarò:

– Ebbene, in questo caso neppure io vi dirò con quale autorità faccio queste cose.

Parabola dei due figli

28 Poi Gesù disse loro: «Vorrei conoscere il vostro parere. C'era un uomo che aveva due figli. Chiamò il primo e gli disse: Figlio mio, oggi va' a lavorare nella vigna. 29 Ma quello rispose: "No, non ne ho voglia"; ma poi cambiò idea e ci andò. 30 Chiamò anche il secondo figlio e gli disse la stessa cosa. Quello rispose: "Sì, padre", ma poi non ci andò. 31 Ora, ditemi il vostro parere: chi dei due ha fatto la volontà del padre?».

Risposero: «Il primo».

Allora Gesù disse: «Ebbene, vi assicuro che ladri e prostitute vi passano avanti ed entrano nel regno di Dio. 32 Perché Giovanni il Battezzatore è venuto ad indicarvi la strada giusta, ma voi non gli avete creduto; i ladri e le prostitute, invece, gli hanno creduto. E anche dopo aver visto queste cose, voi non avete cambiato idea: avete continuato a non credergli».

Parabola della vigna e dei contadini omicidi

33 «Ascoltate un'altra parabola: C'era un proprietario che *piantò una vigna, la circondò con una siepe, scavò una buca per il torchio dell'uva*

e costruì una torretta di guardia; poi affittò la vigna ad alcuni contadini e andò lontano.

34 «Quando fu vicino il tempo della vendemmia, mandò dai contadini i suoi servi per ritirare il suo raccolto. 35 Ma quei contadini presero i suoi servi e uno lo bastonarono, un altro lo uccisero, un altro lo colpirono con le pietre. 36 Il padrone mandò di nuovo altri servi più numerosi dei primi, ma quei contadini li trattarono allo stesso modo.

37 «Alla fine mandò suo figlio, pensando: Avranno rispetto di mio figlio.

38 «Ma i contadini, vedendo il figlio, dissero tra loro: "Ecco, costui sarà un giorno il padrone della vigna. Coraggio, uccidiamolo e l'eredità l'avremo noi!". 39 Così lo presero, lo gettarono fuori della vigna e lo uccisero».

40 A questo punto Gesù domandò:
– Quando verrà il padrone della vigna, che cosa farà a quei contadini?

41 Risposero i presenti:
– Ucciderà senza pietà quegli uomini malvagi e darà in affitto la vigna ad altri contadini che, alla stagione giusta, gli consegneranno i frutti.

42 Disse Gesù:
– Non avete mai letto quel che dice la Bibbia?

La pietra che i costruttori hanno
rifiutato
è diventata la pietra più
importante.
Questo è opera del Signore
ed è una meraviglia per i nostri
occhi.

43 Per questo vi assicuro che il regno di Dio sarà tolto a voi e sarà dato a gente che farà crescere i suoi frutti. [44]

45 I capi dei sacerdoti e i farisei che ascoltavano queste parabole capivano che Gesù le raccontava per loro. 46 Cercavano quindi un modo per arrestarlo, ma avevano paura della folla perché tutti lo consideravano un profeta.

Parabola del banchetto di nozze

22 1 Gesù ricominciò a parlare servendosi di parabole. Disse:
2 «Il regno di Dio è così. Un re preparò un grande banchetto per le nozze di suo figlio. 3 Egli mandò i suoi servi a chiamare gli invitati, ma quelli non volevano venire. 4 Allora mandò altri servi con quest'ordine: Dite agli invitati: Ecco, ho preparato il mio pranzo, i miei tori e gli animali ingrassati sono stati ammazzati e tutto è pronto. Venite alla festa! 5 Ma gli invitati non si lasciarono convincere e andarono a curare i loro affari: alcuni nei campi, altri ai loro commerci. 6 Altri, ancora, presero i servi del re, li maltrattarono e li uccisero.

7 «Allora il re si sdegnò: mandò il suo esercito, fece morire quegli assassini e incendiò la loro città. 8 Poi disse ai suoi servi: Il banchetto è pronto ma gli invitati non erano degni di venire. 9 Perciò, andate per le strade e invitate al banchetto tutti quelli che trovate.

10 «I servi uscirono nelle strade e radunarono tutti quelli che trovarono, buoni e cattivi: così la sala del banchetto fu piena.

11 «Quando il re andò nella sala per vedere gli invitati, vide un tale che non era vestito con l'abito di nozze. 12Gli disse: "Amico, come mai sei entrato qui senza avere l'abito di nozze?". Quello non rispose nulla. 13Allora il re ordinò ai servitori: "Legatelo mani e piedi e gettatelo fuori, nelle tenebre. Là piangerà come un disperato"».

14Poi Gesù aggiunse: «Perché molti sono chiamati al regno di Dio, ma pochi vi sono ammessi».

Le tasse da pagare all'imperatore romano

15I farisei fecero una riunione per trovare il modo di mettere in difficoltà Gesù con qualche domanda. 16Poi gli mandarono alcuni dei loro discepoli, insieme con altri del partito di Erode. Gli chiesero:

– Maestro, sappiamo che tu sei sempre sincero, insegni veramente la volontà di Dio e non ti preoccupi di quello che pensa la gente perché non guardi in faccia a nessuno. 17Perciò veniamo a chiedere il tuo parere: la nostra Legge permette o non permette di pagare le tasse all'imperatore romano?

18Ma Gesù sapeva che avevano intenzioni cattive e disse:

– Ipocriti! Perché cercate di imbrogliarmi? 19Fatemi vedere una moneta di quelle che servono a pagare le tasse.

Gli portarono una moneta d'argento, 20e Gesù domandò:

– Questo volto e questo nome scritto di chi sono?

21Gli risposero:

– Dell'imperatore.

Allora Gesù disse:

– Dunque, date all'imperatore quello che è dell'imperatore, ma quello che è di Dio datelo a Dio!

22A queste parole rimasero pieni di stupore; lo lasciarono stare e se ne andarono via.

Discussione a proposito della risurrezione

23In quel giorno si avvicinarono a Gesù alcuni del gruppo dei sadducei: secondo loro, nessuno può risorgere dopo la morte.

24Gli domandarono:

– Maestro, Mosè ha stabilito questa Legge: *Se uno muore senza figli, suo fratello deve sposare la vedova e cercare di avere dei figli per quello che è morto.* 25Ebbene, tra noi una volta c'erano sette fratelli. Il primo si sposò e poi morì senza figli e lasciò la moglie a suo fratello. 26La stessa cosa capitò al secondo, al terzo e così via fino al settimo. 27Infine, dopo tutti i fratelli, morì anche la donna. 28Ora, nel giorno della risurrezione dei morti, di chi sarà moglie quella donna? Perché tutti e sette l'hanno sposata.

29Gesù rispose:

– Voi sbagliate. Non conoscete la Bibbia e non sapete che cosa sia la potenza di Dio. 30Dopo la risurrezione, gli uomini e le donne non si sposeranno più, ma saranno come gli angeli del cielo. 31A proposito di risurrezione dei morti, non avete mai letto nella Bibbia ciò che Dio ha detto per voi? C'è scritto: 32*Io sono il Dio di Abramo, il Dio di*

Isacco, il Dio di Giacobbe. Perciò è il Dio dei vivi, non dei morti!

³³E la gente che ascoltava era molto meravigliata per questo suo insegnamento.

Il comandamento più importante

³⁴Quando i farisei vennero a sapere che Gesù aveva chiuso la bocca ai sadducei si radunarono insieme. ³⁵Uno di loro, che era maestro della Legge, gli domandò per metterlo alla prova:

³⁶– Maestro, qual è il più grande comandamento della Legge?

³⁷Gesù gli rispose:

– *Ama il Signore, tuo Dio,*
  con tutto il tuo cuore,
  con tutta la tua anima
  e con tutta la tua mente.

³⁸Questo è il comandamento più grande e più importante.

³⁹Il secondo è ugualmente importante:

  Ama il tuo prossimo
  come te stesso.

⁴⁰Tutta la Legge di Mosè e tutto l'insegnamento dei profeti dipendono da questi due comandamenti.

Il Messia e il re Davide

⁴¹Una volta molti farisei si erano riuniti e Gesù fece loro questa domanda:

⁴²– Ditemi il vostro parere sul Messia. Di chi sarà discendente?

Quelli risposero:

– Dev'essere un discendente del re Davide.

⁴³E Gesù continuò:

– In questo caso come si spiega che Davide stesso, guidato dallo Spirito di Dio, dice in un salmo che il Messia è il suo Signore? Egli ha scritto:

⁴⁴*Il Signore ha detto al mio Signore:*
  Siedi alla mia destra
  finché io metterò i tuoi nemici
  come sgabello sotto i tuoi piedi.

⁴⁵Dunque, se Davide lo chiama Signore, può il Messia essere un discendente di Davide?

⁴⁶Nessuno era capace di rispondere, di dire anche solo una parola. E a partire da quel giorno nessuno aveva più il coraggio di fare domande a Gesù.

Discorso contro gli ipocriti

Gesù rimprovera i farisei e i maestri della Legge

23 ¹Gesù cominciò a parlare alla folla e ai suoi discepoli. Diceva: ²«I maestri della Legge e i farisei hanno l'incarico di spiegare la Legge di Mosè. ³Fate quel che vi dicono, ubbidite ai loro insegnamenti, ma non imitate il loro modo di agire: perché essi insegnano, ma poi non mettono in pratica quel che insegnano. ⁴Preparano pesi impossibili da portare e li mettono sulle spalle degli altri: ma da parte loro non vogliono muoverli neppure con un dito.

⁵«Tutto quel che fanno è per farsi vedere dalla gente. Sulla fronte portano le parole della Legge in astucci più grandi del solito; le frange dei loro mantelli sono più lunghe di quelle degli altri. ⁶Desiderano avere i posti d'onore nelle sinagoghe, i primi posti nei banchetti, ⁷essere

salutati in piazza ed essere chiamati "maestro".

⁸«Voi però non dovete fare così. Non fatevi chiamare "maestro", perché voi siete tutti fratelli e uno solo è il vostro Maestro. ⁹E non chiamate "padre" nessuno di voi sulla terra, perché uno solo è il Padre vostro, quello che è in cielo. ¹⁰E non fatevi chiamare "capo", perché uno solo è il vostro Capo, il Messia.

¹¹«In mezzo a voi, il più grande deve essere il servitore degli altri. ¹²Chi vorrà farsi grande, Dio lo abbasserà; chi resterà umile, Dio lo innalzerà.

Gesù accusa i farisei e i maestri della Legge

¹³«Guai a voi ipocriti, maestri della Legge e farisei! Voi chiudete agli uomini la porta del regno di Dio: non entrate voi e non lasciate entrare quelli che vorrebbero entrare. [¹⁴]

¹⁵«Guai a voi, ipocriti, maestri della Legge e farisei! Voi fate lunghi viaggi per terra e per mare, pur di riuscire a convertire anche solo un uomo: ma poi, quando l'avete conquistato, lo fate diventare degno dell'inferno, peggio di voi.

¹⁶«Guai a voi, guide cieche! Voi dite: se uno giura per il Tempio, il giuramento non vale niente; se invece giura per il tesoro del Tempio, allora è obbligato. ¹⁷Ignoranti e ciechi! Che cosa è più importante: il tesoro o il Tempio che rende sacro il tesoro?

¹⁸«Voi dite anche: se uno giura per l'altare, il giuramento non vale niente; se invece giura per l'offerta che si trova sopra l'altare, allora è obbligato. ¹⁹Ciechi! Che cosa è più importante: l'offerta o l'altare che rende sacra l'offerta? ²⁰Chi giura per l'altare, giura anche per tutto ciò che vi sta sopra. ²¹Chi giura per il Tempio, giura anche per Dio che vi abita. ²²Chi giura per il cielo, giura anche per l'autorità di Dio che è in cielo.

²³«Guai a voi, ipocriti, maestri della Legge e farisei! Voi date in offerta al Tempio la decima parte anche di piante aromatiche come la menta, l'aneto e il cumino; ma poi trascurate i punti più importanti della Legge di Dio: la giustizia, la misericordia e la fedeltà. Queste sono le cose da fare, anche senza trascurare le altre. ²⁴Siete guide cieche! Voi filtrate le bevande per non mangiare un moscerino e poi ingoiate un cammello.

²⁵«Guai a voi, ipocriti, maestri della Legge e farisei! Vi preoccupate di pulire la parte esterna dei vostri piatti e dei vostri bicchieri, ma intanto li riempite dei vostri furti e dei vostri vizi. ²⁶Fariseo cieco! Purifica prima quel che c'è dentro il bicchiere, e poi anche l'esterno sarà puro.

²⁷«Guai a voi, ipocriti, maestri della Legge e farisei! Voi siete come tombe imbiancate che all'esterno sembrano bellissime, ma dentro sono piene di ossa di morti e di marciume. ²⁸Anche voi, esternamente, sembrate buoni agli occhi della gente, ma dentro siete pieni di ipocrisia e di male.

²⁹«Guai a voi, ipocriti, maestri della Legge e farisei! Voi costruite belle tombe per i profeti, decorate i sepolcri

degli uomini giusti. 30Voi dite: "Se noi fossimo vissuti ai tempi dei nostri padri, non avremmo fatto come loro, che hanno ucciso i profeti". 31Intanto voi dichiarate, contro voi stessi, di essere discendenti di quelli che uccisero i profeti. 32Continuate! State portando a termine quel che i vostri padri hanno cominciato!

33«Serpenti, razza di vipere! Come potrete evitare i castighi dell'inferno? 34Perciò, ascoltate: io manderò in mezzo a voi profeti, uomini sapienti e veri maestri della Legge di Dio. E voi, alcuni li ucciderete, altri li metterete in croce, altri li frusterete nelle vostre sinagoghe e li perseguiterete in tutte le città. 35Così ricadrà su di voi il sangue di tutti i delitti compiuti contro persone innocenti dall'uccisione di Abele il giusto fino all'uccisione di Zaccaria, figlio di Barachia, che voi avete assassinato tra il santuario e l'altare. 36Vi assicuro che tutto ciò avverrà durante questa generazione.

Lamento di Gesù su Gerusalemme

37«Gerusalemme! Gerusalemme! Tu che metti a morte i profeti e uccidi a colpi di pietra quelli che Dio ti manda! Quante volte ho voluto riunire i tuoi abitanti attorno a me, come una gallina raccoglie i suoi pulcini sotto le ali! Ma voi non avete voluto. 38Ebbene la vostra casa sarà abbandonata. 39Perché io vi dico che da questo momento non mi vedrete più fino al giorno in cui direte: *Benedetto colui che viene nel nome del Signore».*

Discorso sugli ultimi tempi

Gesù annuncia che il Tempio sarà distrutto

24 1Gesù era uscito dal Tempio e andava via. Si avvicinarono a lui i suoi discepoli e gli fecero osservare le costruzioni del Tempio. 2Ma Gesù disse loro: «Vedete tutto questo? Vi assicuro che non rimarrà una sola pietra sull'altra. Tutto sarà distrutto».

Gesù annuncia dolori e persecuzioni

3Quando giunsero al monte degli Ulivi, Gesù si sedette e i suoi discepoli si avvicinarono a lui in disparte e gli chiesero: «Puoi dirci quando avverranno queste cose? E quale sarà il segno del tuo ritorno alla fine di questo mondo?».

4Gesù rispose: «Fate attenzione e non lasciatevi ingannare da nessuno! 5Perché molti verranno e cercheranno di ingannare molta gente. Si presenteranno con il mio nome e diranno: "Sono io il Messia!". 6Quando sentirete parlare di guerre, vicine o lontane, non abbiate paura: bisogna che ciò avvenga, ma non sarà ancora la fine. 7I popoli combatteranno l'uno contro l'altro, un regno contro un altro regno. Ci saranno carestie e terremoti in molte regioni. 8Ma tutto questo sarà come quando cominciano i dolori del parto.

9«Voi sarete arrestati, torturati e uccisi. Sarete odiati da tutti per causa mia. 10Allora molti abbandoneranno la fede, si odieranno e si tradiranno l'un l'altro. [11]Verranno molti falsi profeti e inganneranno molta gente. [12]Il male sarà tanto diffuso che l'amore di molti si raffredderà. [13]Ma Dio salverà chi avrà resistito sino alla fine.

[14]«Intanto il messaggio del regno di Dio sarà annunziato in tutto il mondo; tutti i popoli dovranno sentirlo. E allora verrà la fine.

Gesù annunzia grandi tribolazioni

[15]«Un giorno vedrete nel luogo santo colui che commette l'orribile sacrilegio. Il profeta Daniele ne ha parlato. Chi legge, cerchi di capire.

[16]«Allora, quelli che saranno nella regione della Giudea fuggano sui monti; [17]chi si trova sulla terrazza non scenda a prendere quel che ha in casa; [18]chi si troverà nei campi non torni indietro a prendere il mantello.

[19]«Saranno giorni tristi per le donne incinte e per quelle che allattano! [20]Pregate di non dover fuggire d'inverno o in giorno di sabato. [21]Perché in quei giorni ci sarà una grande tribolazione, la più grande che ci sia mai stata fino ad oggi, e non ce ne sarà più una uguale. [22]E se Dio non accorciasse il numero di quei giorni, nessuno si salverebbe. Ma Dio li accorcerà, a causa di quegli uomini che si è scelto.

[23]«Allora, se qualcuno vi dirà: "Ecco, il Messia è qui!" oppure: "È là", voi non fidatevi. [24]Perché verranno falsi profeti e falsi messia, i quali faranno segni miracolosi per cercare di ingannare, se fosse possibile, anche quelli che Dio si è scelto. [25]Io vi ho avvisati.

Gesù annunzia il ritorno del Figlio dell'uomo

[26]«Perciò, se vi diranno: "Il Messia è nel deserto", voi non andateci. Se vi diranno: "Il Messia è nascosto qui", voi non fidatevi. [27]Perché, come il lampo improvvisamente guizza da una parte all'altra del cielo, così verrà il Figlio dell'uomo. [28]Dove sarà il cadavere, là si raduneranno gli avvoltoi. [29]E subito dopo le tribolazioni di quei giorni,

il sole si oscurerà,
la luna perderà il suo splendore,
le stelle cadranno dal cielo,
e le forze del cielo saranno sconvolte.

[30]«Allora si vedrà nel cielo il segno del Figlio dell'uomo; allora tutti i popoli della terra piangeranno, e gli uomini vedranno *il Figlio dell'uomo venire sulle nubi del cielo* con grande potenza e splendore.

[31]«Al suono della grande tromba egli manderà i suoi angeli ad ogni direzione. Da un confine all'altro del cielo essi raduneranno tutti gli uomini che si è scelti.

Parabola del fico

[32]«Dall'albero del fico, imparate questa parabola: quando i suoi rami diventano teneri e spuntano le prime foglie, voi capite che l'estate è vicina. [33]Allo stesso modo, quando vedrete accadere queste cose, sappiate che egli è vicino, è alle porte.

[34]«Io vi assicuro che non passerà questa generazione prima che queste cose siano accadute.

[35]«Il cielo e la terra passeranno, ma le mie parole non passeranno.

Gesù invita ad essere vigilanti

[36]«Ma nessuno sa quando verranno quel giorno e quell'ora; non lo sanno gli angeli e neppure il Figlio: solo Dio Padre lo sa.

[37]«Come è accaduto ai tempi di Noè, così accadrà anche quando verrà il Figlio dell'uomo. [38]A quei tempi, prima del diluvio, la gente continuò a mangiare, a bere e a sposarsi fino al giorno nel quale Noè entrò nell'arca. [39]Nessuno si rese conto di nulla, fino al momento in cui venne il diluvio e li portò via tutti.

«Così accadrà anche quando verrà il Figlio dell'uomo. [40]Allora, se due uomini saranno in un campo, uno sarà portato via e uno sarà lasciato lì. [41]Se due donne macineranno grano al mulino, una sarà presa e una sarà lasciata lì. [42]State dunque svegli, perché non sapete quando viene il vostro Signore.

[43]«Cercate di capire: se il capo-famiglia sapesse a che ora della notte viene il ladro starebbe sveglio e non si lascerebbe scassinare la casa. [44]Anche voi tenetevi pronti, perché il Figlio dell'uomo viene quando voi non ve lo aspettate.

Parabola del servo fedele e infedele

[45]«Chi è dunque il servo fedele e saggio? Quello che il padrone ha messo a capo degli altri servi per distribuire loro il cibo al momento giusto. [46]Se il padrone, quando ritorna, lo trova occupato a fare così, beato quel servo! [47]Vi assicuro che il padrone gli affiderà l'amministrazione di tutti i suoi beni.

[48]«Se invece quel servo cattivo pensa che il padrone torna tardi [49]e comincia a trattar male i suoi compagni e per di più si metterà a far baldoria con gli ubriaconi, [50]allora il padrone tornerà, in un momento che lui non sa, quando meno se l'aspetta, [51]lo separerà dagli altri e lo metterà tra i malvagi. E là piangerà come un disperato.

Parabola delle dieci ragazze

25 [1]«Così sarà il regno di Dio.

«C'erano dieci ragazze che avevano preso le loro lampade a olio ed erano andate incontro allo sposo. [2]Cinque erano sciocche e cinque erano sagge. [3]Le cinque sciocche presero le lampade ma non portarono una riserva di olio; [4]le altre cinque, invece, portarono anche un vasetto di olio. [5]Poi, siccome lo sposo faceva tardi, tutte furono prese dal sonno e si addormentarono.

[6]«A mezzanotte si sente un grido: "Ecco lo sposo! Andategli incontro!". [7]Subito le dieci ragazze si svegliarono e si misero a preparare le lampade. [8]Le cinque sciocche dissero alle sagge:

– Dateci un po' del vostro olio, perché le nostre lampade si spengono.

[9]«Ma le altre cinque risposero:

– No, perché non basterebbe più né a voi né a noi. Piuttosto, andate a comprarvelo al negozio.

[10]«Le cinque sciocche andarono a comprare l'olio, ma proprio mentre

erano lontane arrivò lo sposo: quelle che erano pronte entrarono con lui nella sala del banchetto e la porta fu chiusa.

11 «Più tardi arrivarono anche le altre cinque e si misero a gridare:

– Signore, signore, apri!

12 «Ma egli rispose:

– Non so proprio chi siete.

13 «State svegli, dunque, perché non sapete né il giorno né l'ora.

Parabola delle monete d'oro

14 «Così infatti sarà il regno di Dio.

«Un uomo doveva fare un lungo viaggio: chiamò dunque i suoi servi e affidò loro i suoi soldi. 15 A uno consegnò cinquecento monete d'oro, a un altro duecento e a un altro cento: a ciascuno secondo le sue capacità. Poi partì. 16 Il servo che aveva ricevuto cinquecento monete andò subito a investire in un affare, e alla fine guadagnò altre cinquecento monete. 17 Quello che ne aveva ricevute duecento fece lo stesso, e alla fine ne guadagnò altre duecento. 18 Quello invece che ne aveva ricevute soltanto cento scavò una buca in terra e vi nascose i soldi del suo padrone.

19 «Dopo molto tempo il padrone ritornò e cominciò a fare i conti con i suoi servi.

20 «Venne il primo, quello che aveva ricevuto cinquecento monete d'oro, portò anche le altre cinquecento e disse:

– Signore, tu mi avevi consegnato cinquecento monete. Guarda: ne ho guadagnate altre cinquecento.

21 «E il padrone gli disse:

– Bene, sei un servo bravo e fedele! Sei stato fedele in cose da poco, ti affiderò cose più importanti. Vieni a partecipare alla gioia del tuo signore.

22 «Poi venne quello che aveva ricevuto duecento monete e disse:

– Signore, tu mi avevi consegnato duecento monete d'oro. Guarda: ne ho guadagnate altre duecento.

23 «E il padrone gli disse:

– Bene, sei un servo bravo e fedele! Sei stato fedele in cose da poco, ti affiderò cose più importanti. Vieni a partecipare alla gioia del tuo signore!

24 «Infine venne quel servo che aveva ricevuto solamente cento monete d'oro e disse:

– Signore, io sapevo che sei un uomo duro, che raccoglie anche dove non hai seminato e che fai vendemmia anche dove non hai coltivato. 25 Ho avuto paura, e allora sono andato a nascondere i tuoi soldi sotto terra. Ecco, te li restituisco.

26 «Ma il padrone gli rispose:

– Servo cattivo e fannullone! Dunque sapevi che io raccolgo dove non ho seminato e faccio vendemmia dove non ho coltivato. 27 Perciò dovevi almeno mettere in banca i miei soldi e io, al ritorno, li avrei ritirati con l'interesse.

28 «Via, toglietegli le cento monete e datele a quello che ne ha mille. 29 Perché chi ha molto riceverà ancora di più e sarà nell'abbondanza; chi ha poco, gli porteranno via anche quel poco che ha. 30 E questo servo inutile gettatelo fuori, nelle tenebre: là piangerà come un disperato.

Il giorno del giudizio

31 «Quando il Figlio dell'uomo verrà nel suo splendore, insieme con gli

angeli, si siederà sul suo trono glorioso. ³²Tutti i popoli della terra saranno riuniti di fronte a lui ed egli li separerà in due gruppi, come fa il pastore quando separa le pecore dalle capre: ³³metterà i giusti da una parte e i malvagi dall'altra.

³⁴«Allora il re dirà ai giusti:
–Venite, voi che siete i benedetti dal Padre mio; entrate nel regno che è stato preparato per voi fin dalla creazione del mondo. ³⁵Perché, io ho avuto fame e voi mi avete dato da mangiare, ho avuto sete e mi avete dato da bere; ero forestiero e mi avete ospitato nella vostra casa; ³⁶ero nudo e mi avete dato i vestiti; ero malato e siete venuti a curarmi; ero in prigione e siete venuti a trovarmi.

³⁷«E i giusti diranno:
–Signore, quando mai ti abbiamo visto affamato e ti abbiamo dato da mangiare, o assetato e ti abbiamo dato da bere? ³⁸Quando ti abbiamo incontrato forestiero e ti abbiamo ospitato nella nostra casa, o nudo e ti abbiamo dato i vestiti? ³⁹Quando ti abbiamo visto malato o in prigione e siamo venuti a trovarti?

⁴⁰«Il re risponderà:
–In verità, vi dico: tutte le volte che avete fatto ciò a uno dei più piccoli di questi miei fratelli, lo avete fatto a me!

⁴¹«Poi dirà ai malvagi:
–Andate via da me, maledetti, nel fuoco eterno che Dio ha preparato per il diavolo e per i suoi servi! ⁴²Perché, io ho avuto fame e voi non mi avete dato da mangiare; ho avuto sete e non mi avete dato da bere; ⁴³ero forestiero e non mi avete ospitato nella vostra casa; ero nudo e non mi avete dato i vestiti; ero malato e in prigione e voi non siete venuti a trovarmi.

⁴⁴«E anche quelli diranno:
–Quando ti abbiamo visto affamato, assetato, forestiero, nudo, malato o in prigione e non ti abbiamo aiutato?

⁴⁵«Allora il re risponderà:
–In verità, vi dico: tutto quel che non avete fatto a uno di questi piccoli, non l'avete fatto a me.

⁴⁶«E questi andranno nella punizione eterna mentre i giusti andranno nella vita eterna».

I capi degli Ebrei vogliono uccidere Gesù

26 ¹Quando Gesù ebbe finito questi insegnamenti disse ai suoi discepoli: ²«Voi sapete che tra due giorni è la festa di Pasqua, e il Figlio dell'uomo sta per essere arrestato e poi lo inchioderanno su una croce».

³Allora i capi dei sacerdoti e le autorità del popolo fecero una riunione in casa di Caifa, il sommo sacerdote. ⁴Insieme, decisero di arrestare Gesù con un inganno e di ucciderlo. ⁵Ma dicevano: «Non possiamo arrestarlo in un giorno di festa, perché altrimenti c'è pericolo di una rivolta popolare».

Una donna versa profumo su Gesù

⁶Gesù si trovava a Betània, in casa di Simone, quello che era stato lebbroso. ⁷Mentre erano a tavola, si avvicinò una donna con un vasetto di alabastro, pieno di profumo molto prezioso, e versò il profumo sulla testa di Gesù.

[8]Vedendo ciò, i discepoli scandalizzati mormoravano e dicevano:

– Perché tutto questo spreco? [9]Si poteva benissimo vendere il profumo a caro prezzo e poi dare i soldi ai poveri.

[10]Gesù se ne accorse e disse ai discepoli:

– Perché tormentate questa donna? Ha fatto un'opera buona verso di me. [11]I poveri infatti li avete sempre con voi; ma non sempre avrete me. [12]Versando sulla mia testa questo profumo, questa donna mi ha preparato per la sepoltura. [13]Io vi assicuro che in tutto il mondo, dovunque sarà predicato questo messaggio del Vangelo, ci si ricorderà di questa donna e di quel che ha fatto.

Giuda tradisce Gesù

[14]Allora uno dei dodici discepoli, chiamato Giuda Iscariota, andò dai capi dei sacerdoti e disse: [15]«Che cosa mi date se io vi faccio arrestare Gesù?». Stabilirono trenta monete d'argento e gliele consegnarono. [16]Da quel momento Giuda si mise a cercare un'occasione per fare arrestare Gesù.

I discepoli preparano la cena pasquale

[17]Il primo giorno della festa dei Pani non lievitati, i discepoli si avvicinarono a Gesù e gli dissero:

– Dove vuoi che ti prepariamo la cena di Pasqua?

[18]Egli rispose:

– Andate in città da un tale, e ditegli: Il Maestro ti manda a dire che il suo momento ormai è arrivato e che viene in casa tua con i suoi discepoli a mangiare la cena di Pasqua.

[19]I discepoli fecero come aveva comandato Gesù e prepararono la cena pasquale.

Gesù indica il traditore

[20]Quando fu sera, Gesù si mise a tavola insieme con i dodici discepoli. [21]Mentre stavano mangiando disse:

– Io vi assicuro che uno di voi mi tradirà.

[22]Essi diventarono molto tristi e, a uno a uno, cominciarono a domandargli:

– Signore, sono forse io?

[23]Gesù rispose:

– Quello che ha messo con me la mano nel piatto, è lui che mi tradirà. [24]Il Figlio dell'uomo sta per morire, così come è scritto nella Bibbia. Ma guai a colui per mezzo del quale il Figlio dell'uomo è tradito. Per lui sarebbe stato meglio di non essere mai nato!

[25]Allora Giuda, il traditore, domandò:

– Maestro, sono forse io?

Gesù gli rispose:

– Tu l'hai detto.

La Cena del Signore

[26]Mentre stavano mangiando, Gesù prese il pane, fece la preghiera di benedizione, poi spezzò il pane, lo diede ai discepoli e disse: «Prendete e mangiate; questo è il mio corpo».

[27]Poi prese la coppa del vino, fece la preghiera di ringraziamento, la diede ai discepoli e disse: «Bevetene tutti, [28]perché questo è il mio sangue, offerto per tutti gli uomini, per il perdono dei peccati. Con questo

sangue Dio conferma la sua alleanza.
²⁹Vi assicuro che d'ora in poi non
berrò più vino fino al giorno in cui
berrò con voi il vino nuovo nel regno
di Dio, mio Padre».

³⁰Cantarono i salmi della festa, poi
andarono verso il monte degli Ulivi.

Gesù sarà abbandonato da tutti

³¹Allora Gesù disse ai discepoli:
«Questa notte tutti voi perderete ogni
fiducia in me. Perché nella Bibbia c'è
scritto:

Ucciderò il pastore
e le pecore del gregge saranno
            disperse.

³²Ma quando sarò risuscitato vi
aspetterò in Galilea».

³³Allora Pietro cominciò a dire:
– Anche se tutti gli altri perderanno
ogni fiducia in te, io non la perderò
mai.

³⁴Gesù replicò:
– Io invece ti assicuro che questa
notte, prima che il gallo canti, tre volte
tu avrai detto che non mi conosci.

³⁵Ma Pietro rispose:
– Non dirò mai che non ti conosco,
anche se dovessi morire con te!

E così dissero anche tutti gli altri
discepoli.

Gesù prega nel Getsèmani

³⁶Intanto Gesù arrivò con i discepoli
in un luogo detto Getsèmani. Egli
disse: «Restate qui mentre io vado là a
pregare».

³⁷Si fece accompagnare da Pietro e
dai due figli di Zebedèo. Poi incominciò
a essere triste e angosciato. ³⁸Allora
disse ai tre discepoli: «Una tristezza

mortale mi opprime. Fermatevi qui e
restate svegli con me».

³⁹Andò un po' avanti, si gettò con la
faccia a terra e si mise a pregare.
Diceva: «Padre mio, se è possibile,
allontana da me questo calice di
dolore! Però non si faccia come voglio
io, ma come vuoi tu».

⁴⁰Poi tornò indietro verso i discepoli,
ma trovò che dormivano. Allora disse a
Pietro: «Così non avete potuto vegliare
con me nemmeno un'ora? ⁴¹State
svegli e pregate per resistere nel
momento della prova; perché la volontà
è pronta ma la debolezza è grande».

⁴²Per la seconda volta si allontanò e
cominciò a pregare, e disse: «Padre
mio, se proprio devo bere di questo
calice di dolore, sia fatta la tua volontà».

⁴³Poi ritornò dai discepoli e li trovò
ancora che dormivano: non riuscivano
a tenere gli occhi aperti.

⁴⁴Per la terza volta Gesù si allontanò
e andò a pregare ripetendo le stesse
parole. ⁴⁵Poi tornò verso i discepoli e
disse: «Ma come, voi ancora dormite e
riposate? Ecco, il momento è ormai
vicino. Il Figlio dell'uomo sta per
essere consegnato nelle mani di gente
malvagia. ⁴⁶Alzatevi, andiamo! Sta
arrivando quello che mi tradisce».

Gesù è arrestato

⁴⁷Mentre Gesù ancora parlava con i
discepoli arrivò Giuda, uno dei Dodici,
accompagnato da molti uomini armati
di spade e di bastoni. Erano stati
mandati dai capi dei sacerdoti e dalle
altre autorità del popolo.

⁴⁸Il traditore s'era messo d'accordo
con loro. Aveva stabilito un segno e

aveva detto: «Quello che bacerò, è lui. Prendetelo».

49Intanto Giuda si avvicinò a Gesù e disse: «Salve, Maestro!». Poi lo baciò.

50Ma Gesù gli disse: «Amico, si faccia quello che sei venuto a fare».

Quelli che erano venuti insieme a Giuda si fecero avanti, presero Gesù e lo arrestarono.

51Allora uno di quelli che erano con Gesù tirò fuori una spada e colpì il servo del sommo sacerdote, staccandogli un orecchio.

52Ma Gesù gli disse: «Rimetti la spada al suo posto! Perché tutti quelli che usano la spada moriranno colpiti dalla spada. 53Che cosa credi? Non sai che io potrei chiedere aiuto al Padre mio e subito mi manderebbe più di dodici migliaia di angeli? 54Ma in questo caso non si compirebbero le parole della Bibbia. Essa dice che deve accadere così».

55Poi Gesù disse alla folla: «Siete venuti a prendermi con spade e bastoni, come se fossi un delinquente! Tutti i giorni stavo seduto nel Tempio a insegnare, e non mi avete mai arrestato. 56Ebbene, tutto questo è avvenuto perché si compia quel che hanno detto i profeti nella Bibbia».

Allora tutti i discepoli lo abbandonarono e fuggirono.

Gesù davanti al tribunale ebraico

57Quelli che avevano arrestato Gesù lo portarono alla casa di Caifa, il sommo sacerdote, dove si erano radunati i maestri della Legge e le altre autorità. 58Poi Pietro lo seguiva da lontano. Poi entrò anche nel cortile

della casa e si sedette in mezzo ai servi per vedere come andava a finire.

59Intanto i capi dei sacerdoti e gli altri del tribunale cercavano una falsa accusa contro Gesù, per poterlo condannare a morte. 60Ma non la trovavano, anche se si erano presentati moltissimi testimoni falsi. Infine se ne presentarono altri due 61che dissero: «Una volta egli ha dichiarato: "Io posso distruggere il tempio di Dio e ricostruirlo in tre giorni"».

62Allora si alzò il sommo sacerdote e gli disse:

– Non rispondi nulla? Che cosa sono queste accuse contro di te?

63Ma Gesù rimaneva zitto.

Poi il sommo sacerdote disse:

– Per il Dio vivente, ti scongiuro di dirci se tu sei il Messia, il Cristo, il Figlio di Dio.

64Gesù rispose:

– Tu l'hai detto. Ma io vi dico che d'ora in poi vedrete *il Figlio dell'uomo seduto accanto a Dio Onnipotente; egli verrà sulle nubi del cielo.*

65Allora il sommo sacerdote, scandalizzato, si strappò il mantello e disse:

– Ha bestemmiato! Non c'è più bisogno di testimoni, ormai! adesso avete sentito le sue bestemmie. 66Qual è il vostro parere?

Gli altri risposero:

– Deve essere condannato a morte.

67Allora alcuni gli sputarono in faccia e lo presero a pugni; altri gli davano schiaffi 68e gli dicevano: «Indovina, o Cristo! Chi ti ha picchiato?».

Pietro nega di conoscere Gesù

69Pietro era seduto fuori, nel cortile, quando una serva si avvicinò a lui e gli disse:

– Anche tu stavi con quell'uomo della Galilea, con Gesù.

70Ma Pietro negò davanti a tutti dicendo:

– Non so nemmeno che cosa vuoi dire.

71Poi se ne andò verso la porta del cortile.

Là, un'altra serva lo vide e disse a quelli che erano vicini:

– Questo era con Gesù di Nàzaret.

72Ma Pietro negò ancora e disse:

– Giuro che non conosco quell'uomo.

73Poco dopo, alcuni dei presenti si avvicinarono a Pietro e gli dissero:

– Certamente tu sei uno di quelli: si capisce da come parli che sei della Galilea.

74Allora Pietro cominciò a giurare e a spergiurare che non era vero e diceva:

– Io non lo conosco nemmeno!

Subito dopo un gallo cantò.

75In quel momento Pietro si ricordò di quel che gli aveva detto Gesù: «Prima che il gallo canti, per tre volte avrai detto che non mi conosci».

Allora uscì fuori e pianse amaramente.

Gesù è condotto davanti a Pilato

27 1Quando fu mattino, tutti i capi dei sacerdoti e le altre autorità del popolo si riunirono per decidere di far morire Gesù. 2Alla fine lo fecero legare e portar via, e lo consegnarono a Pilato, il governatore romano.

La morte di Giuda e le trenta monete

3Quando Giuda, il traditore, vide che Gesù era stato condannato, ebbe rimorso. Prese le trenta monete d'argento e le riportò ai capi dei sacerdoti e alle altre autorità. 4Disse:

– Ho fatto male, ho tradito un innocente.

Ma quelli risposero:

– A noi che importa? Sono affari tuoi!

5Allora Giuda buttò le monete nel Tempio e andò a impiccarsi.

6I capi dei sacerdoti raccolsero le monete e dissero: «La nostra Legge non permette di mettere questi soldi nel tesoro del Tempio, perché sono sporchi di sangue». 7Alla fine si misero d'accordo e con quei soldi comprarono il campo di un fabbricante di vasi, per destinarlo al cimitero per gli stranieri. 8Perciò quel campo si chiama anche oggi «Campo del Sangue». 9Così si avverarono le parole del profeta Geremia:

Presero le trenta monete
d'argento,
prezzo che il popolo d'Israele
aveva pagato per lui,
10 *e le usarono per comprare il*
campo del vasaio,
così come il Signore mi aveva
ordinato.

Gesù davanti a Pilato

11Gesù fu portato davanti al governatore romano. Quello gli domandò:

– Sei tu il re dei Giudei?

E Gesù rispose:

– Tu lo dici.

¹²Intanto i capi dei sacerdoti e le altre autorità portavano accuse contro di lui, ma egli non diceva nulla. ¹³Allora Pilato gli disse:

– Non senti di quante cose ti accusano?

¹⁴Ma Gesù non rispose neanche una parola, tanto che il governatore ne fu molto meravigliato.

Gesù è condannato a morte

¹⁵Ogni anno, per la festa di Pasqua, il governatore aveva l'abitudine di lasciare libero uno dei carcerati, quello che il popolo voleva.

¹⁶A quel tempo era in prigione un carcerato famoso, di nome Barabba. ¹⁷Quando si fu riunita una certa folla, Pilato domandò: – Chi volete che sia lasciato libero: Barabba, oppure Gesù detto Cristo? – ¹⁸Perché sapeva bene che l'avevano portato da lui solo per odio.

¹⁹Mentre Pilato era seduto al tribunale, sua moglie gli mandò a dire: – Cerca di non decidere niente contro quest'uomo innocente, perché questa notte, in sogno, ho sofferto molto per causa sua.

²⁰Intanto i capi dei sacerdoti e le altre autorità convinsero la folla a chiedere la liberazione di Barabba e la morte di Gesù. ²¹Il governatore domandò ancora:

– Chi dei due volete che lasci libero?

La folla rispose:

– Barabba.

²²Pilato continuò:

– Che farò dunque di Gesù, detto Cristo?

Tutti risposero:

– In croce!

²³Pilato replicò:

– Che cosa ha fatto di male?

Ma quelli gridavano ancora più forte:

– In croce! in croce!

²⁴Quando vide che non poteva far niente e che anzi la gente si agitava sempre di più, Pilato fece portare un po' d'acqua, si lavò le mani davanti alla folla e disse:

– Io non sono responsabile della morte di quest'uomo! Sono affari vostri!

²⁵Tutta la gente rispose:

– Il suo sangue ricada su di noi e sui nostri figli!

²⁶Allora Pilato lasciò libero Barabba. Fece frustare a sangue Gesù, poi lo consegnò ai soldati per farlo crocifiggere.

Gli insulti dei soldati

²⁷Allora i soldati portarono Gesù nel palazzo del governatore e chiamarono tutto il resto della truppa. ²⁸Gli tolsero i suoi vestiti e gli gettarono addosso una veste rossa. ²⁹Prepararono una corona di rami spinosi e gliela misero sul capo, nella mano destra gli diedero un bastone. Poi incominciarono a inginocchiarsi davanti a lui e a dire ridendo: «Salve, re dei Giudei!». ³⁰Intanto gli sputavano addosso, gli prendevano il bastone e gli davano colpi sulla testa. ³¹Quando finirono di insultarlo, gli tolsero la veste rossa e lo rivestirono con i suoi abiti. Poi lo portarono via per crocifiggerlo.

Gesù è inchiodato a una croce

³²Mentre uscivano incontrarono un certo Simone, originario di Cirene, e lo obbligarono a portare la croce di Gesù. ³³Quando arrivarono in un luogo detto Gòlgota (che significa «Luogo del Cranio»), si fermarono e ³⁴vollero dare a Gesù un po' di vino mescolato con fiele. Gesù lo assaggiò ma non volle bere. ³⁵Poi lo inchiodarono alla croce e si divisero le sue vesti tirando a sorte. ³⁶Dopo rimasero lì seduti a fargli la guardia.

³⁷In alto, sopra la sua testa, avevano messo un cartello con scritto il motivo della condanna: «Questo è Gesù, il re dei Giudei». ³⁸Insieme con lui avevano messo in croce anche due briganti, uno alla sua destra e uno alla sua sinistra.

³⁹Quelli che passavano di là, scuotevano la testa in segno di disprezzo, lo insultavano ⁴⁰e dicevano: «Volevi distruggere il Tempio e ricostruirlo in tre giorni! Se tu sei il Figlio di Dio, salva te stesso! Scendi dalla croce!».

⁴¹Allo stesso modo, anche i capi dei sacerdoti insieme con i maestri della Legge e le altre autorità ridevano e dicevano: ⁴²«Lui che ha salvato tanti altri, adesso non è capace di salvare se stesso! Lui che diceva di essere il re d'Israele, scenda ora dalla croce e noi gli crederemo! ⁴³Ha sempre avuto fiducia in Dio e diceva: "Io sono il Figlio di Dio". Lo liberi Dio, adesso, se gli vuol bene!».

⁴⁴Anche i due briganti crocifissi accanto a lui lo insultavano.

Gesù muore

⁴⁵Quando fu mezzogiorno, si fece buio su tutta la regione, fino alle tre del pomeriggio. ⁴⁶Verso le tre Gesù gridò molto forte: «*Elì, Elì, lemà sabactàni*», che significa «*Dio mio, Dio mio, perché mi hai abbandonato?*»

⁴⁷Alcuni presenti udirono e dissero: «Chiama Elia, il profeta!».

⁴⁸Subito, uno di loro corse a prendere una spugna, la bagnò nell'aceto, la fissò in cima a una canna e la diede a Gesù per farlo bere. ⁴⁹Ma gli altri dissero: «Aspetta! Vediamo se viene Elia a salvarlo!».

⁵⁰Ma Gesù di nuovo gridò forte, e poi emise lo spirito e morì.

⁵¹Allora il grande velo appeso nel Tempio si squarciò in due, da cima a fondo. La terra tremò, le rocce si spaccarono, ⁵²le tombe si aprirono e molti credenti tornarono in vita. ⁵³Usciti dalle tombe dopo la risurrezione di Gesù, entrarono a Gerusalemme e apparirono a molti.

⁵⁴L'ufficiale romano e gli altri soldati che con lui facevano la guardia a Gesù si accorsero del terremoto e di tutto quel che accadeva. Pieni di spavento, essi dissero: «Quest'uomo era davvero Figlio di Dio!».

⁵⁵Molte donne erano là e guardavano da lontano. Esse avevano seguito e aiutato Gesù fin da quando era in Galilea. ⁵⁶Tra le altre, c'erano Maria Maddalena, Maria, madre di Giacomo e di Giuseppe, e la madre dei figli di Zebedèo.

Il corpo di Gesù
è messo nella tomba

⁵⁷Ormai era già sera, quando venne Giuseppe di Arimatèa. Era un uomo ricco, il quale era diventato pure lui discepolo di Gesù. ⁵⁸Egli andò da Pilato e gli chiese il corpo di Gesù. E Pilato ordinò di lasciarglielo prendere.

⁵⁹Allora Giuseppe prese il corpo, lo avvolse in un lenzuolo pulito ⁶⁰e lo mise nella sua tomba, quella che da poco si era fatto preparare per sé, scavata nella roccia. Poi fece rotolare una grossa pietra davanti alla porta della tomba e se ne andò.

⁶¹Intanto due delle donne, Maria Maddalena e l'altra Maria, stavano li sedute di fronte alla tomba.

Le guardie sorvegliano
la tomba di Gesù

⁶²Il giorno dopo era sabato. I capi dei sacerdoti e i farisei andarono insieme da Pilato ⁶³e gli dissero:

–Eccellenza, ci siamo ricordati che quell'imbroglione, quand'era vivo, ha detto: «Tre giorni dopo che mi avranno ucciso, io risusciterò». ⁶⁴Perciò ordina che le guardie sorveglino la tomba fino al terzo giorno, così i suoi discepoli non potranno venire a rubare il corpo e poi dire alla gente: «È risuscitato dai morti!». Altrimenti quest'ultimo imbroglio sarebbe peggiore del primo.

⁶⁵Pilato rispose:

–Va bene: prendete le guardie e fate sorvegliare la tomba come vi pare.

⁶⁶Essi andarono, assicurarono la chiusura della tomba sigillando la grossa pietra e poi lasciarono le guardie a custodirla.

L'annunzio della risurrezione

28 ¹Il giorno dopo, all'inizio del primo giorno della settimana, Maria Maddalena e l'altra Maria andarono ancora a vedere la tomba di Gesù. ²Improvvisamente vi fu un terremoto, un angelo del Signore scese dal cielo, fece rotolare la grossa pietra e si sedette sopra. ³Aveva un aspetto splendente come un lampo e una veste candida come la neve. ⁴Le guardie ebbero tanta paura di lui che cominciarono a tremare e rimasero come morte.

⁵L'angelo parlò e disse alle donne: «Non abbiate paura, voi. So che cercate Gesù, quello che hanno crocifisso. ⁶Non è qui, perché è risuscitato proprio come aveva detto. Venite a vedere dov'era il suo corpo. ⁷Ora andate, presto! Andate a dire ai suoi discepoli: È risuscitato dai morti e vi aspetta in Galilea. Là lo vedrete. Ecco, io vi ho avvisato».

⁸Le donne partirono subito, spaventate, ma piene di gioia e andarono di corsa a portare la notizia ai discepoli. ⁹Ma all'improvviso Gesù venne loro incontro e disse: «Salve!».

Allora si avvicinarono a lui, abbracciarono i suoi piedi e lo adorarono. ¹⁰Gesù disse: «Non abbiate paura. Andate a dire ai miei discepoli di recarsi in Galilea: là mi vedranno».

L'inganno delle autorità ebraiche

¹¹Mentre le donne erano in cammino, alcune guardie che

sorvegliavano la tomba di Gesù tornarono in città e raccontarono ai capi dei sacerdoti quel che era successo.

12 Allora i capi dei sacerdoti si riunirono insieme con le autorità del popolo e decisero di offrire molti soldi alle guardie dicendo: 13«Voi dovete dire che sono venuti di notte i suoi discepoli, mentre dormivate, e che l'hanno rubato. 14Se poi il governatore verrà a saperlo, noi lo convinceremo e faremo in modo che voi non siate puniti».

15 Le guardie presero i soldi e seguirono quelle istruzioni. Perciò questa storia è diffusa ancor oggi tra gli Ebrei.

Gesù appare ai discepoli e li manda nel mondo

16 Gli undici discepoli andarono in Galilea, su quella collina che Gesù aveva indicato. 17Quando lo videro, lo adorarono. Alcuni, però, avevano dei dubbi.

18 Gesù si avvicinò e disse: «A me è stato dato ogni potere in cielo e in terra. 19Perciò andate, fate che tutti diventino miei discepoli; battezzateli nel nome del Padre e del Figlio e dello Spirito Santo; 20insegnate loro a ubbidire a tutto ciò che io vi ho comandato. E sappiate che io sarò sempre con voi, tutti i giorni, sino alla fine del mondo».